The American
Immigration Collection

Irish Immigration in the United States: Immigrant Interviews

JEREMIAH O'DONOVAN

Arno Press and The New York Times

NEW YORK 1969

*

Library of Congress Catalog Card No. 69-18786

*

Reprinted from a copy in the
Wisconsin State Historical Society Library

*

Manufactured in the United States of America

A

BRIEF ACCOUNT

OF THE AUTHOR'S INTERVIEW

WITH HIS COUNTRYMEN,

AND OF THE PARTS OF

THE EMERALD ISLE

WHENCE THEY EMIGRATED.

TOGETHER WITH A DIRECT REFERENCE TO THEIR

PRESENT LOCATION

IN THE LAND OF THEIR ADOPTION, DURING HIS TRAVELS THROUGH VARIOUS

STATES OF THE UNION IN 1854 AND 1855.

BY JEREMIAH O'DONOVAN.

PITTSBURGH, PA.:
PUBLISHED BY THE AUTHOR.
1864.

INTRODUCTION.

THIS sketch of my travels, properly speaking, requires no introduction or preliminary remarks, as it must be considered a small amount of indigested matter, and the sudden explosion of momentary conceptions ; yet, as it is customary, if not necessary, to write something in the form of an introduction to all histories, I must, of course, comply with an established custom, although such should not be attempted by any whose literary attainments and writings have not been sanctioned by the approbation of profound and eminent writers who have secured to themselves, by means of their gigantic productions, a solid, established, literary fame, which is beyond the reach of calumny and criticism ; for if you show a man of renowned acquirements and literary taste a new work, he reads attentively the Preface; and if such will not square with his judgment, he unceremoniously returns the production to the author with his disapprobation depicted in his countenance. Such, in my opinion, is not fair play, for very often the

Preface and History in style and propriety differ, as the Preface confines a man within certain limits, and compels him to make choice of select and accurate expressions, calculated to reflect brilliancy on the forthcoming History; but the History itself gives more room to wrestle with the subject. We have different kinds of readers in the world, and those possessing the highest order of intellectual culture, and merit, read with patience, and in hopes of discovering some grand idea produced by some powerful explosion of poetic fancy and fiction; and if such they discover, they consider themselves requited. Others, with unspeakable vengeance, and to show the supremacy of their judgments, by the severity of their criticisms, only read to censure and condemn, while another class of readers will take no delight, but in comical songs; and the more comical they are in their applications, the more merriment they excite. However, an account of my interview with my countrymen, during my travels cannot, as I heretofore expressed, be considered a History, as it is no more than an illustration of their conditions and localities in the land of their adoption. Thousands of my countrymen at this time fill with dignity and invulnerable fidelity, various situations of trust and emolument in the land of their adoption; and this they do with unquestionable capacities and religious faith, that preserve integrity from well digested imputations and malicious slanders.

Among my countrymen can be found constellations of scientific men, emitting the purest effulgence in the firmament of science; yet I must acknowledge that many of them have not received the polish of educational refinement, and the cause of this deficiency can be clearly suggested, and as clearly anticipated.

Millions, not thousands, of my countrymen were either starved, hanged, or decapitated by remorseless villains who were sent across the channel by the most repacious, unfeeling, ungodly and cruel government that has been established in any civilized or savage country under the canopy of Heaven, and such of my countrymen as escaped from the meshes of their ferocious enemies were driven like wolves into the wilderness, and kept there, remote from science and society, until they thought them beyond the reach of future improvement, and irrecoverably plunged in barbarity and unspeakable ignorance; and were it not for the indigenous quality of my countrymen and their religious training, they would become savages, but their faith and practice, even in seclusion, rendered them inaccessible to such an odious comparison.

Penal laws were enacted to compel my countrymen and women to acknowledge the supremacy and divine authority of a new and perverting creed commenced by Henry, amended by Edward, and finished in the Gospel Factory of Elizabeth.

No glowing eloquence, no sublimity of thought, no lofty aspirations, or no meretricious ornament can have any analogy with the brief sketch of my travels, as it is a dry, true, travelling statement, or if such a thing could exist, it exists in the fertility of some powerful imagination, that could change the most bleak and dreary winter into spring, the most barren wilderness into a paradise, and the most uncultivated moor into elysian fields, and enamelled meadows:

> Some read to find the place the diamond lies,
> Some read to laugh, and some to criticise;
> Each has, of course, a self-peculiar zest,
> But, he who laughs is happier than the rest.

In the year 1848, when the first number of my History of Ireland, in epic verse, made its appearance from the press, and after supplying all my subscribers in Pittsburgh, I took my departure for Freeport, a small town, beautifully situated on the banks of the Allegheny river, some thirty miles from Pittsburgh, and during my stay in that town I took up my residence at Mr. McCue's hotel, which is pleasantly located on the bank of the river, and quite convenient to the landing. It is no exaggeration to say that Mr. McCue's hotel is fitted elegantly for the convenience and reception of the travelling community, and for others that either design or accident would make them call. His accommodations are indisputably satisfactory, and cannot be surpassed in any other inland town of the same size in the State. His table groans under the weight of substantial meats and delicacies which would satisfy the most fastidious appetite and epicurean habits. As an appendage to what I express concerning Mr. McCue's hotel, there is another advantage should be mentioned, and its omission would be a culpable mistake. Mr. McCue is a gentleman of very agreeable manners, edifying conversation, and is indisputably honest and honorable in all his transactions with the world. His household affairs are in a manner superintended by one of my countrymen, a Mr. Thompson, whose assiduity and arrangement of things must be a great acquisition to any establishment of the kind. Though advanced in years his faculties are not the least impaired or disorganized, and his attention and immovable fidelity are generally acknowledged.

I went the following morning to Squire Gillaspie's residence which is quite convenient to Mr. McCue's, and I sincerely aver if that gentleman's soul be as free from sin as his character is from blemish, by divine permission, after departing this life, he will eternally enjoy the asssociations of angels and saints in the regions of bliss and in the kingdom of Heaven.

I next got acquainted with Mr. Reed, a professor of mathematics in that town; he is a clear and forcible writer, a distinguished mathematician, and an accomplished gentleman, and a man of his acquisition must be of much benefit to the inhabitants of Freeport.

The Catholic population of the place is small, still they have built a church, where the adorable Sacrifice of Mass is offered semi-monthly.

I took my departure and proceeded to Kittanning, the capital of Armstrong county, about twenty-five miles higher up the Allegheny, and beautifully situated on its bank, and I must candidly confess that I never saw before equality's horizontal level more consummate or more even than in Kittanning. It appeared to me that aristocracy had neither a friend, nor a home, nor encouragement in the town, although some of its inhabitants, as in other towns, are very wealthy, and some otherwise, yet no distinction could be seen by the most philosophical eye, in their social and promiscuous assemblies and rendezvous; the rich and poor were alike, which I attributed to the high and profound attainments of the opulent class of its inhabitants. I stopped over night in Mr. John Clarke's well-known hotel. This splendid establishment offers excellent accommodations and the most positive security to the travelling community, and the best description and definition that I could give of Mr. Clarke's assiduity and attention to his friends and visitors would fall behind reality, and therefore cannot be superfluously or hyperbolically considered. A better host, or a better man, is unnecessary. Mr. Clarke rendered me all the assistance he could to promote my design in Kittanning. He introduced me to all the distinguished men of the town, ex-governors, sheriffs, statesmen of incomparable fame, lawyers of acknowledged veracity and skill, doctors and physicians who throw the immortal skill of Esculapius in the shade, aldermen and merchants, gentlemen of conspicuous talents and refined education, and although each of these knows his dignity, he is totally divested of supercilious airs, such as contaminate the most brilliant acquirements and considerations.

In that town I met with a countryman of mine of the name of Mr. Browne, of whom I formed a very favorable opinion before I had the pleasure of having an interview with him, as fame spoke largely and loudly in his praise, and our meeting confirmed the wide-spread circulation which embellished his principle and practice. His appearance is noble, manly and attractive, his symmetry is admirably adjusted for strength, dignity and durability, his disposition amiable and even, and his whole appearance engaging and beautiful, such as to gain the estimation of any civilized person in the world, he is also full of good nature, good humor, and manners, the natural inheritance of a genuine Irishman. Mr. Browne superintends, and I think is bookkeeper and part owner of a large rolling establishment which is in extensive operation in Kittanning, and his skill, moderation and immovable fidelity, add much to the success of the establishment.

I rode in the stage to the Great Western. It was on a beautiful summer's morning in the month of June, when the Supreme Artist embellished the face of nature in that latitude, and "made the wilderness blossom as the rose." We entered the bush and as the morning had been clear, calm and beautiful, the enchanting melody of warblers conveyed ecstacy to the heart, harmony to the ear, and added magnificence to sublunary grandeur, such as the finest creative fancy could not magnify. Although my view in the stage had been partially limited, the solemn gloom and solitude of the forest and their inseparable charms, would cause a poetic inspiration in the most savage breast, uncultivated mind, and frigid imagination, and the most incurious observer, saturated with atheistical conceptions, beholding the combination and diversity of trees that illuminated the woods, and the delicious colors of all the flowers that came under my inspection that morning, would indubitably acknowledge the inimitable power and ubiquity of a Divine Pencil. We rode slowly through the elysian shades which brought us in close proximity to the Great Western, and, when in that vicinity, I thought myself landed in the island of Lemnos, while Vulcan had been forging thunderbolts for Jupiter, the father of the Gods, after he kicked him out of Heaven for his excessive deformity. When I got out of the stage at the Great Western, how altered the scene; the beauties of nature disappeared, and I had been at once confronted by majestic art in all its stupendous magnitude. Forges of the utmost capacity belching forth smoke and fire with terrific grandeur. Trip hammers with unspeakable malediction pounding red iron, men nearly denuded with long pokers revolv- melted liquid in ovens, compact and insufferable by their excessive heat, others with incomparable strength, and sledges of an enormous size, breaking iron for certain purposes, in a word, I thought the herculean labor beyond the reach of our ordinary race. Commiseration at the sight steeled me to the spot of observation, but after a little consideration, I thought to myself that their conditions had not been as lamentable as at first sight.

They all seemed cheerful and satisfied, and the sums they received for their labor had been a sufficient equivalent for the hardship they endured, which established contentment among them. The rendezvous had been of a promiscuous nature, but the majority were Irish and Welsh, and I must say that I was much pleased with the inhabitants of the place. I discovered among my own countrymen indigenous and hereditary habits, viz.: hospitality, friendship, unmixed honesty, and, to a certain extent, sobriety. On a rising eminence, better than a mile from the Great Western is a Catholic Church, I may say, in the wilderness, commendably large and handsome, and the Rev. Mr. Mitchell, the officiating clergyman, had to ascend the incredible acclivity every morning, on foot, to celebrate Mass, a penance worthy of imitation. The reverend gentleman had undoubtedly been, in the prime of life, stout, healthy and vigorous. Mr. Mitchell is a distinguished Theologian, an eminent orator, a prince in principle, and indisputably an Irish gentleman. The Rev. Mr. Mitchell had been, also, idolized by the whole congregation. Seeing the church on a week day, I was struck with astonishment where a congregation could come from, but, attending divine service the following Sunday I found the church full to its utmost capacity, and the congregation displayed, individually and collectively, wealth, health and religious training, all of Celtic origin. I was astonished at the rapid sale of my book, the humble production of an obscure writer, disqualified by years, and who never attempted to write a page in his youth or manhood, some billet-doux excepted, and such were imperfectly written, through excessive love, or ineffable simplicity. My proficiency in the sale of my book can only be attributed to the list of my subscribers, among whom were to be found the most distinguished men of the day. No less a personage than the great and lamented Henry Clay, of Ashland, Ky., headed the list, a name sufficient to cure the venomous bite of any insidious critic. After his name appeared the signature of the honored and lamented Harmer Denny, of Pittsburgh, Pa., whose qualifications were indisputably solid, and after him appeared the signature of His Lordship Bishop O'Connor, of Pittsburgh, Pa. This distinguished prelate, though unpretending, is universally admitted to possess an extraordinary fund of intellectual merit. He is considered a great linguist, an elegant orator, a profound and finished scholar, and the cynosure of theologians. And his incomparable abilities are far beyond the reach of my approbation, and could receive no illumination from what I could say by way of definition than the most remote planet in the solar system could from the smallest ray emitting from the luminary, or revolving satellite that accompanies our globe in its revolutions around the sun. Those three men only, without further reference to all the distinguished men in the subscription list, were sufficient to prevent the wanton criticism of unlettered men. I crossed the Allegheny at a narrow point above the Great Western, and traveled through the wilderness to Red Bank, which is, I think, in Clarion County, and the wild woods through which I traveled would afford an excellent shelter to bears, wolves, panthers and other ferocious animals of the kind, and also an impregnable defence to Jack Sheppard, Dick Turpin, and their formidable and murderous accomplices. I thought of meek Moses during a forty years' sojourn in the wilderness, trying to govern a contumacious and sometimes irreligious people; and how a man can endure hardships and difficulties when he has the grace of God in heart, and has been directed by the finger of providence. This reflection gave me confidence and a religious consolation which reconciled me to my lot. In passing through the bush I came to a large tributary stream flowing into the Allegheny, and had been there some time before I had been discovered from the other side, although I stood as near the water's edge as I could, to signify my intention to cross. After some time I saw the ferry-boat approaching, and a beautiful young lady, with a pair of oars cleaving the liquid element with surprising care, strength and dexterity, and the last extended sweep she made with her oars had driven the skiff high and dry on the shore. I viewed with emotion the delicacy of her frame, for she was tall, straight and slender, and still her whole symmetry indicated strength and agility. She was exceedingly fair, and her raven tresses clustered carelessly and unsettled around her head,—

Her skin was fairer than the driven snow,
Enough to kill or captivate a beau,——

The lady was about twenty-five years of age, and I thought it a shame and a sin to subjugate a lady of her appearance to such a state of degradation. She came out of the skiff and stood on the shore as if determined to push the skiff into the water, and while in that attitude I asked her had she a husband, and she answered negatively; I asked her then, had she a brother, and she answered affirmatively, and added, that age and infirmity were the immovable concomitants of the old

2

gentleman, her father, which rendered him incapable of performing what she had to do in the absence of her brother, though he would make the attempt if she would allow him. This tender affection for her father made me love her on the spot, and, indeed, I could idolize her, and I candidly aver, that if I were in the prime of life our separation would be impossible, if she would condescend to a matrimonial compromise. After some conversation, I helped her to push the skiff into the water, and then we both took our stations; and as she rowed slowly, and the morning being beautifully calm, the creek, or rather an arm of the Allegheny of considerable width, we had an opportunity of asking and mutually solving many questions during our voyage. She said she conjectured I was a professional gentleman, and a stranger in that vicinity. I answered submissively and said I was a doctor and a surgeon of some eminence, and had to attend to a desperate case in my professional career, in the next county, and mentioned, also, that I was after attending to another case of the same nature at the Great Western. She asked me, then, where my wife and family resided, I answered, no where; she asked me, then, had I any certain place of residence; I answered, that I made my home in Philadelphia. Then she looked at me, and turned her beautiful blue eyes to some other object, and after a respectful pause, said, as thus, it is a pity an old gentleman of your appearance and abilities should be without a wife and family. O, my dear reader, what a crushing tendency the word old has, and what a consuming application, be it ever so respectfully directed, when it comes from the lips of an angelic creature, of surpassing beauty; but the pressure of age is evident to all.

> Ladies who cannot read a printed page,
> Can read the press-work of declining age.

To come to a conclusion, we landed safely on the opposite side, and questions arose concerning the ferry fee, as she objected against any kind of remuneration for our sailing voyage. This negative only augmented my generosity, and as my resolution is always, and in all cases, inflexible, I then insisted on her taking what I offered. Now, my dear reader, came the critical moment. After a little voluntary pause, I took her tenderly by the hand, and reverently bowed, bent, scraped, sobbed, sighed, sorrowed and said nothing, and at last, with considerable difficulty and reluctance, I took my departure.

After a tedious journey I came to Red Bank, or the port of destination, and after a momentary survey of the locality, and a little conversation with a few of the inhabitants, I became convinced that if Melpomene attuned her strings in Red Bank, no person there would listen to her inimitable strains, and under that impression, I immediately directed my course towards Kittanning, where I arrived late in the evening quite weary, and took my quarters with my invaluable friend, heretofore mentioned. On the following morning I started in the stage for Pitts, to receive the familiar brand, which can be defined by soot, smoke, sulphur, &c. When I rested a few days at home, I got everything in readiness to take an adventurous tour to Cincinnati, and I selected as salesman and companion a young Irishman, about seventeen years of age, named John Joseph Pender, who is now, I hope, in happy eternity; his manners were agreeable, his countenance fair, his conversation free, friendly and affectionate; he read with ease, elegance and propriety, and he was rigidly and scrupulously honest, and I may say religiously instructed in the duties of his religion. After a pleasant passage down the incomparable Ohio, we landed in Cincinnati. On approaching the wharf, I distinctly saw the shore covered with carts, and their owners, principally from the Emerald Isle. At once, an arrangement had been made with one of my countrymen for a stipulated sum to take my friend, my self and my bulky baggage to the corner of Eighth and Sycamore streets, where a Mr. Griffin, a countryman of mine, kept a large boarding house, which had been celebrated for its propriety and unquestionable accommodations, but I labored, I may say, under an undeniable disadvantage, as I had no introduction to the host or hostess, nor to any of their boarders, whose numerical aggregate exceeded the number of stars contained in Orion's belt. On our arrival there, very fortunately Mr. Griffin was standing at the door and viewed our proximity with silent astonishment, when in civil terms I accosted him, and declared to him my intentions. He answered that no room was vacant in his house, that could afford me satisfactory accommodations. During the conversation, many of his boarders as if of a gregarious nature, assembled where Mr. Griffin stood, among whom was his lady, a woman of irresistible charms and unaffected by supercilious airs; her whole exterior bespoke sound sense and good management, and a better looking couple I hardly met with in my travels. Just at the time, the carter or drayman, held the reins to take some other direction, Mrs. Griffin gave him directions to stop a moment, and turning around to her husband, said, "O! Mr. Griffin, we must try to accommodate the gentleman, he is an Irishman and no way fastidious, I will therefore arrange matters to his satisfaction." "Be it so, my dear," said Mr. Griffin. With that she spoke to her boarders, and in a moment of time, my trunks were under the protection and control of Mrs. Griffin.

Now, my dear friend and reader, consider the unspeakable vanity of placing our affections on the perishable and transitory things of this world. Mrs. Griffin since then departed this life, and at the very moment of her death, her charms also disappeared, and her spirit took its flight on angelic wings to the tribunal of Justice, to await the final decision of an Omnipotent Judge. Ah! my dear reader, reflect seriously on the necessity of having our accounts settled before cruel, unrelenting and irresistible death should call and make us submit to his stern authority. Mr. Griffin and my young friend and fellow traveler also died, and I hope are now in the enjoyment of eternal happiness. The interposition of Mrs. Griffin had been timely and satisfactory, and she offered an apology for not having a more suitable accommodation. I intercepted at once, perhaps a multiplicity of words, and said that any she could give would be considered a luxury. On the following morning, after a cosmetic wash and a hearty breakfast, Mr. Pender and myself set out to try if the Cincinnatians had any relish for lyric poesy, and before we separated to take different directions, I established a custom which should be observed by him without violation, which was as thus, that he should come to his dinner daily, and that any infraction of this injunction would incur my displeasure.

My lyric number showed the woes and afflictions of my countrymen, occasioned by English tyranny, treachery and misrule, and if my production were deficient in its other proportions of poetic standard, I thought I gave, of English attrocities, something like a faithful demonstration. I considered that a picture of the crimes and cruelties committed by the English government to annihilate their ancestors, would arouse an original hatred in their hearts, which would cause them to fly unanimously and without delay to the Tree of Liberty, which was to be planted about that time by W. S. O'Brien and others, for the freedom of the Emerald Isle. I proceeded immediately to the residence of the Very Reverend Mr. Purcell, who unequivocally expressed his disapprobation of my essay, and advised me not to attempt its completion. Although having from my youth complied with the injunction of all reverend clergymen who were in full communion with the Church of Rome to that time, I thought then to establish an anomaly, that is, not to comply with his desire, which I did not. Although his censure or disapprobation I knew would have a crushing tendency and would be a fatal impediment to the sale of my work, I withdrew from the reverend gentleman by no means disheartened, though confident of his decision and the result of his discrimination, as I had in my possession at that time the approbation of eminent critics and distinguished divines.

About the time I left the very reverend gentleman, Sol was nearly on the summit of his elevation, which made me steer towards my boarding house, particularly to see if my young friend had complied with my established injunction, to which I found he had. As he arrived in proper time to be accommodated, I asked my friend about his attempted enterprise, and if successful or otherwise? "Ah, sir," said he, "I met with no success, my countrymen in this city are all Americanized, their indigenous manners and propensities have vanished and I have no anticipation of a future success." I cried ditto, and said, try, try again; you know, my young friend, that one swallow never made a summer, nor one woodcock a winter. You know when our countrymen move to perform any desirable action, they move like a hurricane, striking terror in their foes and hope and confidence in their friends. They say, that Milton's immortal "Paradise Lost" remained in obscurity for two generations, and how could my humble production illuminate my countrymen in an instant, sure, they had neither time for reading nor for reflection, therefore, said I, after dinner we must cheerfully and assiduously try again. At that time, there had been living in Cincinnati, a county and countryman of mine, who is now I hope in the association of happy souls in the eternal Kingdom, that neither prosperity nor adversity could change him in principle or practice. There never lived a greater patriot nor a purer or more incorruptible democrat. He held an office of high importance, trust and emolument under Governor Barkley at the time, which he managed with unimpeached and unsuspected fidelty, and at the end gave a faithful account of his stewardship. After dinner I prepared myself to pay a visit to Mr. Patrick Collins of whom I speak, although I never saw him before, neither had I an introduction to him, yet, I had been confident from his general character, that the hundred thousand welcomes, the familiar phrase that is generally expressed at the reception of an Irishman, would sound in my ears, and that the hand of fellowship would be extended to me with ineffable friendship. Mr. Collins had been married to a namesake of mine, and of course a member of an illustrious family of the Royal house of O'Donovan, and this affinity itself should move his natural impulse with greater impetuosity. I entered his office with freedom commingled with a little urbanity, and when he saw me he cordially extended his hand and invited me to a seat.

After the mutual interchange of friendly terms subsided, he inquired familiarly what brought me to the city. I then told him unequivocally what induced me to come; and at that moment reached him the first number of my Lyric History, together with a poem book, both unquestionably original. When Mr. Collins perused it for some time, a settled indescribable gloom obscured the serenity of his countenance, and he remained silent for a time. When he emerged from this gloomy obscurity, he spoke quite low, and his words were tinged with emotion, and said, "My country is my idol." And after a considerable pause, said, in strong, clear and forcible language, "I would suffer this very instant to be immolated on the shrine of liberty." When his mind regained its horizonal level, he introduced me to a Mr. O'Sullivan, an eminent lawyer, who held his office under the same roof. Although this gentleman left his native country in the state of infancy, he still retained the noble traits of his ancestors. He was exceedingly handsome in person, and his countenance was young and vigorous, and immovably determined to benefit his client. When he returned to Mr. Collins' office again, Mr. Barkley, the Governor's son, made his appearance; a consummate, finished and distinguished scholar and gentleman; and the same as every other great man, he seemed entirely divested of aristocratical affectations, supercilious airs, and all other disgusting externals, with an open, frank, determined countenance, and a brilliant penetrating glance; everything visible to the naked eye bespoke his dignity. Eternity would insensibly steal away in the company of friends. At this time Sol and his coursers had a downward tendency, and had been then approaching the verge of the western horizon. When I stood on my feet to return to my boarding house, which had been quietly observed by Mr. Collins, who cordially invited me to stop and take tea with him that evening, which I respectfully declined, and offered as an apology my anxiety to meet Mr. Pender at his return to Mr. Griffin's, and then he permitted me to return to my harbor of security. My young countryman and I arrived there at the same time, and before terms of civility had taken place, I saw his disappointment deeply engraved on his countenance. "My friend," said I, "have things turned out to your satisfaction this day?" "So much so," said he, "that I am determined to return immediately to Pittsburgh, Pa." "My countrymen in this city," said he, "if not metamorphosed, have lost their indigenous qualities, which died an unnatural death." Now, my dear reader, candidly consider the noble and honest principle of my young countryman; had I a country born in the same situation, his own proficiency would be ahead of all other considerations; and when sure of his wages, he would care but little for my interest. Ah! Island of Saints, in spite of the villifying efforts of heathens, and heretics, of mercenary revilers, and well paid scribblers, your children display inimitable sincerity after landing in this country; but after being vaccinated by crime and immorality, which is the standard and established practice of villains in this country, the vaccination becomes dangerous, and the proper remedy to be applied is the installation of the offender for several years in the penitentiary. No reason could induce my young friend to stop longer in the city; and then, with much reluctance, I gave him liberty to return. After taking his departure, I thought it prudent to remove to another house of entertainment, kept by a county and countryman of mine on the water's edge, named Jeremiah O'Kane, who rests now, I hope, with the blessed in Heaven, as I believe an honester man than he could not be easily found. Mr. O'Kane, at that time, was well advanced in years, and evidently sinking under the superanuating encroachments auxiliary to his age. In my opinion, he was in the last stage of a galloping consumption, and still worse, he married a young wife, which, of itself, was sufficient to provide him a ticket of admission to the chambers of death. Mr. O'Kane I think was confident of his approaching dissolution, as he spent much of his time in prayer and meditation. One evening a journeyman tailor called on me and asked had I seen Mr. P. Scully since my arrival in the city. I answered negatively; and when he gave me the name of the street, and the number of his house I got everything in readiness to visit him. Mr. Scully was a Pittsburgher, and a tailor of the highest grade. Though having his share of the faults and follies of humanity, he was a true and genuine Irishman; had his heart in the right place, and never shrank from extending the hand of fellowship in the hour of extremity to his countrymen, or to others, when it came within his power to do good. Mr. Scully received me with open arms, and warmly introduced me to all his acquaintances; and such made up a large and respectable number. No man could do more than Mr. Scully did to bring my epic production into notice. Mr. Scully, with much earnestness, introduced me to his professional friends, and took me at once to a large and capacious room where, I think, a hundred of these gentlemen worked together, each appearing exceedingly clean and neat, and in the prime of life; and an introduction to so many of that class congregated together, had been gratifying and desirable. I need not mention that they received me with unspeakable kindness and politeness, and with a courtesy that raised my ambition. After taking a hasty survey of the assembled multitude, I distributed many of the numbers among them; and while the first man, to whom I gave a number, had been reading a page, the rest listened in breathless silence and anxiety during the time; and when he had finished the page, he exclaimed, "I'll keep this." "I'll keep this," said another; and so on until many numbers disappeared. As soon as a sale had been effected, the most of them read a page, and I never heard pronunciation more correctly observed; and were it not for seeing them working together, I would take them to be an assembly of collegians. All original error disappeared by the elegance and propriety of their reading. A gentleman named Mr. McManus then withdrew from the assembly, and went in company with me in order to introduce me to another party of the same mechanical class, which resulted successfully. Mr. McManus was an Irishman, of course; and so were they all, with few exceptions. Therefore, through Mr. Scully's introduction, I soon became known to my countrymen in Cincinnati. We are not sufficiently acquainted with those professional gentlemen to judge of them with competent accuracy, as they keep clear of a grovelling community and vulgar associations. No mechanic living thinks less of a dime than a journeyman tailor; or no man is more willing to lend a helping hand to any laudable institution than a merchant tailor. I felt exceedingly sorry that his Grace, Archbishop Purcell, my distinguished and unrivaled county and countryman, had been absent from the city at that time, until I would have the honor of seeing him, as his Grace is universally admitted to be a star of the first magnitude. To these two classes, merchant tailors and their jours; and to boot and shoemakers my future exertions had been devoted, as I anticipated the result to be successful, which anticipation proved rather a prophecy than an anticipation. I acknowledge my indebtedness to the Catholic booksellers of Cincinnati, who are esteemed, and worthy of estimation, by the collective body of all Catholics in the city.

The tailors of Cincinnati instructed me to call on all boot and shoemakers in my travels, and acknowledged the superiority of their intellectual attainments, and acting in conformity with their instructions, confirmed the sincerity of my advisers and after some consideration, I found these were the two hinges to which my future prospects were suspended. After commending myself and my friends in Cincinnati to the care and protection of Divine Providence, I took my passage on board a steamer for St. Louis. The weather was clear, calm, and beautiful, and the Ohio high enough to take us over the Louisville Rapids in gallant style, and with amazing rapidity, this was the cry of all on board, with one exception, as, I considered such of no force or magnitude when compared with the stupendous rapids of the St. Lawrence in Upper Canada, over which I had many a race on rafts constructed of my own lumber. In my travels through life, I had the opportunity of seeing various rivers in Europe and in America, and in my opinion, I never saw so beautiful a river as the Ohio; it is of the same width and not interspersed with many islands to disfigure its surface, and many of them, you would suppose, are formed by nature for the accommodation of the Niades, or alike Ogygia, the fairy residence of Calypso and her nymphs, who baffled the incomparable wisdom of Mentor for a time, in the detention of Telemachus when in quest of his father Ulysses, after the Trojan war.

I must correct my mistake: as I landed in Louisville after leaving Cincinnati, and when the steamer approached the wharf, I saw it covered with carters, and after making some inquiries for an Irish house of entertainment, I was informed a gentleman of the name of Mr. Hughes kept a respectable house of the kind conveniently, and where I could unquestionably be accommodated; this was the first time since I left my native country I found myself in a slave state, and the humility and obedience of the slave at once claimed my sympathy, and were it not for their hereditary bondage, my sympathy would not be extended, as I consider humanity, humility, urbanity and obedience to be the distinctive characteristics of greatness, and the property and satellites of great men. One of the slaves soon landed me at my countryman's residence, and he and his lady received me with much attention and kindness. I soon learned they were both from my own part of the Island of Saints, an island celebrated for its kindness to strangers, and its devotion to God. They came from the sweet town of Bandon, the grand saloon and head quarters in Munster, of William Prince of Orange. Safe and contented I remained with Mr. Hughes until I left Louisville, and in his house I got acquainted with a county Cork man of mine of the name of Timothy Riordain, who diligently sought for daily labor in the city, the best natured poor fellow I ever met with, and after a little acquaintance I found he possessed superior abilities, and if his ambition would equal his talents, he would find some other situation more conformably to his mind than daily labor. My countryman's pronunciation was quite vicious and vulgar; still, he spoke the English language correctly, and grammatically, and whoever came in a mathematical contest with him, would be mathematically defeated. Mr. Riordain being acquainted in the place had been of infinite service to me, as he introduced me to many of my countrymen; among whom I met with many very generous and whose names I carefully inserted in my notes, which, unfortnnately, I lost in my travels, which left me no aid for recollection but a treacherous memory. There is one gentleman in Louisville of the name of O'Niell, a name preeminent on the pages of ancient and modern history, whom.I can never forget. He keeps a large assortment of boots and shoes on the levee for sale, and his establishment is patronized by the leading men and women of the city. Unmistakably, O'Niell is a gentleman in principle and practice, standing in defiance of the foul breath of calumny which is always found in connection with competition. In Louisville, as well as in all my travels, I never had been insulted by a native American gentleman with the exception of one solitary instance—a skeleton which had been pneumatically affected or put in motion, tried to do so, but had been unsuccessful. My unflinching friends, the tailors and boot and shoemakers, displayed the same generosity in Louisville that they did throughout my travels. I took my departure from Louisville on a summer's evening in the month of August, and went over the falls with incredible rapidity; such was the opinion of my fellow travelers, when in the course of time the curtains of night were unfolded and commenced insensibly to spread and to assume more density, until the refulgent rays of the moon, which was then in full blown blossom, rendered the density transparent or caused it entirely to disappear. The excessive heat of the weather, together with a craving avidity to view the face of nature, which was then calm and motionless as death, kept me on deck the whole time during our passage down the Ohio, and in consequence of the serenity of the water, the moon's reflection on it produced a trembling mirror pleasing to the imagination. How awful it is to think that all the beauties of nature must disappear forever, and even the gems that beautify the firmament must dissolve also, while the immortal soul stands guilty of crime, disobedience, and folly, whereas, that soul, before its final defeat, could, by penance and repentance and the hearing of the church, be made worthy of the association of saints and angels in the mansions of bliss, during endless eternity. Early next morning we entered the Mississippi, the mother of waters, and the reservoir of innumerable tributaries, only inferior in magnitude to itself and a few others. At this time navigation, as the river was low, was very dangerous, yet, Providence guided the helm until we safely landed at St. Louis. While ascending the river, I composed the following ode to the Mississippi:

O ! great Mississippi, grand is thy fall,
Thou longest of rivers and largest of all !
How grand is thy surface, how deep is thy bed,
Where often, relentless, thou bury'st thy dead !
Spare a Milesian from th' Evergreen Isle,
To flee from oppression, became an exile,
The bard that had written, proclaim'd it to be
The flower of the earth and the gem of the sea.
What makes all these buzzards to fly in the air ?
Or look for support in the wilderness here ?
'Tis something that floats on thy surface they smell,
For, such is their living, as, nothing they kill.
O ! giant of rivers, tho' grand be thy flow,
Thou hast been the cause of unspeakable woe,
Now, spare me, I pray, and when Erin is free,
Then, act thy own pleasure in dealing with me :

If native inhabitants live on thy banks—
Tho' lonesome their doom, and thin be their ranks,
Ah! there they are shelter'd from bondage and fear,
Since planting the tree of sweet liberty here.

No sooner did I come close to the wharf, than I knew I could be accommodated as, treachery, satanic enactments, and godless tyranny dispersed my countrymen all over Christendom. They can be found in St. Louis in great multitudes. On landing I asked one of them, would he be kind enough to take me and my baggage to some respectable house of entertainment, kept by an Irishman, where I could remain during my stay in the city. "My friend," said he, "I will take you to a very respectable hotel, where you will be inaccessible to intrigues, treachery and insult; where you and your property will be as safe as if at home in your own bedchamber;" "but," said he again, "I must take you some distance from this levee, as very often there have been committed here, theft, robbery and other sanguinary crimes too deplorable for revelation, and at variance with Christian charity."

"All right, my friend," said I, "drive on and I will follow you to that harbor of peace, plenty, prosperity and hospitality." He did so, and brought me to either the Sixth or Eighth Ward Hotel, kept by Messrs. Nugent and King, two gentlemen from the ancient dominion of the renowned O'Neill's, and indeed the most shallow and obtuse physiognomist at sight, would know them to be gentlemen. Mr. Nugent had been married to Mr. King's sister, an amiable lady devoted to industry and entirely divested of any external gloss or affectation, which sometimes accompanies affluence and the want of proper cultivation, which made me at once attached to my new residence. At that time, Mr. King had been an unmarried man, and kept an extensive livery stable, and attended to his customers with great assiduity, and Mr. Nugent attended to the affairs of the hotel, with skill, sense, and economy; both these gentlemen were scrupulously honest, they had plenty at command and knew how to enjoy it, with thanksgiving; in a word they lived happy and contented, universally known and universally esteemed. In consequence of losing my note book I can give no precise or adequate account of my countrymen in St. Louis, as I have nothing to enable me, but a treacherous memory. Although crime is unscrupulously committed in that city, particularly on the levee, still, I think it is the most religious city in all my travels. There my countrymen and women, generally speaking, are friendly, generous, and ineffably hospitable, and it is not in the power of envy to point out a stain in the moral habits of the Catholic citizens of St. Louis. I had the happiness of calling into many Catholic Colleges and religious convents in that city, and in my humble opinion, and it is an indisputable fact, they are the abode of angels and saints: in a word the citizens of St. Louis are beyond the reach of my feeble and imperfect exposition. I met with a gentleman in St. Louis to whom I am bound to make a particular allusion, and whose name is Patrick McKanna, and the best and most accurate definition I can give of him is to say that he is a genuine Irishman, and those who know the true meaning or etymology of the term will sufficiently appreciate his worth. He is free from imperfections and spots which sully the reputation and character of the degraded portion of mankind. Mr. McKanna's residence is within a mile of the city. He is remarkable for hospitality, and his lady has become conspicuously known for her cheerfulness and activity in the administration of this natural and hereditary proclivity. Mr. McKanna is an honor to his native country and a decided advantage to the land of his adoption, and to crown all, he is a sterling, immovable, and incorruptible patriot and democrat.

Convenient to Mr. McKanna's residence dwells another of my noble countrymen, Mr. Patrick

Keegan, a gentleman of full weight and value, who can bear the strictest inspection, and I heard since, that he left his comfortable home and went to the gold regions in quest of a perishable accumulation. On leaving Mr. McKanna's, I called at the residence of Mr. Patrick Hogan, whom I consider to be a gentleman in all his habits and social intercourse with the world, and his residence shows elegance, wealth, and prosperity, and indisputably proves the inimitable taste and cleanliness of its occupier. At the time I called there were four Catholic Priests together at his house, among whom was a young reverend gentleman and a convert to the Catholic Church, whose father had been exceedingly successful in the accumulation of the perishable dust and things of this world, and whose princely residence had been situated conveniently to St. Louis. This rendezvous of holy men is sufficient to draw down a blessing from heaven on the whole territory. Each of them of course became a purchaser, and overlooked the original blunders of my production, as they spoke of it in commendable terms, though not well pleased with the severity of the castigation I gave the English Church and English Government, and strenuously recommended me to observe moderation and Christian charity. The reverend gentleman who had been converted to the church behaved exceedingly generous towards me, though he had been silent on the occasion; may God grant him grace for his own sake, and for the sake of his heavenly mission. One morning while sitting at breakfast it had been emphatically announced that the cholera made its appearance in the city, and had been depopulating it with incurable malignity. This announcement struck the whole with indescribable timidity, and the news spreading with alarming rapidity caused many to come to the conclusion to seek safety in flight, and I acknowledge I had been one of the number. Many of the boarders sounded a hasty retreat, and thinking that there was danger, I added lustily my mite to the confusion. At that critical moment I met with a Pittsburgh gentleman, and a countryman of mine, whose removal from Pittsburgh had been much lamented by those who knew him best. The gentleman was a Mr. Fitzpatrick, lineally descended from the Kings of Ossory, who emphatically advised me to go to Galena, a distance of five hundred miles up the Mississippi. As I knew his sterling worth I consented without hesitation, and immediately got ready to depart from St. Louis. I made no intrusion on my friends, viz.: tailors and boot and shoe makers, as I found the inhabitants uncommonly génerous and brave. Of my ascending passage I had taken notes, and as I lost them, an accurate description is impossible, though I must say it had been critical, dangerous and romantic. Before any further extension of my historic narration, I will make a full, open, and scrupulous confession, even if it should stand a lasting memorial of my infirmity. One day while the steamer with incredible force was ascending the Mississippi, I sat on the most conspicuous part of the boat, to view the inexpressible magnitude of that giant river, and the surrounding scenery which had been indisputably pleasing to the eye of imagination, I observed the water changing from its original color to that of a chocolate, and after some reflection I could not prove the cause from the effect, but making an enquiry, I was satisfied on the subject by an upper Mississippian, who informed me the pine country above had been inundated, and the exudation of the pine was the cause of the discoloration of the river. After some time I was astonished to see some of the passengers drinking the water with avidity, which seemed to me unnatural and disgusting, and considered that sheer necessity compelled them to drink the strange and loathsome beverage. Having the temperance pledge in my possession at the time, and making no use of Satan's distillation for years hitherto, and also thinking a violation of it an abomination to God, I thought myself secured against the use of intoxicating spirits, which had been used immoderately on board the steamer by some of the passengers. On the same day my thirst became so exceedingly great and irresistible that my suffering could no longer be tolerated. No doctor had been convenient to whom I could make an application for the privilege of mixing a little brandy with the pine water to extinguish my inexpressible thirst. Although being conscious of my irregularities whenever I drank a little of that satanic distillation, still, I thought the maturity of my philosophy would enable me to subdue the desire of drinking more than would quench the intolerable thirst I keenly felt at that present moment; but, alas, I found such resolutions were unable to subvert my approaching calamity; my insatiable thirst would admit of no delay, which induced me at once to mix a little of the man-killer with the pine waters of the Mississippi, and take a deadener, which seemed at first unquestionably consoling, but after a little time I felt its indescribable influence and effect. Whether the combination of the pine water and bad brandy, or my long abstinence from intoxicating draughts had been the cause of my sudden and unexpected overthrow, I am not able to determine.

In an hour after I swallowed the poisonous dose, I exhibited all the symptoms of an original drunkard, and kept nibbling at the brandy, though I strenuously endeavored to discontinue the frequent application until I landed in Galena. When I landed in Galena, as my countrymen are all over the earth, I found them in Galena in countless numbers, and I had been taken by one of the carters to an Irish gentleman's house, named Mr. Michael O'Byrne, commonly called Burns, a brave and true Milesian, indubitably descended from the

Chiefs, Champions and Princes of Wicklow, whose incomparable prowess, immovable courage, and determined opposition to English tyranny have been emblazened on the page of history. Mr. O'Byrne is married to his second wife, a decided and finished lady. Mr. O'Byrne is a large, athletic man, whose proportions are beautifully arranged; he speaks calmly, gracefully and with propriety; he is sober, solid and intelligent; he is an incorruptable patriot and a devoted democrat; he is all that can be said to constitute the man and the gentleman—a genuine Irishman. Mr. O'Byrne's name is mentioned with profound admiration by all who have the pleasure of his acquaintance, and I can never forget his assiduity to me in the hour of extremity, that is, when prostrated by misfortune and sickness; speaking collectively of the Galenean's, I think, a more meritorious population is not to be found, or more worthy of applause. Gratitude compels me to acknowledge the many obligations I am under to the population of Galena; particularly to a few of my countrymen who emigrated from my own immediate neighborhood in the Emerald Isle. These gentlemen signalised themselves in watching my irregularities with assiduity and apprehension. A gentleman of the name of Mr. O'Mahoney is one of those to whom I am deeply indebted for his acts of unspeakable kindness, and the other two gentlemen are two brothers of the O'Desmond family, and from the same vicinity with O'Mahoney. These brothers had taken me to their own residence and watched over my misery with sympathy, and administered every comfort for my speedy restoration, without the least hope of any remuneration for their excessive trouble from their troublesome guest. This kindness is hereditary in the O'Desmond's, and no man in America knows it better than I do. Now, my dear reader, mark the result of immoral and disorderly habits, and perhaps it would enable you to avoid the meshes of sinful intoxication.

One evening when sitting in Mr. O'Byrne's, in came a gentlemen, and a countrymen of mine, and used much civility in his conversation towards me, and said he knew me in Pittsburgh, Pa. And was much astonished that anything should upset my original equilibrium, or the stability of my sobriety, and after making many scrapes, bows and genuflections, Mr. Patrick O'Reily and Mr. Jeremiah O'Donovan got intimately acquainted. As he seemed devoted to my present and future happiness, I escorted him to the steamer, on board of which he ascended the river, and he cordially invited me to tarry until I would obtain my lost inheritance or original sobriety. I complied with Mr. O'Reily's request, whom I considered a secondary guardian angel; and this consideration impelled me to give him for safe keeping whatever amount of money I had in my possession, a sum, I think, about forty or forty-five dollars. My secondary guardian angel, Patrick, at once and without much ceremony, at its reception, deposited the money in close communion with his fob, where I thought it had been beyond the reach of the most expert pickpocket. Mr. O'Reily had in his saloon the necessary accommodations, viz.: a flask of a strange construction, hieroglyphically carved, to make its external appearance more pleasing to the eye, which was filled to its utmost capacity of the still-worm exudation. We drank a little, of course, of the invigorating beverage enveloped in Mr. O'Reily's hieroglyphical flask, and swore to the hilt to stand immovably to sustain the stars and stripes, which had been at the time beautifully unfurled by a gentle breçze over our heads, not forgetting our patriotism to the Emerald Isle. Mr. O'Reily's brother and sister-in-law had been passengers on board the same boat, who retired to rest, and left Mr. O'Reily and Mr. Jeremiah O'Donovan in close communion with the hieroglyphical flask, which we enjoyed with much hilarity, without noise, nonsense or intervention until we too retired to rest. I must say Mr. O'Reily drank sparingly, as men of his calibre generally do, and although I frequently sipped, I did so with a delicacy unknown to a confirmed drunkard. Ah, my friend, we retired to rest without saying a prayer, or acknowledging the power and protection of the Divinity who saw my immoral and detested dissipation, and who indisputably made an unerring entry of it in the book of life, against me—"the name of the Lord be magnified." We got up early the following morning, perhaps without acknowledging Divine protection, and after moistening the clay with a few more drops of the still-worm beverage, in order to regain our original elasticity, we left the boat and traveled through the town, inseparably linked, with honesty our motto, and liberty our safeguard. I would never mention a word about my misfortune only to put others on their guard against falling into the calamitous pit of intoxication, and then fall an easy conquest to arrant rogues and ravenous vultures who replenish their pockets by preying on their credulity. I think I remained with my friend or in his company that night, and I am sure my expenses accumulated to a small sum, as my friend would sooner have a taste of the contents of his hieroglyphical flask than of any other beverage, and at the same time it had been disagreeble to my feelings and dignity, though drunk, for I always considered a flask the companion of a detestable and degraded loafer. Mr. Patrick drank, I must say, sparingly, though he often applied his precious lips to the tube of his flask; this proves that he wanted to save the amount he had in his possession. On the morning of the second day, after a little walk we halted, and he said, "Mr. O'Donovan," and at the same time with a brilliant burnish of dishonesty and indisputable rascality around the pupil of his eye, "you had better return immediately to Pittsburgh, for your money is nearly spent." At the sound of his instructions I knew I was in company with one of the most consummate scoundrels that misfortune could send in my way. I asked him, with surprise, how much had been left, and at this interrogation he handed me a five dollar bill, and emphatically said that is all that is left. I asked Patrick where was the remainder ; his reply was, "You spent it." "How could I spend the money you had in your possession?" "No matter," said Patrick, "that is all that is left." I went immediately to Mr. O'Byrne, who knew the amount of money I had in my possession and communicated the defection and unspeakable villany of my countryman. Mr. O'Byrne had him immediately arrested, and brought before a court of law, but my friend promptly denied having any more of my money. The gentlemen who presided to administer justice on the occasion, asked Patrick O'Reily how he swore, and Patrick being well prepared for the examination at once, and without speaking a word, raised his right hand, and with as much dexterity as the best trained pointer would, when making a dead set at a partridge, to signalise to the gunner the immediate locality of the bird, and Patrick's manner of speaking the truth, or proving his innocence testified his defection and rascality, as he attributed no more religious obligation to an uplifted hand, or to swear by it, than if he swore by the rind of an apple. I made no remarks on his manner of swearing, as I made it a point of duty in my travels through life never to make any allusion to any thing touching on religious matters on any platform on which I stood.

An uplifted hand and a hebetated conscience, soon delivered Mr. O'Reily from the meshes of the law, and he left without showing any indignation for the impeachment or the injury done to the reputation of so immaculate a character. I went immediately on board of a steamer moored in Fever river and bound for St. Louis, and never saw or heard of Mr. O'Reily since he left the seat of justice in Galena. May God forgive my dear countryman for his insincerity. Now by taking his defection into consideration it will create astonishment: the illustrious name of O'Reily is unquestionably of Milesian origin, and nobly exalted in the scale of Milesian dignity, and it has given to us as many illustrious Prelates and Priests as any other name, whose immaculate lives and sanctity stand beyond the reach of calumny; and a second consideration is also astonishing, as he came from a county, Cavan, which was, is, and will be the home of men possessing indomitable courage, unstained actions, unbounded generosity, and invulnerable patriotism—a county which was, and would be now in the legitimate possession of the O'Reily family, if injustice had evaporated from the earth, and right could be substituted for might; but that time cannot arrive until the reign of tyrants with their lives will terminate by strangulation or decapitation, as an easier death would be incompatible to the guilt of tyrannical vultures. There are many of my countrymen in Galena worthy of notice, applause, and of approbation, among whom are the following: Mr. Barry, a county and a countryman of mine, who reflects honor on his native land, and adds brilliancy to the land of his adoption; Mr. O'Driscoll, a gentleman of pure Milesian origin, generous, affectionate, and patriotic, and formerly a neighbour of mine in the Emerald Isle; another distinguished gentleman, an eminent physician, who is extensively known by means of his professional skill—he is considered a modern Esculapius, as he can restore health, defeat death, and hinder abortions; and a gentleman of the name of O'Donnell, I think he must be lineally descended from O'Donnell who was Lord Lieutenant of Ireland in the reign of the unfortunate and imbecile James II.—no panegyric can be too brilliant in the description of his cleverness.

I left Galena in low spirits, crushed by debility

and misfortune, and as the timorous hare after a long chase is anxious to return to its original seat, I thought, if possible, to strike for home, and as an addition to my hitherto misfortunes, as the steamboat was descending the river the Captain gave orders to stop at Nauvoo, in order to provide the boat with a fresh supply of water from a spring near the landing place, which is considered clear, salubrious, and invigorating. Though exceedingly sick, and in a state of stupidity caused by unusual intoxication, I was anxious to see the great Temple of Nauvoo, one of the wonderful wonders of America. I asked one of the officers of the boat, could I have time to take a survey of the great Mormon Temple, and he answered affirmatively, and in my hitherto described condition I approached the far-famed Temple, which was situated at no great distance from the bank of the Mississippi, and when proximity made me sensible of its real magnitude, I was struck with astonishment, and allowed at once that hitherto reports concerning it had not been meretriciously exaggerated. My amazement infinitely increased at the following solemn sentence outrageously galvanised over the entrance of the Temple, it read as thus: "This is the Temple of the Lord, and of latter day saints: the world shall bow down and adore it." A treacherous memory may somewhat alter the inscription, though I am of opinion it is correct. I read both the command and the thundering admonition with inexpressible indignation, and after a pause, and after musing on the satanic pretensions of vile rebels against the Lord, I threw myself on my bended knees and fervently prayed to Almighty God, if it were agreeable to his will to lend a favorable ear to my petition, and in the plenitude of omnipotence to demolish that prodigious temple, which is as vile and as hellish as the ancient Pantheon, where heathens congregated to worship their heathen divinities, and where the rites and ceremonies of Paganism were wickedly and irreligiously performed; I also prayed for that deluded people, and for their conversion to the true practice and knowledge of the true religion, which is invariably characterised by faith and good works, the land marks of salvation. After the offering of my petition, I felt some inward compunction, fearing the malice of intention at the time of the presentment or offering, might interfere with the spirit of charity and moderation; for of all the innumerable isms and chisms, the result of private interpretation that have at present distracted the human family, I look upon Mormonism to be the most ungodly, and the most degrading. After arising from my prostration, I walked around the temple astonished at the inexpressible grandeur of that stupendous structure, and more so when I considered the folly and absurdity of the doctrine taught therein. Being somewhat acquainted with the Mormon Bible, which Joe Smith dug out of the mountain of fiction, in the State of New York, which afterwards became Joe's infallible revelation book, expressly and angelically written for the regeneration and salvation of the wicked—when my observations were taken, with weary limbs I returned to the landing place, and to my great grief and consternation the boat had departed, and I saw her gliding down the Mississippi with electric velocity. There I was left alone and condoling, like the mighty Roman among the ruins of Carthage. Being pressed down by debility and declining age, without a house within the limits of my view, or without a living creature to whom I could communicate my helpless and wretched situation, in the midst of desolating wastes, my sensations can be better felt than expressed. At that time the whole town of Nauvoo had been in a state of dilapidation, roofless houses, and not a shed left that could protect me from the assaults of dogs and hogs that roamed unrestrained through the frightful wastes and desolation of Nauvoo; the chickens gregariously flew from field to field the same as partridges; the cattle, as being unacquainted with man, appeared wild and unmanageable; the rabbits left their burrows seemingly astonished at my intrusion. Perhaps imagination heightened the scene, and every thing appeared a mass of confusion, which came within the limits of my inspection. This happened in the month of October, and the weather in that latitude had been getting cool, and rather dangerous to an impaired constitution, without any canopy to resist the inclemency of the weather, and I saw, as I thought, death and eternity in a fearful combination staring me in the face. The thoughts of dying in Nauvoo had been more hideous to me than can be either imagined or described. As prayer is powerful with God, I turned my eyes towards Heaven, and prayed for heavenly assistance to escape from the fearful calamity and danger that surrounded me, and God in his mercy indisputably heard and granted my prayer, as he sent a speedy relief which brought me in safety out of the dismal labyrinth which surrounded me. I then pushed from the river towards the temple again, and selected a spot where I could repose for the night and await the decrees of heaven. It had been then about three in the afternoon. I reclined myself on this selected spot without the least expectation of human assistance until morning, as steamboats never touch at that place except to replenish their casks with an invigorating beverage which is found on the bank of the river, and precisely at the landing place. It appears to me that I fell asleep immediately, and probably slept an hour before I was summoned to arise, by a gentleman of herculean might and dimensions, who took me by the arm and awoke me from my slumbers. I was much astonished at the approach of a human being, as I could not conjecture where he came from, as I could discover no inhabitants within the circle of my inspection. The gentleman spoke exceedingly kind and affectionate to me, and seemed not only to sympathize in my misery, but to share largely in my misfortune; he seemed peculiarly dressed, and his dress was made so as to show his herculean dimensions to advantage, and the serenity of his countenance had been angelically pleasing and encouraging, particularly in the hour of extremity.

The gentleman addressed me as follows: "What brought you here, my friend," said he, "among the ruins and desolation of this inhospitable region?" I gave the gentleman a true and simple statement of the misfortune which brought me within the meshes of despair, without the least equivocation from the truth of the accident which occurred. The gentleman then said: "If you act agreeably to my instructions you will be exonerated from your difficult and perilous situation; and," said he again, "as boats seldom touch at this point, and as there is no hospitable abode to receive you in your present state of debility, you take care not to deviate from my directions, and, if not, your escape can be effected with facility. Fear not, neither be you discouraged." I thought at once of my catechism, whose lessons early in life imprinted on my mind that God is everywhere, and that His ubiquity is indisputable. The cheering intelligence I got from the heavenly messenger restored to me, in a manner, my original motion and elasticity, and I must say, some unexpected strength. I submissively bent to acknowledge my gratitude to my friend and benefactor, and then departed without asking his name, an omission which I consider unpardonable. But before I took my departure I looked all around to avoid hogs and dogs, and other ferocious animals which have been already mentioned, but saw nothing of the kind to interrupt my departure. I need not tell you, dear reader, that I unerringly complied with his directions, which effected my escape with facility from the chambers of despondency and death.

I suppose, dear reader, you would be anxious to hear the instructions I received from my angelic guide, which facilitated my escape from Nauvoo, the original paradise of Joe Smith and the Mormon saints, and that I shall give you with as much infallibility as I can, making an allowance for an agitated and treacherous memory. He took me by the right arm, and pointed to the river and said: "Do you see that high cliff that intercepts the river from your vision?" I answered, "Yes, sir, I do." "Then, said he, go directly towards that 'cliff, and convenient to it you will see a boat manned with four oars, which will indisputably take you across to Montrose, and when you arrive on the other side, you will see in readiness awaiting your arrival, two splendid animals and a fine coach, that will take you with incredible velocity across the country to Keokuk, a distance, I think he said, of 20 or 30 miles, and every care will be extended to your comfort until you are safely seated in your own berth," and added, "you and the boat will come at the same time to the wharf; take courage and fear not." I bowed and departed, and, my dear reader, to be candid in the matter, I attributed no implicit confidence to his assurance, or that such happiness awaited to facilitate my escape, and I considered his language more fabulous than prophetical, but, when I came to the cliff that obstructed my vision, according to his testimony, I saw in the identical place the boat, as heretofore described by my angelic director. So far, so good, but this did not consummate my happiness, as I felt still some inward apprehension of the uncertainty of my position. The men very cordially invited me to jump in, which I did, with alacrity, and there they awaited a few moments, until a gentleman by the name of McDonnell arrived, whose serenity and beautiful countenance dissipated all fears which intrinsically agitated me. He showed the gentleman in full, and seemed to be about thirty years of age. Indeed, I must say, the rest appeared, also, a decent set of fellows.

Although the Mississippi is considered 6 or 9 miles wide where we crossed, they rowed over the space with much rapidity. Though some of the rowers appeared young and wanting sufficient maturity to perform so laborious a task, yet it had been performed with inexpressible ease and dexterity. To corroborate the angelic prediction, as soon as we landed I saw the two animals heretofore described, beautifully harnessed on the landing place, and appeared motionless, without a driver to keep them in such subjection. In a moment the driver made his appearance, ascended and firmly held the reins, which at once demonstrated their avidity to perform the journey, in a word, they seemed unmanageable. With inexpressible courtesy the driver invited me to get in, and as he saw my debility, he strenuously assisted me to do so, and Mr. McDonnell and another gentleman got in also, and the youngsters stopped behind. And with ineffable speed they drove through that wild country without rest or hesitation, until we arrived, about nightfall, in the port of destination. And at that moment the sailors on board the fugitive boat were throwing out a plank to admit passengers to go ashore. This had been an unerring corroboration of angelical instructions.—Then, with the assistance of the two gentlemen, I got out of the coach, and with one under each arm I went aboard, and they cautiously and kindly placed me in the cabin. Ah! dear reader, this had been a critical moment. Overwhelmed with confusion, and without means to recompense the extraordinary kindness and assiduity of the two gentlemen who helped to bring me out of worse than Babylonian captivity, I became speechless, and could not utter a sentence to attenuate my culpability in the estimation of my benefactors. They bowed with unspeakable courtesy, demanded no recompense, and departed. I have, and will during the remainder of my days commend them to divine protection. Now, reader, pause solemnly on my escape from worse than captivity by the intervention of Divine providence, and consider in every dangerous extremity the ubiquity of God, and think the eye of Providence is immovably fixed on you, as if he had nothing else in creation to mind but yourself; and remember, also, that prayer is acceptable to Him who at once can exonerate you from all dangers and difficulties. My dear reader, I have no hesitation in saying that the being who awoke me from my slumbers had been either prophetically or angelically inspired, and commissioned by Divine Providence to redeem me from the impending fate which awaited me in the original paradise of Joe Smith and the Mormon family. Some time in the night the boat took her departure from Keokuk, and gallantly glided down the Mississippi River until we landed in St. Louis, and whatever conveyed the intelligence, the first news I heard, to my surprise, was, that the great Mormon Temple had been demolished by a terrific conflagration, and the news has been corroborated by unquestionable reports. Now, my dear reader, solemnly pause and consider whether the destruction of that stupendous edifice had been effected by spiritual fire, or by the agency of a treacherous incendiary. When I landed in St. Louis I went to see Messrs. Nugent & King, who affectionately invited me to remain with them until my health would be properly restored; but no admonition could make me remain; home I should go, and had been strenuously assisted in my efforts to accomplish my design by an Irish gentleman of the name of Mr. John Gawl, a professional baker. This brave countryman contributed as much to comfort me in time of sickness and prostration as my brother could do. At last, after a tedious and weary passage, I arrived in Pittsburg, Pa., pale, lean and emaciated, and on the very verge of eternity, and without offering a word for the purification of the stains I contracted through imprudence or misfortune. Now, my dear reader, before I close the narration of my downward trip I will tell you of an incident which occurred in a certain town or city during my stay therein, which will show you the diversities of human life, and how soon the scene is changed from the imaginary happiness we enjoy in rambling through elysian fields and enameled scenes, basking in the fallacious brilliancy of an unclouded sun, without reflecting on future impediments. Ah! how momentary and transitory is human happiness, and how fallacious are human enjoyments; how soon they evaporate and leave us a prey to disappointments, misfortune and woe!

The brilliant sun did often disappear,
And sable clouds had occupied his sphere.

Some of my readers will undoubtedly call in question the veracity of what follows, and brand it with the title which is commonly called blagging still. This appellation cannot debilitate its sincerity; and as I have related the vicissitudes I encountered in my travels, I will also relate the imaginary happiness I enjoyed while ranging through the inexpressible regions of bliss, and fed by the smiles of unsullied beauty. In a large town or city, in my travels, I put up at Mr. L——'s Hotel; and Mr. L—— was an Englishman by birth, education, and prejudice, and a very well informed gentleman. But we must overlook his singularities and habits to discover his intrinsic merits. Mr. L—— appeared, to strangers, pompous and haughty, and consequential, self-willed and self-important, and such are the natural characteristics of an Englishman, which made him appear repulsive to some and insufferable to others. But those are not sufficiently acquainted with Mr. L——, and I must acknowledge I had been of this class, until my acquaintance with the gentleman dispelled the absurdity of my opinion. Mr. L—— did not interfere with the affairs of his establishment, no more than any of his boarders, as his mind and thoughts were occupied by the contemplation of some new invention or discovery, which seemed a mystery to all his acquaintances, and even to his wife; and if Mr. L—— had been a member of any Christian community, he practically showed no external sign of his internal conviction. Mrs. L——, on the other hand, had been witty, wise, and facetious, courteous, kind, and entertaining, and an Irishwoman in the bargain; very attentive to her boarders and travellers, and entertained all with respect, comfort, clemency and cleanliness. She was rich in intelligence, and openly professed and practiced the Roman Catholic religion. They lived according to matrimonial laws, in peace, harmony, and contentment, and I never saw before, two so dissimilar in habits, practice, and propensities, display such mutual confidence and affection, or that stood in the same reciprocity of terms. They had no issue, but still were blessed with all the necessaries to render life agreeable. One evening, after returning from my rambles, Mrs. L—— asked me had I been in such a street in the city. I answer negatively. Then Mrs. L—— expressed a wish that I should call to such a number in that street, as there, she said, resides an accomplished young lady who is exceeding fond of reading, and will, unquestionably, patronize your productions. "And my friend, O'Donovan," said Mrs. L——, "I will give you, before you set out, a history of her life and situation, as it might enable you to act with more caution, prudence, and accuracy. Her father," said she, "was an Irishman, and an honest industrious one at that, who, by hard labor and industry, accumulated and amassed a large fortune in this city, and left none to inherit or enjoy it after the mother's death, but an only daughter, the very lady, to whom I am introducing you, Miss Laura. The house she lives in is hers, together with the whole range adjoining it; and in other parts of the city she has a large property, so that her possessions are large, ample, and indisputably solid. Her father, before his death, kept an extensive confectionary in this city, and had been considered an honest, respectable citizen; and Miss Laura, herself, is justly considered virtuous, charitable, good-natured, and an accomplished young lady; and still she is unmarried and sliding down rapidly from the meridian towards the western horizon, where the beauty she possesses so fascinating, and so irresistibly, will, in a few years, set, and there remain beyond the reach of the most sagacious eye, and the most attentive observer; but her assiduity to her personal decoration is a check to that slide, and some of the keenest observers consider Laura only in her teens; but the singularities of her mother's propensities have confirmed her celibacy so far, since the death of her husband as she stands in the market every day, with the exception of Sundays, in spite of the inclemency or the intolerable rays of the sun and weather, to dispose of her candy and other sweet things she has at her disposal; and she was never known, during many years, to take the smallest refreshment to nourish old age and infirmity; she is nothing but skin and bones, and her voice is sharp, feeble, and unmusical; and no gentleman who is acquainted with her mother, would have the timerity to approach Miss Laura in the shape of a wooer, for fear of the acidity of her mother's vocabulary."

"Madam," said I, "that creature must be lineally descended from Shylock, and, of course, possesses or has his natural proclivities; but if you tell me, Mrs. L——," said I, again, "the latitude and longitude of her age, by my knowledge of navigation, I will find the place to a notch; and if Laura is anchored in the vicinity of either of the poles, where I am located myself, I am in hopes of a compromise, or at least, of an honorable reception." Mrs. L—— replied: "The old bachelors are sometimes exceedingly shy; still, I think your accuracy as a physiognomist, is sufficient to tell the latitude of her age." "And my friend and countryman," said Mrs. L—— again, "I am in hopes your astronomical observations will bring all to light," and added, "There is another deficiency, or rather an external blemish observable in Miss Laura, which hinders gentlemen of her acquaintance of paying their addresses to her, as none else would be admitted. I mean men of common magnitude. This blemish is visible, though it seems to overreach the eagle eye of the physiognomist and philosopher." "And my countryman," said Mrs. L—— again, "as I have an extraordinary opinion of the keenness of your observation and unerring conceptions of external blemishes, I will let yourself discover that stain without any enabling preliminary of mine." Enough was said. I retired immediately to bed, not to sleep, but to consider on some infallible mode of discovery. I thought I could divest myself of the distinguishing characteristics of an Irishman; and these are frankness, affability, wit and unbounded generosity. Such marks bear no affinity to pride, pomposity, and presumption, and counterfeit myself a keen, cool, cautious, calculating Yankee, the better to proceed. But this mode of action I deemed impossible, and also incompatible with the virtue and dignity of an Irishman. I at once exclaimed: "I am an Irishman and will act in conformity with his disposition. Her eyes will be my unerring guide, and I will proceed accordingly." I arose early on the following morning, and offering a prayer as a thanksgiving to the Supreme Ruler of the universe, I repaired to the barber's shop to dislodge some external encumberance, and to give delineations of a declining tendency—a cosmetic wash and polish—in hopes they would appear to some advantage in the eyes of Miss Laura, and gave him strict orders how to shave and cut hair in the most fashionable style; also informed him that my future happiness, in a manner, depended on his action, and told him to improve in his inimitable art, to secure that happiness. The barber, being quite a young man, and thought my sentiments corroborated my design, which he considered exceedingly foolish, he too, tittered, during the operation, which had been effected by my vanity, until at last I cautioned him against incissions. After having done at the barber's, I returned to my room, and decorated myself with my best bib and frill, and then, as I thought, my symmetry much improved, and my appearance better, filling my carpet-bag with my books which gave an account of the woes and sufferings of my countrymen, by the penal enactments of an ungodly, unmerciful, and unscrupulous government. All things ready, I directed my steps, alone and unknown, towards the point of attraction, No. 177, to discover some blemish, or spot, disfiguring the Planet Laura, which eluded the telescopic observations of my astronomical predecessors. Before long I came in view of her residence, as being located on the corner of the street. She had a full view of my proximity. I moved with the velocity of a deer to hide my weary slide down the declivity of life, but I came not within the limits of her inspection, as she sat in a careless recumbent attitude, perusing attentively one of Sir Walter Scott's novels. On approaching the door I coughed slightly to indicate my coming, so as to give her time to prepare herself for my reception, and stood motionless awaiting Miss Laura's approach. She immediately made her appearance, beautifully tinged with the exterior sanctity of an angel; and as soon as I got a glimpse of the incomparable creature, I bowed low with humiliation and reverence to acknowledge my devotion to the angelic being that stood before me; and after making a few Egyptian hieroglyphics with my boots on the carpet, with Miss Laura's approbation, I took my seat, and the first glance of her beautiful eye informed me that she was none of those fastidious creatures, rather ethical for common sinners, and this conviction made me instantly touch the most sacred and most musical chord of my Irish harp. Miss Laura was not overloaded with supercilious airs and unapproachable purity, as other creatures are of her sex.

Whether Miss Laura expected any visitor that day or not I cannot say, though she had been in perfect trim to receive such, as the curling tongs performed its own part with inimitable art, and the rich raven tresses that hung gracefully on her forehead were beautifully adjusted; she had a fine set of teeth, which she showed to much advantage when she smiled. She had been cosmetically washed, patched, pruned, pinched and painted, and I am of the opinion that the most unerring inspection would prognosticate the throne of her age to be erected within the circle of her teens. No sooner seated than I commenced my observations; her eye, though slow in its motion, was dark, large, keen, killing and expressive; her features were beautiful and pleasing, and void of repulsion, and no defection or blemish could be seen in her external appearance. Miss Laura inquired if I were a stranger in the city, in the most polite manner imaginable. I replied I was. "I know," said she, "you are an Irishman by birth, and added, I am happy to think my father was one also; my dear, departed father, said Laura, often boasted of being an original Irishman with ecstacy and enthusiasm, which had been no way offensive to my mother, as being a native of that country herself, and on that account I entertain a

5

strong veneration for Irishmen in general." "That is quite natural," said I, and added, "Miss Laura, I can discover a pure stream of Irish blood running through your veins this moment, and I feel myself animated by the utmost veneration for the visible irresistible charms you display, which are the hereditary attributes of Irish ladies." "Sir," said Laura, with a smile, "I should be much surprised at your flattery or otherwise incomparable allusions, only that I know encomiums and admiration of female beauty are as natural to Irishmen, as those irresistible charms you have mentioned are to Irish ladies." Her reply caused much merriment on both sides, and I considered at once that I had met my match. Miss Laura again spoke, and said, "Sir, you seem to be some professional gentleman, and if it should not intrude on courtesy I would wish to know where you make your home." "Miss," said I, "I am a Pittsburgher, which is some distance from here and in the State of Pennsylvania." This information had been an intrusion or rather an insult to her geographical knowledge, but I added, "as thus, which is unqestionably within your understanding, this appendage canceled the enormity or magnitude of the offence," and said I again, "I am professionally a surgeon and physician, and by practicing both I gain my living, when at home in Pittsburgh. "O, my friend," said Laura, "unless reports and communications be unfounded and fabulous, you make your home in a dreadful wicked and dangerous city." I unequivocably acknowledged that there were some dangerous characters in the city, and some atrocious crimes committed there; nevertheless, in it, I said, can be found as honest, as religious, as generous, and as intelligent a population as in any other city in the Union of the same magnitude, and said that Christian denominations of every kind receive the spiritual instructions of their priests and ministers in Pittsburgh with as much assiduity and devotion as the

Christian population of any other city in the United States. Miss Laura coincided with me at once. I spoke again to Miss Laura, and said, "As thus I must inform you of the cause of my perambulation. My native country is now on the verge of a revolution, and I have attempted to write her woes and afflictions to stimulate and animate my countrymen in America, and such as would sympathize in the misfortune of the Irish nation everywhere, or aid and help them in their revolutionary struggles, and I have a number of the work in my possession at present, together with a small poem book containing some fugitive pieces, songs and incidents elucidating my past folly, all original, also my early courtship and sad disappointment in the consummation of matrimony, or a union by its solemn laws with her I so dearly loved; some I sell and some I give away." "Sir," said Laura, "will not your sacrifice interfere with your pecuniary circumstances or worldly affairs?" "Miss Laura, "said I, "nothing can greatly damage my pecuniary circumstances, as my means are already limited and circumscribed, and if my sacrifice should reduce my funds to the lowest extremity for the sake of restoring or helping to restore the freedom and independence of my unfortunate native country to its original basis, the happiness I would intrinsically feel would recompense me for my sacrifice and labor." "Sir," said she, "if you please let me see one of your productions." I handed her immediately the poem book, thinking it would relish better with the avidity of her taste and imagination than the historical events of other days. As luck would have it, the first reading matter that struck her eye, and animated her feelings, was the courtship, and after reading a page or two she raised her beautiful black eyes and looked at me with indiscribable commisseration, read a little more, and her sensation seemed beyond description, and her symptoms and pandiculations confirmed me that sweet Laura had been sunstruck before, and that the arch-boy Cupid hebetated his arrow in her susceptible heart. After some time she closed the book, and asked me in a very serious manner, "was the courtship real or imaginary?" Miss Laura said I, "the courtship is not a galvanized fiction, and you may rely on its authenticity." Then Laura deliberately said, "I need not ask you any question concerning your wife and family, for any person thrown into Cupid's crucible so early in life could never consent to be united afterward in matrimonial bonds with any other." At that moment the clock struck five, P. M., and Miss Laura cried, "it is five o'clock!" I looked with astonishment on Miss Laura, and expressed my surprise at the late hour of the day, as I could not think it more than twelve o'clock or the noon time of the day, and I said, quite sadly, "time flies, O, how swiftly." "Apologetically you can confer compliments, sir," said Miss Laura, "without evident indications." "O, Miss Laura," said I with a modifying tone, "directly or indirectly, they are due without making at the moment any evident personal allusions." "Now," said Laura, again, "sir, you will have a good appetite this evening as you had a long fast this day within this inhospitable roof, which is altogether incompatible with the generous reception which your countrymen give others on the like occasion." "Miss Laura," said I, "I never had a ravenous appetite, and the little I had to nourish nature has deserted me, since I had the honor and pleasure of an acquaintance with so distinguished, so beautiful and so entertaining a lady, as you are," and added, "O, Miss Laura where to find the fugitive I leave you to conjecture." "Thank you, sir, another hint, a compliment," said Laura. At that moment I attempted to rise, but I found myself tied to the seat, fast as Prometheus was to the mountain, by Miss Laura's incomparable charms, but after extricating myself from the difficulty of my position, and taking my carpet-bag in my hand, Miss Laura asked me, as thus, "Sir," said she, "is your carpet-bag locked? if it be," said Laura, "you may leave it under my protection this night, and I will be responsible for its contents in the morning, and I know some in this vicinity who will purchase of you; come again to-morrow." O, my friends, this invitation touched my ears so musically, so harmoniously and so agreeably that my feelings on the occasion I can not describe. I said to Laura, "then I will leave you my carpet-bag, and its key, and had I the keys of that kingdom into which sinners can never enter, without a purification of their original and actual transgressions, you should have them also, so as you could go in and out at pleasure." "Mr. O'Donovan," cried Laura, "go! go! your flattery is rather complimentary for human nature to spurn; go, it is time you should clear yourself; nevertheless, I hope we will have the pleasure of seeing you to-morrow." At once I touched my hat, bowed low, submissively and departed, and in fifteen minutes time found myself moored in Mrs. L.'s hotel, who no sooner saw me than she and those who were acquainted with the matter came running to know did I excel my assiduous predecessors in discovering Laura's external repulsive and objectionable blemish. After Mrs. L.'s inquiry I informed her no visible deformity existed in Laura's disk, and that I considered her the most finished creature in the framework of nature. "O, my dear countryman," said Mrs. L., "there is an external blemish, but it appears it is invisible to human inspection." I retired after some time to bed with a full determination of making another trial the following day. My rest had been interrupted by a thousand strange stratagems of discovery, and I summoned my ingenuity to bring things in contemplation to maturity. And after breakfast the following day I steered for the observatory, and had been again received by Miss Laura with a calm dignified and respectful attention.

After the courteous interchange of terms ceased, Laura asked me several questions, which I strove to answer with caution and fidelity. Then I thought I would take an accurate and unerring observation, which would put me in possession of her visible deformity, if such a thing existed, still nothing of the kind had been discoverable. After a little while Miss Laura arose and went into an adjoining room and brought me some kisses as she did the day before, with a liberality verging on insanity. O desperation, the first kiss-paper I read was mortifying, I pretended to read it with anguish, tribulation and anxiety, and the thing appeared evident to Laura, who asked the cause of my embarrassment. I reached her the kiss-paper, accompanied with a mournful glance, and a sad countenance which she indisputably observed; it read as thus:

Old folks oft' woo, but get no recompense,
Which shows old folks are destitute of sense.

This couplet I contrived to get in a newspaper the evening before, and when Laura read the couplet she blushed, and then, with a forcible though mild reasoning, commenced exonerating herself from any participation or previous knowledge of the little poetic effusion which was imprinted on the kiss paper. I tried to find her guilty of murder in the first degree, but her defence had been so legally and logically conducted, that I withdrew the suit, paid all expenses and passed a graceful apology for my unsupportable suspicion. All peaceably settled, I considered a closer proximity would be attended with greater accuracy, and that my view would be more comprehensive and unerring at a reasonable distance. The cause of her sitting at such a distance from me will be made evident before the conclusion of this narrative. Still, at that distance eternity itself would steal away from any man in company with her, and I thought myself, while in her company, ranging through the

Elysian fields of imaginary happiness, or roving through the aromatic groves of the Ganges, but, alas! I was soon awakened from my imaginary gyration as the old clock again struck five in the afternoon, and sounded the mournful signal of my departure, and the doleful intelligence of our separation. I then slowly and with much reluctance arose from my seat, but, O! in what a condition; with a debilitated constitution, a broken heart, a dismal countenance, and with an instinctive assurance that I should never see her again in this world, and with doubts conscientiously impressed, that I could not see her in the next. When ready to move, Miss Laura spoke again as follows: "Mr. O'Donovan, I had better not pay you this evening for the books, for, while the money is due, I will expect you to come this way again in expectation of getting it; you come to-morrow, and your money and books will be at your command." O, my dear reader, a reconciliation of this kind was easily effected, and I said to Laura, you have paid me a thousand times for them, and received more than their value, when you consented to read such indigested and dispirited a production, and as a matter of course, I cheerfully consented. Miss Laura brilliantly polished my composition with her approbation. After going through observed gemuflections and other hieroglyphics pertaining to courtesy and fashionable habits, I departed. After my arrival at my boarding house, Mrs. L. with much avidity inquired if I had any better success this day than I had yesterday; I said, "no better, madam." "Well,," said Mrs. L., "if you say so, I will unravel the whole mystery to you." "No, madam," said I, "I will make another experiment, and if not successful, I will relinquish the idea of any further prosecution of the blemish in question." "Well then," said Mrs. L., "I can inform you of another street leading to the observatory, as you call it, and the foliage of the trees would cause a refraction of the solar rays, which are now irresistibly felt." This advice I afterwards considered to be providential, as it had a preliminary tendency to the discovery. I had a much clearer view of her by going the new road, and therefore had an opportunity of viewing her position while reading, with more certainty. As Laura did not notice my close proximity until I came close to the door, I saw clearly by the inclination of the book to the left eye, that she was perfectly blind of the other; having taught so many boys and girls laboring under the same disadvantage, confirmed me in my opinion. Laura received me once more with unbounded applause, and openly declared her happiness in seeing me return. I thanked her for her kind and incomparable reception, and expressed my willingness, if it came within my dominion to offer her an equivalent for her ineffable courtesy, and for the urbanity she showed, altogether unmerited by an accidental stranger. When I sat down, the gyrations of my imagination were exceedingly big and circular, in search of some solid spot whereon I could rest my Archimedian lever, to take an infallible telescopic observation, or rather, human inspection of all parts exposed to occular demonstration, of female beauty, to discover a deformity, or blemish, on the disc of one of the handsomest planets, though of modern discovery, that had been as yet signalized; an obscurity rendered invisible by some unaccountably fortunate impediment which I am not able to elucidate. Laura's manner was highly pleasing and polished, and that matured by a high order of intelligence and superior judgment would render her pleasing and acceptable to any gentleman, as a wife, neighbor, or companion. Miss Laura spoke freely of the characteristics of my countrymen, and indeed, favorably so, though I acknowledged to her that I had a thousand faults, follies and deficiencies, yet, among that heterogeneous combination ingratitude could not be discovered. As Miss Laura was an early riser and an attentive artificer, her external appearance showed to the best possible advantage, and I sat at the same distance from her that I usually did, and looked slightly and earnestly at her right eye, but could observe neither a defection, obscurity or blemish within the range of my inspection. I immediately thought of another stratagem which could give me an opportunity of a closer examination: I summoned at once the little discretion, modesty and urbanity, and other little preliminaries necessary for the enterprise, and after pouring forth a thousand well directed encomiums on her personal beauty, and particularly on her raven tresses, asked Laura, my infatuating jewel, permission to touch, and only touch, with my finger the wonderful and inimitable silken curls, which clustered around her head, and descended gracefully on her snowy neck. Miss Laura acquiesced with ineffable cheerfulness, and when permission was granted, I moved, and modestly sat at the blind side of my angelic Laura, and again poured forth my admiration of her beautiful features, raven locks inimitably adjusted, and some other perfections peculiar to herself, which were neither feigned, forged or fictitious, but natural and agreeable to circumstances. Laura, submitting to my examination of her incomparable locks, still knew too well how to hide her deficiency or blindness, and render it inaccessable to my diligence, as she, during the time, half closed her eyes. Being baffled by the ingenuity and skill of Miss Laura, so far, I thought still to come closer to her eye, and pour out more laudations on the curve and beauty of her eyebrows, commencing at the left and coming round to the right, uttering slowly, "O! what a beautiful eyebrow! O! when have I seen such a beautiful eyebrow before? Never, never!" Still, all my accuracy proved vain and fruitless, as Laura had her eyes entirely closed when I had finished my revolution. Her artful fortification of her blindness only helped to confirm my opinion of the obscurity. Not wishing to bė impertinent, and after acknowledging the obligation I was under to Miss Laura, I removed to my usual seat, and took another accurate view of her eye, which appeared as immaculate as the other, or, perhaps in more appropriate terms, as brilliant as the star Femalhaut, which is placed in the eye of the Southern Fish. So situated, I must candidly confess that days became moments in her presence, and in turning round I saw that the common disturber of my happiness, the old clock, would signalize its intention, and I observed to Laura that in a short time I would be under the disagreeable necessity of bidding her a final adieu. This remark caused a solemn silence on both sides, which lasted for some time, and when Laura observed my sad contemplation, she seemed much confused at my indescribable infatuation and suffering; she unquestionably considered I got implicated in her invulnerable meshes, and seemed lost in meditation for some time. Miss Laura after recovering from her solemn silence, walked slowly and thoughtfully into an adjoining room and brought me out my carpet bag and books, without trespass or intrusion, and also the amount due for the books she bought, which I obstinately refused taking; but all negatives proved an abortion. Before I had time to bid Laura a final farewell, she spoke as follows:

"O'Donovan, my friend"—for all other terms and compliments were suspended, such as Mr. and Miss and all other preliminaries denoting politeness or distinction, were cancelled on both sides, I mean the superfluous encumbrance had been entirely rejected or forgotten—"you had better come to-morrow, it will be the last day of the week, and charge me, or the commonwealth with the sacrifice, and if you leave me the carpet bag, I will expect you to come, otherwise I despair of your returning. Ah! sweet Laura well knew that a rope of sand 'or of mountain snow, could pull me back to hear the unwelcomed sound of the old clock again, whose predictions with unerring certainty made a sad revelation of my hour of departure from my earthly Paradise, then I gave her back again my carpet bag, with all its contents, then bowed submissively and departed. This operation caused an immediate reaction in my constitution, and while on my way to Mrs. L.'s, I thought some desperate effort should be made to regain my freedom, and thinking of the lamentable condition of Telemachus when Minerva the goddess of wisdom, in the shape of Mentor, threw him with obstinacy and determination into the ocean, to have him escape from the long captivity intended for him by Calypso and her nymphs. When I arrived Mrs. L—, her train of servants and boarders came running together to inquire about my success in my last discovery. I softly whispered in Mrs. L—'s ear, the word "blind," and then placed my finger on my right eye, to signalize the accuracy of my discovery. At this intelligence, my countrywoman, Mrs. L— displayed more joy and gratification than I could have expected. She ran to her husband and informed him of my infallible discovery, of Laura's incurable blemish, which indisputably pleased him to a notch. He showed himself exceedingly happy in consequence of my incomparable diligence, perseverance and industry, and acknowledged my telescopic observation, more certain, more forcible and more infallible than any taken by my predecessors. When inquiries and merriment subsided, I went into my room and composed the following poem, which I intended to send her that evening, with a little runner, who had been kept in the hotel for the same purpose, but after a second consideration I avoided doing so. It is as follows:

Why gaze on you on that ill-fated day,
When some misfortune drove me in your way,
The first fond glance that I bestowed on thee,
That glance has proved unfortunate to me.
The smallest ringlet of your glossy hair,
Would save my life and banish my despair;
The gloomy thoughts of my approaching doom,
Now drives me headlong to my silent tomb.
Can't other duties my affections draw?
'Tis better die than violate the law.
How strange to read upon historic page,
That man can love in his declining age!
Yet so it is, and so has been the case;
With one doom'd man among the human race.
In mossy dells where hermits love to pray,
And wood-nymphs often rendezvous to play,
I'll range alone to dissipate my woes,
Or climb the mount to where Parnassus flows,
And there convenient to the sacred spring,
I'll find contentment where the muses sing;
But no contentment is existing where
My Laura cannot have an equal share.
O! Laura, Laura, my unceasing theme;
'Tis not your riches, but your smiles I claim.
Dear Laura tell me, where am I to go
To spend my days in misery and woe?
Ah! beauteous Laura, beauteous are thy charms,
I fear they'll fade in some unworthy arms,
And I, unconscious of your future fate,
Repining sadly in another state.

O'Donovan.

This poem, as I said before, I intended to send to Miss Laura the same afternoon, by a little runner kept in the hotel for that identical purpose, but after a second consideration I declined doing so, not knowing the effect it would have on her mind, but when I took my departure from the place, I gave it to Mrs. L. with strict injunctions to have it conveyed to her.

I went the following morning according to arrangements made and provided to the observatory, and found my angelic Laura, beautifully decked, rigged and cosmetically finished; her tresses inimitably adjusted, and her whole exterior much improved, by art and other fascinating ornaments, that added much elegance to her original appearance, and perfection. She received me with mournful silence, as I suppose she thought our final separation approximating. On my side of the question could be seen a gloom and conceivable stillness beyond the reach of demonstration, and on Miss Laura's side, were half-stifled sighs and other inconsolable symptoms, evidently acknowledging her situation. As thus, we spent the day in a kind of dumb philosophy, but, a little time before the old clock was determined to declare its intentions, which would, perhaps, indisputably signalize our final separation, I took my carpet bag in my hand with mournful reluctance to bid my Laura my last adieu, who sat diametrically opposite, as I thought with downcast eyes and a nervous constitution, when in rushed the sea-serpent, her mother, and to describe the configuration of that specimen of blighted humanity, is unquestionably impossible, and when she saw me sitting opposite her darling daughter, she uttered a fearful, outlandish and inhuman scream, which put my whole constitution in commotion. Though being well fortified against its influence by the information I received of Mrs. Skinflint, from Mrs. L— who did her some justice in description. She frightfully asked Laura what brought that man here; poor Laura seemed prostrated with ineffable shame and confusion. "Who is that man or what brought him here?" asked the sea-serpent again. She continued, "who made him acquainted with you—drive out the villain Laura; drive him out instantly." She seemed a mere skeleton, very tall but miserably bent, screwed and twisted, and showed the unscrupulous and devastating assaults of time; her thin gray hairs falling down her narrow and attenuated shoulders in sad disorder and irregularity, and her dress was neither rich, rare nor expensive. Poor Laura—though in deep agony—approached her mother with attention, respect, assiduity and affection, and the obedience she displayed on the occasion, enlarged my attachment to her a thousand fold. Poor Laura said mildly and calmly, "O! mother, dear mother, this is Mr. O'Donovan, a gentleman of unquestionable habits, an eminent physician and surgeon, and my dear mother curb your temper and get acquainted with the gentleman; he is also your own countryman. This request only excited her sentiments and anger to a tremendous pitch, and she yelled furiously, "A countryman of mine, Laura; many a fine rascal my country has produced, and I think he is one of them; drive him out Laura, he seems to be an old broken-down lawyer who is in quest of a wife to support him in his old age and infirmity, whose misfortune and misspent life compelled him to adopt the appellation of physician and surgeon. Laura! Laura!" cried the old serpent again, "that man could not cure Calander Digby's brindle cow," she continued, screaming and cautioning against my future intrusion, until her words became utterly or altogether indistinct. I sat motionless all the time attentively viewing the spasmodic efforts and strange symmetry of the old serpent, until at last I took advantage of Laura and made a farcical grin at the miserable miser, which made her understand the contemptuous opinion I entertained of her, and which made her a thousand times worse, for when she made an attempt to signalize to Laura my disrespect for her, her confusions and convulsions had been so great, that her language became a mystery to her darling Laura and indisputably so to me.

I approached the door, when I thought her convulsively strangled, to take my departure, but oh, my! sweet Laura followed me, and begged of me most earnestly, not to be offended at her dear mother's singularities, but when the old tape-worm saw with what tenacity her dear Laura clang to me, I thought then unquestionably that death was inevitable, and that my dear Laura could futurely hold the reins of government herself, and regulate her dominion during the remainder of her days. I then bid a tender farewell to Laura, and walked slowly and sorrowfully down the street, musing sadly upon the condition of poor Laura, and being confident that our separation had been finally established, then and for ever; and after going some distance from the paradise lost, as if lineally descended from Lot's wife, I looked back and saw poor Laura in the same position that I left her, and I conjectured by the downward tendency of her head and other unmistakable symptoms, that she was in great agony and confusion by the meanness of her mother's strange and terrfic contortions and convulsive struggles, and more so through her mother's insolence and insufferable behavior towards myself, and on that spot I took the last sorrowful glance of paradise lost. I considered it a happy circumstance for the fair sex, that Laura kept within her castle, as they would appear in her presence dim and diminutive as stars of inferior magnitude appear in the vicinity of a full moon, when under the influence of the magnificence of her lustre. On my way home, I was thinking of the lamentable state of a miser. Indeed, I came to the conclusion that a miser is a useless encumbrance and a dishonor to society, for if his relative, friend, or neighbor, had been reduced by the vicissitudes of fortune to low and limited circumstances and to make an application to him for some assistance to help him out of his difficulty the result would be an abortion, and a refusal, and his application would be attended with no acquisition to help his pecuniary deficiencies. The miser's accumulation is inaccessible to either piety or pity. Now, my dear reader, this is a fearful consideration, as every man must know that whatever sum or amount he would deposit in banks or leave behind him of that perishable and mineral production, avails him nothing, but whatever sum he deposits in "Thy Kingdom come," and beyond human control, that sum he will indisputably receive with compound interest. Now, my dear reader, I have candidly narrated to you my tribulation and imaginary, or perhaps, real happiness, and I leave you to conjecture if one compensates the other. I returned immediately to Mrs. L——'s Hotel, settled my accounts, had my baggage taken on board, and then took my departure from the regions of bliss, without any expectation of seeing again my ever lost Laura, which is the cause of the following poem.

O, Laura, Laura, fare thee well,
Adieu forever more,
In wood, in glade, in cave and dell,
Your memory I'll adore.

When fate directed me your way,
Of me my fate denied,
'Twas then I saw the Queen of May
With Cupid at her side.

He took his aim, his arrow sped,
It pierced a tender part,
And I thought then, that I was dead,
Or lived without a heart.

I closely viewed the radiant fair,
No blemish could I see,
But raven locks and ringlets rare
Which hung down gracefully.

I viewed, and viewed, and viewed again,
The peerless goddess there;
Her brilliant eye and swan-like skin,
Her forehead high and fair.

Ah! Laura's notes then gently fell
Upon my listening ear,
Alike the notes of Philomel
Which steeled me to the chair.

The first fond glance of her I took
Had much deranged my mind,
And I could swear upon the book,
That Cupid is not blind.

Eternity would steal away
From me, I'll tell you how,
Could I gaze both night and day
On her angelic brow?

The clock struck then to let me know,
Which did disturb my mind,
The very hour that I should go
And leave my joy behind.

The awful news the sound conveyed
Methinks I hear it now,
Then to the beauteous native maid
I made a courteous bow.

She said, as time we cannot stay
To mitigate all sorrow,
I hope, I wish, I beg and pray,
That you may come to-morrow.

To her I calmly made a vow,
I kept unbroken too,
That I would come, then made a bow,
And bade Miss L——, adieu.

I hastened home to Mrs. L——,
Who wanted to be wise;
And said my friend, now can you tell
Where Laura's blemish lies.

O, blemish, madam, she has none,
She is divinely fair,
As pure in thought as any one
Who's under angels' care.

My friend, said she, I'm better tell
Where Laura's blemish lies,
It will dispel the magic spell
She placed upon your eyes.

Ah! Laura, madam, I revere,
And can define her state;
Alas, alas, you sent me there,
Or else, avenging fate.

For some repose, I went to bed,
No sooner closed my eyes
Than my fleeting fancy fled
To Laura's paradise.

When Sol had tinged the mountain's brow
And forest warblers played
I thought I should fulfil the vow
To Laura, I had made.

To see my Laura was my lot,
The fairest of all creatures,
And down I sat upon the spot
To gaze upon her features.

Adam with his peerless queen
In Eden's blooming bower,
I do believe, had never seen,
So beautiful a flower.

With caution and prudential skill
  I viewed her o'er and o'er,
And she appeared more radiant still
  Than she appeared before.

Ah! time insensibly would fly
  To bear my ills away;
And golden hours would never die,
  Could I with Laura stay.

Pleasure has a transient reign,
  And fickle fortune too;
Still, nothing then, could give me pain,
  While Laura was in view.

The time again, that we should part,
  The clock announced with care,
Which gave myself a broken heart,
  And threw me in despair.

Now, said I, I must depart,
  This time we both will sever,
I'll keep your image in my heart,
  Adieu, adieu, forever.

Then Laura spoke without delay
  To dissipate my sorrow,
Ah! this can't be our parting day,
  Oh! do come back to-morrow.

With my request, said she, again
  I hope you will comply,
As I would think 'twould be a sin,
  If you should say good-bye.

To her, submissively I said,
  Be sure I will obey,
Then kiss'd her hand, and bowed my head,
  And homeward bent my way.

My hostess met me at the door,
  And ask'd in great surprise,
Did I ever since explore
  Where Laura's blemish lies?

I said dear madam, tease me not,
  My jewel is so fair
That neither blemish, stain, or spot,
  With her could interfere.

Then Mrs. L——, again replied,
  You're better try no more,
For you can't find what others tried
  A thousand times before.

Or, if you do pursue your course,
  There is a better way,
Where shady trees will blunt the force
  Of every solar ray.

'Twas indeed my lucky lot
  To go the other way,
And acting so, I found the spot
  Where Laura's blemish lay.

When near her place I saw at once,
  And clearly did espy
The book she read, tho' not by chance,
  Inclining to one eye.

Then I exclaimed, Laura, dear!
  Oh! what I heard is true,
And to my grief, that one so fair,
  Could have a blemish too.

Without delay I entered in
  To view her dazzling beauty,
And bow'd, as I consider'd then
  It my incumbent duty.

'Twas then I thought a nearer sight
  Would banish my surprise,
But Venus never beam'd so bright
  As did both Laura's eyes.

I calmly said to her as such,
  Oh! lovely goddess, fair,
Would you permit me now to touch
  Your locks of silken hair?

With all my heart, said Laura, dear,
  I'll grant you your request,
And yet it's nought but common hair,
  If you should try your best.

I then approached with modest air,
  And sat convenient by
Where Laura sat upon a chair,
  To look into her eye.

Ah! wicked Harry's* heart would melt,
  Tho' obdurate before,
If he could feel what I had felt,
  He would behead no more.

I soon removed unto the chair
  On which I sat before,
Though I knew full well the stain was there,
  I loved her still the more.

I gently touched her tresses rare,
  Her forehead fair and high,
But she with an exceeding care
  Had mostly clos'd her eye.

There she sat in beauty's glow,
  Fair, innocent, and meek,
The blushing rose and virgin snow
  Contending in her cheek.

---

* Henry VIII., the wife-killer.

Oh! what a solemn silence reign'd,
While hearts were beating high,
Tho' she surprising courage feign'd
She could not stay her sigh.

While in this mood her mother came,
And slowly she drew near;
Ah! soon her wild outlandish scream
Had made me quake with fear.

Tho' far in years she did advance,
Still loudly she did shout,
And cried to Laura, rise at once,
And turn that rascal out.

Miss Laura met her at the door,
And said both clear and strong,
If you but knew this man, I'm sure,
You would restrain your tongue.

Have patience mother, for a while,
And try to act your part;
He is a star from Erin's Isle,
Who knows the healing art.

She said outrageously again,
Believe not what he feigns;
He's one of those intriguing men,
Who is in want of means.

Then Laura said, that can't be so,
He calumny defies,
His fame is like the virgin snow,
That on the mountain lies.

Thro' all this time, I did not wag,
Unmindful of my duty,
But viewed this ugly, hateful hag,
As if she were a beauty.

With much reluctance I arose,
Abandon'd to despair,
The screaming Bedlam's vocal blows,
I could no longer bear.

Then Laura held me hard and fast,
To banish my regret,
Alas! that grasp as being the last,
I never shall forget.

The strangest news I have to tell,
And which I can't deny—
I could not say to her, farewell,
Nor could she say good-bye.

'Twas then I tried with courage rare,
Consistent with my duty,
To gaze on that angelic fair,
Envelop'd in her beauty.

On trembling limbs I then withdrew,
  Repining at my lot;
Altho' I could not say adieu,
  I will forget her not.

O'DONOVAN.

I have no doubt but Laura, after my departure, had been informed of my pretending qualifications as a physician and surgeon, and if so, it will teach her, and teach others of her sex into whose hands this production must fall, not to attribute infallible certainty to the romantic productions, or pretensions of a rambling stranger.

As I mentioned before, I returned from my downward trip much debilitated and with a shattered constitution; still after two week's rest at home, good attendance, and the necessary nourishment for a speedy recovery, I felt immeasurably better, and being disappointed and dissatisfied, and naturally of an unbending, indefatigable disposition, and not easily subdued by adversities, though somewhat discouraged by declining age, I came to the conclusion to take another trip to the Eastern cities, and I acted according to my determination although the winter had been momentarily expected, and navigation nearly suspended. I sent my books before me to Philadelphia, and took the canal as far as Harrisburg myself, and lodged with my friend and countryman Mr. Hogan, who kept and perhaps still keeps, a splendid and respectable hotel in that capital. Mr. Hogan is one of the most amusing and pleasing landlords I met with in my travels, for accommodation sake speaks a little of every language; he sings and whistles harmoniously, and is considered by every man, who is acquainted with him, exceedingly honest, and although the gentleman at that time, (1848,) was sixty-five years of age, hardly a man could be produced who could put him on his back. Mr. Hogan possessed herculean strength in his manhood, and an uncommon share of activity, as no young man in his neighborhood could out-run him at the forementioned age. After breakfast, the following morning, I called on the Rev. Mr. Meagher who officiates as a Catholic clergyman in Harrisburg, and when I entered his residence there was seated, immediately before me a reverend clergyman, a distinguished divine, an eminent theologian, a prince in principle, and as an appendage to this luminous combination, an illustrious Irishman. The reverend gentleman received me with admirable attention and kindness which are the peculiar attributes of the holy priesthood, and clergymen generally speaking, and after interchanging a few terms of civility, I mentioned to the Rev. Mr. Meagher my errand to the capital of Pennsylvania. The reverend gentleman bought one of my books and paid a very generous price for it. I objected to the amount, but my objection proved ineffectual. I was glad the reverend gentleman bought the book by the cover, without further examination of its merits. On parting, the reverend gentlemen gave me a note of introduction to the Rev. Mr. Lane at Phildelphia, who also received me kindly. On the following Sunday I went to hear mass in Harrisburg, and where I could hear the Rev. Mr. Meagher preach distinctly to his congregation, and the elegance of his language, the sublimity of his ideas, and the religious spirit which he introduced in the subject, are beyond the reach of my elucidation, and the most inflexible skeptic, if he were in attendance, would, or should, be convinced of his lamentable condition in the sight of heaven, and of his vain and obstinate opposition to the established and unerring laws of the Catholic Church. During my stay in Harrisburg I was highly pleased with the inhabitants of the capital. In fact, they seemed courteous and kind, and the American ladies and gentlemen of that town, such as came under my inspection, were of a high order, and of a superior grade, and entirely divested of pride, presumption and prejudice; and if my judgment be competent, in all my travels met not their superiors. I called at Mr. Burke's residence, in Harrisburg; although in several instances pride is the offspring of riches, but in this case it is not so, and, indeed, the most superficial observer could prove that it never entered into Mr. Burke's dominions, as it found no encouragement from himself or from his lady, and therefore could not vaccinate the family. Mrs. Burke seemed very busy herself, arranging her furniture and making other preparations within her princely mansion. I had not seen her daughters nor any of her family, with the exception of one young gentleman who had one of his eyes accidentally injured at that time by the explosion of a gun; and him I considered a finished young gentleman. By inquiry I heard afterwards that he got perfectly retrieved from the injury he sustained, which information gave me unspeakable pleasure. Mrs. Burke is one of the best-looking women, taking her age in consideration, that I met with in all my travels. I then took my departure for Lancaster, in the cars, and arriving there I took up my quarters in Mr. Bernard McGran's splendid hotel, where I enjoyed, during my stay in the place, peace, plenty and protection, and to utter a word in his praise in this rambling sketch, is, I must say, unnecessary, as Mr. McGran's universally known, and being universally known, is universally esteemed. He is an honor to the land of his nativity, and an acquisition to the land of his adoption. I entertain a good opinion of the whole family, particularly of his son, who was, at the time (1848), bordering on maturity or manhood. He was then, unquestionably, a promising young fellow. Shortly after my arrival in Lancaster,I paid avisit to the Rev. Mr. B. Keenan who officiated there as a Catholic priest, and the first glance I had of him I was struck with reverential awe, as I thought I saw an angel in the place and person of the aged gentleman. Ah! the ease and harmony of his language, his calm and heavenly composure, his simplicity, commingled with the dignity of his appearance, then on the verge of eternity, the length of time he officiated as a Catholic clergyman there, and the servant of God, caused a great sensation in me, which is incompatible to my powers of description, and beyond the reach of my talent. These heavenly attributes secured in his behalf the love and veneration of all Lancasterians indiscriminately, and of all others, as well, who had the pleasure of his acquaintance. I departed in peace, after receiving his benediction. I made no great stay in Lancaster, though I found my countrymen there exceedingly clever, and many of them fond of poetical effusions.—From Lancaster I took my departure for the City of Brotherly Love, and safely arrived at No. 17 Chestnut street, which was then a respectable hotel, kept by a respectable widow lady named Mrs. Murphy, a countrywoman of my own, and a more honest, clever, or a better hearted landlady never crossed the Atlantic Ocean. She kept excellent accommodations, and her boarders fared sumptuously every day, and her hotel was a harbor of security and comfort. She had two sons and a daughter with her at the time, all well instructed and educated, and a cleverer young man than her son could not easily be found in Philadelphia. I had been introduced to this hotel by a gentleman of the name of Mr. Wallace, a wine and liquor merchant of that city, and an Irishman, with whom I formed an acquaintance in Harrisburg, at the residence of Mr. Richard Hogan; being a bachelor himself, had boarded there at that time, and I must confess candidly, that he possessed the reputation, habits, and dignity, of a finished and consistent gentleman; and his appearance would indisputably recommend him to any respectable society; and, as luck would have it, we boarded together at Mrs. Murphy's during three months.

After a few days rest in the harbor of peace, plenty and security, I put myself in motion to circulate among the Philadelphians an Irish history in lyric verse, containing an account of the woes, afflictions, sufferings and privations of my countrymen and women, by the most unjust, atrocious, and barbarous enactments of the most dangerous, cruel, intriguing and unscrupulous enemies that ever governed either a barbarous or a Christian nation since the commencement of the Christian era. My first visit was made to the residence of a distinguished Irish gentleman by name William Moroney Esq., as I lost my note-book, perhaps this is not the identical name, but any individual acquainted with the illustrious Celtic race, would know the gentleman to be a Milesian of a superior grade, and a full, finished, indisputable gentleman, whose appearance would be a passport and a letter of recommendation for him to all civilized and meritorious people on the face of this earth. Mr. Moroney made himself conspicuously known in Philadelphia and other parts, as being a treasurer to the Repeal Association in Philadelphia, during O'Connell's time, and the sacrifice he made to bring it to a speedy maturity had been prodigiously calculated, but having abundant means of his own and a generous heart to shell it out, sheltered him from any inconvenience—more about him hereafter. I soon discovered that my countrymen in Philadelphia participated in the noble habits of their ancestors, and their social intercourse and rank, owing to their high order of intelligence, exacted a large and an honourable praise from friends and foes, which calumny cannot cavil or time obliterate. Many of my countrymen in that city, are lawyers, doctors, scholars and critics of the keenest discrimination; and although I saw countless errors in my history when printed, which escaped me in manuscript, the critics on the work saw them more clearly, when pulverized in the crucible of literary criticism, which incontrovertibly showed all its faults and frailties. Still they all considered it a stupendous undertaking, and with all its errors, worthy of countenance and support, and added, as it had been the first of the kind that ever had been attempted, that I was entitled to their praise and approbation. In Philadelphia I met with a gentleman of the name of Mr. Collins, a classical scholar, a professional lawyer, a clear and forcible writer and an Irishman—in full. I knew his father and mother in the Island of Saints, and I shall not belie them, as I suppose they are both before this time in happy eternity. They lived honestly, respectfully, religiously, irreproachably, and I hope died happily. A young gentleman of the name of Mr. Dunn, who was studying law with Mr. Collins at that time, and will in the course of time display great abilities in his professional career, saw at once a grammatical blunder in my history of Ireland in epic verse, and charitably criticized on it, and when he did, I uttered not a word in its defence, as it would admit of no palliation. I saw the impropriety of the sentence as evident as he did, but considered it a poetic license, and considered such toleration was sufficient to cancel its impropriety. The blunder can be seen in the following verse where the satanic foes of Catholics, wrote to King Charles to oppress them and keep them from any office of trust or emolument. It runs thus:

Though still contending for your restoration,
Be sure you claim of them a decimation
Of what they're worth, for to support the crown,
This adds a jewel to your own renown.

"For to support the crown," for, in this sentence is improper, as crown being a noun in the accusative case, governed by the verb in the infinitive mood, to support, leaving the preposition "for" without government or its legitimate jurisdiction.

This manifest blunder I had seen in the poetical works of eminent and distinguished writers, poets, and divines, it is to be found in fiftieth page of Ward's Cantoes in Queen Elizabeth's prayer book, "for to eat manna;" and even in Catholic and Protestant Testaments, 16th chapter and 4th verse of the Acts of the Apostles, "And as they went through the cities, they delivered them the decrees for to keep," &c., and still, with all this, we must consider it a manifest grammatical blunder. I met with another gentleman of the name of Mr. Dunn, another lawyer in the vicinity with Mr. Collins, of whom I have every reason to speak in the most respectful manner, as I found him to be generous and kind; and I was informed then that his professional abilities had been of a very high order. Thence I took my way to another Irish gentleman's house of high Milesian blood, Doctor O'Brien; this gentleman is descended from the Kings of north Munster, and to attempt to set forth his cleverness would require a Homerian pen to do him justice, and his professional skill is also entitled to the greatest applause. This brave man is from the universal county of Cork, and from the town of Bandon, the beautiful saloon and head-quarters of Billy, Prince of Orange, in Munster. I visited my countrymen individually in Philadelphia, and found them as Irishmen should be, generous, liberal, courteous and kind. Being one day in a certain hotel in that city, silently and accurately taking notice of the assembled party, and of their manners and habits, all had been handsomely dressed, and in proper trim, I knew, after a momentary consideration, that they were tailors, my original friends. In this opinion I was not mistaken, and although I sat alone, and thought unknown, and undistinguished on a remote seat, I was recognized by a gentleman in the assembly, who approached and accosted me as follows: "My friend," said he, "I think I know you?" "Perhaps so," my friend, said I, and added, "your features are quite familiar to me, although your name escapes my memory."

"Your name," said he, "is Mr. O'Donovan." "Yes, sir," said I, "and I hope you will be kind enough to inform me of your own, so as to calm the intensity of my feelings." "My name," said he, "is Michael McAfee, and I am a Pittsburgher too." When he said so, we affectionately shook hands, and other tokens of friendship caused a momentary exhibition and mutual affection; the rest of the party paid afterwards particular attention to me. That young gentleman unquestionably was a Pittsburgher, whom I knew from his infancy until approaching maturity. He was slender, tall, and handsomely formed, and beautifully organized in symmetry; his guileless manner, unaffected affability, fascinating features and gentlemanly conduct would render him conspicuous in any honorable assembly. He was also a devoted Catholic, a good husband, a fond father, and an excellent mechanic, an acquisition to the community, and an honor to Pittsburgh, and to his parents, who brought him up in the ways of religion and truth. He is now beyond the reach of flattery, and I hope in communion with the blessed in heaven. Mr. McAfee suspended business at that time, and traveled with me through the city for a few days, and introduced me to all his friends, and to others who were within the limits of his acquaintance. Mr. McAfee learned his trade of his uncle, Mr. Peter McAfee, a merchant tailor in Philadelphia, of whom I will immediately speak; at least, I have every reason to do so, and that in the highest terms imaginable. Mr. Michael McAfee died a few years afterwards, plunging his parents, and a host of relations, friends and acquaintances in an ocean of sorrow, and unspeakable anguish, and left behind him in this vale of tears, an affectionate wife, and two small children to lament the death of an affectionate husband, a kind father, and a generous provider. As soon as my friend had done with his introductory mission, his uncle, Mr. P. McAfee, left nothing undone, that could be done by an honorable introduction, so that through the means of the aforesaid gentleman I became acquainted with my unflinching and original friends. Tailors are indisputably an honorable class of citizens throughout the Union. Mr. P. McAfee was then a merchant tailor of high standing in Philadelphia; he is an Irishman by birth, one in principle, and one in practice, who never stained the land of his nativity by treacherous advantages, or dishonorable actions, and though the Emerald Isle is oppressed, calumniated, and I may say motheaten, from the most wicked, cruel, and unjust enactments, framed by the most unholy, unsparing, and damnable government that ever framed a constitution, to govern either a civilized or a barbarous people, since civilization has been constituted by Christian intelligence. Ireland still produces men of mind, magnitude, learning, and indomitable courage, and women of immaculate purity and religious habits, who are to be found, felt, and distinguished in every scientific department and religious community on the face of the earth. I met with another merchant tailor of the name of Mr. Ceasy there, whom I considered exceedingly clever. Among this class, and among boot and shoe makers, there is no lack of intelligence, patriotism and generosity. I met with a certain gentleman named Mr. Donagan, in Philadelphia, also a boot and shoemaker, from whom and his lady I received every mark of disinterested friendship; they love their country and countrymen, and would sacrifice what they possess for the restoration of the Emerald Isle, to its original freedom and prosperity. I met with another gentleman there, also a boot and shoe maker, of the name of Mr. Queen, and our language has not mentioned the name of a cleverer man or a greater patriot. I would have given a more satisfactory and brilliant account of these two useful and respectable classes, viz., boot and shoemakers and tailors, were it not for accidental impediments, these are occasioned by the losing of my note book; I could use no language in praising my countrymen and women in Philadelphia, should be considered superfluous. The inn-keepers of the city, generally speaking, are gentlemen whose attention and meritorious habits secure to themselves the good will and applause of the citizens of the City of Brotherly Love, and also of the traveling community. Among the Hotel keepers of that city I met with an Irish gentleman of the name of Mr. Conroy, and nobly he merits the name of an Irish gentleman; Mr. Conroy kept a great and splendid Hotel in Fourth street below Chestnut, and the man who would consider him contrary to what I have stated, must be superficially acquainted with the character of an Irish gentleman. I consider him a finished one, without a stain or blemish; I got an introduction to a gentleman in Prince street, New York, named Mr. Collins, from Mr. Conroy, or rather an introductory note, of whom I will speak with the respect due to Mr. Collins hereafter. In Kensington, which is entirely inhabited by Irishmen and their families, I met with another of the name of Mr. Donelly, and a worthier man is as unnecessary as he is rare; he kept a respectable Hotel in Kensington, and gave ample and general satisfaction to the citizens of the place, and also to the traveling community. In Kensington I met hundreds of Bandonians, principally mechanics and owners of large manufacturing establishments, all clever, generous, national, and meritorious patriots and democrats, of the right sized calibre; the notes I had taken of those disappeared, either by accident or bad management. I took up my quarters for some time in Richmond, near Kensington, at the house of a gentleman of the name of Mr. McCarthy, he is a native of the place, and his lady is also a native, and of German extraction, and I candidly confess I never saw through all my travels a man and wife pull together more evenly, more affectionately, or more harmoniously. The kindness and affability which he showed to all that came within the limits of his sphere, had been well seasoned by the amiable qualities, pleasing manners, and unremitting attention of his lady, and you would judge by a momentary decision that they received their training in the same school, and from the same unerring disciplinarian. Another gentleman who lived conveniently to Mr. McCarthy's residence, and kept a book store, for whom I entertain the greatest friendship and the most profound respect, is of course an Irishman, and his wife is justly entitled to every mark of veneration due to her sex, and duty and courtesy impel me to make this acknowledgment I paid a visit to the Rev. Mr. McLaughlin's residence, and fortunately he happened to be at home at the time of visitation; Mr. McLaughlin was in 1848, and I hope is at present, the officiating Priest in Richmond; and the time I called at his house another Reverend gentleman had been in company with him, who officiated conveniently to Richmond; both the Reverend gentlemen were young, and full of original, or rather natural inheritance and native goodness, and spiritually saturated with the theological virtues of the Priesthood; they were venerated, and if the term could religiously bear inspection, almost idolized by their parishioners, and by all who had the honor and pleasure of forming any acquaintance with them; Rev. Mr. McLaughlin had an Irish thrush which sang sweetly, and cheered the surrounding neighborhood with Irish melody, of which I took some notes that disappeared in the catastrophe, which will be made manifest after a little. Omitting the name of another gentleman I met with in Philadelphia, would fasten the seal of ingratitude upon my memory, and that I consider the greatest stain and stigma that could be impressed on a man's character. I had been intimately acquainted with his father and mother in the Island of Saints. They are now I hope in blissful eternity, and in communion with the blessed in Heaven, enjoying the unspeakable happiness secured by a virtuous life, devotional duty, and persevering industry. The gentleman of whom I speak, at that time, was bordering on manhood, and had been then well provided for; he knew no wants which would render life disagreeable or unpleasant, and received no instructions that would jeopardise his eternal welfare; his name is William Rodgers, a Bandonian, and a mason by trade. I think he is married to the second wife, and has no issue. I will desist from further particulars respecting the Philadelphians after giving a hasty sketch of a few more of my countrymen, citizens of that city. Mr. O'Keane is one of the gentlemen, a fine-looking Irishman, whose external appearance speaks with confidence in his favor, and his interior qualifications and kind disposition corroborate externals; all nations if possible would eagerly claim him as a countryman of their own, but this they cannot accomplish, as the most incurious eye can identify him at first glance to be a genuine Irishman; there are two of his cousins in Pittsburgh, Messrs. Michael and Henry O'Keane, and I emphatically say that they reflect honor and distinction on their native land. I am now to speak hurriedly of an Irish gentleman who had no parallel in his day in America, or if he had an equal, I have no hesitation in saying that he had no superior. The gentleman to whom I have reference departed this life in 1854, and as faith and good works are the two hinges on which our eternal welfare rests upon, it is to be hoped that eternal sunshine illuminates his soul, in the communion of the blessed in the kingdom of his Father. The gentleman of whom I speak was Rodger Brown, Esquire, a wealthy merchant and grocer who carried on business extensively in Market street, Philadelphia; more about him hereafter. I left Philadelphia and visited a town within a few miles of it, called Manayunk, and stopped over night in a gentleman's house named Mr. Gallagher, an Irish gentleman of course, who kept a respectable inn in that town, for the accommodation of citizens and travelers. I found Mr. Gallagher exceedingly generous and kind, and had every accommodation necessary to accomplish his purpose, and such as could satisfy the greatest epicurean, or the most fastidious appetite. I called the following morning on the Reverend gentleman who officiated there as a Parish Priest, and he and the Rev. Mr. Sheridan of Philadelphia, I thought were the best looking gentlemen I saw in my travels, whether clerical or secular. I think the Reverend gentleman's name is Mr. Doran; he is unquestionably an honor and an acquisition to the Holy Apostolical Church. I met another gentleman in that town of the name of Mr. Thomas, and meeting with an Irishman of splendid intelligence, lofty aspirations, and brilliant conceptions, comparatively speaking, is the same as seeing a star of the first magnitude in the Heavens in the vicinity of inferior ones, or those of inferior magnitude, whose astonishing brilliancy obscures the inferior lights, and renders them invisible to the naked eye; so will a noble, kind and generous Irishman obliterate the venial stains, follies and freaks of his countrymen, if located in the same vicinity with himself. Any man acquainted with Mr. Thomas will acknowledge him to be a man of that quality.

Now for higher regions, Pottsville; the coal trains from Pottsville to Richmond had been at that time, (1848,) under the superintendence of an Irishman of the name of Cornelius O'Sullivan; I only knew Mr. O'Sullivan by name, through which by a momentary pause I considered to be a finished gentleman, and also came to the conclusion from what I had heard that he could have no coal bank of his own, owing to his liberal propensities. To demonstrate the cleverness of O'Sullivan would require an abler pen than mine, as my dear friend is the bravest of the brave. I was strongly advised to go to Pottsville, as thousands of my countrymen were there, in various employments; and an opportunity immediately occurred which gave me the extreme pleasure of an interview with Mr. O'Sullivan, and a few minutes in his company convinced me that what I heard concerning him had been no exaggeration; Mr. O'Sullivan strenuously advised me to go to Pottsville with himself, in the cars, and that he would do all that could be done to render my journey safe and profitable. I embraced the opportunity with evident alacrity, and immediately got on, and he ordered steam to be applied to the iron Pagasus, in the month of February, 1848, with the immutable intention of going to Pottsville, a considerable distance from Richmond. Although a train of cars had been attached to our puffing Pagasus longer than the tail of the most formidable comet yet discovered, Mr. O'Sullivan and his Irish brigade paid more attention to me than they would to an Oriental Prince, or to some foreign Plenipotentiary bloated by pride and presumption through his elevation by his potential sovereign. We arrived at the place of destination about 10 o'clock at night, and on leaving the cars I was prevailed upon by Mr. O'Sullivan to remain at his own residence that night, which was situated on the declivity of a hill or rising ground, a small distance from the track; but the intervening space had been coated with one solid sheet of ice, and the night being exceedingly cold, dreary, and dark, and as both my hands were engaged with my trunks, when assisting Mr. O'Sullivan and another gentleman to bear them up the acclivity, both my feet gave way, and as if prostrated by an electrical shock, down I fell suddenly on my face, on a knotty piece of black oak, which was partly embeded in the solid ice, which left my face in a fearful and deplorable condition; there I was, bruised, dangerously cut, and bleeding profusely, and my unsufferable condition and anguish of mind can be more easily imagined than described, when I saw a pure stream of Milesian blood descending the dreary declivity of Pottsville, commingled with coal, soot, cinders, and snow. O! what an awful scene, and what a dreadful recollection. Though old and almost superannuated, I entertained the same veneration for my features that the Romans of old did, who always preferred a wound in the body to a scar in the face; and in that lamentable condition I was introduced to Mrs. O'Sullivan, an amiable, accomplished, and tender-hearted lady, who unquestionably regretted my sorrowful fate. I requested Mr. O'Sullivan to accompany me to Pottsville, a mile distant, to have an interview with one of the sons of Esculapius, so as during his inspection I could have an opportunity of hearing his approbation of my accidental deformity caused by the forementioned injurious prostration. The blood ceased running from my wounds, for excessive freezing stayed the current.

All the inhabitants of the town had been lulled in the arms of Morpheus, notwithstanding, we soon affected a resurrection of an extraordinary size, and of an unparalleled magnitude. When O'Sullivan knocked at the door I heard tremendous heavy steps, coming down stairs, which made me think I was then in the vicinity of Lemnos, or else some prodigious hippopotamus was approaching, and that immediate destruction was inevitable. The door was opened, and a blazing candle placed on the table which was in the room. The night was exceedingly cold, and the fire in the last stage of consumption. There was the doctor standing, and I was struck with admiration when I took a hasty glance of his stupendous size, and in the contemplation of his gigantic form, Herculean shoulders and beautiful symmetry, I forgot my own confusion for a time, I thought then that he and the Rhodian Colossus were cast in the same mould, and that it would require another earthquake or some indescribable natural explosion to upset the doctor. He expressed no surprise at the enormity of my wounds, and gave no prescription for the speedy restoration of my face to its original appearance; he did nothing, but applied a piece of sticking plaster to my wounds, and as the fire had expired for the want of coal, the plaster could not be sufficiently heated to stick to the wounds, but in the application of it, he placed his thumbs to my forehead and his fingers to the back part of my head, and by the compression I thought my eyes fled from their sockets, alike two fiery balls and passing with the velocity of meteors causing the plaster to stick fast to the wound and become immovable. Mr. Rider sat down, for such is the doctor's name, and his company was agreeable and edifying, as he spoke the English with invariable fluency and propriety. I do, and will respect his memory. The doctor gave our conversation a political turn, and grievously deplored the lamentable bondage of my countrymen by the perfidious legislation of the English government. I soon discovered him to be a democrat of the finest calibre, and of an incorruptible grade, and it is no fiction to say that we agreed politically. Dr. Rider is an American by birth, and in my opinion of Irish extraction. Mr. Eugene O'Sullivan and I departed and allowed the doctor to return to his slumbers. On the following morning I mentioned to O'Sullivan and his lady, so as to be more convenient to the doctor, that I would take up my abode in the town of Pottsville as there was much danger to be apprehended in going from their residence to

Pottsville in hard freezing weather, and my wounds might be affected by the severity of the weather. Mr. O'Sullivan and lady with much reluctance consented. Another motive which induced me to remove, I mean to demonstrate. Had I remained in Mr. O'Sullivan's house during three months, no remuneration would be accepted, as such would imprint an indelible stain on the escutcheons of the O'Sullivan and the O'Driscoll families. My friend O'Sullivan, accommodating enough, accompanied me to Pottsville, by way of introducing me, and it would require some respectable testimony to exonerate me from the stigmatical suspicion of a finished toper and loafer, as my broken face confirmed the suspicion. After the host and hostess were convinced of my accidental calamity, they seemed to bear half my woes upon their shoulders, and their commiseration and sympathy were made manifest by their assiduity and attention to make my deplorable condition to myself, as comfortable as possible. Both were natives of the Emerald Isle, and the landlord's name was Mr. Daniel Harkins, a gentleman universally known and respected, and I emphatically say, not by the way of puffing or exaggerating, that they displayed in this hour of extremity that sympathy and feeling which are the natural inheritance of the genuine Irish. The same day I paid a visit to the doctor, and his recommendation was, that the application of a few leeches would unquestionably be followed by a decided improvement. In Pottsville, there could not be found then a professional leecher, but a German barber, in the place for accommodation sake, and after a diligent search I found him, being invited to his place by a pole hieroglyphically painted and posted at his door, and after making my intention known to the barber, he made immediate preparations to set his blood-thirsty leeches to work, and to give them an opportunity of drinking copiously of a royal Irish fountain, or in other words, of Milesian claret. The gentleman spoke previously of their extraordinary execution, in the highest terms imaginable, and I thought by the thundering applause of his leeches that the little drop which remained in my veins would be immediately drained by the insatiable gluttony of the monstrous epicureans. At the first glance of the leeches, I entertained a very unfavorable opinion of their usefulness, and I was not mistaken, although the gentleman tried different times to bring them to action, but, impossible, as they were useless, lifeless and worthless, and if a coroner's inquest had been held at that time on the leeches, the verdict would have been death from consumption, or some other incurable disease beyond the reach of the most powerful medicine. However ineffectual and abortive the attempt proved to be, the gentleman demanded seventy-five cents for his professional skill and experiment, which I paid without hesitation or reluctance. I immediately returned to my room and sat gloomily there, musing on my state and condition, until the thoughts of my situation had driven me to the verge of despondency. At length I came to the conclusion to pay the doctor for his professional services, and make no further application to our modern Esculapias, and there was no fear that I would make a second trial of the barber's long, lean, lank leeches. I went instantly to the doctor and demanded his bill, and to my astonishment his bill was merely nominal, which I unquestionably paid, and also thanked him for his incomparable skill and assiduity during my visitation. I then returned to my room to habituate myself to seclusion. Ah! confined and confused, I sat on the stool of repentance, and everything that could facilitate my improvement or the restoration of my mutilated features to their original amplitude, had been tried by Mrs. Harkins, my kind and amiable countrywoman, and after a few days melancholy meditation in seclusion, I observed with gladness, a decided improvement in the deformity of my features; scabs, scratches and contusions began to disappear, and my physiognomy showed its original relations and natural form. I soon commenced my usual occupation, and I must honestly acknowledge, though the inhabitants of Pottsville were not all poets, that they were fond of poetic inspirations, and indeed, I found them all exceedingly courteous, generous and friendly. I had taken notes of all the clever fellows I met with in Pottsville, but, they unfortunately perished with the rest, which causes a deficiency in my illustration of the Pottsvillers. I think Mr. Potts must have committed some stupendous crime when he selected that dreary seclusion, in the vicinity of Pottsville, as his residence; a place at that time inaccessible to human society, and the rendezvous of bears, wolves, panthers, and all other hideous and savage animals; or else he must have possessed an honest disposition, at variance with the lying machinations of the political intrigues, of an unworthy combination; and, notwithstanding the seclusion of the place, he left a numerous progeny behind him, and very respectable at that, to commemorate his singularity in the choice of his selection and seclusion. Pottsville is surrounded by stupendous mountains and one of them requires a particular description:—

In summer time, or else the story lies,
That mount uplifted, cleaves the cloudy skies,
And through the clouds, a night-cap made of snow,
Appears conspicuous from the plain below,
And stranger still, a mountain flood or tide,
Comes tearing, tumbling down the mountain's side.

Within ten miles of Pottsville, in a dreary and desolate region, hundreds of my countrymen were engaged in laying out railroads for the convenience of hauling coal to Richmond, and the contractors of the road were of course, Irishmen. One of them was an O'Riley, from the great and noble county of Cavan, a gentleman who would reflect dignity ond renown on the dismal regions of Tartary, if such were the land of his nativity. The other was an O'Collins, a Waterford gentleman, whose urbanity and impressive manners would ensure him esteem and success among the Hindoos, if he resided among them. The other gentleman was a Burke, from the county of Limerick, and a branch of that illustrious race who displayed no friendship or acknowledged no affinity with Elizabeth of immortal memory; he was unquestionably generous to a fault. One and all exerted themselves and made use of mild, insinuating language to all the hands in their employ, inducing them to patronize myself, but, all proved to be an abortion; unfortunately, the grade of my countrymen employed in those sections, with some honorable exceptions, would prefer a quart of good Monongahela whiskey to all Homer's poetical inventions. During my stay in that barren region, in the month of February, I stopped at the place of a gentleman of the name of O'Donahue, who was married to Mr. Eugene O'Sullivan's sister, of whom I have spoken. Mr. O'Donahue was a countyman of mine, the same as O'Sullivan, and was born and educated near the haunts of my childhood, and the same sterling, original friendship and hospitality prevailed within his dwelling that could be naturally expected from a place occupied by a man of the Milesian family.

I was rolling in clover during the time I remained under the friendly roof of Mr. O'Donahue's residence, without paying anything for my entertainment to either host or hostess. I returned to Pottsville without delay and made immediate preparations for returning to the City of Brotherly Love. I got into the cars at Pottsville, and came with incredible velocity to Germantown, and stopped there over night, and when I understood there were but few of my countryman in that town, I considered it labor in vain, and that there was as much probability of gathering wool in a goat's house as to sell poetic effusions among the Germans of Germantown. The following day I stopped in the celebrated town of Phœnixville, within twenty-seven miles of Philadelphia, where I found my countrymen in shoals. I stopped over night at the private residence of one of my countrymen, who entertained me with ineffable hospitality. Ah, the peculiar characteristic of the genuine Irish. I must and will respect his memory, and that of his family, though I forget his name, although I think it is Mr. Kelly. I met with many clever men in that town. The following day brought me to my old quarters, No. 17 Chestnut street, Philadelphia, where I was affectionately received by the amiable and generous Mrs. Murphy, proprietor and hostess of that flourishing mansion. After a short stay in Chestnut street, Mr. Wallace, my original friend, strenously advised me to go to Wilmington, Delaware, and spoke of the place in the most encouraging manner, and said as much as if my success would be inevitable. I got immediately into the cars to see the splendor of the place, and also to realize a proficiency or something bordering on a small fortune. The winged Pagasus moved with incredible velocity, and less than two hours brought me to the place of destination, and both my animation and ambition cooled at my proximity to Wilmington. I thought at first sight the most befiting appellation the town should get would be that of "hard scrabble." I put up that night at Mr. McGovern's tavern, indisputably an Irishman of the primitive stamp, though I thought he had a greater appetite to accumulate money, though far advanced in years, than he had for reading poetic effusions, although the poetry had been originally Irish, and Irish poetic aspirations. The season of the year I arrived in Wilmington had been very unfavorable to its appearance. As it happened in the month of February, when nature displayed its utmost desolation, as it had mantled the town with snow, ice and other disagreeable inconveniences, which deprived it of its natural and artificial beauties, yet at the approach of Spring its natural transformation would be pleasing to its visitors. I sold in the town but one history, or as I should say, one number of the metrical history of Ireland, and that to a gentleman of the name of Mr. McDermoth, a wine and spirit merchant in Wilmington, and indisputably an Irish gentleman ; this I judge from conclusions drawn from externals. There is a splendid Catholic College in the vicinity of Wilmington under the government and superintendency of the Rev. Mr. O'Reily, at which I thought I should have a peep before I would leave Wilmington. The reverend gentleman was fortunately sitting in his studying room when I entered, and it is no fiction, or no vain or imaginary assertion to say, emphatically, that his appearance as a gentleman, even if disconnected with his theological acquisitions, and ecclesiastical indications, would do honor to any Christian of the primitive stamp in the Christian world. Mr. O'Reily was a purchaser, of course, and he no sooner opened the number than he observed the manifest grammatical blunder, which I have mentioned before, and indeed it had been the most manifest blunder in the whole composition. No man has a better sight, more knowledge, or a keener discrimination to see our errors than a Catholic clergyman. though generally speaking humility and humanity forbid the exposure. After pointing to the blunder or infirmity of the sentence I felt satisfied, as imperfections are discovered in the works of the most learned and profound writers, and consequently they must be found in feebler elements. No man can be a judge of his own production as partiality is expected to have a tendency to self-production. When the reverend gentleman read a little more of the work, he seemed better satisfied, as the spirit displayed in the work would hide a multitude of errors and sins also. In that college I got acquainted with the Rev. Mr. O'Neill, for whom I entertain the most profound veneration. As much as I could do while in the presence of those venerable and venerated clergymen is to suppress my feelings when thinking on the original history of my native country, and the desolation that mantled it by the devasting hands of ruthless strangers. There were two reverend gentlemen before my eyes, far from their native land, lineally descended from Irish royalty, and Milesian nobility; one the hereditary Prince of Tyrone, and the other the hereditary Prince of Cavan, injustly deprived of their vast dominions by the unscrupulous and perfidious injustice, and tyranny of an ungodly government, that lately discovered easy, lucrative, yet damnable avenues to heaven, and framed dangerous and hypocritical laws to sustain a railroad to that celestial kingdom, which they constructed at the expense of virtue and religion. These two noble Milesians, or their ancestors, were unjustly deprived of their vast possessions, which still remain in the hands of their unrelenting enemies, for no other reason than their immortal attachment to the faith of true Catholics, which faith is founded on Apostolic authority, and is a light and a guide that will infallibly show us the way to heaven. Such gloomy thoughts were sufficient to obscure the most lofty and towering imaginations. I returned with all possible speed to Philadelphia, and got everything in readiness to visit New York, and in the middle of February, 1848, I took my departure for that city; and being disappointed in going in the morning train, I had to go a part of the way by water, I think as far as Amboy, and by so doing, it happened late in the evening when we arrived in that city. My countrymen, as usual, were there in attendance with all kinds of vehicles to convey men, women, and all kinds of commodities from a needle to a thunderbolt to the respective destinations of those who hired them, and I was placed within a neat cab to take me to the place of my destination, which was a respectable boarding house kept by a Mrs. Flemming, in No. 177 Grand or Grant street, a lady of excellent habits, intelligence, and accomplishment, and to crown her felicity she was then a widow. I had a letter of introduction to her from the Honorable Judge McKenna of Pittsburgh, who boarded with her himself for a considerable time, and who knew the comfort and protection her house afforded to every one who valued his own dignity and reputation. The Honorable Judge strenuously recommended me to Mrs. Flemming, and he knew how, as having no deficiency in heart, head, or hand, to complete the intended introduction. Mrs. Flemming, nor her boarders had not been in bed when I arrived, and after producing my introduction and expounding preliminaries, I was received with courtesy and exultation, and let me add approbation more benefitting an Oriental Potentate than Mr. O'Donovan. All Mrs. Flemming's borders emigrated from the Emerald Isle, with the exception of one American gentleman of the name of Taylor, with whom I was exceedingly well pleased during our acquaintance. The ladies who boarded there supported themselves respectably by their superior skill in needlework, and made themselves distinguished and admired by various accomplishments, all young and unmarried. A gentleman of the name of Mr. Daniel O'Kavanagh, one of the borders and a countymen of mine, played beautifully on musical instruments, and one of the boarding ladies also played to perfection on the piano, so when they played in concert, time passed insensibly away. As a community we lived indiscribably happy, clear of sorrow, of sickness, and hunger, and it is to be hoped sinless. The winter of 1848 had been remarkably severe in New York, and after a few days inactivity or recreation I walked out to view the citizens of New York, the far famed empórium of the Western World. I soon discovered the kind of population that inhabited the city : indeed it would require a man universally acquainted with the different races to give an accurate description of the heterogeneous mass that populated that city. I got much astonished at some things that came under my notice, and I candidly confess I never before saw humanity so lamently degraded as I saw in New York, and a man or woman of tender or noble feelings would regret, after inspection, that he had been made of the same materials. Still as a counterpoise to this lamentable wretchedness, there are not many cities in Europe that richer, nobler, greater or more honorable men and women can be found than in the same city, taking into consideration both the native and adopted citizens ; after a little consideration I thought the suggestion in holy writ had been infallible, where it says, that, "the tares and wheat grow together." After some short time I got acquainted with officers and policemen in the station in Grand street, and a cleverer set of men never existed, all I may say from the Emerald Isle, purely Celtic, purely distilled and rectified in Milesian worms which cleared them of all impure encumbrances and contamination, which have polluted modern times and modern inventors. These gentlemen were very useful to me, besides a generous encouragement by purchasing, they recommended me strongly to others, and as being acquainted through all the city their recommendations contributed greatly to my welfare. Then I got acquainted in the Gas Works, with all the gentlemen engaged in them, and with all the superintendents in the whole establishment located in Centre street, all Irishmen and countymen of my own Cork, and the two overseers were from the birthplace of the celebrated Counseller Curran, one of them had been called Mr. Foely; and the other gentleman's name I forget. Although I took particular notice and notes of both the gentlemen's names and cleverness, and to avoid superfluous encomiums I make use of the Yankee phrase, "they can't be beat!" From this establishment I was directed, and by the forementioned gentlemen to the East River Gas Works, which were superintended also by Messrs. Downey & Cassady, both Corkmen from the borders of Dunereal. I found these, and the men under their inspection or government uncommonly clever and generous, with one exception. I could do nothing among tavern-keepers, grocers, and private citizens in New York, which compelled me to make an application to my undying, undeviating, and unflinching friends, viz.: tailors, boot and shoemakers, and I frankly, emphatically, and honestly say that my application did not turn out to be an abortion. The same unmistakable, honorable, generous and hereditary impulse that actuated those two classes of our community throughout my travels in America, animated them in New York, and perhaps in a more inspiring and animating manner. The tailors of New York, in communities, in societies, and in fraternities generally make the second or third story of some edifice of splendid appearance, their place of rendezvous, in some places they number one hundred, in other places two hundred, and in other places more or less; here they remain remote from public confusion, working together in harmony and peace; all apparently young men, and beautifully dressed and arranged in due order, familiarly, formidably, fantastically, and accomplished, and well qualified to display the perfections of their professions; they work with ease, elegance, and exactness, and among them are to be found statesmen, politicians, lawyers, metaphysicians, and gentlemen. The ladies who work in the same board can be easily distinguished by their situations in the ranks; every lady either works for herself or for her husband, and often for her employer, and handsomer ladies, married or single, than they, are not to be found, or could bear closer inspection, as respects beauty, than the ladies of whom I speak, that worked in those establishments. By introduction from one establishment to another, I got mostly acquainted with the principal establishments in the City of New York, and also with the private professional gentlemen, or in other words, with the gentlemen who worked in their own dwellings, and discovered they too, had the same calibre. I took notice of many things I saw in New York, and in fact took notes of them, and particularly those who interfered in any manner in the proficiency of my publications, or helped the sale of them, and of various other things pertaining to the city, yet all inevitably perished or disappeared. I met with a gentlemen of the faculty in the city, of the name of Mr. Brady, from the county Cavan, who had been of infinite service to me by the way of introduction among the fraternity; he was a generous, finished, stainless Irishman, and from this noble and praiseworthy class I turned my attention to the second hinge on which hung my dependence and hopes, viz.: boot and shoemakers, and met them in New York, as elsewhere, respectable and generous; they were the two poles which supported my wandering revolution, and outside these poles nothing appeared to me, with few exceptions, but objections, sterility, and an uncultivated wilderness, and I defy any man, who will be presumptuous enough to issue any kind of a literary production before the community or the world at large, to overthrow this testimony. I met with two of my countrymen in New York, to whom I am bound to make a particular reference, as they deserve the highest and most unbounded applause. One of these gentlemen was a Mr. Fox or Cox, a Limerick gentleman, who filled the qualities of a sexton and teacher in the Catholic Church, called St. James Church, in that city; his appearance is exceedingly pleasing, and his serene countenance and symmetry spoke triumphantly in his favor, and his whole frame had been mathematically adjusted. From the short interview I had with the gentleman, I judged him to be a genuine Irishman of the primitive stamp, and after taking my departure from Mr. Cox, I found wherever I mentioned his name that he was universally known and esteemed, that is, as much as the term or word "universally" can have any reference to the City of New York. He bought an armful of my books without inquiring into the merits of them, but merely by the appellation they bore, and as he knew I had been the first who attempted to give the History of Ireland, or any other country in epic verse, and if the attempt bordered on abortion he considered it merited some applause and encouragement. The other gentleman was a Mr. O'Byrne, a gentlemen from the ancient dominion of the valiant O'Neill's, in the province of Ulster. He is indisputably of a pure Milesian stock, and a lineal descendant of the Princes and Chieftains of Wicklow, and the most inveterate enemy that English Edward met with when he attempted to subjugate Ireland. Mr. O'Byrne is a fine-looking Irishman, and displays much dignity and courteous manners, in a superior degree, both in his countenance and conversation, such as would entitle him to a seat among the most illustrious and distinguished associations. Mr. O'Byrne had been then connected with the far-famed and well-known establishment of Roach Brothers & Company in New York. I met with hundreds of my countrymen, also, that ought to be noticed, but must be omitted in consequence of a treacherous and uncertain memory. I passed over to Brooklyn, and found that my countrymen there possessed a generous feeling, superior still to the New Yorkers, and their patriotism more intense and immutable. The first gentleman with whom I got acquainted in that city, was a Mr. O'Callaghan, a merchant tailor, and as an appendage to his professional career, an Irish gentleman. Mr. O'Callaghan, without solicitation, gave me every information respecting the fraternity to which he belonged, which contributed very much to my welfare in Brooklyn. I learned of him not only the streets, but the numbers of their places of rendezvous, and among them I found the same hereditary propensities, that I did heretofore in the same class throughout my travels.

In Brooklyn, I met with a noble countryman of mine, of the name of Mr. Creaton, and he and and his brother being extensively engaged in the boot and shoemaking line, assisted largely to dispose of my publications; they used every honorable means to do so; that class of mechanics were, in Brooklyn as elsewhere, intelligent, generous and patriotic. Another brave countryman of mine, and a native of the ever-memorable county Clare, and an adopted citizen of our glorious Republic, Mr. McNamara, kept a respectable inn, in Brooklyn, then, is a gentleman indeed, in principle and practice, much esteemed by his friends, and admired and beloved by a large circle of acquaintances; and his wife, an Irish lady, is an ornament to her sex, an honor to the land of her nativity, and an acquisition to the land of her adoption. Speaking of my countrymen and women, in Brooklyn and Williamsburgh, I found them in both places in their original element, facetious, witty, generous, full of indigenous habits and undiminished hospitality. I left New York, in the cars, for Newark, in New Jersey, and stopped in Mr. Boyle's Hotel, in that City, an Irishman's son, and though, being a little out of the original track, maternally, that little did not impair his propensities, or that un-

9

bounded generosity which was his indisputable inheritance by his paternal side of the question. The extraordinary friendship and cleverness of my countrymen, such as I met with in that City and and in other parts of the State, require an abler pen than mine to demonstrate the glory and applause to which they are entitled. The notes I had taken of my countrymen in Newark disappeared in my travels, and left me a pensioner on a treacherous memory. From Newark I went to Paterson, and after coming out of the cars in Paterson, I inquired of the by-standers if any of my countrymen kept an inn, or house of entertainment in that town. I was answered in the affirmative, and then I wanted to know the name of each respective inn-keeper; the names repeated being heterogeneous to originality, or old Irish names. I asked again if any other name could be given. Yes, was the reply, there is a gentleman of the name of Mr. Lynch, who keeps one in Paterson, a gentleman of an irreproachable reputation, who will indisputably accommodate you. That finished my interrogation, and I repaired immediately to his residence to take shelter under the friendly roof of a Milesian mansion, where I expected to find shelter, prayer, piety and protection, disunited and disconnected with the impurity of irreligion, or, mongrelism, which would stain, directly or indirectly, the clear, pure primitive and unpolluted fountain of original instructions, and ascending, the evening shades of life, accompanied by the setting sun of his existence, had obscured nearly Mr. Lynch's mortal career; notwithstanding all this, he still possessed the warm heart of an Irishman, and though advanced in years, he had been in the enjoyment of good health, and all his faculties seemed undiminished, and to add to all this, he lived in the estimation of all the citizens in Paterson. Mr. Lynch was also blessed with ample means or, in other words, with an abundance of such necessaries as would render life agreeable. Mr. Lynch was then a widower, and without issue, yet he had relations enough to enjoy the great accumulations of honest and persevering industry. I remained for ten or twelve days in Paterson, highly satisfied with its population, both native and adopted, as I thought their habits were good and regular, their manners ineffably pleasing, and their conversation afforded pleasure and edification. I visited the Passaic Falls, which would delight the most incurious eye after a moment's contemplation; and as my countrymen are to be found everywhere on this globe on which we move, as if possessing the power of ubiquity, assuredly, I met with one of them at the Falls, and I think he had some command over the place, to keep something in good order that wanted his vigilance, as art is beautifully combined with the enchanting scene, or natural harmony of the Falls. His name, I think, was Mr. Chapman, and from the renowned and ever-to-be-applauded county of Wexford; he was an Irishman, indeed, possessing the invaluable inheritance and bravery of his countrymen. He demonstrated the construction of art for the direction of the water with mathematical precision, and Euclid himself could hardly give more unerring definitions. I met with another gentleman from the county of Waterford, in Paterson, of the name of Mr. Powers, who was extensively engaged in business, or in the mercantile line, and much esteemed and admired for his unspeakable integrity and business capacity, and also for his obliging habits as a neighbor and citizen. A gentleman of the name of Coult,—Roswell Coult, Esquire,—had a splendid mansion on the verge of the town of Paterson, and to whom the town principally belonged; he had a good many swans on a pond or creek convenient to his mansion, displaying their supercilious majesty on the water, and often their awkward strides on land, seemingly training their twilight signets to do the same. The Catholic Church, erected in Paterson, is a great ornament to the town; it is a splendid edifice, with a spire majestically rising to a great elevation, on whose extremity is erected a gorgeous cross, pointing to the cold heart and heedless sinner, the crucifixion of our Lord on Mount Calvary, for the salvation and redemption of all the human race, and whispering to all beholders, the necessity of penance and repentance. The Rev. Mr. Quinn was the officiating clergyman in Paterson, in 1848, and I thought then, as I do now, that he was the most sinless clergyman I ever saw; he is now in eternity, I hope in the happy communion and fellowship with angels and saints, as a reward for his spiritual labors and spiritual assiduity to the edification of his flock. I returned immediately to New York, which is eighteen miles distant from Paterson, and took up my abode with my incomparable friend, Mrs. Flemming. During my stay in New York, I had no opportunity of seeing his grace, Archbishop Hughes, as he had been absent from the city at that time, though it would give me unspeakable pleasure to see so illustrious a personage, and so distinguished an ecclesiastic from the Island of saints, whose literary pen has shed so much lustre on the pages of history, that time, with all its accumulation of arts, sciences and improvements, can neither improve nor impoverish. After a few days rest in New York, I came to the conclusion of paying Albany a visit, the capital of the State; and agreeably to this decision, I took my departure in one of the opposition boats, universally known by the appellation of Rip Van Winkle, and to give a proper and vivid description of the vast and heterogeneous multitude that was on board that steamboat, on her passage from New York to Albany, would require a more graphic, a more romantic, and a more celebrated pen than I wield; men and women of every hue, from various climes, of various creeds, and of different political opinions, met promiscuously on that boat; some appeared lively, some shrouded with religious solemnity, and some apparently with sorrow. No beds could be had for love or money, and on that account the deck had been unusually crowded; such as were from the same country met together in separate communities, speaking the same language, and passing dull hours away. I immediately commingled with the saints from the Emerald Isle; and thank Providence, and not the atrocious and detestable enactments and legislations of Queen Victoria, we had the majority, while others sat in the shade of minority. Though many a year past and disappeared since I left my native land, I brought along an inexhaustible fund of the Celtic language to the wilds of America, which, in spite of time and adversities, I preserved without much decay, and which the combination of both had no tendency to destroy. About eight o'clock the following morning, old Van stretched her side along the Albany wharf, and before the planks could be properly adjusted, the multitude that had been standing on the wharf, rushed on deck, crying aloud with stentorian lungs, "I'll carry your trunks to your lodgings;" each grasping the richest piece of furniture he could see on board, as he considered it a substantial proof of its owner's wealth, or the magnitude of his purse. The old chest, roughly constructed, that I had on deck, displayed no attraction that would draw the attention of those men who were in quest of gain, until all the rich movables were carried away; and still many were on deck who got nothing to do, and were anxious to do something rather than to be entirely disappointed, rushed together to lay violent hands on my old chest; and as I stood sentinel to avert such unlawful encroachments, I soon made them sensible of the danger of the unwarrantable liberty they were taking, and my uncouth logical rebuff made them sensible that I was an old coon, somewhat Americanized, who would not suffer the least intrusion on my old hippopotamus. At that moment I observed, on the wharf, a drayman, whom I determined, by inspection, to be an Irishman, and asked him then, could he convey myself and my chest to a certain street in the City, as I had an introductory note to a gentleman resident in such a number in said street, in the City of Albany, from a very respectable gentleman in New York. He frankly answered affirmatively, and in less than ten minutes I found myself under way to the place of destination. After arriving at the place, the gentleman to whom my introduction referred, had moved, and none of the neighbors could identify his whereabouts. Being thus disappointed, I then informed the gentleman to take me to some countryman's house, as I intended to remain a month or more in Albany. He said he could indisputably do so, which proved to be a fact. After some considerable driving through the City, we came to a respectable Hotel, situated in the western extremity of the City; and as I lost my notes of the place and travels, I forget the name of the street; and the moment we arrived the landlord made his appearance, and strenuously assisted in taking my baggage into his own house and placing it in his own custody. The landlord's first appearance made me sensible of my security and comfort, and also made me bear, with perfect resignation, the disappointment I met with; when I saw together, the landlord and the gentleman who brought me to his house in close proximity, by a single glance, I identified them to be brothers. The landlord's name is Mr. Patrick Murphy, whose countenance displays originality and candor, and his old lady showed all the remarkable characteristics of a genuine Irish lady. No hieroglyphics, or no humbug could exist under the same roof with Mrs. Murphy. Mr. Murphy has accumulated a handsome fortune, and has only one to inherit it after his death, who then had been called home from a Catholic College, under the supervision of his grace, Archbishop Hughes, in consequence of his father's indisposition. The boy then showed laudable habits, and amiable and agreeable manners; and it really appears to me, and it is my candid opinion, when maturity establishes its own sway, and indelibly stamps its impressions, the boy will display some brilliant abilities. When night approached with her commanding stillness, and the latest rays of the sun seemed drooping in the last stage of consumption, many of the respectable citizens, including native and adopted, assembled in Mr. Murphy's Hotel, and caused a reaction in their constitutions by shallow draughts, after the occupations of the day, and remained until ten at night, and then were shown the way, by the brilliancy of our nocturnal lamp, or by other necessary accommodations to guide them through impenetrable darkness, to their respective homes. In that respectable assembly I observed a countryman of mine, by the name of Mr. Brady, commanding much respect and attention from every one in company; his frame was large and his proportions had been harmoniously adjusted; he was witty, affable, and exceedingly generous, and possessing the attributes and peculiarities of a true Milesian Irishman; he lived conveniently to Mr. Murphy's residence, and his family was well provided with all necessaries that could render life happy and comfortable.

The population of Albany, though large, as far as I could judge, or any casual observer, is sober, settled, temperate and orderly, clear of the vices and corruption which contaminate society in other cities; and all denominations in Albany agree well, and dwell in mutual harmony together. The Catholic churches in Albany are indisputably in a flourishing condition, and thousands of her members there, are, indeed, rich and respectable. I went different times to see the Rev. Mr. McClusky, a distinguished divine and orator who officiates in St. Patrick's Church, but found no opportunity of speaking to the Rev. gentleman, as it appeared to me he was busily engaged in the Christian duties of the priesthood at the time, that could not reasonably admit of an intrusion on the sacred functions of his officiating capacity. Mr. John McClusky, who is a brother to the Rev. gentleman, and a citizen of Pittsburgh, is considered one of the wealthiest merchant tailors west of the mountains. I met with a gentleman in Albany, of the name of Mr. Newman, and if my talents would coincide with my inclination, I would do him justice; but as his cleverness is inaccessible to my grovelling description, I will miscarry in the attempt. Mr. Newman had the control or management of one of the most flourishing hotels, or mansion houses, in Albany. All trunks, baggages, and valuables, were placed under his care, until the owners took their departure from said hotel. A better or an honester man than Mr. Newman could not fill the situation; and, as an addition to his sincerity and vigilance, he is one of the best penmen I met with in my travels. His penmanship had been of a superior order. I met with another gentleman in Albany, of the name of Mr. Jordan, a wine and liquor merchant; and I candidly consider him a constituted gentleman; and so are his brothers, who follow the same business in East Troy. I was strenuously introduced to a gentleman in Albany, of the name of Mr. Cooney, a merchant tailor, who received me with unspeakable courtesy, and also displayed towards me all the cleverness pertaining to his fraternity, a society saturated with generosity, consideration, and intelligence. I will make some reference to another merchant tailor in that city, and I will have done; I forget his name, but I think he came from the inimitable county of Tipperary. He married a lady of French extraction, whose father has a large grocery in Albany;

a cleverer man never existed; and as he belonged to the Montgomery Guards, he wanted me to compose a few verses suitable to the purpose, which he could sing occasionally when the company met, which I did, but had no opportunity of seeing him, as I rather suddenly took my departure from Albany. Here they are. I composed them on no particular air; and those who are acquainted with music must supply that deficiency themselves.

A SONG

Written impromptu at the request of a friend in Albany, for the Montgomery Guards, and for the purpose of singing it occasionally at their place of rendezvous.

You brave sons of Erin, whose nature and notion
Are bent on promotion, come hear to my strains,
And think of that Island, the gem of the ocean,
That sighs with emotion in bondage and chains;
And think of the heroes* that slumber in glory,
With heads white and hoary who marshal'd in glee,
And told the bold tyrants this beautiful story,
Come, clear in a hurry, we want to be free.
And think of that Island,
That green little Island,
That dear little Island, the gem of the sea.

As fortune divorced us from British oppression,
We'll kneel with discretion on liberty's shrine,
And take a fine view which will leave an impression,
Of the bright stars of freedom that brilliantly shine.
Here tyrants can't trample on any devotion,
Inspir'd by that notion we crossed the wide sea;
And here we can breathe without fear or emotion,
In the land that is glorious, because it is free.
Oh! think of that Island,
That green cover'd Island,
That sweet little Island, the gem of the sea.

If Vulcan's huge cannon should cross the wide ocean,
And Mars take a notion to manage the fleet,
How soon we would rally, with zeal and devotion,
And stain his promotion wherever we'd meet;
Each tyrant existing in grandeur and glory,
Like all other cronies, should forfeit his fee;
And chains and dark dungeons could live but in story,
And venomous tories should certainly flee.
Oh! think of that Island,
Our own little Island,
Our dear little Island, the gem of the sea.

---

* American Revolutionists.

Oh! think of the hero who fell in December,
And ever remember, Montgomery Guards;
If fortune had favored the town should surrender
Tho' all its defenders were nobles and lords;
And think of our sires* in an iron-bound bandage,
How often they struggled for their liberty;
And steer for that nation in chains and in bondage,
And angels will aid you to set them all free.
Oh! steer for that Island,
That beautiful Island,
That down-trodden Island, the gem of the sea.

O'DONOVAN.

During the time I boarded in Albany, I was much delighted with an Irish gentleman who boarded in the same house; I forget exactly the name; something similar to Mulholland; yet, this much I know, that he possessed superior abilities; and although his reputation as a gentleman and scholar was universally admitted, and indisputably sanctioned, still he had his own difficulties to surmount, as his means had been somewhat limited, and perhaps narrowly circumscribed, too much so, for a man possessing the dignity of mind that he did. Though under the rigid control of humility, he had been then preparing himself for the priesthood; and confident I am, with the intervention of Providence, that his commendable efforts and perseverance will raise him to that dignity; and if so, I have no hesitation in pronouncing emphatically, that he will sustain the purity and dignity of the Church of Rome, which has been kept immaculate since St. Peter, the fisherman of Galilee, with divine authority, laid the foundation of Christianity in that city, which has been ever since the capital of the Christian world. However, I thought it prudent to take my departure from Albany, and pay a visit to the venerated Trojans, or East Troy. This had been a necessary decision. After landing in Troy, I put up at an Irishman's house, one of the name of Mr. Patrick Pursell, from the immortal County of Tipperary. Mr. Pursell has been long and favorably known by all

---

* United Irishmen

the citizens of Troy; and his fortitude, faith and fidelity, well and indisputably established, as he possessed the genuine feelings of an Irishman; and as I lost the notes I had taken of Troy, I can't say much about its inhabitants, as having no aid but a treacherous memory; still, I will make use of the Yankee phrase again: the Trojans can't be beat. This is only an abbreviation of what I would say in their favor had I retained the notes I had taken of the most conspicuous of its inhabitants. In fact the Trojans, east and west, are exceedingly kind, brave, hospitable, friendly, and generous in their homes, and unflinching in the hour of extremity.

Both native and adopted citizens of Troy are regular and orderly in their habits, and show without a deficiency the strict obligations of citizenship. The two gentlemen of whom I spoke before, of the name of Jordan, displayed much kindness to me during my stay in Troy, particularly the younger, who seemed very fond of the hints introduced in my production, as they honestly and politically revealed the abominable and unsufferable tyranny of the English government and the treachery of British legislation, and also the duplicity and perversity of the lords and rulers of my impoverished and unfortunate native country. One morning in May, 1849, whilst traveling in the western extremity of East Troy, I entered a house, or rather a grocery, which was full of my countrymen; the most of whom were exceedingly well dressed, and drinking moderately, and during a hasty and stealthy inspection, such as would evade impertinence, I observed among them an Irishman, whose mien, prudence and language uttered an admirable testimony in his favor. I thought then that he had been soliciting their votes for his own elevation, or that of his friend. As soon as I entered he turned his attention to the stranger, Irish fashion, and asked me some courteous questions, which gave me an opportunity of declaring my intention, and the cause of my perambulation. "Sir," said he, "you are the first of the human family, as far as I know, who attempted to give the history of any nation in verse," and he added as thus, "and this attempt entitles you to the respect and consideration of your countrymen, and also to the notice of all literary men, who know the stupendous difficulties you had to surmount." Such sentiments gave me an ample testimony of his attainments as a scholar. "Sir," said he, again, "let me see a number of your history." I courteously complied with his request, and without hesitation he read a few verses with such harmony, nicely observing pronunciation and prosody, and covering all mistakes and improprieties with his superior style of reading, that in fact, I was agreeably surprised, and thought the number was all brilliancy; so much for good reading. The gentleman pronounced it an admirable production, and although flattery is agreeable to our nature, I thought otherwise. His approbation contributed to its sale at that moment, and probably his approbation was intended for the same purpose. At that moment an old woman who sat in a remote corner of the house viewed me with suspicion, and immediately gave vent to her cogitation, or as she thought it, a prophetical consideration, as she said confidently, as thus, "My countryman, you are not the author; and in fact," added she again, "I'd wish to know what you follow for a living; I suppose you carry some holy tracts in your carpet bag, also; and, my countryman, this is no place for the likes of you; and the Lord be between us and harm, you are too smooth to be holy, and, indeed, I don't like your looks." There ended the grunting judgment of the old beldam, and although she heard the verses read, she knew nothing concerning their meaning, which at once confirmed her ignorance. I shot an indignant glance at the old hag, which she seemed to disregard, and my singular appearance, I think, gave rise to her vituperations and remarks. I was at the time wrapped in a druidical green overcoat, which resisted the inclemency of many a hard winter, and was otherwise disqualified by old age, or an overgrown maturity. Her remarks conclusively proved her ignorance, though her insinuations substantially proved the immutability of her faith, and her repugnance to the dissemination of tracts. She unquestionably thought my books were tracts. However, I forgave her, though her ignorance inevitably appeared, her sentiments and remarks conclusively proved the solidity of her faith, and I came to the conclusion if she had her faults, she also had her redeeming qualities. As she thought my books were intended for the perversion of Catholics, or for the reclamation of some refractory pets who were not within the limits of religious admonitions, and evidently considered my doctrine more imaginary than true. My friend paid much attention to her scruples, and reprimanded her logically, which for a time put a stop to her audacity, as he found that I was silent on the occasion. I spoke to the gentleman in hopes of extenuating her faults and her uncalled for intrusion, and said, that as she had not been enlightened with any burnish of literary attainments, that we should cheerfully forgive her, and that forgiveness was an incomparable virtue. This had a powerful tendency to cool her avidity for some time, but soon she showed greater signs of contumacy than ever, and a greater desire of putting my abilities to a test. "My countryman," said she, "I promise to buy one of your books, though I can't read or write, if you compose one verse for me now, about Troy. If it should beggar old Molly, if you do it, just now, I will buy one. Come, do it, now." My friend again with some indignation spoke to her and said that this place at present seemed very unfavorable for sudden poetical explosions. Still, all objections only caused an accumulations of demands, and made the beldam more determined, to prove me an impostor. When I found that there was no avenue left through which I could honorably make my escape, though somewhat embarrassed by her importunities, I said, "Madam, though silence and solitude are the most befitting places for the inspiration of poetic explosions, I will attempt to gratify your desire. I asked for pen, ink and paper, which I received with some reluctance from my friend, and as soon as Molly saw me making some preparation to write something concerning Troy, she again said by way of interruption, "Indeed, I want it right away, without patching or scratching at all, at all." My anger had not been meridian high then, though for some time ascending, until I viewed the rotundity and dimensions of old Molly, whose grunting metaphy sical powers put me to so much trouble, and then without much hesitation I wrote the following verse on Troy:

> Another Helen may exist
>   To mar her husband's joy,
> And through her means some daring hand
>   May set a match to Troy.

I made the gentleman write down the verse so as he could read it with poetic ease, and after doing so, he read it aloud for Molly, who seemed very much surprised, and highly satisfied, though much confounded at the recollectien of her temerity. My friend indisputably seemed pleased in consequence of Molly's disappointment. Old Molly was as good her word, and all the men who were present purchased, and Molly's unwieldy courtesy and genuflections, expressive of her sorrow for her unfounded presumption, and her snbmissive manners to myself were evidently humiliating, and the contrition she displayed on the occasion sufficiently compensated for her unwarrantable importunities and obstinacy, and she and I on the spot became friends of no ordinary cement. I say, therefore, that it demonstrates insanity in a certain degree, or at least ridiculous folly, to pretend to some qualifications which are inaccessible to the pretender's knowledge, or at variance with his mental abilities. In Troy I met and got acquainted with an Irish gentleman of the name of O'Rourke, a name made familiar by historical revelations, showing the treachery and insatiable cruelty of an illegitimate queen, the impious daughter of Henry the 8th. O'Rourke kept the best beef and mutton, and the most extensive and best supplied store in the city of Troy. O'Rourke is a man of fine proportions, and possesses herculean strength. He is generous, friendly and determined, and also, an honest man, a good neighbor, a worthy citizen, an unflinching democrat, and a patriot of the highest grade. I then crossed the river to West Troy, to try the calibre of my countrymen in that part of the city, and there I found them full of friendship, of fine feelings, and of every attribute which would constitute genuine Irishmen. In prosperity and adversity they prove themselves Irishmen. In West Troy I got acquainted with an Irish gentleman of the name of John Brady, Esq., a wine and liquor merchant, in that part of Troy. I could color no language in his praise that could be considered an exaggeration, and no sentiments could be uttered in his favor which could overreach the mark, or no encomiums could border on flattery when applied to him, or in describing so valuable a character. Mr. Brady is a married gentleman, and has no issue, which I consider a loss to society, if they should inherit their father's disposition, qualities and propensities. Mr. Brady has few equals, and, although he is very wealthy, he knows neither pride, pomposity nor vanity. He is blessed with an even, religious wife, good health, and all other necessaries to render his existence comfortable and happy. Mr. Brady made me acquainted with the

Reverend gentleman who officiated in West Troy at the time, and whose name is Mr. O'Reilley, and is indisputably lineally descended from the princes of that name who governed with universal applause the County of Cavan, which should be in the possession of some branch of that family to this day, and one look at the Rev. Mr. O'Reilley irrefragibly proves the elevation and dignity of his ancestors. I then took my departure from Troy with a determination to visit Waterford. A few miles only intercept their proximity, and, after taking a ramble through the town, I found the whole population to be Irish. I stopped a little while at a gentleman's house in Waterford of the name of Mr. Kelly, and had a pleasant conversation with his amiable wife and two beautiful daughters. They seemed friendly and courteous, and spoke the English language fluently and properly. They lived unknown to pride, affectation and fantastic habits, and lived, as I thought, comfortably and happily. Convenient to Waterford lies the most grand and stupendous scene, or natural curiosity, with one exception, in the world, bearing the name of Cohoos, a prodigious cascade, or waterfall, whose terrific velocity conveys grandeur and sublimity to the eyes of the beholder, which no language can paint, or no eloquence define. A little to the west of the dreadful cataract is a small town, or village, wherein are established several foundries of different kinds, and different magnitudes, and where, as in all other establishments where heavy labor is required, my countrymen are employed in hundreds, and the most of them young, stout, healthy, determined and sober. Convenient to these establishments, in a small town dwells an incomparable Irish gentleman of the name of Mr. Flint, from that invulnerable County of Tipperary, and it was within the limits of his hospitable mansion that I had taken my repose the night I stopped in town, and I found Mr. Flint much like the rest of his countrymen, exceedingly generous and clever, and his wife peculiarly favored with all the nobleness of virtue and cultivation necessary to qualify and embellish a woman. This town had been my Arctic Circle, and Napoleon's retreat from Moscow was nothing in comparison with the rapidity of my flight, after leaving it, until I arrived in Baltimore, and my hippopotamus only equalled me in speed. After coming out of the cars in Baltimore, I requested, as usual, one of the bystanders to direct me to some Irishman's house that had been signalized for the reception and accommodation of travelers. With much courtesy he complied with my request, and strenuously directed me to Mr. Daniel Shannon's house of entertainment at Marsh Market, and after some time I found myself seated in the commodious mansion owned by Mr. Daniel Shannon. I soon discovered that Mr. Shannon had been long and favorably known in Pittsburgh, Pa., and, in consequence of our previous knowledge of each other, we got, as Irishmen will get, familiar and friendly towards each other. When I found myself exonerated from the fatigue of my journey I commenced the sale of my productions through the city, and after a few days' traveling I was struck with amazement at the vast number of my countrymen who are citizens of that impregnable city, and I defy any man, in all his travels, to meet more generous, more hospitable, more friendly, or finer, or more incorruptible patriots than he will meet in Baltimore, and I may add, that the most of them are intelligent and well educated. After reflecting on the calamity of my countrymen at home, and thinking of the geographical dimensions of the Island of Saints, and making a due allowance for the havoc that famine caused, and the results of pestilence and wars, and taking also into consideration a more depopulating plague, engendered by the foul, false, fallacious, floundering, ungodly acts of an unscrupulous government—a government that devised unparalleled cruelty for the extermination of the Celtic race, without compunction or the fear of God; taking all these destructive elements into consideration, I am astonished at the multitude of my countrymen that are still on the face of the earth, and in every country, and each and all wishing and praying for the restoration of the Emerald Isle to its legitimate owners, and for its rescue from the unrelenting grasp of despots and strangers. I think with the immortal Dr. Brownson, that the Irish are a missionary race, scattered all over the globe for spreading the unerring doctrine of the primitive church among heathens and infidels, and that it is for that very purpose that they are so numerously preserved by Divine Providence. I remained in Baltimore until I was attacked by my periodical sickness, which pushed me to the verge of eternity, and caused me to write home for my son, who came to my relief as soon as possible, and were it not for his strength and assiduity, I would never be able to reach home.

[END OF MY FIRST TRAVELS.]

I had not been very long at home when I found myself perfectly retrieved from my insufferable sickness, and as soon as I found the restoration of my original equilibrium, at the solicitation of my friends I attempted to finish the History of Ireland in epic verse, as the first number extended only to the termination of the ever-memorable battle of the Boyne; and on the 12th of March, 1854, I took my departure from Pittsburgh in the cars for Philadelphia. The weather was unusually warm at that season of the year, and fires in the stoves were considered an insufferable nuisance, rather than an accommodation for passengers. The iron horse pursued its course with incredible speed, and we were soon removed from the smoke and other inconveniences pertaining to Pittsburgh. We soon observed the irresistible darkness of night approaching, which soon shrouded us with an impenetrable mist. A solemn stillness triumphantly reigned, and all were busy in selecting some place where they could settle themselves comfortably for the night, to take a comfortable nap; the God of sleep invisibly came, and drew the curtains over every individual's eyes, and soon they were in the enjoyment of sleep, roving with ineffable delight through the Elysian meads of imaginary happiness, unless occasionally disturbed by the terriffic alarm given at our proximity to some station, which only served to electrify the system and settle the nerves. In this blissful state we continued until the sentinel vociferousiy cried, Altoona! Altoona! Myself and a few more made our resurrection from the gloomy caverns of sleep, but the most of them remained in a torpid state, and I thought then, it would require more than human agency to restore to them their usual activity. No interruption prevented the incredible velocity of our iron horse until we were within forty miles of Philadelphia, when of a sudden its motion had been checked, and from the observable confusion, some derangement or interruption was anticipated. After some anxious inquiries, we were in possession of the cause of our invisible detention, and our terriffic confusion, as we were informed on good authority that another train under full sail had been coming against us, which was delayed by the breaking down of a bridge, which in its construction had been weak and imperfect, which rendered it incapable of supporting such a stupendous weight, and our communicator demonstrated that, if we attempted to cross the bridge of Asses, that death and destruction would be the inevitable consequence. Some indisputably returned thanks to Divine Providence for his succor and intervention in the hour of extremity, and the train became motionless until the bridge underwent a temporary repair, which admitted us to pass over in safety.

The evening star displayed unusual brilliancy when the cars arrived in Philadelphia, and the starry host with unerring accuracy, commenced their siderial revolutions, bright and newly born. As I possessed a degree of agility not often in the power of men of my age, I proceeded to the residence of Mr. John O'Brien, No. 232 South Fourth Street, where I knew a welcome awaited me. I got acquainted with Mr. O'Brien's son in the Birmingham of America, (Pittsburgh) in the residence of Mr. John Crowly, an Irishman and a mechanic of steady habits, fine intelligence, and unquestionable integrity, to whose sister-in-law Mr. Patrick O'Brien is married. After some tedious traveling and earnest enquiries, I found Mr. O'Brien's residence, and after making the customary alarm before entering, I discovered the person that opened the door and cordially invited me to walk in, was the wife of Mr. Patrick O'Brien, whose maiden name was Miss Smith, a lady of refined education, taste and manners, and in addition to such accomplishments, she possessed a noble and generous disposition, who no sooner knew me, than she ran towards me with that warm feeling and affection which is hereditary to the noble inhabitants of the Emerald Isle, and pressed my hand tenderly, as a token of respect and kindness for her Pittsburgh acquaintance—and then with telegraphic dispatch communicated my arrival, and in a few minutes I found myself in the presence of Mr. John O'Brien and in the presence of his lady, and candidly speaking, before I could distinctly identify my friends with the unerring glance of a true physiognomist, the reverberating sound of a thousand welcomes saturated my ears, and hebitated my hearing; and then followed the friendly invitation of "sit down, make yourself comfortable." This made me feel as happy as if I had been under the umbrageous shade of a venerable tree in the Garden of Paradise. So situated in the old chieftain's house, and one of the hereditary kings of North Munster, or at least, should be one; when this explosion of Irish hospitality subsided, his son, Mr. Patrick O'Brien confronted me, with whom, as I stated before, I formed a friendly acquaintance in Pittsburgh, before his marriage with Miss Jane Smith, who with uncommon kindness received me and added by his ecstacy and congratulations to the unparalleled reception I received from his wife and generous parents. O! Irish hospitaity, O! imperishable treasure, still in existence in every clime where Milesian inhabit, in spite of unrelenting tyranny and savage barbarity, since days gone by, that thought to stifle and suppress you.

Mr. James O'Brien, another son of the chieftain, and a watchmaker by profession, with whom I had no acquaintance, and living in Philadelphia, came and crowned my reception with gentlemanly and affectionate expressions, and who was then, after returning from the land of his nativity with a young and beautiful wife, who is an ornament to her sex, and an honor to the country that gave her birth, and if virtue, prudence, extensive education and polished manners were properly appreciated, which indisputably must be, she would be considered an acquisition to society. This Miss O'Reily, now the wife of Mr. James O'Brien, a finished gentleman, is, and so are all of whom I spoke in connection with the O'Brien family, from the ancient town of Ross Carbary, in the south-west extremity of the County Cork, a town famed for the intelligence of its population, and indeed they could not be otherwise than intelligent, as the great and celebrated John Collins of Myres, taught for many a year convenient to Ross, and that in succession, one of the greatest mathematicians, grammarians, Irishians, poets, and antiquarians that existed in his day, not in Ireland, but in Europe; and the celebrated Daniel Hearlehy taught in the town for more than twenty-five years, who was deemed one of the best classical scholars and teachers in the country, and under the instructions of such men, it is no wonder its inhabitants were well educated. After some time I retired to bed and comfortably fell in the arms of sleep, and there remained swimming in an ocean of imaginary happiness or ranging through Elysian fields undisturbed, until the sun's bright rays aroused me from my slumbers. The following morning after a plentiful and delicious breakfast, I received a pressing invitation from Mr. John O'Brien and his kind lady to remain with them and partake of their hospitality free of cost and encumbrance during my stay in Philadelphia. The invitation was no astonishment to me, nor to those who were acquainted with the hospitality of his house, as such had been customary with Mr. O'Brien, and such had been practiced within the capacity of his residence, and I must acknowledge that Mr. O'Brien is in easy circumstances and knows nothing con cerning pecuniary embarrassments. This invitation of course I declined, with such courtesy as I could command, and indeed, it is seldom that courtesy becomes my subsidiary when necessary, as having no acquaintance or communion with one another.

There was a gentleman of the name of Mr. Terrence Griffin, residing then at No. 90 Locust Street, Philadelphia, with whom I formed an intimate acquaintance in Pittsburgh, at the house of Mr. Samuel Nolan, a professional baker and a particular friend to Mr. Griffin, who is also a baker of eminent skill and professional qualifications, and when I entered his house in Locust Street, his lady informed me that Mr. Griffin was absent from home on some unavoidable business, and said she expected his immediate return. Since I arrived at maturity,

I considered myself an infallible physignomist, and the first glance I got of Mrs. Griffin, communicated to me that my friend enjoyed the greatest happiness arising from matrimony, that is, an amiable wife, as her countenance vindicated virtue, humility and a religious glow, and this opinion was afterwards confirmed by the watchful observance of her religious habits. I was not long seated when my friend Mr. Griffin made his appearance and extended to me the hand of friendship and fellowship, and then I told him of my intention to remain in the city for some time, to commit the history of my ill-fated country to press, which I attempted to write in epic verse, and had been looking for a boarding house where I could comfortably remain until I could accomplish my design. Mr. Griffin at once cordially invited me to remain with himself as long as it suited my convenience. I readily embraced the offer, and the next thing which was to be considered was to make an immediate arrangement to get my history printed.

After making some inquiries, I was directed by an Irish gentleman of the name of Mr. Timothy Lynch, who is now I hope in happy eternity, to the large and long established printing house of Messrs King & Baird, located at No. 9 Sansom Street, Philadelphia. Mr. Lynch accompanied me to this establishment, and was himself at the time keeping an extensive Catholic book store in the city, and also, held the agency of the Boston Pilot. Mr. Griffin my invaluable friend, always accompanied me until I got matters arranged, and seemed as anxious as myself to facilitate my proficiency.

As I have spoken before of my great skill and ability as a physiognomist, as soon as I saw Mr. King's manly form and countenance, I entertained a very high opinion of his goodness and veracity, which, I thought were visibly depicted in the glow and serenity of his features. Mr. King's symmetry is admirably well adjusted and commands much dignity; he smiles gracefully, has a fine set of teeth he shows to advantage whenever he chances to smile, and to crown all, I think he has one of the finest mathematical heads I ever saw on any man's shoulders. After some time, I concluded to get my history printed in that great establishment, and my deficiencies were rendered harmless by his indulgence, and the kindness of Mr. John O'Brien, who generously advanced a sum of money, and would cheerfully advance more, if I acquiesced with his wishes. Some time after the book made its appearance from the press, in pamphlet form; still I thought it better to get it bound, and after doing so, the next consideration was, how to get purchasers. An obscure author, unknown to popularity and of shallow abilities, indisputably stood in the shade; and if his abilities were of a high order, and heretofore unknown as a writer, would labor for a time under a great disadvantage respecting the sale of his publication. However, the subject I grappled with was strange, novel, and stupendous, but my worthy and unflinching friend, Mr. Griffin, sounded the alarm, and as it is conceded by every one who is acquainted with Mr. Griffin, although a practical baker of the highest grade, that he is a man of intelligence and intellectual merit. The first person who handseled generously my poetic history of Ireland, had been my friend Mr. Griffin, and the second handsel had been given by Mr. John Smith, from the same county, (Wicklow,) with Mr. Griffin, a gentleman, if I mistake not, from the town of Bray, who had been my bed-fellow during the time I boarded in Mr. Griffin's house. Mr. Smith undoubtedly was young, strong, handsome and generous, and reflected in himself great credit on the land of his nativity. Thousands from the county of Wicklow and many from the town, who were neighbors at home, are now living in Philadelphia, and all, either acquainted with Mr. Griffin, or drawn towards him by the ties of consanguinity, affinity, or good fellowship, and I discovered all to be well-informed, genteel, admirably clean in appearance, and indisputably generous.

Convenient to Mr. Griffin's residence, lives a gentleman of surpassing kindness, of the name of James Semple, a professional painter of high standing in society, and universally admitted to stand at the summit of his profession, a profession he carries on extensively and profitably. Mr. Semple is also a noble-looking gentleman, an honest neighbor, a good citizen, an incorruptible democrat, a fond father, and a faithful husband until death caused their separation.

Mr. Semple I think is from Neury, the nursery of good and faithful men. This acquisition I gained by the introduction of Mr. Griffin. Mr. Semple introduced me to many of my countrymen of high and noble bearing in society, who subscribed with alacrity to my metrical history; among them had been a gentleman from the county of Galway, named Mr. Michael Hill, an architect of skill and experience, who combined theory with practice, and elegance with solidity, and is a carpenter or master builder of rare professional abilities. A brother to this gentleman of the name of Mr. John Hill, had taken a very active part in my affairs in Philadelphia, he purchased himself, and animated others to do the same, he is a genuine Irishman, and a patriot. Mr. John Hill invited me to take dinner with him, and this, as I accidently met him, I complied with his courtesy and kindness; and when we arrived at his house he politely introduced me to his lady, who with unspeakable courtesy and marked veneration, I must acknowledge received me; she possesses rare beauty and accomplishments; no doubt we feasted deliciously on a sumptuous, plentiful and well served dinner. Many carpenters who worked at St. Catherine's Church, in that city, with Mr. Hill, pursued the same course, and purchased cheerfully; and the same gentlemen were from different counties in the Emerald Isle, and all gentlemen of professional merit and intelligence; one was from the county Carlow, of the name of Thomas Dempsey, another from the county Derry, of the name of Mr. Patrick McLoughlin, another gentleman from the county Dublin, of the name of Mr. Joseph Rowen, another gentleman from the county Donegal, of the name of Mr. O'Dougherty. I met with another gentleman who worked at St. Catherine's, from Mullingar, of the name of Christopher Lestrange, who also purchased one of my Irish Epic History, and showed himself a true patriot in the bargain. And in the most of all the carpenters I met with, I discovered an imperishable love and veneration for any production having a tendency in demonstrating the woes and sufferings of the inhabitants of the Irish nation. I returned to Mr. Griffin's, where every comfort awaited my arrival, as a cleverer man and a cleaner or more hospitable housekeeper could not exist in any country or clime than Mrs. Griffin, and I emphatically say, that Mrs. Griffin is matchless. Living in Race street, in the City of Philadelphia, are the mother and sisters of Mr. Griffin, the old lady, though at an advanced age, displays dignity in her appearance and wisdom in her counsel, and it requires no philosophic eye to judge her at the age of eighteen to have been a paragon to her sex. And it is no flattery, neither can it be superfluous, to say, that her daughters are a credit to the land of their nativity, and light and instruction to the land of their adoption, and if either corruption, ingratitude, or infatuation, could induce me to forget or deny my country, one glance at those three sisters would repair my deficiency and unquestionably bring me to my original declaration. Their names are Miss Mary Ann, Miss Bridget, and Miss Esther Griffin, and all unmarried, as yet, although they are exceedingly handsome, intelligent, religious, and surpassingly industrious; they take the lead of all the ladies in the City of Philadelphia, in point of fashion, and no lady is considered dressed in a fashionable style unless she will call at the great and fashionable emporium, where the latest fashions from France, and all other countries of note, will be exhibited to her view. Race street is her ground, and when fitted out there she will be fit to be seen at any public exhibition in Europe or America. The father of these ladies is dead, and I hope in communion with the blessed, in the everlasting Elysian of the just; and I am credibly informed that he was in high standing in society, and a gentleman that would require a princely income to support his liberality; still he always had abundance, and left a property behind him in Ireland for the benefit of his family. I am writing in epic verse, (which I think will be my last attempt,) a pamphlet on a few I met with in my travels, who distinguished themselves with indefatigable industry to promote the sale of my publication, and I expect in that to give the ladies their due. Among my subscribers has been a gentleman of the name of Mr. Dennis Ryan, who lived opposite the Pennsylvania College, in Ninth street, an amiable gentleman and a genuine Irishman. Thence I went to Mr. Logue's, a hatter in Market street, another purchaser, and a gentleman, who, with his lady and family are distinguished and respected in Philadelphia. Convenient to his place in Market street, is another gentleman, and an encourager of the publication, and a merchant tailor; and all the merchant tailors in Market street, with very few exceptions did the same. Their names are as follows: Mr. O'Donnell, a gentleman of noble appearance, and of a noble origin, of high Milesian dignity; Mr. McGuire, a descendant of the Lords of Farmanagh; Mr. Francis Timmins, an indisputable gentleman and patriot; Mr. William O'Gorman, a gentleman of high position in the scale of Milesian dignity; and many more in the same standing in society, whose names have slipped my memory: all merchant tailors. I then called on my friend, Mr. Dennis O'Kane, in Quince street, of whom I have spoken rapturously in the first number of my travels, who acted his part as usual; and a friend of his, and a namesake, a bootmaker professionally, showed unbounded friendship in my cause and used his influence to introduce me to his friends and acquaintances. There is something in a name, or rather a surname, that some will not stain, under any consideration. Thence I directed my steps, accompanied by Mr. James Semple, to a young gentleman of the name of Mr. James Carr, who keeps a commission office or agency, not far from Washington Square; he is a Philadelphian by birth, and a more amiable, or a more gentlemanly young man, has no existence in society; the polish of his manners and dignity of his countenance are letters patent to Mr. Carr, wherever he goes. Thence I directed my steps in company with Mr. Semple, to Hudson's alley, where we came to a large carpenter shop, kept by a Mr. Brown, a county and countryman of mine. Mr. Brown is from near Mallow, in the county Cork, and I fear not that any of his acquaintances will disapprove of my approbation of Mr. Brown, as he is an honest, modest, unassuming gentleman, whose bearing stands high and distinguished in society, and has also an amiable wife, and a proper and well-educated family. Thence I directed my steps to a gentleman of the name of Mr. James Clark, an Irishman, a gentleman, a patriot, and a democrat, built upon an incorruptible bottom, made of incorruptible Irish oak, and as durable as the Pyramids of Egypt. Mr. James Clark was then clerk to Mr. William McLaughlin, between 4th and 5th streets. He is from the county Meath, near Tara, where patriotism is indelibly cherished in the hearts of all the brave men from that part of the Emerald Isle.

I made a mistake in connection with Mr. Brown's establishment, as not speaking of a converted gentleman to the Catholic faith, who mechanically worked in the establishment; his name was Mack something, which I sincerely regret to forget, as a more sanguine friend to advance the sale of my publication I had not met with in my travels. The gentleman is a Catholic, principally and practically. The husband had been sanctified by the wife. Thence, to Mr. Kelsh, corner of Spruce street; he is a distinguished Irishman, a gentleman, and an unsurpassable patriot. Thence to Mr. Magee, a noble Irishman from the noble north, and the provincial men of that part of the Emerald Isle, are noted all over the world for their kindness, courage, and patriotism. Thence to Mr. Bernard Nolen's, a Meath gentleman, and indisputably a brave and kind-hearted Irishman; and on returning home I met with Mrs. Taylor, of Moyamensing, an amiable lady from the county of Wicklow, and a near relative of Mrs. Griffin. Thence to Miss Smith, a sister to John Smith, of whom I have spoken as my friend and bedfellow. She was then in an extensive fancy dry goods store, and I do not exaggerate when pronouncing her to be a model of her sex, and also an ornament; she is charitable and religious, and her modest appearance unquestionably qualifies the expression; Miss Smith was then unmarried. Thence I steered to pay a visit to James McCann, Esquire, and in company with my unflinching friend, Mr. James Semple. Although Mr. McCann is extravagantly rich, he is not enveloped in that impenetrable mist which is sometimes the concomitant of wealth; Mr. McCann, encouraged me by purchasing my publication. Now, my dear reader, I am to describe a gentleman of indisputable worth, and it would require the pen of a Fenelon to do justice to the meritorious habits, character, and ineffable goodness of said gentleman. I have spoken, in my travels in 1848 of him, and that in the best and highest terms I could command; and I called again on him in 1854, and found him as before, immovable in all his grand and noble designs of doing good whenever an opportunity afforded him the satisfaction of doing so without the least observable change, and I emphatically say, and aver, that a few men of same calibre and standing in society would cancel the manifest faults and follies of thousands of Irishmen. This gentleman signalized himself a true patriot, and had been Treasurer of the Repeal Association, in O'Connell's time, contributed himself, generally, and animated others to follow his example; his residence is not far from the Post Office, in Philadelphia, and his name is William Moroney, Esquire, and if I mistake not, he is son-in-law to James McCann, Esquire, of whom I have spoken, or if not, there is some close affinity subsisting between them. In my next epic publication I intend to say more about Mr. Moroney;* this is one of Ireland's noblemen, and one of my reserved stars. Thence I directed my course to Mr. James McDonough's residence, who keeps a hotel of a high order in 6th below Shippen street, and as he is one of Erin's noble sons, it would require the most flowery and eloquent expressions to point out his true character to the public. All his habits are original, natural, and indigenous, and this combination at the command of a gentleman who knows occasionally how to direct it in due order, renders his company not only acceptable, but desirable. Mr. McDonough stands high in the estimation of the native citizens of Philadelphia, and indisputuably in the estimation of all the adopted citizens in the whole city, and the veneration his own countrymen entertain for him is beyond the reach of my pen. As *Mr. McDonough is a star of the first magnitude*, I hope I will do him justice in the forthcoming epic poem. Mr. McDonough,

*** Mr. Moroney, I think, was born in County Kilkenney.**

I think, is a native of the County of Roscommon; he is however, from that province. Mr. McDonough has another brother in Philadelphia, who bears an irreproachable character, and stands high in public estimation. Now, my dear reader, I am going to introduce to public notice another gentleman, and unquestionably a star of the first magnitude, or rather a comet, who became renowned for his hospitality, goodness, and unspeakable generosity, as he contributes largely to every religious and laudable institution, helps to support the widow and her orphans, keeps an open house to entertain his friends and neighbors. Yet as Providence would have allotted it, he is wealthy, or at least in easy circumstances, and such he acquired by honest industry and perseverance. Mr. Semple, my friend in every extremity, took me one night to this gentleman's house, and after he read a little of my publication, and that he did with force, elegance, and propriety, as his education is of high order, he purchased an armful of my books, and paid me in California gold, on the spot. His wife is a splendid Irish lady, who reflects lustre and honor on her sex, and unspeakable renown on the land of her nativity. My dear reader, the name of the gentleman of whom I speak is Mr. Michael Comber, a distinguished Irishman from the County of Galway, the home of great men and virtuous women. Mr. Comber has a brother, who is entitled to the same panegyric, and nothing superfluous could be said in his praise. This brother, I believe, lives near the Schuylkill, in the City of Philadelphia, in which place he is admired and respected. I had been introduced by Mr. John Comber, to a gentleman from the City of Cork, of the name of Mr. O'Keefe, and I judge from the little acquaintance I had with him, that he is deserving the name of a genuine Irishman. Then I directed my steps to the residence of Mr. Quinn, a grocer, near South street, and a native of the county Galway, and it is my honest opinion, that a better hearted man never crossed the Atlantic Ocean. He indefatigably exerted himself to be of service to my cause; he purchased himself, of my books, and made others do the same. Mr. Quinn is rich and respectable, and may he live long and die happy, which is the wish of his obedient servant, O'Donovan,

The following Irish patriots purchased, with avidity: Mr. Peter Nolan, boot and shoemaker, 331 Shippen street; Mr. Edward McCann, boot and shoemaker, Sixth street, Philadelphia. This is another brave Irishman, and a sound unadulterated patriot and democrat. I love and cherish his memory; and I consider him one of my reserved stars. Mr. Jeremiah Bergin, Gafney's alley, a boot and shoemaker; Mr. Dunn, a constituted gentleman from the inimitable county of Tipperary, 183 Seventh street, Philadelphia, another boot and shoemaker. Mr. McCoy, a professional hatter, corner of South street; Mr. Fillen, another gentleman, hatter. I honestly assert that this mechanical class, as far as I could discover, is wholly saturated with fine feelings, democratic principles, and immovable patriotism. I then directed my steps to Mr. Sweeney's residence, foot of South street, a noble Irishman of commanding appearance and intelligent powers. Mr. Griffin and he are married to two sisters; and it is not superfluous to say that Mrs. Sweeney is an ornament to her sex, to society, and to the land of her nativity. She is exceedingly handsome, generous, courteous, charitable and benevolent; applauded by her neighbors; beloved by the poor, and respected by the clergy. The last time I saw Mrs. Sweeney, I thought she was a little inclining to corpulency, which I regretted, thinking it would interfere with her symmetry; a symmetry which nature, or nature's God, so beautifully adjusted. I then steered my course to pay Mr. Smith a visit, who lives in George street above Eleventh, and is a glass stainer by profession, a constituted gentleman, and an Irishman to boot. Next to Mr. R. Cunningham, Thirteenth street above Vine, another gentleman, and an indisputable Irishman; thence to Mr. Patrick Healy, Dock street, another gentleman of a Milesian stock; thence to Mr. Ferdinand Quinn, grocer, corner of George street and Shippen. I have spoken already of the cleverness of Mr. Quinn; still, he is worthy of all praise, as he reflects great honor on his native land by the kind feelings he possesses, and the liberality he displays indiscriminately, and to every one according to his vocation. He is kind, candid, and romantic, wealthy and considerate; and no man could be admired more for strict integrity than he. He is very popular among all classes, particularly among his countrymen. Mr. Quinn, I think, is a native of the noble and distinguished County of Galway, and is one of my reserved stars. Mr. Charles McCarthy, No. 2 Dock street. This is an illustrious branch of the great McCarthy family, and of the Kerry Sept; and take him any way you please, he is an indisputed gentleman. Mr. Woodlock, at Mr. O'Keefe's, No. 102, South street, a learned and promising young gentleman. Mr. O'Keefe, is an original son of a Milesian stock. Mr. David O'Sullivan, corner of Third and German street, basking in a high place of Milesian dignity. Mr. Kinney, grocer, below Shippen, another gentleman whose honor and dignity will stand examination. Cornelius Danver, a shoemaker, of that incomparable class of our community; he resides in Flower street, Benton avenue. Mr. McMahon, No. 86 George street, another of Ireland's nobleman. I wonder if he be anything in kin to Mackmahon, chief commander of the French army? Alderman Carew, South street. Mr. Carew is much respected and distinguished for his honest administration of the law, and for strict integrity, and able decisions.

Mr. O'Connell, South street near Sixth. This gentleman is a countyman of mine, and nearly from the same part that I came from; and I am happy to have it in my power to aver emphatically, that Mr. O'Connell is a constituted gentleman, distinguished and admired by a large circle of acquaintances. Mr. O'Connell is united to an amiable lady from his own place in the Emerald Isle, and has a son in College, a promising young gentleman who is intended for ecclesiastical distinction. May God grant him grace to accomplish his design. Mr. Rossider, from the inimitable County of Tipperary, in Mr. Diamond's liquor store, another of Ireland's noblemen. I will mention a lady subscriber. Mrs. Boylan, (but nothing in kin to Ann Boylan, Henry's daughter and wife,) who lived at the time with Mrs. Griffin, during a part of the time that I boarded there. She is one of the most religious old ladies I think I met in my whole travels. Miss Annie Stephens, corner of Pine and Second street. This is quite a young and affectionate girl who, I must say, exerted herself in a strenuous manner to sell my books, or a part thereof; and who succeeded admirably in doing so. Her disposition is beautiful, and her temper even and unruffled. Her dear father, who departed this life, and I hope is now with the happy in Heaven, was an Irishman of the same calibre. Mr. Highland, Tenth and Washington streets, a gentleman of the right stamp. Mr. Highland keeps the Jackson hotel, for the safety and comfort of all visitors, and for his own honor and benefit. Mr. Edward Morris, from Yougal, County Cork. This luminary is another countyman of mine, and is a tributary branch of the boot and shoemaking class, who is distinguished for their unbounded generosity and intelligence. Messrs. Glinn & Mackdonnell, Richmond. These gentleman are merchant tailors, and like the rest of that class, they are liberal, patriotic noblemen. Mr. Moore, another merchant tailor of the same die, and possessing the same qualities. Mr. Pattent, in Richmond, is worthy of all praise; and, like the rest of the boot and shoemakers, his imperfections, if any, are but nominal. Mr. Pattent is reserved for my forthcoming epic poem. Mr. O'Keane, another gentleman of high Milesian dignity. Mr. Alexander McFadden, Richmond. This is one of Erin's blessed and unblemished sons. Mrs. Wood, corner of Wood and Devlin streets, and formerly of Pittsburgh, is a lady in every sense of the word, and has a benediction from Heaven for her livery. Mr. Kelly, another young gentleman from Pittsburgh, and now located in No. 147 Second street, Philadelphia. Mr. Kelly is an ornament to our iron city. Mr. Andrew Diamond, bookseller, a few doors from Market street, towards Chestnut, a full, fledged, finished, famous, Irishman. Mr. P. McGoughagan, grocer, Richmond street, Richmond. This gentleman of noble feelings, and nobler qualities, is an Irishman of unspeakable patriotism. Mr. P. McCormack, another merchant tailor, William street, Richmond, is another distinguished Hibernian, and one of her favorite sons. Richmond, unquestionably, can turn out as clever men as I met with in all my travels; and if there be another congregation under the spiritual jurisdiction of a finer priest than the Richmond congregation, they must have a special unspeakable blessing. Rev. Mr. McLaughlin is their spiritual adviser in Richmond. May God spare him over his flock, and sustain his labors to promote the spiritual welfare of his congregation. My worthy friend, Mr. James Semple, directed me to a gentleman of the name of Mr. Thornton, who had, in a manner, the government of the Girard House, in Philadelphia, at his own hands; and a finer specimen of an Irish gentleman, though young, I never saw before. He purchased immediately, and inspired others to follow his example, which they did with amazing alacrity, whose names respectfully will appear in my forthcoming epic poem. Afterwards, I proceeded to Mr. William McMullen's hotel, corner of Eighth and Emeline streets. This young gentleman became universally known for his courage, determination, and pugnacious propensities in the hour of extremity, and would accommodate a bluffling bully with a few well-directed blows to settle his stomach, and charge him nothing for his scientific method of doing so. Mr. McMullen is a Pennsylvanian born, though always the unflinching supporter of Irishmen. Mr. McMullen, I would judge, is about twenty-five years of age; has handsome features, and stands as straight as an arrow; his frame is well adjusted, and his nerves are made of iron; he is also both generous and manly. Thence to Mr. Costilo, in Carpenter street above Eighth. This young gentleman I never saw; but I was credibly informed that he promises fairly to be an ornament to the bar, and an honor to his native country. Mr. John Smith, grocer, corner of Eleventh and Milton streets. Mr. Smith emigrated some time ago from his native land; and is from near Coothill, County Cavan; and I have neither scruple of conscience nor hesitation in avowing that he is one of the cleverest men I met with in my travels. He is generous, patriotic, and friendly. Mr. Smith did more to benefit my cause than perhaps my brother would, were he placed in the same situation; and, in his kind undertaking, he admirably succeeded. Mr. Smith is one of my reserved stars, and will appear in my epic poem book, a luminary of the first magnitude. Mr. N. Donelly, Catholic bookseller, near St. Paul's Church, Moyamensing, is an indisputable gentleman; friendly, affectionate, and patriotic. Rev. Mr. Sheridan, officiating Catholic pastor in St. Paul's Church. I have spoken of this Rev. gentleman in my first travels deservedly, in glowing and complimentary terms. May God bless him and grant him long life and a happy death. Rev. Mr. O'Brien; this gentleman officiates also in St. Paul's. May a benediction from Heaven shield him from all danger. Rev. Mr. Cantwell, officiating Catholic pastor in St. Philip's Church. This Rev. gentleman, though one of the finest specimen of humanity, is both humble and humane, and clothed with the grace and humanity of an ecclesiastic. Rev. Mr. Lane, Catholic pastor of St. Catherine's Church, Philadelphia. I was strenuously recommended, per note, to this Rev. gentleman, by Dr. Magher, of Harrisburg; and it is unnecessary to say that the Rev. gentleman received me with that sincerity and kindness which are the peculiar attributes of a Catholic clergyman, and remains since, on all occasions, my unflinching friend. Rev. Mr. Mullen, of St. Patrick's Church, near Schuylkill, is an amiable young priest, full of affection and tenderness. May Divine Providence keep watch over him. Captain McGoey is a native of the County Longford, and a credit to all Ireland. He keeps a respectable hotel at the foot of Walnut street, which is frequented by the better class of our citizens. Mr. John O'Byrne, a native of the city of Dublin, and grandson of John O'Byrne, Esq., of Wicklow. This gentleman, now a worthy citizen of Philadelphia, is one of Ireland's defenders, who fled in 1848, to avoid the damnable tyranny and cruelty of the blood-hounds of Queen Victoria. He is a perfect gentleman, and one of my reserved stars. Mr. Barr keeps the Globe Inn, near Washington Square; has in his hotel one of the longest and most beautiful counters I saw in my travels. He is an Irish gentleman, and, of course, much esteemed and distinguished by the citizens of Philadelphia. Mr. John McAdams, carpenter, a generous son of the Emerald Isle. Mr. John Bready, another Irish gentleman, and also a carpenter, from the County Derry. Mr.

Bready assisted in doing the carpenter work in St. Theressa's Church, Catherine street, Philadelphia. Mr. A. Green, who is barkeeper in the Girard House, is a native of Coothill, County Cavin, and an amiable, young, beautiful youth. Mr. Green had another young gentleman assisting him, in the same situation, as fair and beautiful as himself; and also as generous. I think he is from Tipperary. Ah! my country, how fair are thy sons, and how beautiful and immaculate thy daughters. Mr. Thomas Whealan, carpenter, from the County of Carlow; Mr. Patrick Whealan, carpenter, from the County Donegal; Mr. Charles Judge, carpenter, Ballynahinch. Every one of these gentlemen deserve praise and commendation for their loyalty to the faith cherished by their forefathers; and also for their patriotism and unbounded generosity. Mr. Patrick Woods, from the banks of the ever memorable Boyne, another nobleman from Erin's Isle. Mr. Charles Cahill, grocer, in Lombard street, an indisputable Irish gentleman. Mr. O'Neill, counsellor at law, near Washington Square. This is a distinguished gentleman, as well in his moral intercourse as in jurisprudence. He is an illustrious scion descended from illustrious progenitors, who immortalized themselves in opposition to Queen Bess of blessed memory.

Mr. Gallagher from the county Donegal and parish of Rossgray. Mr. Gallagher keeps a hotel and is much beloved and respected. Mr. Daniel O'Dougherty, county Donegal, and a grocer of the first magnitude, in Vine street, Philadelphia, and as an appendage, an unexceptionable gentleman. Mr. William Murta, from the beautiful city of Dublin is now carrying on business in south Second street very extensively. Mr. Murta possesses a fine disposition, an unruffled temper and pleasing countenance. His lady is a native of Philadelphia and of Irish parents, and possesses every quality that adorns a woman. Her maiden name is Gallagher. Mr. S. Henry, Broad street; this gentleman is an Irishman and a sound patriot; he is from the north of Ireland where patriotism preeminently reigned, is reigning, and must forever victoriously reign. Mr. John Bastible, West Philadelphia: this gentleman is from my own part of the Emerald Isle, and proud I am of the acknowledgment, as he is an honor to society, and reflects much credit on the land of his birth. His lady is also unsurpassed in anything touching or having a tendency to cleverness. Mrs. McCullough—this is another lady residing in West Philadelphia, and is an affectionate, nice lady, full of kindness and clemency and deserving of a high praise. Mr. Bastible, a near relative, if not a brother to the aforesaid, is also living in West Philadelphia, and is entitled to every encomium. Mr. Bastible, and I am certain a brother to the first spoken of, is a gentleman standing high in the approbation of all his acquaintances; though I had not the pleasure of seeing himself I had the pleasure of seeing his lady, a very good substitute indeed, and I esteem her for her kindness, and admire her for her generosity; her maiden name is Gallivan. I knew many of her friends, and a powerful clan and connection they were in that part of the Emerald Isle, where, in my golden days, I had been best acquainted. On crossing the bridge which directed my steps into West Philadelphia, I saw at the termination of the rising acclivity a splendid hotel, and from external appearances, I conjectured the occupants had taken delight in taste and elegance, as the scenery which surrounded their abode made a charming appearance, and seemed inaccessible to the arrangement of vulgar ambition. I entered, and the first object which attracted my notice, was a beautiful lady, sitting in a musing, melancholy posture, with a sick child in her arms, and a doctor sitting conveniently. A close physiognomist watching attentively every sign and alteration of the child's countenance, which would disclose to him the actual disease which affected it, in order to provide a remedy for its expulsion. If I am not mistaken, the doctor's name was Mr. Flynn, an indisputable gentleman in appearance, and I have no hesitation in saying, was one in principle and practice. After a pause, although solicitous for the speedy recovery of her darling child, which appeared manifest in her beautiful, but somewhat melancholy features, she turned herself around and asked me some questions which gave me an opportunity of declaring to her the cause of my perambulation; though her anxiety for the speedy restoration of her darling child was unspeakable, still, patriotism, or at least the love of liberty, and the wish of restoring my beautiful though unfortunate country to its primitive distinction among the nations of the earth, was evident in her countenance, which caused her to become a ready purchaser, and insisted or, rather advised the doctor to imitate her example, which he did without reluctance. The notes I had taken of this lady disappeared in the catastrophe, and in my forthcoming epic poem, God willing, I mean to do her justice, where her name* and nativity will be blended in close communion together. I had not the pleasure of seeing her husband, as he was from home on some unavoidable business; his character is irreproachable, and as far as I could learn, he is a profound gentleman. Another gentleman of the name of Mr. Donoughue keeps a grocery there, and a cleverer Irishman is not wanting. There are many more gentlemen in West Philadelphia whose names are omitted, which will appear in the forthcoming work, and I emphatically aver that I met with as clever ladies and gentlemen in West Philadelphia as I did in all my travels: more about them by and by. Mr. John Coyle, grocer,

---

* Mrs. Gorman.

Tenth street below Milton, Moyamensing. This is an honorable son of Erin's venerable Isle. Mr. Philip Divine, inn keeper, Tenth and Christian street, Moyamensing. Mr. Divine is indisputably a gentleman and a star of much brilliancy, more about him hereafter. Mr. Casey, Tenth and Carpenter streets, Moyamensing: Mr. Casey is a man of very extensive knowledge, a poet and a clever man; he is advanced in years, and is blessed with beantiful daughters, intelligent, modest and admired. Mr. Coleman, marble cutter, Eleventh and Catharine streets, another of the Irish patriots and comets. Mr. James McPeake, grocer, No. 9 Catharine street, Philadelphia; this is a gentleman well known, esteemed and indisputably revered and admired, he is one of the handsomest young men I met with during my whole travels, and the beauty of his countenance and well defined symmetry would give him admittance into the most distinguished society; he is from Londonderry, on which he has reflected much honor, and not only on that, but on the whole of Erin's Isle. Mr. McPeake* proved himself to me an unflinching friend; he is also unmarried, which makes him a great favorite with the ladies; more about him hereafter. Mr. J. Boyle, grocer, Ninth and Christian, Moyamensing, I think is a native of the county of Leitrim; it matters not what part of the blessed Isle he is from, as no panegyric would overreach his cleverness. Mr. Jeremiah Henesey and son, boot and shoe makers; I think the old gentleman is a native of the county of Limerick, and father and son are strictly clever and religious: I remarked when sitting in Mr. Henesey's shop, when St. Paul's Church bell rang twelve at noon, both the father and son suspended work and cautiously offered up a silent prayer in honor of the immaculate mother of our crucified Lord, and such is manifestly their religious habits. Mr.

---

* Mr. McPeake is a Lieutenant in the Montgomery Guards.

Thomas Savage, merchant tailor, Seventh below Catharine; this gentleman is highly cultivated and very intelligent, exceedingly clever in his social intercourse with his fellow man. Mr. Thomas Kearney, No. 3 below Christian, Moyamensing, another gentleman from the Island of Saints. Mr. James Dever or Dwire, from the county of Cork, now in Richmond, Philadelphia; whoever would say that he is not a constituted gentleman, would incur my displeasure, as he is a countyman of mine, and of course must be a constituted gentleman. Mr. Roger Brown, Esq., grocer, No. 323 Market street, between Ninth and Tenth, Philadelphia. Now, my dear reader, I am determined to speak of the greatest Irishman that existed in his day, with one exception, of which I will speak hereafter; I have no allusion to ecclesiastics or to church dignitaries, but to a layman, who had hardly a parallel in cleverness, and who is now, I pray and hope, in the enjoyment of eternal happiness and in company with angels and saints in the everlasting Kingdom of God, and it would require a more brilliant pen than I wield to speak of his merits or do him justice in description: Roger Brown, Esquire, was unquestionably an Irishman of surpassing qualities; he possessed all the noble elements and attributes which constitute a genuine son of the Emerald Isle, or in other words, an Irish gentleman; he was generous, hospitable, kind, consoling, facetious, agreeable, learned, and strictly honest in all his dealings and social intercourse; he contributed to the wants of his fellow man without distinction, and the recollection of the widow and orphan always found indelible shelter within his heart's core; he was a good neighbor, an unerring citizen, an incorruptible democrat, and the love and veneration he cherished for his countrymen and native country would prove invincible to any opposition or external force that cruel tyranny could devise; he contributed largely to every laudable institution; he was religious, and died as he lived, in close communion with the Church of Rome. Ah! and the Church of God, whose benedictions ascended with him to heaven; he was a dutiful husband, an affectionate father, and a noble provider; he left behind him a modest, unassuming wife and six children, mournfully and bitterly lamenting his loss together with a large circle of relatives, friends and acquaintances who monrn in anguish the loss of departed worth. A little before I took my departure from Philadelphia for New York, which was on the 6th of July, 1854, I asked Mr. Brown, in his own office, could he recommend me to the notice of any gentleman in New York city; he answered affirmatively and without hesitation, and said he would give me an introduction to one of the best Irishmen in all America; a gentleman, said he, who can, and will do more for your interest than any other in that metropolis. A glow of cheerfulness was evident in his countenance, and he turned to his desk and wrote with manifest facility and despatch an introductory note to Cornelius Dever, Esq., who is associated with one of the greatest firms in New York, located in No. 10 Pearl street. Cornelius Dever, Esq., is the Achilles of the Irish race in America. Mr. Brown handed me the note, which was well worded and beautifully written, and indisputably to the point, and I aver, that that note crowned my future success throughout all my travels, and what Mr. Brown said, seemed to be prophetically delivered, for the gentleman to whom he introduced me, in goodness baffles all description, and that gentleman is Cornelius Dever, Esq., who lives in a princely mansion in 42 ——— street, Brooklyn. Mr. Roger Brown was a native of the noble county of Tyrone, the place of original loyalty, fortitude, bravery, and determination, and so is Mr. Dever from Tyrone, and two handsomer gentlemen I had not seen in my travels, taking their large symmetries into consideration. I intend, if Providence spare me, to write in epic verse a book containing some thousand verses on the merits of these two gentlemen, and also on the merits of others who signalized themselves in my behalf during my travels. I have written a few verses in commemoration of my departed friend, Mr. Brown, they read as thus:

The human grove has lost a lofty oak
That early fell by an untimely stroke;
Alas, alas! he left a vacant space,
That none hereafter can befit the place.
For that one mould in which he had been cast,
Is either broken, or, forever lost.
Each helpless widow must lament and mourn—
Ah! this sad change and this disastrous turn,
She will through life his memory revere,
To swell her grief and deepen her despair:
Who'll help her orphans in the time of need?
Who'll clothe the naked, and the hungry feed?
O! cruel death, why not avert the blow,
And spare our friend to mitigate her woe?
Let some great bard inscribe upon his tomb
The love he cherished for the Church of Rome.
In all his dealings he was straight and even,
And being admitted to a seat in heaven,
From holy hands he got a wreath and crown,
The much lamented, honest Roger Brown.

I will only say concerning Mr. Brown, that he died lamented at the age of forty-two. I know my faults and imperfections are many, still, ingratitude never found a moment's harbor in my bosom. The forthcoming epic poem will exclusively illustrate the merits of the luminaries that I met with in my my travels, and for whom I entertain the most profound veneration. Mr. M'Cawly, grocer, William and Callowhill streets; this gentleman is a distinguished son of the inimitable county of Tipperary. Mr. Neagle corner of Twelfth and Pine streets; this gentlemon keeps an extensive grocery, and was almost a neighbor of mine in the Island of Saints, and I must say with unbounded joy, that he is a credit to the land of his nativity; he is rich, and has an amiable lady for his wife, and a pious and respectable family. Mr. Mulholland, grocer, corner of Thirteenth and Carpenter; this is another of Erin's distinguished sons, and no person will dare refute my approbation of him. Mr. Edward Carroll, county Farmanagh, was the only journeyman tailor who encouraged my publications in Philadelphia; my friend is now in the land of gold. Mr. Duffin, grocer, Richmond; I verily believe a bad or an ordinary man could not live in Richmond; however, Mr. Duffin is a gentleman of worth and renown.

Mr. John Connelly, grocer, from the City of Dublin, between Twenty-fourth and Biddle streets; I always thought that a man coming directly from that city, before adulteration could take place, had something of a superior manner and cleverness which appeared to advantage to a sagacious eye, and Mr. Connelly is one of them. Mr. P. O'Conner, grocer, corner of William and Cole streets; this gentleman is without a doubt one of the cleverest gentlemen that I met with in my travels; more about him hereafter. Mr. O'Doherty, Richmond; this gentleman descended from some one of the original chieftains and defenders of his native country against foreign invaders; he keeps a large establishment comprising boots and shoes of every kind and quality, and is well liked. Mr. McCauliffe from Donerale, County Cork, a gentleman in every sense of the word. Mr. Muldrew, Schuylkill; this gentleman keeps an extensive grocery on Lombard and Beach streets, and indeed I never had the pleasure of seeing himself still; in all my travels I never met with a cleverer lady than his wife; Mrs. Muldrew is a pious lady, and has a son in College intended for the priesthood, may God grant him grace to accomplish his desire; more hereafter. Mr. Peter Dempsy from the County Kildare, corner of Lombard and Beach streets; this is a fine and noble-looking Irishman, the young Mr. Dempsy is most respected for his cleverness on all occasions. Mr. Brady, grocer, Beach street; whether this gentleman be a native or not I will not attempt to illustrate, but it matters not where he was born, as he is unquestionably a man and a gentleman; more hereafter about him. Mr. William Joice, from the Parish of Cong, county Mayo, the burial place of Roderick O'Conner, Monarch of Ireland; in Cong the remains of the unfortunate King repose unheeded and unknown; O the misery of the Irish since his reign is unspeakable and indescribable. Charles C. Collins, Esquire; I spoke of this gentleman in my first rambles in the favorable manner he deserved. Mr. Daniel Jeffries; this gentleman has the control and management of the Washington House in Chestnut street, I think he is a native of the county Donegal, still it matters not where he is from, as he is great among the greatest, possessing a pure patriotic principle, and an honorable mind. Mr. Michael Madden, a Limerick gentleman, in the aforesaid Washington House, an earnest and faithful son of the Emerald Isle. Mr. Jeffries is chief steward in the Washington House, as Mr. Thornton is in the Girard House; in this house was then engaged twenty-six young and beautiful girls, and about the same complement of the handsomest young men, altogether beautiful and comely. Mr. Patrick Walls, in said house, is of county Derry, a gentleman of indisputable cleverness. Mr. Miles Kehoe, a county Wicklow gentleman, is young, comely, and promising. La Pierre House, Broadway, or Broad street, Mr. James Bird, from the inimitable county Tipperary. Mr. McLaughlin, boss carpenter 410 Hamilton street, from the county Derry, one of the noble and flourishing sons of the Island of Saints. Mr. James Burke, of the illustrious House of Burke, keeps a respectable inn on the corner of Callowhill and Second streets, is also from the inimitable county of Tipperary; and like the rest of her sons, is generous, courageous, and worthy of all praise; more about these gentlemen hereafter. Mr. Edward Campbell, from the county of Derry, and grocer in Richmond; O! Richmond your population is exceedingly clever, and worthy of the highest panegyric. Mr. Leahey, store-keeper, Richmond street, Richmond; this gentleman is from the county of Cork, and a gentleman of distinguished merit, also possessing a mild and unruffled disposition. F. W. Higgins, Esquire; this young gentleman of distinguished abilities is a Virginian by birth and education, is now practicing law in Philadelphia; his father was a Waterford gentleman, and his mother was of the illustrious family of the great McCarthy, of the Kerry sept. Mr. Higgins is one of the cleverest young gentlemen perhaps in the City of Brotherly Love, and to illustrate to the world his merit is beyond the reach of my pen; he did every thing to advance the sale of my publications; I must acknowledge the supremacy of the Philadelphia lawyers and Doctors over all of that class I met with in any other city in my travels; by supremacy I mean encouragement to literary pursuits. Mr. Hartly, grocer, in Richmond street, Richmond, another irreproachable gentleman. Mr. Arthur Donelly, from the renowned Tyrone, the home of great men and beautiful women. Mr. James Lousey, a Cork gentleman, and from that part of it called Ballyvorney. Mr. Gallagher, inn-keeper near Schuylkill bridge, is a noble Milesian and an amiable gentleman; more about him by-and-by. Mr. E. P. O'Driscoll, Quince street near Pine; this gentleman had been a neighbor of mine at home, and has been a long time engaged in one of the Philadelphia Banks; the name stands high in Milesian dignity, and as far as I could learn he bears an irreproachable character. I speak confidently so far as to say that Mr. O'Driscoll has an amiable wife, and a very respectable family; more about him hereafter. Doctor McLaughlin, Tenth street, between Pine and Lombard streets ; this is a finished gentleman, a gentleman in his expressions, one in manners and habits, and one in principle and practice, and if I mistake not, a native of Philadelphia ; more about him hereafter. Mr. McGennis, stevedore ; this gentleman is from the loyal county of Donegal, and I had not the pleasure of seeing him, though being at his residence, still I was credibly informed that he was soul and body an Irish composition ; he is also a patriot and an incorruptible democrat. I had the pleasure of seeing his lady, an amiable women, free of pride, presumption, or folly ; more hereafter respecting them. Mr. George Murphy, at the corner of Twentieth and Market streets, a native of the county of Derry, and an unquestionable gentlemen. Mr. James Lee, a professional carpenter, and a gentleman of course, Mr. Lee had been working at St. Theresa's Church, Philadelphia, at the time ; he is a native of the sweet county of Carlow. Robert Walsh, Esquire, No. 34 Front street above Chestnut. Whether Mr. Walsh be a native or an adopted son of our Commonwealth, I am not able with certainty to determine, but it appears to me that he is a full fledged, finished Irishman ; and in my travels through life at home or abroad, I never met with a more perfect model of a gentleman ; he is extravagantly rich and responsible, and his refined conversation and gentlemanly manners are unsurpassed ; his popularity is solid, loud, lasting, and extensive, and he is entirely divested of the slime and mist of aristocracy. Mr. Walsh bought my Irish History in epic verse, and handed me a piece of Gold which admitted of no division, as Mr. Walsh refused to take back any change ; more about him hereafter. Mrs. Ryan, Tenth street below Master ; this lady is another from the inimitable county of Tipperary, and a lady in every shape and form. My friend

Mrs. O'Brien, South Fourth street, introduced me to the two Misses O'Mahoney; they are from that part of the Emerald Isle, very familiar to recollection, bearing the name of Bandon, the galvanized and luxurious saloon of William, Prince of Orange. These two young ladies possess social accomplishments in a very high order, and reflect much credit on the land of their nativity. Bandon is a part of the vast possessions owned by the ancestors of these young ladies, though now in the hands of tyrants and strangers. Mr. Patrick Turner, Mallow, county Cork; Mr. Turner is a gentleman dyed in the wool, and in all his actions he proves himself a man. Mr. Michael Monohan, La Pierre House, Philadelphia; Mr. Neal McLaughlin, county Caven, La Pierre House; Mr. John Weldon, ditto, also from the county Cavan; every one of these gentleman is entitled to unbounded praise and commendation. This house and the Girard House are the property of Mr. Edwards, and are considered the most magnificent and most accommodating establishments of the kind in all America. Mr. Thomas O'Leary, Second and Coates streets, Philadelphia; this gentleman was born in said city, and keeps a large grocery at the above mentioned place; he is a little giant in strength, and his proportions harmonize beautifully with each other; he is unquestionably a gentleman in full; more about him hereafter. Doctor Crowly, Second and Chestnut streets; I knew this gentleman's father before the Doctor knew himself; a gentleman he was of noble habits, fine acquirement, and bore an irreproachable character. The Doctor was not at home when I called, being on his professional tour to examine his patients, but his sister was there, a guileless, comely, and beautiful young girl, who displayed much courtesy and kindness when I entered her residence. Mr. James Trainer, corner of Eleventh and Pine streets; it is no exaggeration to style Mr. Trainer an Irish gentleman, in part and in parcel, no better disposed man crossed the Atlantic ocean ; he is from the county of Cavan, the home, the nursery, and cradle of patriots and gentlemen. Mr. Fullum, county Longford, Parish of Collumkill ; Mr. Dalton, King's county ; these two gentlemen are an honor to themselves, to their native land, and also a benefit to the land of their adoption. Mr. James Doyle, South Third street ; this is a gentleman to whom I was introduced by Mr. Terrence Griffin, who is his brother-in-law, and indeed it would require a brilliant pen to demonstrate fully the splendor of his qualities ; though unknown to himself as being one of the most unpretending men perhaps in my travels. Mr. Doyle is married to an amiable lady, who is his second wife, and has a daughter, the offspring of the first marriage, who is in my opinion a modern Venus, as the serenity of her countenance shows both grace and benevolence ; but external charms, under the control of religious training, are beyond the reach of impudent and improper insinuations ; devotion, rightly understood and practiced, is an impregnable fortification and safe protection of unsullied innocence and spotless virtue. Miss Doyle has been lately married to Mr. Dominick Bradley, of pugilistic renown, whose acknowledged prowess in the ring as champion, makes bullies quake and shrink from competition,—

He, Hector like, although without a shield,
Enters the ring and makes ambition yield ;
With matchless might he strikes the fearful blow,
And wins the prize from his defeated foe.

Mr. Charles Cahill, grocer, corner on Lombard and Beach streets ; this gentleman is from the county Lowth, and not only an honor to Lowth, but to all Ireland. Mr. Cahill is one of Erin's favorite sons. There is another gentleman of the name of Mr. Woods in the same vicinity with Mr. Cahill, and from the banks of the Boyne, of whom Ireland should be exceedingly proud, as he never tarnished a feather of her fair fame. Mr. Doyle directed me across the street to a gentleman of the name of Mr. Dougan, who is an extensive Druggist in South Third street ; he is from the City of Dublin, and speaking with unerring confidence in this point, I emphatically pronounce him a constituted gentleman, friendly, affectionate, and generous ; he is young, handsome, unmarried, and wealthy ; attributes sufficiently capable of captivating some beautiful young lady, possessing a lofty ambition, and in easy circumstances. Mr. Dougan left his native country when young, and still he entertains the strongest veneration for the land of his birth ; more about him hereafter. Mr. Daniel O'Donovan ; this gentleman is concerned in a hat establishment in Market street, Philadelphia ; indeed he is a perfect gentleman ; he came from Timelague, in the county of Cork, a place where many of that illustrious name reside. Mr. William J. Turner, born in the Parish of Ballygarrick, county Wexford, Ireland ; I had the pleasure of forming an acquaintance with this amiable young gentleman in Chestnut street, Philadelphia, and there is not a country in the world of any kind of civilization, but would be proud of claiming him as her son, or being the birth-place of such a luminary.

Oh, incomparable, invincible and invulnerable Wexford, what inexpressible valor your sons displayed in the hour of extremity, in opposition to unrelenting demons and voracious vultures ; more about him by and by. In Philadelphia, I met with Mrs. O'Donovan, from the ancient town of Ross, in the southwestern extremity of the county Cork, (Mrs. O'Donovan has been a widow for some time,) of which I spoke before as being eminently known by means of its literary population. She is comfortably located near St. Malachy's Church, and has two sons living with her, both young and unmarried, universally esteemed and popular ; they are fine mechanics, well educated and moral; a credit to the land of their nativity and an acquisition to the land of their adoption. Mrs. O'Donovan, herself, sprung from the ancient and illustrious house of O'Donoghue; more about them hereafter. The ancient aud Milesian name of O'Rourke; three of this noble name dwell in Richmond and Stormy-hill, and certain I am, that the pure current of Milesian blood freely circulates in their veins; these are patriots and gentlemen of the highest grade. Mr. James Patterson, Richmond; there is no man in existence in any country, who has a warmer heart for the land of his nativity than this gentleman, or none more deserving of applause and the congratulations of his countrymen. Mr. Bleaney, cork cutter, between Spruce and Pine streets; this gentleman, I have the honor to acknowledge, is a county man of mine, and although he left his native country quite young, he still retains great affection for the land of his birth, and an immortal hatred for the oppressors of his race. Dr. O'Neill, near the corner of Sixth and Spruce; this is indisputably a gentleman, and is unquestionably saturated with that hereditary dignity which, by right, was in the possession of his ancestors, and should be now, in the possession of their descendants. No name is more worthy of veneration, or more deserving of applause than that of O'Neill. Mr. More, merchant tailor, Richmond; this is another Irish gentleman, a great reader, a great patriot and an undoubted democrat. There are, in Richmond, many more who contributed to advance the sale of my publications, but the notes I had taken with a lead pencil, suffered obliteration by friction, and prohibits a full description of things and transactions which escaped my memory, or disappeared in the wreck. Mr. Bernard Lee, grocer; I had taken notes of this gentleman, which suffered from mutilation; but Mr. Lee is the bravest of the brave. Mr. Quigley, in Ross street; this gentleman keeps an accommodating hotel, and is, in principle and practice, a genuine Irishman. I mentioned before, that on the 6th of July, 1854, I took my departure, in the cars, from Philadelphia for New York, and as I attributed implicit confidence to the honest testimony and sincere sentiments expressed by Mr. Brown, concerning the goodness and patriotism of Mr. Dever, I felt exceedingly anxious to see the gentleman myself, owing to my opinion of my infallibility as a physiognomist, and this vanity, or superficial opinion, was only supported by my own imaginary justification. When I landed in New York City, and when my trunks were removed to No. 64 Montgomery street, the residence of Mr. Cornelius O'Sullivan, and being well satisfied with my reception, I repaired immediately to No. 10 Pearl street, as Cornelius Dever, Esquire, had been incorporated with that solid, responsible and ancient establishment, which is considered founded on an immovable base. And, although, since I grew to the years of maturity, by either accident, design or introduction, I had been ushered occasionally in the presence of gentlemen of high standing in society; still I always showed some embarrassment or timidity in my first interview, and probably this weakness arose from my own knowledge of my deficiencies, which I thought were visible to others as well as to myself. Although laboring under this disadvantage, I entered the office with Mr. Brown's introduction or letter, and I candidly aver, although Mr. Dever's back had been turned to me, that I knew him to be an Irishman, and the first sight I got of his beautiful features, and of his fine, large and expressive eye, my usual confusion in such cases, immediately evaporated, for Cornelius Dever, Esquire, like all other good and great men, is entirely divested of pride, prejudice, presumption, pomposity, and nonsense. I found myself perfectly happy and in a wholesome atmosphere, as I can never endure to inhale the foul air of aristocracy.

So situated, I reached him Mr. Brown's introductory letter, and when he read it, I saw a glow of joy and satisfaction illumine his countenance, at receiving a communication from his distinguished friend. Mr. Dever immediately asked me, had I any of my books along, and when I answered affirmatively, I reached him a publication of each kind, and without even opening them, he paid me well for them. This testimony is unquestionably candid. Mr. Dever then gave me the number of his residence in Brooklyn, and invited me, with that courtesy and hospitality, exclusively his own, to take breakfast with himself and family, on the following Sunday, and after some deliberation, that he would suggest a plan to facilitate their sale. After signifying my approbation of his kindness, and my acceptance of his invitation, I withdrew, and returned to Montgomery street, intrinsically convinced of my future success, as being well aware that any undertaking in the hands of such a gentleman as Mr. Dever could not prove an abortion; no more about that gentleman until the following Sunday morning. Before I left Philadelphia, I got acquainted with a young gentleman of the name of Mr. P. O'Reily, and better known by the appellation of Captain O'Reily, as he is a distinguished character in military discipline, and had been, then, Captain of the Exiled Guards in that part of the City, and providentially had been my bed-fellow during my summer stay in New York City. This gentleman, before my arrival, informed my countrymen in that vicinity that I would pay them a visit, which prepared their minds to receive me with applause and approbation. Mr. O'Reily is a native of the town of Ross, of which I spoke before, in consequence of its literary population, and Mr. Cornelius O'Sullivan is also a native of the same town, and so is Mrs. O'Sullivan, a branch of the ancient, illustrious and royal house of O'Donovan. Mr. O'Sullivan had a few select boarders, and all were of high Milesian stamp. Their surnames were as follows: O'Sullivan, O'Neill O'-Reiley and O'Donovan, and to take into consideration the etymology and ancestral dignity of that little group or community, sitting down together at one table, and driven from their hereditary possessions by strangers and a godless government, would cause a lamentable sensation; still, all seemed glad to get clear of that beautiful Island, poetically styled, the Gem of the Sea, and as drifted wood, got clear from the control of an oppressive government. The second gentleman that bought a publication, was Captain Thomas Moynahan, also from the town of Ross, and I emphatically say, that Mr. Moynahan is an Irishman, an l also a gentleman, and one of the best singers I heard in all my travels. Mr. Moynahan is married to the second wife, a beautiful lady, Irish of course, who possesses amiable qualities, prudence, wisdom and economy, an honor to her native Isle, and a delight to the land of her adoption. I will hereafter speak of Mr. O'Sullivan, and of Mr. O'Reily, and show their assistance and kindness. When Sunday morning came, I crossed the East river, encased in a superannuated suit of black cloth, and a hat in the last stage of consumption, a pair of carpet shoes and a tolerably clean shirt; and add to this incomparable exhibition, old age, and then picture to yourself my fascinating appearance; and in this trim and condition I directed my steps towards the residence of Cornelius Dever, Esquire, located at No. 42 Wychoff street, Brooklyn City. After making the customary alarm at the door of his mansion, a young girl made her appearance and ushered me into the sitting room, where I had an opportunity of drawing a comparison between my carpet shoes of different colors, and the gorgeous and foreign carpet on which they rested. In the course of a little time Mr. Dever made his appearance, and received me with unbounded affection and kindness, exclusively the inheritance of the natives of the Emerald Isle.

After a little conversation breakfast was announced, and we prepared immediately to do justice to ourselves by partaking of a sumptuous breakfast, which afforded me an opportunity of seeing Mrs. Dever, the most modest, graceful, artless, and beautiful lady that I saw in all my travels. Mrs. Dever, I think, is from the metropolis of Ireland, and had been a Miss Finn before her matrimonial alliance with Mr. Dever, and a relation of the celebrated counsellor Finn, who practiced with admirable success at the Irish Bar. Mr. Dever and his lady have largely contributed to shed lustre on the meritorious character of the genuine Irish, and may that lustre never fade. After breakfast was over, Mr. Dever and myself proceeded towards St. Paul's Cathedral, which is convenient to his residence, and at that early hour thousands were congregated in the vicinity of the Church, and no sooner did Mr. Dever make his appearance than many approached to shake hands with him which made me sensible of his universal popularity, and before the expiration of thirty minutes, through the unspeakable kindness, and strenuous introduction of Mr. Dever, I became well known to the multitude, who with pious attention came to worship in St. Paul's Cathedral. The first gentleman to whom he introduced me was an O'Sullivan, from the learned and musical county Kerry, and the second introduction was to Eugene O'Sullivan, Esquire, indisputably, the hereditary prince of Bare Haven, located in the western extremity of the county Cork, a constituted gentleman, who is admired for the dignity of his appearance, renowned for wisdom, though young, and revered for his social habits, and moral intercourse. Next comes Doctor O'Sullivan, a native of the town of Killarney, a young and beautiful gentleman of distinguished abilities, and rises above Esculapius in the healing art. Mr. O'Sullivan is generous, friendly, and cheerful, a patriot and a democrat, a gentleman and an Irishman, and although those gentlemen afforded some accumulation by purchase, the influence they possessed was still greater, and which they extended to me with unbounded alacrity. Mr. Dever gave me a list of some of the nobility of Brooklyn, I mean some of the most distinguished gentlemen in that healthy and splendid city, and I commenced the prosecution of my labors with an internal evidence of success; and the moment I informed them of my intention, and mentioned the name of Mr. Dever, all original blunders and typographical errors disappeared, and it seemed there was no room left for criticism, therefore, it is impossible to tell or conceive the advantage arising from the commendation of one distinguished gentleman whose popularity is universal. Before we parted Mr. Dever warmly and affectionately invited me to dine with him that day, which invitation I modestly refused, as having elsewhere some unavoidable business to attend to, and which would admit of no protraction, but before I left him, he wrote impromptu a general introductory note, which was well written, and written with caution and ability. It read as thus:

"The bearer, Mr. Jeremiah O'Donovan, is highly recommended to me by a valued friend *in Philadelphia. He is the author of an Irish history in epic verse on various subjects, and he visits New York to make sale of his books. Not having read them, I cannot speak knowingly of their merits, but I have not the least doubt they will prove interesting, and are well worth the price he asks for them; the subjects being chiefly, if not altogether Irish. All who value them on this account will, I am sure, encourage their author, even, should his

* Roger Brown, Esq.

attempt be ever so humble to those who know me, I have but to say, that, whatever they may do to aid him in disposing of his books will be a great favor conferred on me.

"CORNELIUS DEVER."

This introduction coming from such a man as Mr. Dever must command great influence; another thing must be considered as Mr. Dever is a gentleman of literary taste, and can recite in whole or in part the productions of the most eminent poets, and such men know the weakness of erring humanity, and consequently are willing to forgive mistakes and deficiencies. Now my intention is, if Providence spare me, to write a small book in Epic verse on the late and lamented Roger Brown and on Mr. Dever, and also on others who strenuously and cheerfully exerted themselves in my behalf during my travels. This subject will give me an opportunity of displaying my abilities, if any I possess, as every subject I grappled with before limited my thoughts and ideas from soaring into the regions of poetic fancy, or Elysian viewing scenes capable of affording inspiration to a drooping imagination, and cause a reaction in despondency. I will endeavor to give the names of those gentlemen who patronized my publications in Brooklyn City: Doctor O'Byrne, Dr. Branigue, R. D. Clansy, Esq., J. Finegan, Esq., Dean street; J. O'Donnell, Esq., corner of Hicks and Columbia streets; James O'Sullivan, Esq., doing business in Wall street, New York City; Peter O'Hara, Esq., near State street; ——— McKanna, Esq., St. Paul's Cathedral; H. G. O'Hara, Esq., near State street; Patrick O'Neill, Esq., navy yard; Dr. Little, Myrtle avenue; Squire Mulligan, Atlantic street; ——— Doyle, Esq., ditto; Mr. Doyle keeps an extensive establishment comprising a variety of boots and shoes; James Collins, Esq., Willow street; F. Bannon, Esq., corner of Hick street;

——— Bradly, Esq., brother-in-law to Cornelius Dever, Esq., Captain McCarthy, William Doherty, Esq., ——— Coleman, Esq., ——— Quinn, Esq., merchant tailor; Mr. Caffey, York street, merchant tailor, near the navy yard; Mrs. O'Mahony, Mrs. O'Doherty of whom I will speak hereafter; Miss O'Sullivan, and Miss Hickey, although Miss Hickey is entitled to an O, but as she has neglected the application of it herself I will participate in the same indulgence. Those ladies, whose names I have mentioned are ornaments to their sex, and an acquisition and light to society; they are also accomplished, beautiful and intelligent, the married and the unmarried. Speaking individually of the gentlemen I have named is unnecessary, as they are all in high standing in society; some are of high professional abilities, and the whole admired and respected for their moral accomplishments, strict integrity and high attainments, and no panegyric in their favor could or should be considered an exaggeration, and if merit had been properly appreciated I could find as many esquires in the City of Brooklyn as would make a volume of considerable magnitude, but such titles are not frequently made use of in historical composition. Mrs. O'Doherty is a widow, young, handsome, modest, and fascinating; she is both a milliner and dress-maker, and has a house full of young ladies sewing for her, and I feel myself under an extraordinary compliment to a young lady from the immitable county of Tipperary, who was learning of Mrs. Doherty at the time. Mrs. O'Doherty gave me a list of my countrymen, and her name will appear in my forthcoming poem book. To omit the name of an Irish gentleman from county Galway of the name of Michael Burke, Esq., would constitute an unpardonable sin, and show much ingratitude on my side of the question. Mr. Burke, if merit and education would be appreciated, is more fit to be President of the United States than to be interrupted in his towering inspirations by juvenile annoyance. He teaches in the Orphan Asylum in Brooklyn, which is indisputably a meritorious and laudable vocation. Mr. Burke is both a scholar and poet, and composes in the Irish language admirably. The first glance Mr. Burke had taken of my publications, in the midst of his hurry he sat down and wrote his approbation of the work as follows:

"The bearer Mr. Jeremiah O'Donovan called upon and introduced himself to me as the person so highly recommended by Mr. Dever. I took the opportunity, amidst the hurry of my calling, to read some passages of his work; I feel satisfied that the Poem, independent of its historical facts, breathes through it the noscitur poeta. Could I command my countrymen en masse, I would say to them all, come on, patronize and buy, you shall be amply compensated, and struggling genius in some measure rewarded for his toil and patriotism,

"MICHAEL BURKE,*

"*Roman Catholic Orphan Asylum, Brooklyn.*

"P. S.—I bought one copy of the Epic Poem."

There is an undoubted gentleman of the name of Mr. Fields, keeping a respectable tavern near the landing place in Brooklyn when you cross from Grand street on the Ferry. He is an Irishman in soul and body, in principle and practice, and I am determined to show him profound respect in my forthcoming work. I was directed to him by Captain Moynahan of Montgomery street. I am going to make mention of another Irish gentleman to whom I had been introduced personally by Captain Moynahan, as he is another Mr. Moynahan, and I neither violate my honor or conscience when I proclaim him a finished gentleman; he is a native of the learned county Kerry, and strenuously recommended me to Mr.

* Mr. Burke is truly classical.

O'Dougherty, an extensive grocer in the same street, whom I found to be a gentleman of a high grade and cultivation; and also, to another gentleman in the same line of business, living conveniently to Mr. O'Dougherty. The notes I had taken of him disappeared in the accident I met with in my travels, which will shortly appear in this work; all I can say at present is this, that I believe him to be an irreproachable gentleman, and that I intend to do him justice hereafter. Mr. Patrick Lennin, 83 Baltic street, Brooklyn, from the parish of Carigden, county Longford. No eulogy is too extravagant, or no praise too superfluous having a tendency to describe this gentleman. Mr. Lennin's name should be placed among the archives of the great men of Ireland, and I would rather pass by this gentleman until a more favorable opportunity would enable me to do justice to his worth; more of him hereafter. Another gentleman from the county Galway of the name of Mr. James Nolan, and now residing in Williamsburg, to whom I was introduced by Mr. Lennin, is entitled to the same praise and veneration, and I do not exaggerate when I say that he should, if possible, be embalmed, so as to perpetuate his identity in my forthcoming epic poem; I will give these gentlemen a double burnish. Mr. Nolan has a son, a promising young man, to whom I will refer hereafter. Mr. Lennin also directed me to a gentleman of the name of Mr. James Johnson, living conveniently by, a professional baker and an unquestionable gentleman in all his habits and transactions. Colonel Colbert is a Cork gentleman, and I think, one of the greatest patriots in all America; I believe his residence is on Atlantic street. I partook of a sumptuous dinner with his lady and himself, and found them exceedingly hospitable and generous, more hereafter. Miss O'Donnell, Charles strèet, is a young, accomplished, and beautiful lady, who received me with much courtesy, as such is always at her command when it is necessary to show it. Miss Bannon, another of the fair sex whose affectionate reception I cannot forget. I left much grieved at the lamentable appearance she displayed for the loss of her dear little brother. I had not the pleasure of seeing her father, who bears the fairest reputation among all who are conversant with his irreproachable habits.

Another brave and generous Irishman, a Mr. Hickey, who lives near Mr. Bannon's residence, is one of the untarnished sons of Erin. Colonel Powers is a native of Waterford and now living in Williamsburg, is highly esteemed, and distinguished for his good qualities, democratic principles, and invincible patriotism; there is a squire living conveniently to Mr. Powers, a Galway gentleman, and to my sorrow I lost the notes I had taken of him in the great accident I met with, but as his popularity is unquestionably imperishable, we judge that his actions and habits are inaccessible to uncharitable remarks and envious criticism. I found him to be a very clever man, and I intend to bring his name before the public hereafter. There is another gentleman of the name of Mr. Thomas O'Reilley living in Williamsburg, a carpenter by profession, a prince in principle, a patriot in heart, an Irishman in habits, and an incorruptible democrat in the time of election; he is from the town of Clonakilty, in the southwest part of the county Cork, and is married to a lady of the illustrious house of O'Donovan. All that keeps Mr. O'Reilley from enjoying some office or post of distinction is the want of extensive means, for all other accomplishments are at his command. Ungrateful generation! Mr. Roderick D. Clancy; this gentleman is living in Boyd street, Brooklyn, and is from the incomparable county Tipperary. I say incomparable because they resist tyranny and shoot down aristocracy without cheating the target. I was directed to this gentleman by my invaluable friend Mr.

Dever, who spoke of him in high terms, and by that means I felt exceeding anxious to see him; as I knew Mr. Dever's honor and dignity of mind were repugnant to exaggeration. When I arrived at his residence he was not in, but his amiable lady courteously directed me to where he was. When I saw Mr. Clancy, I admired his herculean frame, and when nature made him she must have been in good humor, as his proportions were beautifully arranged, in a word, a better, or a nobler minded man never crossed the ocean. Mr. Clancy gave me a letter of introduction to his cousin, Mr. Looby in the city of Salem, Mass., one of the richest men in all Salem, it read thus:

"BROOKLYN, NEW YORK.

"MR. LOOBY,—SIR: I do recommend to your special notice, Mr. Jeremiah O'Donovan, as a gentleman and good Catholic; he has for sale a most interesting poetical history of Ireland, written by himself; you will be so kind as to introduce him to the good Catholics of Salem, and the Reverend Clergy, and much oblige your affectionate cousin,

"RODERICK D. CLANCY."

His approbation of the work is as follows;

"BROOKLYN, *August*, 1854.

"I have read with pleasure the History of Ireland in epic verse, written by Mr. Jeremiah O'Donovan; It is a work that no well wisher of that country should do without. As to poetry and history, it is a most interesting work; it is got up in good style, and its cheapness will, I am confident, induce many of my countrymen who still love the land of their birth, to provide themselves with a copy. Mr. O'Donovan is a gentleman of the highest recommendation and his work is worthy of the most extensive patronage.

"R. D. CLANCY."

There are three gentlemen, teaching in connection in St. Paul's Cathedral in Williamsburg, that have shed lustre and immortal brilliancy on their native land: one is Mr. M'Carthy Ready, from that part of the Emerald Isle that gave birth to the illustrious and ever to be lamented Daniel O'Connell; Mr. M'Carthy Ready's brilliant qualifications are well known and established, and his public speeches and orations are of a very high order; together with such qualifications, his appearance commands respect and approbation; his kindness to me will appear ere long on the page of history, with as much animation and glow as the declining lamp of an affectionate Irishman can command. The other gentleman's name, I think, is Mr. Mackelroy, whose shining qualities and qualifications are much esteemed by scientific men. This gentleman is from the county Tyrone, and having no more knowledge of him than knowing him to be a Tyrone gentleman would make me almost swear to his cleverness. O! Tyrone, Tyrone! the dominion of the Neills, the place in which valor and patriotism were sustained by military skill in days gone by. The other gentleman's name is Mr. O'Donnell, from the classic soil of Kerry, and is entitled to the greatest encomium. The united efforts of such men under the piercing eye of reverend theologians must be of unspeakable benefit to any school, college or seminary. The Rev. Mr. Wallace, who officiates in the Cathedral, bought one of my Irish histories, although being himself a poet of the highest grade, and his spiritual poetic composition is a production of poetic talent. I met with an Irish gentleman named, I think, Mr. Coffee, in Mr. O'Reilley's house in Williamsburg who will appear shortly in poetic costume. Adieu to Brooklyn and Williamsburg for a time. No man could live happier than I did in Mr. O'Sullivan's house among the illustrious Irish descendants I have mentioned, as a cleverer man than O'Sullivan never existed, and he is blessed with a wife of the same attributes as regards affection and hereditary kindness.

O'Sullivan keeps a large grocery in 62 Montgomery street, New York City, which is attended by himself and his sister-in-law Miss O'Donovan, who is young, beautiful, prudent, religious, and incontrovertibly honest. Mr. O'Sullivan, Mr. O'Reily, and Mr. Moynahan contributed strenuously to dispose of my publications; but to give individually the names of all my subscribers in New York, would make a history in bulk larger than any of the Asteroids making their revolutions between Mars and Juniper for preserving the harmony of the universe, though it should swell to that considerable magnitude every single name would appear, were it not for the accident which caused them to disappear, and which accident will be made manifest by and by. Cornelius Dever, Esq., is the sun, and centre of all the luminaries that assisted the sale of my publications; he is the main planet, and from him irradiated the brilliancy that warmed and animated all the surrounding bodies that assisted in the dispersion of the impenetrable mist which surrounded my humble publications. Mr. Henry McGuigken, (I may be wrong in the orthography of his surname,) plumber and gas fitter, 166 Ninth avenue. This is an Ulster gentleman, and I honestly aver one of Ireland's noblemen, and so is his clerk, whose name I forget. Mr. McGuigken is one of those kind and liberal Protestants, who are ornaments to society, social order and religion, and entirely clear of sectarian animosity. Mr. McGuigken will appear in my forthcoming Epic poem, and in that I mean to bring my galvanic battery to bear on himself and on his praiseworthy clerk. Mr. Francis McGowen, Thirty-fifth street, east of Ninth avenue. I acknowledge myself under extraordinary compliments to this distinguished Irish gentleman. Mr. McGowen is exceedingly wealthy, esteemed and popular, and is free from all offensive and preposterous airs that accompany some of our aristocracy; he has two beautiful and lovely daughters saturated with shining accomplishments; more about them hereafter. Mr. P. Tracy, N. E. corner of Fifth avenue and Forty-second street: Mr. Tracy is a native of the inimitable Tipperary, and that is evidence enough to prove him to be a gentleman. God willing, we will hear more about him by and by. Mr. James Devlin, Sixth avenue, east side, one door north of Twenty-fourth street; this gentleman, comparatively speaking, is a young man, although married, and perhaps one of the most popular young men in the city; it would require a powerful pen to do justice to his merits, as he is a good neighbor, a noble citizen, an undying patriot, an invincible democrat, and a friend of literature. The great friendship he displayed towards myself I am not able at present to demonstrate, but hereafter I mean to try. John C. Devlin, a counselor at law in Broadway, near Barkley street; this is another gentleman young in years and full of promise. Mr. Devlin has distinguished himself by his able advocacy in some critical cases at the bar or in Court, and it is generally expected that time and practice will develope some powerful abilities he possesses. Although a native of the City of New York, it has been always his pleasure and practice to shield Irishmen from unjust imputations, an abundant crop produced by unscrupulous enemies and sectional malice. Mr. James McLaughlin, plumber, Sixth avenue and Thirty-sixth street; this gentleman and his lady are indisputably clever, kind, affectionate and patriotic; they are very popular and bear truly irreproachable characters, I will think of them hereafter. Plumbers—this generous mechanical class taken as a mass, should be much respected, and are so, I acknowledge with satisfaction and pleasure. Mr. Walters, No. 10, St. Luke's place; this gentleman is a distinguished Irishman, and to see him is to detect his greatness. Mr. James Dillion, 417 Ninth avenue; this gentleman took more interest in the sale of my books than perhaps my brother would if he were in his situation.

Before Mr. James Dillon got entangled in the meshes of hymenial bonds, he spent much of his time in selling Catholic religious books, which made him acquainted with those who were likely to purchase; and, with kindness, patience and perseverance, every time I would call at his store he had a list prepared, and the name of every one on whom I would call with a probability of success, and did this with a cheerfulness beyond the reach of illustration. The love and respect I entertain for Mr. Dillon are lasting, solid and imperishable. Mr. Dillon is from the noble and patriotic county of Caven; the county whose natives gave me the greatest patronage of any county in my travels. Mr. Dillon is blessed with an amiable wife and a fine young family—more about him hereafter.

Mr. Doren, merchant tailor, opposite Mr. Dillon's like every other merchant tailor, is clever, generous, patriotic and brave. Merchant tailors are fit to associate with the most intelligent and distinguished men of our country—more about them hereafter. Mr. Wheelan 16th Street, between 8th and 9th Avenues. This is another gentleman of honor, integrity and distinction, and one of my reserved stars. Mr. Daniel O'Donovan from Ross Carbary; it is enough to say, that he descended from the illustrious house of O'Donovan, to vindicate his greatness. Mr. Levin, boss carpenter, 125 Avenue A; here is another of the distinguished mechanics of New York city; he is exceedingly popular and worthy of the unanimous approbation of all his acquaintances, which by his social habits he has secured to himself—more hereafter. Mr. Baker, corner of 23d Street, between Avenues A and B; Mr. Baker is a young gentleman who deservedly supports the character of a gentleman; he is a watchmaker, professionally, and a sober intelligent, industrious young man. Mr. Mulkeen, or otherwise, Captain Mulkeen; this is a gentleman from the city of Limerick, and a generous, magnanimous member of the Garryowen Confederacy. I was introduced to him by Captain O'Reily, and an acquaintance with such a gentleman is both agreeable and profitable. Mr. Barry, from ancient Ross; this gentleman is now located in Montgomery street, much respected for his moral habits, intelligence and patriotism, I found him to be exceedingly clever. Mr. O'Farrell, Sherry Street; this is a county Cork gentleman, and as far as I could hear and see, Mr. O'Farrell is distinguished and admired for his even temper, temperate habits and industry. Mr. O'Crowley from the ancient and scientific town of Ross Carbary, a branch of the Milesian dynasty. Mr. Roirdain, Peck Slip; this young gentleman is a plumber, and a very promising youth; though young, he is much respected for his rectitude, sober habits and industry. Mr. Connelly, 40th Street and 9th Avenue; Mr. Connelly keeps a respectable inn in said location, and is remarkable for his integrity and for the hospitable reception he offers to all his friends and customers; more hereafter. Mr. Daniel O'Sullivan, Leonard Street; this young gentleman is barkeeper in this street, and the dignity depicted in his countenance would introduce him into any office, and like the rest of the O'Sullivans, I found him uncommonly generous, clever and full of patriotism. Mr. Patrick Hays, grocer, 449 between Avenues A and B; this is another from the ancient town of Ross Carbary and of its learned population, and I may add, one of Ireland's noblemen. Mr. John Murphy, boss carpenter, 9th Street near Avenue B; this is a gentleman of undoubted veracity, and if all the honor and manliness which have formed a combination in his heart's core, were in divisions and sub-divisions, divided among ten thousand of the most degraded rascals in our community, each of them would be able to hold a respectable position in society, and if I live to finish the poetic history of my travels, I am determined to summon all the little abilities I can command, to let generations to come, know that such a gentleman as Mr. Murphy lived in my day. Mr. Murphy is from the town of Bandon the rendezvous of the satelites of William, Prince of Orange, in modern times. Francis Ceasy, merchant tailor, No. 4 Leroy Street; here is another gentleman of that noble class of mechanics, who, by their generosity, have earned for themselves unbounded popularity and applause. Mr. Duffy, corner of Spring and Broadway, New York; this young gentleman is cutter in one of the most fashionable establishments kept by any merchant tailor in New York city, and is as much the gentleman internally and externally, as any other young man in the city. I was directed to this young gentleman by Mr. Mackey, who keeps an extensive boot and shoe store, on 9th Avenue between 21st and 22d Streets, whose illustration of his character was in glowing terms, and indisputably to the purpose; more about him hereafter. Mr. Mackey is a classically bred gentleman from the Isle of Saints, and possesses every accomplishment that constitutes a gentleman —more hereafter. Mr. Daniel Draddy; this gentleman is from the City of Cork, and keeps an extensive marble establishment in 23d Street near the East River. To see Mr. Draddy is unquestionably to venerate him; his stature is noble and commanding, his proportions evenly adjusted, his conversation is agreeable and edifying, and his language correct and positive; he is a mechanic of the highest grade, has a well cultivated mind, he is a great historian and writes the Irish language druidically, in a word, he is an honer to his country. Mr. Draddy gave me a letter of introduction to a gentleman in Boston, and I thought it the most perfect explosion of momentary conceptions I ever read. I am sorry it is not in my power to lay it before my readers—more of Mr. Draddy hereafter.

> This nobleman, his noble mien and size,
> His fine proportions and expressive eyes,
> Reflect much honor on the noble race,
> Who claim that city as their native place.

Mr. Morgan, victualler, University Place, between 11th and 12th Streets; this is a true incorruptible Irishman of irreproachable habits and character; he is very popular and seems to do a great deal in his line of business. I believe him to be a great patriot, yet I am not able to judge of his political propensities. While standing in his meat shop, a lady entered and cheerfully purchased a history, and so did likewise a young gentleman who seemed to be earnestly at work in the shop—the lady's name and his, will appear hereafter. Mr. Devlin, baker, Frankford Street, New York; when I called at Mr. Devlin's residence, he was absent from home on some unavoidable business, but after having some conversation with his lady, I discovered her maiden name was Macken, and a sister to a gentleman of that name whose residence is in Pitsburgh, Pa., a near neighbor of my own when at home or located in that city. Being acquainted with Mr. Mackin and knowing him to be a constituted gentleman, I considered she had a right to inherit the same unerring qualities that he did, and so she has, and indeed, if possible, in a superior order. Mrs. Devlin is religious and affectionate, and much esteemed and venerated by a large circle of acquaintances. She is also wealthy, and gives of her abundance to subvert poverty. I afterwards had the pleasure of getting acquainted with Mr. Devlin himself, and found him to be a worthy, affectionate and patriotic Irishman; more about them hereafter. Mr. McCarthy, blacksmith, in Water Street, is either from the county Cork or county Wexford, it matters not where he is from, as he is an Irishman, and a Milesian of high renown and antiquity taking his progenitors into consideration, and he himself stands high in public estimation. Another young gentleman who worked in his establishment proved generous in the encouragement of any attempt bordering on literary adventures—his name will appear hereafter. Mr. John Dunn, South Liberty Street; this gentleman stands high in the estimation of thousands who are acquainted with his merit and worth, in New York city, and I can say from my own slight acquaintance with him, that he is a finished gentleman. Mr. Slane, No. 8 Platt Street; this is a perfectly finished Tyrone gentleman, and any testimony that proves by a circumstantial or positive conclusion, that he is from Tyrone, proves him conclusively to be a gentleman. Mr. Ferguson is another distinguished son of that blessed Isle'

Where snakes can't live since Patrick blest the land,
Alas! now curs'd, and by a stranger's hand.

Mr. Faherty, grocer, corner of Rutter and Water Streets. I was recommended to this gentleman by Captain O'Reily of Montgomery Street, who spoke of him in glowing terms, and truly he corresponds with his definition of him—more about him hereafter. Mrs. Quinn, milliner, 8th Avenue near 19th Street, is a beautiful widow, O! how charming—

How beautiful, how charming, and how kind,
Is this fair widow with a generous mind.
Seek all creation for the fairest lass,
An Irish lady will obtain the toss.

O'DONOVAN.

Mr. O'Neill, who keeps a livery stable, in 12th street, is from Tyrone, the ancient dominions of the O'Neill family. I need not illustrate his habits or patriotism, as you know him to be a lineal descendant of that illustrious house; more hereafter. Captain O'Leary, corner of 25th street and 8th avenue. This gentleman is from either the City or county of Waterford, and stands foremost in the ranks of his countrymen. In New York he is universally respected for his patriotism, and an unflinching Irishman in the hour of danger or extremity; he is one of my reserved stars. Captain More, grocer, 10th avenue near 26th street. This is another honorable captain, and a true Irishman.

Oh may some captain rise and free that land,
In chains and bondage by a tyrant's hand,
Who fears not God, and fell away from grace,*
The scourge and captor of the Irish race.
Don't blame the Queen, but that polluted land
Who made vile laws, but not at her command.

O'DONOVAN.

Mr. Clark, 23d street, near the East river. This gentleman keeps a splendid hotel in high order and of the first magnitude, and is an honor to society, to his country, and to himself; in my poetic history I hope I will do him some justice. Mr. O'Connor, 9th avenue and 44th street. This gentleman is from the county Cork, and a brave branch of an illustrious Milesian family.

Since Ireland fell, the bravest Macks and O's
Are but the victims of their English foes.

O'DONOVAN.

Mr. Walsh, a boss carpenter, who lives conveniently to Mr. O'Connor's residence is another of the noble sons of the Emerald Isle. Mr. Walsh is popular, warm-hearted, and patriotic; more about him hereafter. Mr. Corney is another gentleman, I met with in New York, who is much esteemed by his fellow citizens. Mr. William Cleary, No. 11 Jacob street, New York City. This is a gentleman whom I highly esteem, and whom I consider worthy of applause; he is a sincere friend, faithful to his promise and punctual in his compromise; more about him by-and-by. Mr. Cronin; this gentleman keeps an Intelligence office in New York; he is from Needeen, in the county of Kerry, the soil of music, poetry, and song; there is no need for a

---

* This verse was penned the time Lord John Russel was in office.

cleverer man than Mr. Cronin; in a word, he is a genuine Irishman of the primitive brand; he gave me a note to his lady, who lives at No. 10 Amity Place, to purchase one of my publications, which she did with much alacrity. Mr. Cronin keeps his office in Broadway, and I counted seventy of the most beautiful girls I ever saw, in his office, looking for situations—all from Ireland. After departing from the office I looked mournfully towards heaven, and let the reader be assured, that I had still one prayer in reservation for the government which was the cause of their banishment from their native land; more about them hereafter. Mr. James McDonald, born in the town of Monanghan, and a resident of the United States during eleven years; this is another of the illustrious sons of Erin. Mr. J. O'Donnell, Harrison street, another unblemished gentleman from that fair isle. Miss E. C. O'Donnell, 18 years old, is a young, gay, and beautiful lady she is unquestionably as good as she is handsome.

Women have been good, but the one alone,
The bastard monarch* of the English throne.

Mr. McCarthy. This gentleman is from the County Cork, and now stands in Washington Market, with every kind of produce. Although a branch of the illustrious family of McCarthy, were, or in other words, an exiled branch of the illustrious house of McCarthy; he is wealthy, affectionate, and saturated with patriotism. I am determined, if Providence spare me, to point out his worth in my forthcoming poem. Mr. Collins stands in the same market, and follows the same business; a county Donegal gentleman, and I neither lie nor sin, when I say that he is an unblemished son of the Emerald Isle. Mr. Larkin stands in the same market, holding the same commission, and I emphatically say, for his candor and uprightness that he deserves the same applause with his two country-

* Elizabeth of blessed memory.

men. I had been directed to these gentlemen by Mr. O'Neill, 33d street, New York, to whom I am under such compliments, and to whom I owe such an extraordinary amount of gratitude, that I cannot express myself on the occasion now. Mr. O'Neill is an honor to his country, and is blessed with an amiable wife and a fine promising family; more about them hereafter. There is another young man who stands also in the same market, to whom Mr. McCarthy introduced me, a perfect gentleman he is, and his name will appear poetically in my next. Lieutenant Cooney, corner of Centre and Pearl streets; I consider no applause could overreach the manifest qualities of this gentleman; I will speak of him hereafter. Mr. Harris, grocer, corner of Pearl and Gay streets. This noble Irishman is from the county Down, and has been seven years in this country; his merit is well considered by his countrymen in New York. Mr. McGuire, grocer, 7th avenue and 32d street; this is one of the most amiable young men in all New York; he is universally respected, and by his manner and bearing, I believe him to be descended from the Lords of Farmanagh. There is a gentleman of the name of Mr. Toomey, living conveniently to Mr. McGuire, and is a native of the county Cork. I believe him to be one of the most hospitable Irishmen in America. He is a gentleman in manner, in principle, and size. Mr. Thomas Coughlin, 11th avenue and 49th street. It is no sin to call this gentleman a genuine Irishman, and that title covers a multitude of sin. He has a very respectable family, and one of his sons plays harmoniously on the Union Irish bag-pipes; more about them hereafter. Mr. Michael Connelly, cooper, No. 229 39th street. I have the honor of claiming this gentleman as a countyman of my own, universal Cork; he is an unflinching patriot, and an untarnished son of the Emerald Isle. Mr. Patrick Mc'Ginn; this gentleman is a

Professor in Holy Cross Church, 42d street, New York. It would require time and talent to show the interest this gentleman had taken to dispose of my publications. He is like the rest of the faculty in New York, a learned professor and an incorruptible patriot. Here follows his approbation of my History of Ireland; "I take great pleasure in noticing O'Donovan's Poetic History of Ireland, being always happy to see and encourage every advance made in bringing before a descerning world the unspeakable injustice the history of our ill-fated country must record. Having read and compared it with other authentic histories, I consider it correct, and therefore recommend it to all true lovers of fatherland.

PATRICK McGINN."

Here is the approbation of another learned professor on its merits:

"I have examined the Poetic History of Ireland, by Mr. Jeremiah O'Donovan, and have the great pleasure of recommending it to all my countrymen, and to others who wish to read the true account of that desolated and misgoverned country, and I sincerely hope that my countrymen will think it their incumbent duty to have such an excellent work in their families, and to read with sorrow of those tyrants and oppressors who have made our country the sympathy of all nations.

"JOHN ROGERS,
"*17th St., Corner of 10th Ave.*"

I think Messrs. McGinn and Rogers are from the County Louth, though it matters not, they are both Irishmen, and their sentiments show it. O, my country! my country! what luminaries you have produced, despite of tyranny, persecution, and every other disadvantage you had to encounter. Mr. E. McShoy, Domore, County Tyrone, 19 years from home, and in New York. This is another of the illustrious sons of Tyrone. Mr.

Edmund Walsh, Lisnacen, Parish of Dromtariff, County Cork. Wherever I met with Mr. Walsh I met with a constituted gentleman. Mr. Edward Clarke, No. 50 Catherine street; this gentleman ranks high among all citizens in New York, particularly among his countrymen; Mr. Clarke inherits the greatness of his ancestors; more hereafter. Mr. Patrick Ward, born in Dublin, and has been five years in America, now located in James street, New York; this is a noble Irishman, inaccessible to the foul breath of calumny; more hereafter. Mr. John Bannon, Rathmullin, County Donegal, another of Erin's noble sons and well-wishers. Doctor O'Reilley, Oliver street; this gentleman is one of the most eminent in his profession that I met with in my travels; he cures the most malignant diseases, and even checks the direful and irresistible stroke of death for some time. I think Dr. O'Reilley is from the noble County of Cavan, and must be a descendant of the illustrious princes of that name who were, and should be now, the rulers and owners of that part of the Emerald Isle; more about him hereafter. Doctor O'Donnell; I think this gentleman's office is in White street, New York, and is himself unquestionably one of the sons of Esculapius, and if a better man exists, death should spare him as a specimen of one man of the human family that did much and injured none. Dr. O'Donnell is from the city of no surrender, Limerick. These two doctors are the Castor and Pollox of the age, and should be distinguished for their eminent professional knowledge and extraordinary abilities. Mr. Michael McDonnell, born in Liexlip, County Kildare, which he left seven years since for the land of promise; Kildare forever! Mr. Edward O'Connell, County Derry; this gentleman keeps an extensive grocery in New York, and no man can contradict me when I say he is a gentleman; more about him hereafter. Messrs. Caffery &

Walters, No. 26 Henry street, New York; these are gentlemen of a true, unfading stripe; nay, more, they are patriotic Irishmen, with a fame unsullied and hearts without alloy; we promise more about them by and by. Mr. Daniel Quinn, teacher and sexton in St. Columbia's Church, Twenty-fifth street, New York, born in the Parish of Pomeroy and Donoughmore, County Tyrone, and has been six years in America. My dear reader, I am, I candidly confess, at a loss to command a sentiment equivalent to his merit. Mr. Quinn's being from Tyrone is one step towards the elucidation of his greatness. Still, he is greater than the great, and whatever could be said in his favor could not overreach his worth. Mr. Quinn, I am sorry to say, has not means sufficient to correspond with his generosity and benevolence, and an accumulation that would suffice should be no small amount. In my forthcoming Epic History of my Travels, I will try honestly to do Mr. Quinn some justice. Mr. William Deleany, who is only eight months in our land of liberty has been his assistant teacher. He was born in Blandalkin, County Dublin, and is a young man of great promise and abilities. Mr. Daniel J. Buckley, Liscarrol, County Cork, six years in America; this young gentleman, who is fit, according to his mathematical abilities, to be a professor in Trinity College, Ireland, is wandering through the streets of New York for the want of employment. His religion nailed him to the counter, and will give him no admittance into any institution otherwise than Catholic, and such are already supplied with men of eminent abilities. I met with another gentleman in Albany from Mockroon, in the County Cork, whose universal knowledge of mathematics is of a high order, laboring under the same disadvantage; his name was O'Leary. Mr. Williams is carrying on extensively in the grocery line in New York, in a street called Depeyster, and is universally popular; indeed, deservedly so. Mr. Williams is also President of the long-shore men, the most powerful association of the kind in New York. He is a man of excellent attainments, of moral, social and political integrity and habits; he is an Irishman and a gentleman. Mr. Howard is doing considerable business at the East River near Montgomery street; a better hearted Irishman never existed; more about these gentlemen hereafter. Mr. Kilduff, Sixth avenue, No. 84, near Eighth street; this gentleman is a merchant tailor of much worth; his manner is pleasing and his kindness is valuable. Mr. Kilduff is a patriot of the widest calibre, and, like the most of the merchant tailors, he is generous and patriotic. No man could be more popular than he, and to add to his happiness, he is married to an amiable lady. Messrs. McGovern and Taggart, in Mr. Brown's eating house, Water street, near Wall, New York. When I paid a visit to these gentlemen, Mr. Taggart was absent on some unavoidable business, but another gentleman in the same department supplied the deficiency. Mr. McGovern did everything in his power to advance the sale of my publications, and so did the other gentleman, also, and I sincerely regret that I have not his name to mention, yet I hope I will hereafter. Such patriots reflect much honor on the land of their nativity. I mean in my forthcoming Epic History to exhibit to future generations the indescribable cleverness of said gentlemen. Capt. Butler, watchmaker, No. 7 Pearl street; this gentleman is from the inimitable County Tipperary, and has been universally admired and respected for his patriotism and social intercourse. In the revolution of 1848, in which our magnanimous and honored countryman, W. S. O'Brien distinguished himself, Capt. Butler took a decided part, and for doing so the Queen offered a large sum for his apprehension. However, this encouragement proved abortive, as Captain Butler managed, with strenuous activity to avoid the Queen's detectives until he landed under the protection of the stars and stripes of American freedom, where he is now an invaluable citizen of our blessed commonwealth; we will hear more about him after some time. Mr. Daniel O'Doherty, boot and shoemaker, Chambers street, New York; this gentleman is of Milesian extraction, and is descended from the potent princes of Enisowen; he is an Irish gentleman without spot or wrinkle. One day, when traveling in Broadway, N. Y., I espied conveniently a superb building, new and magnificent, and of considerable magnitude. I also saw that it was full to its utmost capacity of gentlemen, which induced me to enter, to take a magnifying view of its interior. I soon found that it was a merchant tailor's establishment, or in other words, the head commercial mart of New York. In this emporium the gay and gaudy aristocracy of New York ornament themselves exteriorly, and suit themselves in any article that is costly, and fashionable. This establishment belongs to a full finished gentleman of the name of Devlin, a name worthy of veneration and applause, who keeps more gentlemen tailors at work than would take Sebastopol, provided they had a consummate general to lead them, and I have no hesitation in saying that he could be found among them; more hereafter will be said concerning this commercial establishment and the noble mechanics pertaining to it. Mr. Samuel Mitchell, bootmaker, from the Barony of Duhallow, in the County Cork; I met with this young gentleman in New York, and found him an Irishman in mind, body and soul. He wrote as thus, his approbation of my Poetic History of Ireland, and in these mournful lines you will see his patriotism:

"I heartily approve of the History of Ireland, written by O'Donovan in epic verse, and wish that half the spirit running through its lines would run through the veins of my countrymen, and the independence of the Emerald Isle would be ere long established." Here is the approbation of Mr. James Nolan, of Williamsburg, of whom I have spoken already: I "have read Mr. O'Donovan's metrical History of Ireland, and I cheerfully concur with the sentiments therein, more especially in those which relate to Lord John Russell, and I respectfully recommend it to all true Irishmen." This gentleman is from Eyrecourt, County Galway. Mr. Connolly, inn-keeper, Fortieth street and Ninth avenue, New York. This gentleman is a true friend to the land of his nativity, and his patriotism is immovably established; more about him by and by. Mr. P. Boylan, from the County Longford, residing in this country for seventeen years; this gentleman keeps an extensive grocery near Anthony street, and is much respected by all persons who are acquainted with him; he is a gentleman of confidence and integrity; more about him hereafter. Mr. Johnston, Beekman street, New York; this gentleman keeps a mammoth bakery, and is much respected for his social improvements, as well as his social intercourse. He is exceedingly popular, and is unquestionably deserving of the like. Mr. Johnston is from the beautiful banks of the Boyne, of hallowed memory. Poetically we'll describe him. Mr. P. Lynch, No. 30 West Twentieth street and Seventh avenue, N. Y.; this gentleman, of Milesian dynasty, is one of the brave sons of Erin; he is that morally, socially and politically. Mrs. Rider, from Kilmalock, County Limerick; this amiable Irish lady is living at present in Thirty-fourth street and Seventh avenue, N. Y.; she has been during twenty-two years in this country, and perhaps in New York. She is a rich widow, bearing an irreproachable reputation, and I have not the least doubt of her truly deserving that brilliant and imperishable monument she has erected herself to her memory.

I hope to do her justice hereafter. Mrs. Rider possesses in heart and mind the noble attributes of a lady, namely,. tenderness, affection and sincerity; women are good, though

> History tells, that Elizabeth had been
> A vile, licentious and invidious queen.

Mr. Bernard O'Niell, from the county Sligo, now living between Thirty and Thirty-fourth streets, Seventh avenue, New York; this gentleman left his native country twenty-two years since, I have spoken of him before, and, God willing, I will speak of him again, as I consider him a noble Irishman. Mr. O'Lone, 598 Broadway, New York; this is a worthy gentleman, and said title is indisputably due to his merit. Mr. O'Lone keeps the most splendid establishment in the city of costly articles which overreach my description. Mr. P. O'Neill from Granard county, Longford, twenty-six years in this country; to say his name is O'Neill is enough to elucidate his dignity and Milesian origin; in a word he is a genuine Irishman. Messrs. Crow & Flynn, No. 15 Cherry street, New York; these two gentlemen are, I may say, living under one roof, and kinder or more patriotic Irishmen are very rarely to be found; they are exceedingly popular, admired and respected. Mr. Thomas McCormick, near avenue A, New York; this gentleman is as much respected as any man could be by all his acquaintances, and a better Irishman is unnecessary. Mr. Constantine Duffey, grocer, No. 323 Twelfth street, between avenue A and B; this gentleman is another illustrious Irishman, he is wealthy and his heart is fully saturated with patriotism; more about him hereafter. Mr. Martin, No. 11 Luke's place, New York; this is another of Ireland's stars, and of the first magnitude; Mr. Martin is worthy of all applause. Mrs. Crowly Thirty-third street, between A and B; she is from Kilbarry near Dunmanway, in the county Cork. This lady appeared to me to be exceedingly clever, and she could hardly be otherwise, as she was morally, honestly and respectably brought up by prudent, conscientious and respectable parents. I knew them well in the Island of Saints when I was gay, young and unmanageable. I had not the pleasure of seeing her husband, but the knowledge I have of his father and friends demonstrates his cleverness no doubt; in my forthcoming poetic history of my travels I will give a clearer definition of Mr. and Mrs. Crowly. Mrs. Brady, Edgerstown, county, Longford; this lady lives at present in 32 West street, where she keeps an extensive dry goods store, and is one of the most amiable ladies in New York. Mr. Brady, her husband, was in Ireland at that time for the benefit of his health; may he safely return to her fully recovered from his indisposition. There is another lady living conveniently to Mrs. Brady's residence, I think of the name of Mrs. Collins, and I confess she is a woman of extraordinary cleverness, an acquisition to her sex and an honor to the land of her nativity; I am happy to acknowledge that she is from the same county that I am myself; this lady's husband had been from home but left an excellent substitute behind. Mr. P. Cuff, corner of Twenty-sixth street and Eighth avenue; this is another of the Irish nobility and a faithful son of that ill-fated country. Mr. Fitzsimmons, Fourteenth street; this worthy young gentleman is bar keeper to a respectable widow lady in this locality, though young he loves the land of his birth. Mrs. Duffy, 44 Filbert street, Philadelphia—I forgot to mention this lady among the Philadelphians—where she is generally known for her benevolence and christian charity; I believe one of her sons has taken holy orders, may God grant him grace; none of her children are at home with herself; she is rich, responsible and respectable, blessed by the poor and and cherished by the rich; more hereafter. Mr. Patrick Turner from Mallow in the county Cork;

this is another mistake, Mr. Turner is living now in West Philadelphia, and enjoys an honest reputation; he stands high in good society, and has the invaluable blessing to be married to one of the most amiable of her sex.

Mr. Collins,* grocer and innkeeper in Ninth Avenue near Thirty-sixth street, New York. Rev. Mr. Kelly, officiating Catholic clergyman in St. Malachi's church, Philada. Affection, benevolence, and sociability, are incontrovertibly the qualities of a Catholic clergyman, and all persons acquainted with the Rev. Mr. Kelly must say that he is abundantly supplied with such attributes. I called on this Rev. gentleman in my travels, and he received me with marked veneration, such as I thought that neither myself nor my publications merited. The Rev. Mr. Kelly is an amiable young priest, who is, if I could make use of the expression, not only venerated by his parishioners, but idolized; he is much beloved by all persons acquainted with his social accomplishments, and he is a strenuous laborer in the vineyard of his Divine Master; may God spare him for the spirtual benefit of his congregation.

Mr. Dennis McCarthy Sheehan; I spoke of this gentleman before, and as he can bear inspection I will again. This gentleman is maternally descended from the illustrious McCarthy family. He is from Kenmare, county Kerry, and now a citizen of Philadelphia. Mr. McCarthy is a little giant, still his proportions are beautifully adapted, and no man acquainted with him but will acknowledge that generosity is his predominant passion. Mr. Whelan, Sixteenth street, between Eighth and Ninth avenue. This gentleman is both rich and respectable, and he and his lady and family breathe in the purest atmosphere; I mean, God willing, to

---

* Mr. Collins in every sense of the word is a gentleman, and truly maintains the dignity and reputation of a gentleman; I will say more about my friend hereafter.

give an illustration of him in my forthcoming epic history. Mr. Rhodes, No. 161 Broadway, New York City. In my travels through the United States I believe I never conversed with any man who shows more of the gentleman in his conversation and appearance than the gentleman whom I have mentioned, and he is indisputably worthy of that respect and veneration which are and should be due to great men. Mr. Rhodes is what I consider and term a perfectly finished American gentleman, who is always in the sun and never in the shade, because he cannot breathe the infectious air of aristocracy. Mr. Rhodes is of German extraction, polished and refined, and his literary attainments are of a very high order; he is an ornament to his native city, which is, if I judge accurately, New York. I will give a better illustration of Mr. Rhodes in my forthcoming history. Mr. William O'Shea, Rutter street, New York. This gentleman is very popular in that part of the city, and his abilities are highly and extensively appreciated, and as he hails from the inimitable county Tipperary he must be worthy of encouragement and of some office of note and distinction. His attainments are solid, his manner pleasing, and is made of some Irish oak; more about him hereafter. Mr. William Clifford, Cherry street, New York. This gentleman, and I have no hesitation in saying so, is one of the greatest patriots in the land of his adoption, and a warmer friend to his countrymen never existed, and if one of his loaves (he is a baker by profession,) is as big as his heart, he could indisputably feed all the hungry men and women in New York city. Mr. John Crowly from the southwest extremity of the county Cork. This is another untarnished son of the Emerald Isle, brave generous, and kind. Mr. Shanahan, boot maker, Montgomery street. I fearlessly say that this gentleman is an honest, industrious, sober and patriotic Irishman. I have the pleasure of being a countyman of his;

more by and by. Mr. James McCabe. This gentleman is living on Beach street, Philadelphia, and is from the county Galway, the home of the lion of the tribe of Juda,—Archbishop McHale,—and a cleverer Irishman is not every day to be met with. Mr. McCabe is justly esteemed and respected. Mr. McGeary, Beach street West Philadelphia, this gentleman to whom I was directed is a clever fellow, and a polished gem of the Emerald Isle. Mr. McGeary will not impoverish the reputation of his fair native Isle. This gentleman supplies the most part of the city with lime, and he is heaping wealth together of considerable magnitude. —— Slevin, Esquire, Philadelphia. This gentleman is one of the Brothers, and perhaps belongs to the firm of Slevin & Brother of Cincinnati; this establishment, although the principal is in Cincinnati, has its tributary branches in various cities and in different States, and is immovably considered by any external force or opposition. He, as well as the rest of his brother, have contributed prodigious sums for the completion of Catholic churches and other religious institutions. This gentleman and his brothers are worthy members of the Catholic church and this Christian institution, they vindicate principally and practically. Mr. Slevin of Philadelphia and Mr. Edwards, if I mistake not, are brothers-in-law. Mr. Edwards is a citizen of Philadelphia also, and a man of stupendous wealth, and that, with his talent and social accomplishments, has gained for himself the highest esteem and respect of every distinguished and reputable citizen in Philadelphia. Mr. Edwards owns the La Pierre and the Girard House, two establishments that cannot be excelled by others of the kind in any city in America. Therefore the house or firm of Slevin & Brothers, or Slevin & Co., in Cincinnati, by taking into consideration the responsibility of its foundation, and all its ramifications, collaterals, and revolving satellites must be considered impregnable.

This house is strong, and never means to fall,
'Tis built on pillars, with a granite wall;
Let what will come, from either East or West,
There is abundance in the iron chest—
To pay the whole, no matter what amount—
The nicest way to settle an account.

Fairmount, Philadelphia.—I have taken notes of all my contributors in this part of the city with a soft lead pencil, which, after a little friction, became entirely mutilated, and this unavoidable defect I am ashamed to acknowledge; however, I candidly confess I never experienced more generosity, kindness, or courteous expressions among my countrymen and women than I did among my friends at Fairmount. Mr. John Farrell, who lived in Pittsburg and is now in California, has two brothers living at Fairmount, and I blush not, neither do I debauch my conscience, by saying that they are gentlemen and Irishmen too, and indeed of a superior grade; and add that they are, as they should be, popular, respected, and appreciated. I met at Fairmount with a gentleman of the right kind of calibre, of the name of Mr. Brinnan, a boot and shoemaker. Oh, what patriotism is imbedded in his heart's core! what affection in his bosom, and what friendship in his conversation! I recollect a gentleman who had been there on the night-watch, came into Mr. Brinnan's shop, (the Queen's county is where he hailed from,) to whom I had been introduced by Mr. Brinnan, took one of my publications and read a few pages of it with evident correctness, and then purchased a copy with manifest alacrity. There is another gentleman of the name of Mr. O'Doharty living at Fairmount, I think a liquor merchant and grocer; and many others also who are entitled to the most exalted panegyrics and extravagant encomiums for the patriotic and sterling feelings they cherished, which is the natural inheritance of genuine Irishmen.

Williamsburgh and Brooklyn.—Mr. McClean, who keeps a large establishment, comprising boots and shoes, in Fulton street, Brooklyn, is a generous and noble son of the Island of Saints; he reflects honor on the land of his birth, and is very popular in the land of his adoption. Messrs. Quirk & Smallfield, Williamsburg.—These are unquestionably two young patriots of extraordinary promise, who would sacrifice anything and everything for the restoration of the land of their nativity to its primitive elevation; both boarded in Second street, Williamsburg. I forget the names of the two young gentlemen, tailors professionally, who worked for Mr. James Quinn, Myrtle avenue, Brooklyn; they emigrated from the parish of Kilabeg, northwest extremity of Donegal, which is also Mr. Quinn's native place; however, these two gentlemen possess indelible patriotism and regard for the land of their nativity. Cornelius Dever, Esquire, a native of the town of Straban, parish of Camus, County Tyrone, Ireland, and is now thirty years of age; his residence is in 42 Wychoff street, Brooklyn. Now my reader, before I bid adieu to Brookyn, I will make a few remarks: it is my intention, if providence spare me, to write my travels over again in epic verse, in order to signalize those who distinguished themselves in my behalf during my travels. The two hinges on which it will rest will be made manifest in the work, one of the hinges will be the late and much lamented Roger Brown, Esquire, who resided in Market street, Philadelphia, and the other will be Cornelius Dever, Esquire, of Brooklyn, New York, and of course others will receive their share of applause with as much attention and fidelity as my limited and superficial abilities will allow. Claudius Bradley, Esquire, No. 165 Myrtle avenue, Brooklyn, Eugene O'Sullivan, Esquire, hereditary prince of Barrec Haven, though being deprived by the irresistible force of godless tyrants and strangers, of the vast possessions of his ancestors, he is still justly entitled to the appellation.

Mr. O'Sullivan cordially invited me to take tea with him at his residence some evening before I would take my departure for Boston, Massachusetts, and said that he would give me a note of introduction to James O'Sullivan, Esquire, a resident of Boston, and a descendant of the same illustrious family with himself; with much alacrity I acquiesced with his invitation ; and one evening afterwards I proceeded to his residence, which is in Atlantic street, a magnificent mansion in which an oriental potentate could revel. Mr. Eugene O'Sullivan is quite a young man, and his mother a widow lady. On my arrival I had been affectionately introduced by Mr. O'Sullivan to his mother, to his sisters, and also to his brother, who received me with disciplined experience, and inimitable hospitality, which is only known to the natives of the Emerald Isle. Oh, what happiness I felt that evening in company with that brilliant, artless and distinguished family, whose innocence and friendship increased my admiration! Early in the night I departed with a letter of introduction from Mr. O'Sullivan to his revered friend in Boston, and was escorted by Mr. Eugene O'Sullivan, by his brother, and also by Doctor O'Sullivan, of the same illustrious house, to the far distant termination of Atlantic street, where, after giving and receiving benedictions, I crossed the South Ferry, got into an omnibus, and soon found myself in No. 62 Montgomery street, under the friendly roof of Mr. Cornelius O'Sullivan's residence. On the following day I took my departure for Boston, on board the Bold Commodore, a fast sailing steamboat of incredible strength, and every object receded with the incomprehensible velocity of electricity, which made us leave behind Blackwell's Island, Hellgate, and every other point of annihilation, torture, and destruction. After some time her course lay due north, and sometimes north-by-east; this I ascertained by the north star. The Commodore kept majestically on her course until sometime in the night, which I cannot exactly determine. The cry Stonington reverberated from the approximation of some invisible solid, which aroused every individual from a balmy and refreshing repose, and from the imaginary bliss that is felt while ranging through Elysian fields and enamelled meadows; and after some little delay and confusion we were all comfortably seated in the cars for Boston, and in a few hours the flying horse carried us safely to that city. The internal capacity of the cars became magically animated. All persons were in motion at once and repairing for their destination. I stood on the platform near the cars without a friend, with a prodigious chest full of books, together with some other bulky baggage, under the insufferable rays of the sun. I soon was redeemed from the intricacy of my position by the approach of two of my countrymen, who asked me had I a trunk or any kind of baggage I would wish to have taken to my port of destination? Answering them affirmatively only made them more inquisitive, and in a friendly manner strenuously recommended me to a boarding-house kept by Mr. P. O'Neill, which was within a few rods of the platform. The sound of O'Neill inspired an intrinsic gratification. I felt better than I could describe, not being far from the place where the immortal Warren fell a victim to English cruelty, and where the Pilgrim Fathers landed to show the violence of British tyranny, my sensations could be better imagined than defined. However, before these considerations vanished from my mind, I found myself sitting comfortably in Mr. O'Neill's first class boarding-house, seriously ruminating on future operations. After I had taken breakfast the following morning I went to South street, where Mr. John O'Sullivan resides, and where he keeps an extensive establishment, including groceries and liquors of every kind and quality. Mr. O'Sullivan received me with that unspeakable kindness which is the natural inheritance of the O'Sullivan family since Christianity found shelter in society. On leaving Mr. O'Sullivan, he gave me the names of some prominent men in Boston, which had been the immediate preliminary for commencement, and if genuine Irishmen are to be met with, you will find them in Boston and throughout the State of Massachusetts, and any attempt that I would make to give their character its deserving burnish, would prove an abortion, not for the want of fidelity, but the want of talent. The names that Mr. O'Sullivan gave are as follows: Mr. Jeremiah O'Kelly, Gough street, Mr. P. Holly, South and Kingland streets, Mr. John O'Sullivan, Albany street, Mr. O'Conner, South street, Mr. Mac, in the Navy Yard, Charleston. These are all countymen of my own, Cork. Each and every one of them stands high in distinguished societies, is unquestionably popular with a character as fair as unsullied snow.

Mr. Jeremiah Kelly, Gough street, Boston.—This gentleman left his native country when quite young, and landed I believe in Boston; he came from the southwest extremity of the County Cork, the ancient locality of distinguished men of the Milesian order, and by his education, behaviour, religious habits and social intercourse, which constitute the man and the gentleman. Mr. Kelly has ever since filled with applause an office of trust, honour and emolument in Boston, Massachusetts, and his character is as free from stain, after holding this office for thirty-three years, as the flower that grows on the bank of the Ganges, or that grows in his own native Emerald Isle. Mr. Kelly married a lady of French extraction, and that day kind providence laid the foundation of his future happiness and poured down a blessing on his head which will follow him to his grave, and illumine his direction to Heaven. Mr. and Mrs. Kelly studied very much the improvement of their family, and for that reason they are religious, virtuous and refined, and their education and accomplishments are of a high order, and their daughters play harmoniously on the piano, the youngest as well as the oldest, and are also obedient to parents and pastor. Mr. Kelly's eldest son died not long since, after arriving at the age of maturity and was universally lamented as being a young man of great promise, and the patience and resignation they displayed on that sorrowful occasion was admirable, and nothing else could have produced such christian fortitude, but the love of God and an entire resignation to his holy will. When I called at Mr. Kelly's residence he was in his office at the time, but his lady was there, a noble and generous substitute, who with alacrity bought one of each publication and paid a heavy price, as she would accept of no change, but this liberality was only the beginning of the end, which the following candid acknowledgment will sustain. Mrs. Kelly invited me to dine at her house the following day, and expressed that Mr. Kelly was very anxious to see me; I sanctioned with evident alacrity the invitation, and went to his house at the time appointed, and after a little time Mr. Kelly made his appearance and received me with open arms, and welcomed me a thousand times in our own vernacular tongue; and although Mr. Kelly and I were for many years from our native country, we still possessed an inexhaustible mine of that copious and expressive language. When ready to take my departure Mr. Kelly called me into his room and insisted on my taking a ten dollar gold piece composed of the purest California dust, and all objections to the contrary proved unavailing. Mr. Kelly is in the fifty-fourth year of his age, and a finer looking man of that age is hardly in the country; he has a gigantic frame handsomely modelled, a noble and commanding bearing, and a pleasant countenance. While sitting in Mr. Kelly's I could not turn my eyes to any part of it without gazing on some object that cautioned me to avoid sin and prepare for eternity, as the room had been hung with venerated pictures. I will say no more about this noble family until the poetic history of my travels will make its appearance, and then I promise to bring up the rear.

There is a young gentleman living conveniently to Mr. Kelly's residence of the name of Mr. William Cullin from the county Leitrim, a truly religious young man, and his social habits and amiable conduct have rendered him one of the most popular young gentlemen in all Boston; more about this young man hereafter. Mr. J. O'Sullivan directed me to a gentleman in Charleston, of the name of Mr. Mack, who is an officer of some distinction in the navy yard, and I hesitate not in saying that he is an incorruptible patriot and a genuine Irishman; more about him also. I was directed by Mr. William Cullin to a gentleman of the name of Mr. J. O'Conner, who is engaged to fill some special office in the Revere House, Boston. In this gentleman, and in others, also connected with the same popular establishment, I discovered undying democracy and invincible patriotism. Oh! the land that gave birth to such men must arise from its melancholy slumbers, and hold a distinguished position among the nations of the earth. Here are their names: Mr. J. O'Conner from the parish of Killoraglin, county Kerry; Mr. John Horan, New Castle, county Limerick; Mr. John Gallavan, Dromnakill, county Cavan, and Mr. Peter Williams, parish of Killaney, county Louth.

Perhaps these comets would hereafter show,
And give the British an astounding blow.

In another popular and long established house in Boston, called the Adams House, I met a young gentleman of the name of McCarthy; this young man is unquestionably a branch of the illustrious

McCarthy family ; this information I adduce from his manner and honorable principle, and to say he is from the county Tipperary, at once identifies his quality. Mr. McCarthy is head steward in this splendid establishment, and a better selection could not be made by its governor or proprietor. There is another young gentleman in the same establishment, I think he is from Limerick, the city of no surrender; no matter where he is from, as he is one of Erin's favorite sons—we will hear more about these gentlemen, God willing, by-and-by. From there, by the direction of Mr. McCarthy, I went to the United States Hotel, and there I met with two brave sons of the Emerald Isle, and well she may be proud of them. Messrs. Powers and Flynn, such I believe I may call them, they are Irishmen however, warm, ardent, inflexible patriots, anxious for the restoration of the Island of Saints to its original grandeur. I also met with two other young gentlemen, in the American House, in Hanover street, Boston, pure unsullied gems, with fair skins and clear countenances; one of these young men, named Mr. Brosnehane, was from Kerry, and the other from the county Tyrone, of the name of Mr. Dooling, as handsome a young gentleman as I met with in my travels; no praise favorable to them, would be considered superfluous, as they have deservedly secured the applause of all their acquaintances that appreciate merit. There are two young, splendid fellows now bordering on maturity, and working in a marble yard in Boston, named Powers and Dunn, of whom I have formed a very favorable opinion. Mr. Powers is a native of Boston, still he adores his fatherland, and would venture his life for its freedom. These two gallant young men sigh for the emancipation of the Green Isle from the claws of vultures.

I presented Mr. Flemming with the note of introduction which I received from Mr. D. Draddy of New York city, who received me with evident attention and kindness. I look upon Mr. Flemming to be a gentleman of wisdom and understanding, and his very appearance would sustain his respectability; he has an extensive marble establishment in Washington street, Boston. Mr. Patrick F. Manning, merchant tailor, from the parish of Kilrush, county Clare, Ireland; Mr. Manning imigrated from the Emerald Isle, seven years since and is now located at No. 3 Gridley street, Boston. Every person who knows Mr. Manning, indisputably respects him, as being the true representative of the man and the gentleman; I will write more about him. P. O'Reily, Esquire, a professional lawyer, I think, and a Bostonian by birth and education, but an Irishman in principle, practice and affection, as he is completely divested of that strange, distant and frigid reservation, peculiar to some American gentlemen; his person is as clean as his character is from stain, and that is as clear as the brightest ray of Hesperus of a calm summer's evening, when there is no interruption in the atmosphere to cause a refraction, but an immediate proximity is invited by his friendship and condescension. Mr. O'Reily holds some office of distinction in the court house, and I believe him to be one of Boston's popular gentlemen, and I acknowledge myself under a weighty obligation to Mr. O'Reily for the unspeakable friendship I received at his hands in Boston. Mr. O'Reily is one of my reserved stars. Mr. J. Powers and Mr. Flynn; Mr. Powers is from the parish of Bray, county Wexford, and Mr. Flynn from Naise, county Kildare, both living in one house in Boston.

To this lady and gentleman I am much indebted for their kindness; also, they are deserving of my respects and best wishes, as the patriotism of Mrs. Powers is beyond description; more about them hereafter. There was another gentleman in Boston to whom I was strenuously directed, I think of the name of Mr. Bresney; he is in a leather store and is full of kindness, affection and courtesy. Mr. Bresnry hails from the county Kerry, the nursery of intelligence, poets, and learning; I will think of him hereafter. Mr. Joseph O'Kavanagh, from the parish of old Ross, county Wexford. This gentleman landed in Quebec in 1842, and married in Canada to a French lady, who is pious, virtuous and beautiful, but living now in Boston, happily and comfortably. Any man acquainted with Ireland's woes and history must know the fidelity, bravery, and patriotism of Wexford men, for such is emblazoned on the pages of history, and time itself cannot deface it, and the aversion they entertain for the English government is, as it should be, invincible, incurable, and irreclaimable. This gentleman is young, strong, handsome, active, and determined, and a warmer-hearted Irishman is unnecessary. Mr. O'Cavanagh is a coachman to a distinguished gentleman in Boston. I claimed through a mistake Mr. Holly as a Cork man, I must with some reluctance surrender him to Waterford, and like his countrymen, he is noble, generous, unassuming and wealthy. Mr. Holly has a strange foreign bird in his place called the Minee bird, and in size it would answer as a mean proportion between a blackbird and a crow. In the hearts of my country girls in Boston I discovered the greatest patriotism, and their enthusiasm verges on insanity. These ladies fill various situations, according to their capabilities, and I have no hesitation in saying that many, very many, of these young ladies, can compete in beauty, virtue, and loveliness, with any other ladies moving in the same sphere on the habitable globe, and I say again that they show more affection than others moving in the same sphere in any other country, Ireland excepted, under the sun. In the forthcoming poetical history of my travels, more will be said about them. Their names are here arranged, Mrs. Gately, county Cavan, Miss Bridget Shellling, county Donegal, Miss Ellen Fenly, county Kilkenny, Miss Gleason, county Waterford, and in No. 70 Beacon street, Miss Catherine Powell, county Longford, No. 37 Chestnut, Miss Eliza Curry, county Cavan. I met with another young lady, I think in Beacon street, from the county Cork. Oh, what a beautiful and fascinating creature she is! I knew her grandfather in my early days, a gentleman of distinguished professional abilities, who justly acquired great popularity. I met a young gentleman in that street named Mr. Philip Maguire, one of the hereditary chieftains of Farmanagh. I also got acquainted with a gentleman by the name of Clarke, who occasionally visited Mr. O'Neill's place, a perfect and constituted gentleman. Mr. O'Neill directed me to Mr. Doran's residence, in consequence of Mrs. Doran being his aunt. Mr. Doran, though being absent, has an amiable lady, who assumed the responsibility and well supplied the deficiency on that occasion. Mrs. Doran sat calmly and contented in her own magnificent mansion, inaccessible to pride or its worthless concomitants; she is as happy as she ought to be. Mr. O'Neill's niece had been conveniently married, another encourager of poetic powers, and I think one of the handsomest ladies in all my travels. Mr. O'Neill is from the parish of Myshall, county Carlow, and married in Boston to an amiable lady who fills his heart with comfort and his coffers with treasure, as she is industrious, prudent, and attentive to her own affairs. Mr. O'Neill keeps a large grocery and a respectable boarding-house in No. 70 Church street, Boston, and I would advise all travellers going that way to give him a call, as he is a finished gentleman, and his wife is a lady of much worth; here every comfort is administered to boarders. Mr. Peter Williams, one of the gentleman in the Revere House, whose name I have already mentioned, gave me an introductory letter to his two sons, respectable mechanics in the city of Lynn, and I am very sorry that I cannot place it before my readers; although it was written at the impulse of the moment, it could be honorably compared with some of the productions of the most eminent writers, and adding his qualifications to his patriotism, would render him a valuable man in the hour of Erin's difficulty, and with the assistance of such men, I say, Erin must awake from her slumbers and sit in power and dignity, to give laws and learning as she did before, to all nations. And if that will come to pass, as unquestionably it must, Irishmen are in duty bound to erect a substantial and suitable monument in commemoration of such men as Mr. Williams. Mr. Williams also directed me to Mr. James O'Brien, a county Cork gentleman, and a boot and shoemaker in the city of Lynn, whose name and cleverness are proverbial in the city and out of it, and indeed he has a brother of the same stamp and character; they reflect honor on the land that gave them birth. The Catholic population of Lynn are sound patriots and undying democrats.

In my travels through the State of Massachusetts I was directed by a distinguished countryman* of mine in Boston, to another of the same calibre residing in the city of Lynn, of the name of Mr. Griffin, who keeps a large establishment, comprising a variety of boots and shoes, in that city. Mr. Griffin is much esteemed by all who have the pleasure of his acquaintance; no doubt he is worthy of the applause which has been awarded him, as his habits, social intercourse, and intellectual culture have been highly appreciated. While searching for Mr. Griffin's residence, I got by way of a mistake into another superb and capacious dwelling, which had been opened at the time, and before entering I made a loud demonstration of my design by pulling stoutly at the alarm bell; still all to no

* Mr. Peter Williams.

17

purpose; no person approached to give me an invitation to that magnificent mansion; when my patience had been somewhat exhausted I walked in and sat in a beautiful and well furnished room which stood on my right, in which sat a beautiful table, on which had been placed a newspaper, with an excellent assortment of splendidly bound books. I made free to take up the newspaper, and then commenced reading it, so as the solitary hours would imperceptibly pass, as I thought every moment an hour, until such time as some person would appear who could inform me had I been in the wrong box or not. After a moment's perusal, I caught sight of a well digested editorial, which gave an awful description of Christianity during the dark ages, and of the enormities of the Church of Rome during sixteen hundred years, until the blessed reformation illuminated millions of this benighted body. The writer sympathized in the calamitous and irreligious cloud which envelopes millions of them as yet; still, he hoped the blessed reformation would by degress shine on all, so as to incorporate them with Luther's heresy, or with the corruptible doctrine of Henry VIII. the wife-killer. The writer seemed to have no special preference for any individual sect, as he covered the whole with his approbation of the blessed reformation. Although, if they were to be added together, it would require an arithmetician of more than ordinary abilities to enumerate them. The writer excluded none but the one holy, Catholic and apostolic Church, which is now as immutable and incorruptible in her doctrine and decrees, as when first established by divine authority. I continued reading until the hired maid made her appearance, who informed me that the owner of the gigantic building, with his family, had been on a visit in Boston. I retired under many obligations to the young, gay, and beautiful maid, who gave me the information, and went in quest of Mr. Griffin's residence, which I found. Such has been the cause of the following:

Would God have left us sixteen hundred years
To grope our way among the weeds and tares,
Till Luther came to preach his heresy,
And jolly Kate to grace the jubilee,
Soon after Henry had divorced his Queen,
And married Ann, who had a comely mien;
A thousand isms from their union came,
Unlike in faith, and all unlike in name;
He loved her wiles and her fantastic dance,
And all the airs she had acquired in France;
She was his daughter; did that curb his lust?
No, he was frail, and nothing more than dust;
Such is the course of all the sects on earth—
Such is their source, and such has been their birth;
Alike a hive that in the garden lies,
That once a month from it a swarm flies;
One sect breeds many in one single year,
When they dissolve some other sects appear;
Though every ism monthly dies in peace,
Another ism monthly fills its place.
Church made by man, must tumble and must fall,
The Church of God can never change at all.
They rave and fret, to propagate a lie,
Alas! alas! that they are doomed to die;
All split on faith, the same as erring men,
Still curse the Pope, and all will cry amen;
Such is their faith, their prayer, and their creed,
To get to Heaven, such is all the need.

O'Donovan.

Convenient to Mr. O'Brien's residence are more gentlemen of that faculty who are deserving of having something said in commemoration of their cleverness; and I also met two lovely ladies Misses O'Neills, in Lynn. They keep a Catholic, book store in the city, and are from the noble county Tyrone. O! Tyrone, how generous are thy sons, and how lovely thy daughters.

From the city of Lynn I steered my course towards Salem, and then to the residence of Thomas Looby, Esq., in said city; and, by its magnificence, it was easily discovereed; and, fortunately, Mr. Looby was at home at the time. Mr. Looby is a stout built man whose outward appearance bespeaks dignity and determination. After preliminaries and courtesy subsided, I presented him with Mr. R. D. Clancy's letter of introduction, which he read with avidity and attention, and affectionately invited me to spend the evening with him. The splendor of his residence confirmed the magnitude of his purse; still, neither his manner nor his mind seemed the least affected from the combination of both. Mr. Looby is from the inimitable county of Tipperary, and is about forty-three years of age, with a strong and powerful frame, and a healthy appearance. Mr. Looby gave a list of the following named gentlemen who are in high standing in the community, unsullied by reproach, and are even beyond the reach of the foul breath of calumny. Mr. Daniel O'Daniel, Mr. Martin O'Connell, Mr. Dennis Lynch, Mr. John Collins, Mr. James McGeary Danvers, Mr. Timothy O'Shea, Mr. John Murphy, and Mr. Ceary. Each of these gentlemen maintained his post with admirable alacrity. Mr. John Collins did everything that would contribute to dispose of my publications. He is wealthy, patriotic, and generous. Mr. Timothy O'Shea is from Bantry Bay, famous and full of historical events; and the scene of my gay, airy, and early days, when shadows caused no obscuration in the horizon of youthful imagination; and Mr. O'Donnell, from the county of Limerick, who is both admired and venerated by the community at large, as an honest, religious man, and a good citizen; also as an excellent neighbor; did as much as came within the limits of his power to facilitate the sale of my books. All the gentlemen whom Mr. Looby mentioned, proved equal to his definition of them; and I challenge any other city in the Union, inhabited in part or in whole by my countrymen, to show more uncorruptible patriots than the city of Salem, better citizens, or more unflinching democrats, according to its Irish population. The mention of all my subscribers in Salem would be attended with a vast amount of labor. Notwithstanding, I will give the names of a few of my friends. Here they are: Mr. P. Quinn, Derby street. Mr. Quinn is incontrovertibly an honorable countryman of mine; and I emphatically aver that I leave no room for contradiction when I use the expression.

Mrs. Shaw, Union street. This lady is from the county Cork, and a lady of great intelligence. She reflects honor on the land of her nativity, and is an ornament to her sex. Mr. David Harding, Union and Derby streets. This is a gentleman that no encomium could overreach. He is universally known by his varied qualifications, and particularly for his ineffable desire to restore the Emerald Isle to her former elevation. Mr. Timothy O'Connell keeps a large establishment of boots and shoes in Essex street, Salem city; he is from the city of Cork, and who would dispute his patriotism and cleverness must be insane, or the aberration of his mind, by inspection, must appear evidently. Mr. O'Connell is exceedingly popular, and is doing great business. He is considered one of the best and most fashionable, professionally speaking, in Salem. Mr. Timothy O'Donovan is also from the county Cork; and by his manner and habits, which render my friend exceedingly popular, I knew him to be an offspring of Milesian dignity, and indisputably descended from the illustrious house of O'Donovan. Mr. Jeremiah Deasy is another gentleman from the universal county of Cork; better known by the title of Captain Deasy, as he is one of the most aspiring military characters in Massachusetts, and has instructed all the young men in that city in military evolutions. Mr. Deasy distinguished himself in my behalf in that city, and introduced me to his friends, who are numerous and worthy in Salem. Mr. O'Heagarty, from the city of Cork, has a large currying establishment in Salem. He is a young gentleman of intelligence and mental culture. He is also distinguished for his manliness, generosity, and patriotism; more about these gentlemen poetically. Mr. Jeremiah McCarthy, Worth street. Mr. McCarthy, gardener, Danver Port, and another gentleman of the name of McCarthy, living in Danver, a few miles from the city of Salem. I have omitted saying much concerning these gentlemen, as the illustrious name of McCarthy is emblazoned on the pages of history since time immemorial; still, I am urged by a natural impulse to say something at present demonstrating the original dignity, grandeur, and unlimited power of the McCarthy family in days gone by; and as my mother, grandmother, and great grandmother, &c., were of that illustrious race; then, of course, there is a something of a natural tendency or feeling which makes one cling with an indescribable tenacity to that illustrious name. The McCarthy families were kings, princes, and rulers of South Munster, since time immemorial, and governed those parts with unlimited power until the usurpation and tyranny of ungodly strangers cancelled with indescribable animosity and savage barbarity that power, and banished them from their territorial estates without compunction for the enormity of that cancellation. The O'Brien's swayed North Munster, and often contested supremacy with the McCarthys. Yet, the irresistible followers of McCarthy sustained his supremacy until Elizabeth ascended the British throne. The powerful O's of South Munster, among them O'Donovan, who held vast possessions had to acknowledge his superiority by a tacit submission to his injunctions. The illustrious family of McCarthy, in my opinion, degenerated more than other distinguished families of Milesian origin, though there are some stars here and there of the first magnitude, emitting rays of pure splendor that bespeak the original generosity and greatness of their progenitors, among whom are these gentlemen I have spaken of in Salem, Massachusetts, and in its surrounding vicinity. The cause of this degeneracy in the posterity of that illustrious family is easily demonstrated, as the McCarthy's governed, unrestrained, and had vast possessions. Queen Elizabeth, the unrelenting tigress, with immoral vengeance, cancelled every vestige of their prerogative in Munster; and it made no matter whether a McCarthy had been living in a castle or in the meanest cabin. The ferocious tigress pursued them with undying vengeance until she had driven them into the wilderness to spend the remainder of their days in anguish and misery. I intend, God willing, to say more about this illustrious family in my forthcoming poetic history. Mr. Maurice Power. This aged and venerated gentleman is from the county of Waterford, and is well known as an honest man and a religious liver. Mr. Power is respected for his age, and admired for his candor. This little epitaph poem should be written on his tomb:

Here lies the body of Maurice Power,
Whose faults no mortal could discover,
As being to prayer given.

He loved his neighbor as himself,
And never bent to pride or pelf,
For which he is in Heaven.

There is a gentleman in Salem, an extensive currier of the name of Mr. Cusick, who showed me unspeakable friendship during my stay in Salem. Mr. Cusick was born in the parish of Relehan, county Galway, in the memorable year of 1829, when Catholic emancipation was sanctioned, and at an early age freed himself from the meshes of a Godless and tyrannical government, and sought his freedom in the Elysian fields and enchanting groves of America. Mr. Cusick got married to a Miss Wheatly from the county Meath, and is now the father of a large and promising family, he is also exceedingly popular and very much distinguished for his social habits, urbanity and intelligence; he is familiar with friends and generous to strangers—more about Mr. Cusick, poetically.

There is another undisputed gentleman in Salem, a professional stone-cutter from the city of no surrender, (Limerick,) who is a confirmed gentleman, an honor to his native country and countrymen, and an acquisition to Yankee enterprise. There is a merchant tailor in Salem, from the city of Limerick, a full-fledged finished gentleman, who inherits all the kindness and blessings and generosity, which are the characteristics of that noble class, whatever country or clime they inhabit; I forget this gentleman's name, to my regret; I know, however, he is an Irishman of no ordinary calibre. Mr. Thomas O'Reily is superintendent of an extensive bleaching establishment in Danvers, at present, and was born in the county of Armagh, and Mrs. O'Reily is from Cady, and if a more sound and substantial patriot left the Emerald Isle, than Mr. O'Reily, I am mistaken. His hospitality is well established and accredited, and none who know him, can have the boldness to deny my affirmation. Mrs. O'Reily is also fully saturated with feelings of the noblest quality—feelings natural to the genuine and philanthropic Irish. Mr. Rabit, another gentleman from the universal county Cork, is in this vicinity, and is an honor to his country, as being an incorruptible patriot and a gentleman of moral habits and intelligence. Mr. O'Conner from Bantry, a small town near the south-west extremity of the county Cork, and now living in Essex street, Salem; the name and Milesian dignity which are inseparably connected with the name, unquestionably confirm the elevated reputation of this gentleman, and his lady, whose maiden name was Miss Denis, is an honor to her sex, to her husband, and to her country—more about Mr. and Mrs. O'Connor poetically. Mr. Mynahan from the same county, and now living in Cork Avenue, Salem; I had not the pleasure of seeing this gentleman, but in Mrs. Mynahan, I found a generous and noble substitute. Mrs. Mynahan is from the county Kerry, the learned and poetic home of many ladies and gentlemen I met with in my travels. In the same lane, is another lady from the same place, of the name of Miss Pundy, and also another young lady from Cork; they are young, beautiful and accomplished, generous, affectionate and patriotic, I will describe them poetically. There is a famous young gentleman living near South Fields, I think of the name of Mr. Kelly, a widow's son, who will ascend to some elevation of distinction ere long; although young, he promises fairly to fulfil such prophetic inspiration. Not to mention the name of Mr. Lonergan, who keeps an excellent stall in Danvers, would cause a stain on my memory, or at least, would be an unpardonable omission; he is from Tipperary, and a noble scion of that inimitable county. The ladies of Salem are matchless in any part of America, I think, Boston excepted, they are famed for beauty, virtue, humility and religious habits. Misses Julia and Margaret O'Donovan, from Mallow in the county of Cork, now in Danver Salem, Mass., Miss Denis from Bantry Bay in the county Cork, also in Danver; Misses Ann Smith and Stanly, in Chestnut street, Salem; Miss Mullen, at Mr. Stone's, Salem, Mass.; individually and collectively, this galaxy of incomparable beauty are entitled to the most exalted panegyric, not altogether for the external splendor of their incomparable display, but for their virtue, industry and religious habits, which no temptation can contaminate, nor no familiarity can stain.

I met with another of my countrywomen in Salem, No. 17 Chestnut street, and she showed more Irish hospitality—that genuine hospitality which is natural to the Irish—than I have talent to demonstrate. Mrs. Maguire is her name—long may she wear it. If I forget any of my friends in Salem I ought not to forget her. I faithfully promise them a strong and poetic notice in my forthcoming Epic History. Messrs. Batters & Shaly, Derby street. These are two brave and noble gentlemen, and I have the privilege, pleasure, honor and assurance that they are county and countrymen of mine. They are an ornament to society, good neighbors and irreproachable citizens. There is no fear that they will tarnish the land of their nativity; more about them hereafter. During my stay in Salem, Mass., I boarded at the house of Mr. John Hurly, in Derby street, and this is my honest impression, that an honester boarding house is not in the State of Massachusetts, nor a more secure harbor from violence or imposition. Before I left Salem for Lawrence City I went by invitation to see Mr. Looby, and received from him a letter of introduction to John O'Hea Cantillan, Esquire, an honorable Irish gentleman, and a valued and distinguished citizen of Lawrence, Mass. Mr. Looby wanted to hear my opinion of the Salemites, and when I expressed very favorably my opinion of the Irish population of Salem, he gracefully smiled and said, "Mr. O'Donovan, you will think very little of us here when you go to Lawrence, for there you will indisputably meet the cleverest set of Irishmen in any part of the Union." Animated by such assurance from a man of such weight and consequence as Thomas Looby, Esquire, induced me to enter the cars almost instantly, and in an hour's time I found myself landed among my incomparable countrymen in the City of Lawrence. As my decision is always momentary I pushed forward to the city with unusual rapidity, still enquiring for Mr. John O'Hea Cantillan's residence. There was no fear of much perambulation, as good men are as manifest in cities, and as well known and distinguished from other citizens as the planet Jupiter is distinguished on a frosty night by the naked eye from stars of inferior magnitude. Mr.

O'Hea Cantillan was at the time absent from his office, which caused me to follow him to his residence, which is located in the extremity of the city. I entered unquestionably with confidence in Mr. Cantillan's cleverness, as Mr. Looby's testimony was sufficient to explode any other impression. Still, having such a great opinion of my own infallibility as a physiognomist, made me anxious to have a glance at the gentleman myself, by way of an ocular demonstration. I pulled; and the bell announced my approximation, which was attended to with assiduity, and instantly quite a young lady, with that calm gentleness, the result of good training peculiar to her sex, demanded my intention, and after informing her of my desire to see Mr. Cantillan, with much courtesy she introduced me into the sitting room, and in less time than I expected, Mr. Cantillan made his appearance, and the manifestation of his countenance, his noble bearing, and the friendship and familiarity of his conversation, made me judge instantly that no pharisaical hypocrisy was blended with his good nature, and that the most trying adversity could not crumble or subdue the honest independence of his mind, or the most elevated situation could not reduce the powers of his mind to the degeneracy of despised aristocracy. After the interchange of some terms of civility I presented Mr. Cantillan with Mr. Looby's introductory letter, and after he read it he desired me to call at his office at such an hour, and that his consideration at that time would be better adjusted, and courteously begged me to excuse him for withdrawing so soon, as the Mayor and Council had been arranging some business or city regulations, and that he wanted to be there at the time. I requested Mr. Cantillan to direct me to some respectable boarding house where I could take shelter during my stay in the city. Although in his hurry he acquiesced with my request, but where he directed me to take my rest proved an abortion, as the lady who kept the boarding house informed me that her boarders were so thick in number that her house would indisputably swarm, but, said she, as Mr. Cantillan directed you here, I must find you some safe and commodious boarding house, if it be in the city. I followed the footsteps of this amiable countrywoman of mine, and the next house we came to labored under the same inconveniency; her house was overflowing, but she said she knew of a boarding house which unquestionably would afford me every facility, but after arriving there, also, I drew a blank, but that lady also swelled the train, and found an excellent house. This numerical army that cheerfully went in quest of a boarding house for myself, showed the respect they entertained for Mr. Cantillan; the proprietor of the boarding house was a widow named Mrs. O'Reilly, from the County Cavan, and a very religious and kind old lady. I went to his office at the time appointed, and found Mr. Cantillan surrounded by many who came to transact some business, and as soon as he saw me he invited me to draw near, and after I did so he expressed himself as thus: "Mr. O'Donovan, be here with me at nine o'clock in the morning and we will strenuously commence operations." I submissively acquiesced and calmly withdrew to my boarding house, and promptly returned the following day and at the time appointed. All right; Mr. Cantillan had his beautiful vehicle at the door, and when he and I got into it he drove with more than ordinary rapidity through a great part of the city where my countrymen were located, informing them of the cause of my coming to Lawrence City, and also solicited their patronage and encouragement to sustain my poetical works. Of course I was mute and had nothing to say on the subject. It was pretty late in the evening when he returned to his office, where many awaited his return, and ere he commenced business he again expressed himself and said: "Now, my dear friend,

I will give you into the hands of another gentleman of the name of Mr. Patrick Murphy, whom you will find to be a sincere friend on this occasion." Ah! my friends this was a prophetical inspiration, for Mr. Murphy was the gentleman who knew how to act. Mr. Patrick Murphy was born in the Parish of Dromtariff, or in the township known by that name, near Kanturk, in the western extremity of the County Cork, the home of brave men and strong and beautiful women. Mr. Murphy was at that time a watchman in the City of Lawrence, and a better man could not be appointed for the same situation, as he was loved, liked and respected and I do not exaggerate when I say that Mr. Murphy is a fine looking gentleman, with a broad chest and expansive shoulders, whose strength is unknown to others, unless demonstrated by supposition, and also in a manner unknown to himself. Mr. Murphy called at my boarding house and asked me how many copies of my publication I had with me. I told him the exact number, and he regretted I had not as many more, and said that he would not be long in disposing of that complement. This was a true prediction, as you soon will hear. Mr. Murphy took an armful of my books, and I filled to suffocation a large carpet bag of the same, and the first gentleman that he met with he reached him one of the books and said, "Take this—so much;" met with another and said, "Take this—so much;" and my friend continued the game the same as chess playing, until the number we both took out together had been sold. I got into the cars and immediately returned to Boston for a fresh supply, which were successively disposed of in the same manner by my friend, Mr. Patrick Murphy. This magical disappearance created an internal surprise in myself, and in others also; but Providence and Patrick were at the helm, and indisputably secured the speedy sale of my publications. When any of his friends said, "I have no money with me,"

Patrick said, with seeming alacrity, "I will pay it, and you pay me when convenient to yourself." Mr. Murphy silenced every objection by his extraordinary liberality, and his ineffable desire to make sale of the works, and at the sound of "I have no money," he pulled out his purse and instantly paid me the amount. Now, my dear reader, the incomparable cleverness, liberality and inexpressible patriotism of the Irish population of Lawrence City, Mass., should be transmitted to posterity, and indelibly written in letters of gold, so as to inspire succeeding generations to follow their footsteps and imitate their virtues and cleverness. I would let generations to come know, if this history would survive impediments, the individual names of my contributors in Lawrence City, were it not that Mr. Murphy and myself had taken the names of many with a soft lead pencil, which by some unaccountable friction suffered cancellation, and this impediment prohibited me from doing a duty which I ought to have done; and as I could not give their names in full, I thought it more prudent not to mention the names of any. But by this acknowledgment you can judge of my countrymen in Lawrence, as out of the whole three only refused to encourage the production of my humble pen.

By the advice of my friends in the city, I called on the reverend Catholic clergymen, who powerfully sustained me, and who are truly pious and benevolent, and not only venerated, but almost idolized by their parishioners. May God grant them length of days to watch diligently the spiritual welfare of their flocks, the Rev. Mr. O'Donnell kept two or three of my books, and paid a very liberal price for them, and the Rev. Mr. Taiffe kept one, and paid me five dollars in good currency for the same, and courteously and affectionately said, if he were not building a very large Cathedral at the time, he would certainly have given more. This is astounding liberality. I have to say a few words concerning a county and a countryman of mine, a modern Hercules of the name of James Cullinane, from Millstreet, county Cork, he lives a small distance from the city, in a small village composed of one story houses, erected by the Irish to avoid the payments of heavy rents. This gentleman exerted himself beyond description, to dispose of my production in this village, and succeeded too. These small buildings are handsome strong, and comfortable, and the village population have accumulated wealth chiefly by honest labor and constant employment in the magnificent mills erected close by the village. A few words more and I will have done with Lawrence, which is the arctic circle of my revolutions. John O'Hea Cantillan, Esquire, is from Upper Glanmire, county Cork, which is indisputably as beautiful and as enchanting as Ogygia, or the garden of Eden, Ogygia, that spot of enchantment where Calypso and her nymphs made use of all the power, of fascination to detain Telemachus from pursuing the discovery of his lost lamented father, Ulysses. Mr. Cantillan flourished in a high degree of respectability in his own native land, but, like all other responsible and good men, he had to bear somewhat his share of the stripes, as the spoiler came with unjust digested laws, and defiled in great measure his Paradise Lost, which caused him to seek for shelter in the glorious land of his adoption. Mr. Cantillan is united in marriage to a wealthy lady of the name of Miss Roberts, who lived conveniently to his own home, whose parents were highly respected, and associated themselves with the best families in that part of the country, and were admired and venerated for their liberal feelings and sentiments towards those who differed in religious opinions with them. Mrs. Cantillan has been converted, and is a devoted member of the Catholic Church, and is now with affectionate assiduity instructing her own children in the ways of religion and truth. There is a lady now living in

Lawrence, to whom I must make an allusion despite of my contracted limits, I mean Mrs. O'Callaghan. I can assure you dear reader, that there are more hopes entertained at present of Queen Victoria's emigration to America, than there was of Mrs. O'Callaghan at the time of her birth. This alteration in human affairs had been lamentably effected by bad laws and a tyrannical government.

Although I made an inflexible resolution not to speak individually of my countrymen in Lawrence City, Massachusetts, as some of the notes suffered cancellation by friction, and others disappeared in the shipwreck I sustained while going from Philadelphia to Baltimore, which will evidently appear in the course of this history, if it can be properly so called ; yet a second prudential consideration impels me to break through my inflexibility, and from the shallow resources in my power to mention the names of the persons that survived annihilation. Every man in Lawrence, with few exceptions, is entitled to the highest and most extraordinary praise and respect, not only, for all the kindness they showed me, but for the unparalleled liberality they have displayed towards the promotion of every laudable institution, religious and political. In a word, Lawrence shines as a star of the first magnitude among the citizens of our glorious Commonwealth, the land of our adoption. Their names are as follows : Mr. D. Canniffe, five years from home ; he is a native of county Cork, and married in this country. Mr. Daniel O'Hanlon from the parish of Drumtariffe, county Cork, is unmarried, and is three years from home. Mr. Thomas McMahon, from Bruf, county Limerick, married in this country. Mr. Patrick O'Conner, parish of Abbyfail, county Limerick, one year in America. Mr. William Penrose, parish of Aughlis, county Cork, married in Lawrence. Mr. John M. Baker, Mr. John E. Barrat, county Cork, parish of Balihea, landed in America the 18th of May, 1845, now married about five years. Mr. Dennis Spillane, from the City of Limerick, and has been three years married. Mr. Edward Roche, from Glenmire, county Cork, four years from home, married in Ireland. Mr. Hector P. Linn, native of the parish of Rutherglen, Lanarkshire, Scotland; Mr. Edward O'Neill, from the county Carlow, fourteen years in America, married in Boston; Mr. Richard Long, from the parish of Desert, county Cork, four years from home; Mr. Daniel O'Sullivan, Feresa, county Kerry, eight years in America, still unmarried; Mr. Daniel Griffin, Kingeagh, county Cork, three years in his adopted land, unmarried; Mr. Owen Reily, parish of Anno, county Cavan, ten years from his native home, married in freedom's home; Mr. Naughton, a perfect gentleman; Mr. Richard Long, another of Erin's noblemen; Mr. John O'Brien, a native of Lowell, Massachusetts, still unmarried; Mr. Terrence Murphy, a gentleman, and an indisputable Celt; Mr. Roger Ashe, Listohel, county Kerry, eight years from his dear Erin; Mr. Michael, Murphy, parish of St. James, county Cork, fourteen years from home, married in America; Mr. John O'Sullivan, from the parish of Killrittain, county Cork, thirty years from home, married in America; Mr. George McNamarra, county Cork, about eighteen years from home, married; Mr. Patrick Murphy, from the parish of Dromtarriffe, county Cork, married in the Emerald Isle, and three of his children were born there, namely Patrick, John, and Mary. I have, spoken already of this gentlemen, resident in America during eight years; Mr. John Stow, county Tipperary, eight years residence in freedom's home; Mr. John O'Sullivan, parish of Dromtarriffe, county Cork, four years a freeman, married in this country; Mr. Patrick O'Rourke, Castletown Roache and Barony of Fermoy, diocese of Glanmire, and two years in the State of Massachusetts; Mr. Thomas Mullin, Erin's favorite son; Mr. John J. Piquett, parish of Liscarroll, county Cork, left Ireland in 1824, and has been since a resident of Lawrence; Mr. Patrick Collins, from the parish of Kilbam, county Donegal, left home in 1843; Mr. Bartholomew Carick, parish of St. John, Sligo, eleven years in this country; Mr. James Hays, parish of Innishannon, county Cork, left home in 1842; Mr. John O'Conner, from the City of Glasgow, Scotland; Mr. Patrick O'Conner, parish of Banagher, county Derry; Mr. Willian O'Sullivan, born and educated in Bandon, and married in the City of Lawrence, Massachusetts, one of the great railroad contractors in America; Mr. John O'Sullivan, from the parish of Millstreet, county Cork, another distinguished gentleman of an illustrious origin; Mr. Daniel O'Sullivan, this gentleman teaches in the male department in the Catholic school in Lawrence, he was born in Temple Roe, county Kerry, May 7th, 1822, and married in Boston, June, 1844; Mr. Joseph Andrews, born in the City of Dublin, September, 1830; Mr. John McDonough, parish of Killow, county Longford, eleven years in America, and nine in the Elysian of matrimony. This list of names is imperfect, owing to what I have heretofore stated, and to other causes which will be hereafter elucidated, but all I have to acknowledge, candidly taking everything into consideration, is, that the Irish population of Lawrence can not be excelled in fortitude, faith, and fidelity.

The men of Lawrence bear a noble name
And space can't limit their unbounded fame,
Well now, my friends, to make the matter square,
Go where you will and speak of Lawrence there,
'Tis then you'll hear of Lawrence with applause,
Give brilliant tribute to a noble cause.

O'DONOVAN.

Before I took my departure from Lawrence I received a note of introduction from John O'Hea Cantillan, Esq., to George Moloy, Esq., a distinguished Irish gentleman, and citizen of Lowell, whose fame is widely circulated, and when I came out of the cars in that city I proceeded immediately to his residence, and soon discovered that Mr. Moloy was absent, but his absence did not render my reception uncourteous or inhospitable, as he left an excellent substitute at home in the person of his amiable lady, who informed me that Mr. Moloy was at his store, and as dinner hour was at hand that he would indisputably, as was his customary habit, make his appearance in a few minutes, and courteously invited me to take a seat, which advice without ceremony I accepted; only a few minutes elapsed when Mr. Moloy made his appearance, and no sooner had he seen the stranger than he extended his hand to me, and with that friendship, hereditary in Irishmen and in the Irish character, which they emphatically display at the reception of strangers, he invited me to dinner. No allegation could avert his pressing and cordial invitation. I then unquestionably acquiesced, and before we sat down to a sumptuous dinner, which was sufficient to please a voluptuous epicurean, or a fastidious potentate, for it had been more deserving the name I give it than a casual dinner, I reached Mr. Moloy Mr. Cantillan's introduction, and if any thing could add to his former friendship it would appear manifestly then, as the cheerfulness of acceptance plainly demonstrated the veneration and respect he entertained for Mr. Cantillian's introductory note. Mr. Moloy read with avidity the note and promised he would indefatigably exert himself to promote the sale of my publications. After dinner I went in company with my new made friend to his store, where he immediately prepared a list of such as he thought would appreciate my poetic history of Ireland, and he also gave me some necessary instructions he considered conducive to my interest; I applied unerringly to his instructions, and while in conversation with Mr. Moloy a gentleman came into the store whose appearance attracted my notice, as much as it commanded distinction and dignity, his words though few communicated intelligence, for they were properly arranged and accurately adjusted. After the courteous interchange of words Mr. Moloy politely introduced me to the gentleman and explained to him the cause of my visitation and accompanying the revelation he handed the gentleman my Epic History of Ireland, and after reading a few verses of it which perhaps, escaped original blunders, the gentleman said that he would give a favourable notice in his morning newspaper of my invaluable history. Of this incomparable sheet which was daily printed he was editor and proprietor himself, which vindicated the power and infallibility of democratic principles; such a favourable notice I considered would ensure success, but the blowing of the fifth trumpet which hurled Luther from his heavenly meridian to the bottomless pit could not arouse, in my opinion, a poetic propensity in the population of Lowell. The following favourable notice appeared the next morning in the Lowell Advertiser, No. 43 Central street:

"History of Ireland in Epic Verse, by Jeremiah O'Donovan, Pittsburg, 1854. This is a book of 300 pages and is divided into two numbers; the first number contains an account of the woes, afflictions and sufferings of the Irish people, from the commencement of the reign of Roderick O'Connor down to the battle of the Boyne; the second number treats upon the same subject from the termination of the battle of the Boyne to the present time: We have not had an opportunity to examine the work as thoroughly as we could wish; but from the hasty glance which we have given it we are satisfied that the author is not only a poet of a high order, but that he thoroughly understands the subject on which he writes. The author, Mr. O'Donovan, is now in the city and has the work for sale; we would advise those who take an interest in the study of Irish history to purchase a copy.

"James J. Maguire, Publisher."

Still to amend this great defection, I found in Lowell some honourable exceptions, which I will mention hereafter. During our conversation I seemed at a loss to identify the gentleman's place of nativity. In his manner and language he was entirely Americanized; notwithstanding this peculiarity his open and free expressions, facetiousness, wit, urbanity and indisputable friendship would demonstrate him to be an Irishman of no vulgar calibre. After the gentleman withdrew I inquired of Mr. Moloy his name and country, in order to dissipate the mist or doubt that hovered over my imagination concerning the departed gentleman. Mr. Moloy answered my interrogatories and said his name was Mr. Maguire and a Bostonian by birth, but unquestionably of Irish parents; Mr. Moloy's information corroborated my anticipations at once. I got up early the following morning to read the morning news, and the first thing that struck my eye was Mr. Maguire's favourable notice and high approbation of my Metrical History of Ireland: though sententious it had been lucidly, logically and liberally written, and its coming from the fountain of a literary reservoir, I considered would have a tendency to cancel the one half of its original blunders or leprosy though of a different hue, and indisputably secure an encouragement for the sale of it among my countrymen in Lowell City, Mass. I went, as was habitually my custom, to pay the first visit to the Rev. Mr. O'Brien, whose name and fame encouraged me to do so, and soon espied an amiable priest of gigantic size, whose well adjusted proportions harmonized handsomely, and conclusively showed him to be an Irish gentleman. I made manifest to his reverence the cause of my coming to Lowell, the city of spindles, but poverty is the revolving satellite of a priest, and poverty one of the characteristics of the church of God; the reverend gentleman having also a large and beautiful church unfinished and wanting funds to complete it could have nothing to spare and would rest contented if he could command funds enough to finish such a stupenduous edifice; this disappointment checked my impetuosity a little, and it seemed very strange to me as it differed widely from the most generous encouragement I received at the hands of the Catholic clergymen of Lawrence the day before; I went to another reverend gentleman who immediately bought one of my books, and I am sorry to say the reverend gentleman's name was destroyed or disappeared in the ruins of Carthage, which will hereafter be made manifest. After relinquishing the idea of making any further application to the Catholic clergymen of Lowell, and being also informed that some of them were absent from the city, I turned my attention to a few of the primary planets that were in the list which Mr. George Moloy had given me on the previous evening; but, from the truths adduced from former demonstrations and after a momentary pause, I came to the conclusion that a good bucket full of hydrant water would be more acceptable to many of the inhabitants of that city, than a puncheon full drawn from the soul inspiring fountain of Parnassus; this sentence is to be read with some honourable allowance. I met with a gentleman of the name of Mr. M'Loughlin in Lowell, whose ability as a lawyer elevated his profession, or the avocation which distinguishes him from other citizens, and placed him among stars of the first magnitude in the line of jurisprudence, this added to his social intercourse and other admirable qualities, placed his future happiness within the limits of his reach, and to prove his abilities solid and unerring, although an Ulster gentleman himself, he studied in Munster; Munster is not only a college for all Ireland, but for all the world. I had a letter of introduction, as I mentioned before, from a young gentleman of the name of Dowling with whom I met, I think, in the American House in Boston to a young gentleman in Lowell who had been a bookseller himself, and who received me with no hypocritical pretensions. He did everything in his power to animate his friends in that city to encourage my adventures, although the success had been partial, contrary to his wishes. Among his friends in that city there dwells a Hibernian of herculean dimensions, of the illustrious house of Burke, who received me with marked veneration befitting my age, if not my talent; this gentleman suffered from a destructive conflagration which happened in the city previous to my arrival, notwithstanding, he has a grocery of considerable magnitude, and is very popular among the citizens of Lowell. Mr. Duffy the brother-in-law of Mr. Moloy, is a distinguished flower that grew in Erin's verdant soil, but now a citizen of Lowell, who exerted himself to inspire his countrymen to encourage any production, be it ever so humble that would shed lustre on the land of his nativity. I met with others deserving of applause

During my stay in Lowell, through the recommendation of Mr. Moloy, I stopped at the widow Donoughue's boarding house, and a better selection could not be made in my favor; for if such a house as she keeps would be kept in every village, and a few of the kind kept in every town, the travelling community would be safely and comfortably entertained, fidelity would triumphantly reign, and fear and suspicion would unquestionably evaporate. During my short stay at Mrs. Donoughue's I was much pleased and edified by the devotional exercise, and penitential appearance of an Irish gentleman, who boarded there at the time, of the name of Mr. Horn; he was then selling patent medicine of his own composition, a medicine he compounded himself in conjunction with his brother; the composition was very much prized by all the citizens of Boston, and it had been universally considered of much importance, to stop the career of diseases of malignant tendencies, such as the

Cholera, Cramp, Croup, Convulsions, Hysterics, and Rheumatic affections. We slept in the same room, and his devotions were sufficient to induce infidelity to renounce its errors, and embrace with avidity the Christian religion, in order to find everlasting rest within its celestial sanctuary. The gentleman kindly made me a present of a bottle of his invaluable medicine for the preservation of my health, which I gave in the hour of extremity to others, and to my knowledge it had the desired effect, and the result was fortunate. After taking my departure from Lowell, and bidding adieu to my friends, I mounted my Pegasus, and in a very short time I found myself in No. 40 Church street, under the friendly roof of Mr. O'Neil's hospitable residence. After remaining a few days among my freinds in Boston, I entered the hollow cavity of mount Etna late in the evening, and took, as I conjectured, a southwest direction, although having no guide but an occasional glimpse of the stars to ascertain with accuracy our true direction, and in a few hours we safely arrived at Stonington, ninety miles distant from Boston, where the majestic telegraph No. 2, awaited our arrival, and had been in full blast puffing occasionally, which showed her readiness to take us to New York, the city of our destination. This was about the middle of December, and in that latitude the weather had been exceedingly severe, the snow fell fast and heavy, and to use the common phrase of a sailor, we sailed in the wind's eye; still the steamer kept her course with admirable firmness, and pushed forward with unspeakable majesty in spite of all impediments and opposition, and this inspired all aboard with confidence and security. After some time the snow ceased, the stars became more manifest and transparent, and the blue vault of heaven in beauty and transparency, baffled description; the fixed stars, and a few of the planets that were visible, did shine with amazing splendor, even stars of the sixth magnitude displayed splendor and pleasing serenity sufficient to attract the attention of the most incurious eye. At that time, and in that position, I sincerely wished to have on board, or in company, some atheist to whom I could give a rough illustration of the distance, motion and individual magnitude of such of the planets and fixed stars as were then visible to the naked eye in the heavens, and by pointing to him the unerring revolution of the greater and lesser bear around the polar star, which appeared visible at the time. I think would or ought to convince him, that such great luminaries did not happen by chance, but by the eneffable power of omnipotence and divine authority. They sprang into existence when an omnipotent God said, let there be light, and there was light; since then they continue their motions with unerring certainty, and without interruption, and so shall they continue until the dissolution of all things, as well as time. Such illustrations would in spite of predjudice, unfounded reason, vulgar conjectures, and false philosophy, make him a Christian, and cause him to believe that there is a Creator who created all things.

After some time I retired to bed, and very early the following morning I heard, on deck, the awful cry of Hell's Gate, which made me jump up to have a peep at the terrific gate, the impassable barrier of his satanic majesty's dominion. This place received the appellation of Hell's Gate, as it caused the destruction of many steamers and other vessels sailing towards that point. After passing this fearful place, we were soon abreast of Astoria; left Blackwell's Island on the right, and steamed with incredible speed, down the East river, among ships, steamers, crafts, and every description of sailing vessels, until we safely anchored at Pier No. 2, in the North river, early on the following morning. Being acquainted with the facility of conveyance in New York, I soon found myself, bulk and baggage, and other appendages, in No. 64 Montgomery street, where I once more found shelter, friendship and accommodation, in Mr. O'-Sullivan's hospitable home. My reception was indisputably very cordial and affectionate, and without the tincture or the infusion of hypocritical demonstrations, and after the mutual interchanging of courteous expressions, we sat down to a sumptuous dinner provided by Mrs. O'Sullivan for the occasion, and as every one who dined there together had an indisputable title and claim to distinction and Milesian dignity, we felt exceedingly happy on the occasion; conversed merrily until we retired to rest. After breakfast the following morning, I proceeded to No. 10 Pearl street, to see my inimitable friend, Cornelius Dever, Esquire, which could not be considered a venturesome proximity, as the goodness of his heart never allowed him to meditate harm, or encourage evil against any of the human race, and why should an individual whom he served fear approximation. I fortunately found him in his office at the time, and although in company with some other gentlemen belonging to the establishment, he immediately espied me, and extended his hand, which was as fair as the drifting snow and as soft as silk, full of delicate veins, containing and conveying the pure blood of an Irish gentleman to his heart, which I shook with much respect and affection; and after one revolution of his large, beautiful and expressive eye, over my features, he gracefully smiled, and anxiously inquired concerning my success since I took my departure from New York. I can give no illustration of my feelings at the time, as the weight of gratitude steeled me to the seat. When I found myself in the presence of my sincere friend and benefactor, and when I considered that I had nothing in my power to requite the kindness he showed me in Brooklyn, New York, and throughout all my travels, such deficiency caused some embarrassment of the mind, which precluded the power of utterance. I remained with my inimitable friend and countryman until some unavoidable business called him away, and that he postponed for some time, as you will presently anticipate. Precisely at the time of my departure, and while bidding him adieu, I asked him had he any friend in Baltimore, to whom, with his usual alacrity, he could introduce me; and after a momentary pause or consideration, he exclaimed, with ecstasy, "I have," and added, "and one of the cleverest men in all your travels."

Mr. Dever sat down and gave me an introductory note to Patrick McLaughlan, Esquire, a citizen of Baltimore, a lawyer of much eminence and professional ability, and an Irishman to the heart's core. Very much affected, I took the last farewell of my inimitable friend, though I expect, God willing, to see him again, and without delay, proceeded to Wall street, to see the noble and kind-hearted Cornelius O'Sullivan, Esquire, the hereditary Prince of Bare Haven, whom I found in the enjoyment of good health, and also in possession of all the necessaries that would render life happy and comfortable. After leaving Mr. O'Sullivan's office, I went to see Doctor O'Sullivan, a native of Killarney, and another scion of the illustrious house of O'Sullivan, and found him, as usual, calm, kind and contented. I then crossed the East river to Brooklyn, the locality of great men and handsome women, and paid a flying visit to my unflinching friend and countryman, Roderick Clancy, Esquire, and to many of my distinguished friends in that city. I then re-crossed the East river, and found myself, in a very short time, in No. 64 Montgomery street, making everything, and all things, ready to take my departure, on the following morning, for the incomparable City of Philadelphia. Accordingly, in the very hour I intended, I entered the cavity of the iron horse; I did so at Jersey City, and proceeded, with incredible velocity, towards the City of Brotherly Love; and after the lapse of a few hours, I found myself comfortably seated in Mr. Griffin's hospitable residence, where a thousand welcomes awaited my arrival.

The proximity of Christmas caused me to delay in the city until the holidays were over, and as a jubilee had been held in all the Catholic Churches in the city, at that time, I considered myself conscientiously bound to participate in its solemnities. Mrs. Griffin, matchless in her religious devotions, attended Church during the whole time, and such of her children as were capable, in point of maturity, attended also, with unmistakable devotion. Mr. Griffin had been, then, from home on some unavoidable business, but Mrs. Griffin performed his share of the devotional observances, for fear that neglect, or the want of a favorable opportunity would divert himself from his duty. I visited many of my friends in the city, and particularly Robert King, Esquire, of the firm of King & Baird's extensive printing establishment, No. 9 Sansom street, Philadelphia, whom I found in excellent health, which, indeed, gave me unspeakable pleasure. Some thousands of my books, in pamphlet form, had been insured in this establishment, and when I returned, after a long absence, I found them in excellent condition, and I must acknowledge the gratitude I feel for Mr. King, for his assiduity, indulgence and kindness. Such of my books as I got bound, I put into a large chest, and took my departure for Baltimore, and had also my books along, rather than trust them in the care of any forwarder; but alas, this was a mistaken imagination, as you will instantly anticipate. Late in the afternoon, and some distance from Baltimore, a gentleman entered the cars, of the name of Donaldson, and inquired of the passengers, had they any baggage they would wish removed to their boarding houses, or homes in Baltimore, and said he would, for some pecuniary consideration, accomplish the task with faith and fidelity. As I had a bulky baggage to remove, I immediately agreed with him to take my enormous chest to Mr. Nolan's boarding house, where I intended to stop during my stay in Baltimore. Although I rode in cars before this time, some thousands of miles, still, there was a deficiency in my knowledge of traveling, which I am going to mention for the special benefit of the traveling community.

A traveler, after he gets a check or a declaration of deposit from the baggage master, is unquestionably secured for any accident or calamity that would subsequently happen; the check of course, should be safely preserved, so as to have it ready for presentation on demand, or in the hour of extremity, and when coming to any station, provided, he has no facility for taking his baggage to his boarding house, or place of destination, he should not be particular about it, or trouble himself concerning its safety. He should leave it at the station house, in charge of the baggage master, until such time as all inconveniences would be removed, as the baggage master is bound to keep it safely in his custody until leisure and opportunity will enable the owner to call for it, and the company would be accountable for all the damage and deficiency pertaining to it.

When I emerged from the cavity of Pegasus, in Baltimore, and as it was late in the night, I proceeded immediately to Mr. Nolan's residence, and at my arrival there, there was no account of my chest, neither could I get boarding there, as he was inundated with boarders at the same time. But Divine Providence, (though unworthy of Divine interposition,) always came to my assistance in all my difficulties and danger, and although invisible to mortal eyes, is every where present. Being respectfully introduced to the notice of Mr. Nolan, by an introductory letter I presented him, and which I received from Mr. James Doyle, of Philadelphia, and having also, a verbal introduction from the same gentleman, to Mr. O'Byrne, a respectable citizen of Baltimore, and one of the hereditary Princes of the county Wicklow. It happened providentially, that a son of Mr. O'Byrne was sitting in Mr. Nolan's house, at the time I entered, who with much kindness and alacrity accompanied me to his father's residence, where unspeakable friendship and hospitality awaited my arrival. On the following morning I returned to Mr. Nolan's to ascertain something of my books, and on entering his residence, I saw to my surprise, chagrin and confusion, a desolating scene, more dismal than the ruins of Carthage. There I discovered my huge chest, in bulk and form like the hippopotamus, turned bottom upwards, with a belt not much inferior to the inward ring of saturn, around it, so as to keep it from falling asunder, as it bursted longitudinally, for the want of assiduous care, and the notes which I had taken of every city, during my travels, and kept in separate packages, lay intermixed in the chest, in one promiscuous heap together, and many of them entirely disappeared. My anger at this time was at its height, my fury unbounded, and I could hardly restrain my tongue from making use of insufferable language, but to find out Donaldson, and go to law with him, would be an interminable and unprofitable undertaking. I stood contemplating my situation, with despondency, for some time, and then looked back at the losses I had sustained in early life, and comparing both together, I cooled down at once, my anger evaporated, and my original gravity seemed to return to its original consequence and position. I commenced tying up the bleeding wounds of my chest, which I did with more caution than ever Esculapius tied the wounds of his patient, and completing my undertaking I went in quest of a boarding house, wherein I could cast anchor during my stay in Baltimore. I was directed to Mrs. McDevitt, who kept a boarding house at the corner of Pratt street and some other street that has slipped my memory. Mrs. McDevitt was a widow then, and the fidelity and applause of her house, found an uncontestable position and security in the universal approbation of the traveling community. I introduced myself to my countrywoman Mrs. McDevitt, whose personal appearance, though being without extra reflections, or gorgeous drapery, convinced me of being perfectly safe in her custody, during my stay in Baltimore; I communicated to her my design and my wants, and as I had no external illumination to attract her attention, or introduce me to her notice, she viewed me all over, and after a careful examination, she considered that there was a something in my druidical figure and form worthy of reception, and then said, that although she was encumbered with more boarders than she wanted, or perhaps could conveniently accommodate, that she would at all hazards, take me as an appendage to the rest of her boarders. I thanked her most kindly, and answered that my wants are easily satisfied, which Mrs. McDevitt afterwards acknowledged to be the case. I then returned for my books, and when that Pandora's box was placed in the entry, if it were only full of building stones, it would be a sufficient security for one month's boarding money, so all doubts and uncertainties, if any she entertained, were expelled from her mind. After my participation in a sumptuous dinner, I directed my steps immediately to Mr. P. McLaughlin's office to present to him the introductory letter I had in my possession, and on which, in a manner, depended my proficiency in Baltimore. Providentially, P. McLaughlin, Esq. was in his office at the time, which is near the Washington Monument, analyzing and contemplating on some of Blackstone's Commentaries, so as to enable him in the hour of extremity to bring his client's case to a favorable issue.

Mr. McLaughlin is a lawyer of considerable

merit, ability and knowledge, and his fidelity and assiduity to every knotty lawsuit he takes in hand, or pertaining to his profession, established his reputation on an immovable construction or solidity more durable than Queen Victoria's reign. Mr. McLaughlin, when I presented him with my introductory letter, opened it, and when he saw the signature of his esteemed friend Cornelius Dever, Esquire, the joy and alacrity with which he read it gave an additional brilliancy to his placid countenance; such was an indication of the respect he entertained for his invaluable friend and countryman, Mr. Dever. Great and good men, much like the primary planets that sustain the harmony of the universe, sustain and balance each other. Were it otherwise, inferior satellites could never support their existence or position, and would indisputably be an encumbrance to themselves and society. After some questions concerning Mr. Dever had ceased, Mr. McLaughlin asked me to show him one of my books with a courtesy peculiar to himself, which I did, and after glancing over a few pages he became a purchaser—nay, did more, as he gave me a list of some of his personal friends in Baltimore, with whom, as he said himself I could with confidence make an application, and yet added that he would with unbounded pleasure assist in making sale of some of my books in Baltimore. As his promise is considered impregnable, I felt intrinsic confidence respecting the resolution he had taken. I withdrew as soon as discretion impelled me, fully saturated with respect and gratitude for Mr. McLaughlin for the kind reception he gave me. As the evening shades had been drawing nigh and the brilliancy of the sun's rays getting into a state of declension, I returned to Mrs. McDevitt's boarding house and waited impatiently for the arrival of her boarders, as their appearances would be a convincing testimony of the house they boarded in, and if respectable would conclusively prove the house was respectable too. The first that made his appearance I viewed with unerring accuracy and a philosophic eye, and so continued my observation until the last of the train arrived, and I judged each of them, from his appearance, to be a mechanic of some description, and I afterwards discovered that my opinion had been well founded. I retired to bed at an early hour, and comfortably reposed in the arms of Morpheus until the bell-ringer gave the alarm to every boarder to hold himself in readiness for breakfast. None omitted the call and none grumbled, and without exception there was a general attendance, and individually and collectively did justice to the craving appetites of the assembly, whether it had been done to Mrs. McDevitt or not. When breakfast was over I got myself in readiness to visit the gentlemen to whom Mr. McLaughlin directed me, and paid the first visit to William McLaughlin, Esquire, a county man of my own, and a gentleman, too, universally venerated by all who had the pleasure of his acquaintance. Mr. McLaughlin is an honest, unflinching Irishman, who left his native country in 1832, and after various ineffectual rambles through Canada and other States, established his residence in Baltimore, and during his residence there he never violated or made the least infraction on the established laws of either ecclesiastic or constitutional authority. Mr. McLaughlin always complied with all the essential conditions of citizenship, and has amassed honestly and energetically a large and ample fortune in Baltimore; not by intrigues, or by any dishonorable stratagem, but by an honest application to business. Mr. McLaughlin keeps a large bottling establishment, together with other works in full blast, at the corner of Exeter street and Eastern avenue, where a combination of men, women and children get daily employment in various occupations in this establishment. Many of them are from his own neighborhood in the

Emerald Isle, and relatives at that. All are fed, educated and supported by means of his patronage. Mr. McLaughlin has opened a school at his own expense and responsibility, for the benefit of those who are in his employment, and also for the benefit of the poor who are living in the same locality, hires a teacher of laudable abilities, and also teaches himself in conjunction with him when time and opportunity will permit him to do so. Instructions are extended to the poor without charge or comment, or without reference to their religious or political considerations or tendencies, and to show his unutterable repugnance to the pride and arrogance of aristocracy engendered by wealth and superfluities, his own children receive their education in the same school.

Mr. McLaughlin is a gentleman in appearance, an Irishman in principle, and a Roman Catholic in practice. I would speak more generally and emphatically on the subject, but I intend, God willing, to write the history of my travels in epic verse, where I can do more justice to my friend and countryman than in this present historical sketch. After I left Mr. McLoughlin I directed my steps to the residence of the Rev. Mr. Dolan, adjoining the church of St. Patrick in that city, and where the Rev. gentleman officiates as a Catholic clergyman. The church is an edifice of a superior grade and capacity, and is located in the most healthy and beautiful part of the City of Baltimore. It is surrounded by Catholics of worth, wealth and religious propensities, and it would unutterably display my folly in the superlative degree if I attempted a description of this venerated priest, who commands the respect of all his parishioners, and secures the friendship and popularity of all who have the happiness of his acquaintance. Notwithstanding, as I always fed myself with the idea of being a profound and unerring physiognomist, I thought I would take a stealthy glance at the Reverend gentleman whose name conveyed applause and satisfaction throughout the Catholic city. Very fortunately I found the Rev. Doctor at home, and as soon as I declared my intention he received me with indescribable kindness, and an occular demonstration corroborated all the incontrovertible testimonies I previously received in his favor. His frame is of Herculean dimensions, his countenance beaming with goodness, and his heart full of religion. When seen, accidentally or otherwise, his appearance would command esteem and veneration among the most ferocious and uncivilized Indians in North America. The Reverend gentleman directed me to Dr. O'Donovan, and desired me to tell the Doctor that his reverence strenuously recommended me to his notice. This injunction had been given and placed on my shoulders for fear an abortion would be the result of my application. I withdrew from his reverence with my heart full of gratitude for his kindness and liberality, and on the following Sunday attended mass in St. Patrick's Church, and candidly speaking, the elegance of his language, and his convincing proof of Catholic authority would cause all the isms now in the world to evaporate, and induce all the multitudinous denominations in the world at present to conform to the uncontaminated doctrines of the Catholic Church. Happy are his hearers, and long may he live to watch over their spiritual welfare in the City of Baltimore. I bowed with acknowledged reverence and gratitude to the Reverend gentleman and proceeded according to direction to Dr. O'Donovan's office, where I found him at the time, and on the verge of taking his departure to visit a patient who earnestly solicited his assistance in the hour of extremity and danger. I calmly acknowledged my desire for seeing him, and unfolded to him my business in Baltimore, and indisputably delivered the injunction his reverence left in my safe keeping to my illustrious namesake. The Doctor received me with that unspeakable friendship, which is the natural inheritance of the genuine Irish. Though an American himself, this inheritance had been naturally transmitted, and descended from the father to the son, which on all occasions appears brilliant, consoling and satisfactory. My distinguished friend cheerfully became a contributor to my metrical works, and also recommended me to others, with full permission to make of use of his name whenever or wherever I considered my proficiency or advantage required it.

Dr. O'Donovan, professionally speaking, is consulted in all extreme and critical cases; and his world-wide reputation entitles him to ample patronage. The Doctor, I should judge, is on the verge of fifty years of age, and looks healthy and vigorous. The Doctor recommended me to Mr. James Laun, an extensive flour merchant in Baltimore, and President of the Benevolent Irish Society of that city. This gentleman, with whom I had a long interview, is, in my opinion, an American by birth and education; still, as zealous and as unalterable a Catholic as I met with in all my travels; and his charitable donations indiscriminately extend to all sufferers who make an application to him in the hour of extremity, of pecuniary embarrassment, or to the funds entrusted to him, or to his care. His Christian disposition for the extension and support of Catholicity is well known and established in Baltimore; and a better President than he could not be made by the Benevolent Irish Society in Baltimore. More will be heard concerning this gentleman in my forthcoming epic history of my travels. There is another distinguished gentleman in Baltimore, favorably known, Colonel Logue, or Professor Logue; the latter application he acquired by means of his scientific attainments; and the other by his military skill and commanding adventures. I was warmly recommended to this gentlemen; and as soon as I entered his paradise, he received me with indescribable urbanity, and immediately and generously became a contributor to my publications; and as an appendage to his liberality, he instantly sat down and gave a list of his friends, and emphatically expressed his determination, and enjoined on me that I should inform them that he sent me. Colonel Logue is a widower, and his accomplishments are beyond the reach of my hebetated description. The Colonel has a young and brilliant little family; and I think the eldest is about ten years of age, a very promising child. I paid particular attention to her, as she appeared to be a gem of unparalleled promise and brilliancy. This child, at the time, I think was learning music under the tuition of her father; and I observed a splendid piano in the room for her instruction and embellishment; and I was informed whenever he touched, with inimitable skill, that instrument, that Apollo rejoiced, Orpheus retired to the shade to mourn his incompetency in the musical art, and own the superiority of Mr. Logue's inimitable strains and musical science. When I left the Colenel I paid a visit to Mr. William Murry, who keeps an extensive boot and shoe store in No. 68 Market street. Mr. Murry was born in Dublin, and landed in Baltimore August 27th, 1833; got married in Baltimore in 1840, to a lady whose maiden name is Miss Margaret McDonald, and Providence has blessed them with a numerous and promising family, consisting of seven children whose wants are liberally supplied by the same Providence that created them. Mr. Murry is one of Erin's generous sons, and a useful acquisition to the land of his adoption, and also a credit to the land of his nativity. Mr. C. O'Donnell, No. 55 South Frederick street, three doors from Pratt street. This gentleman is from the renowned county of Tipperary, and stands inaccessible to the most malignant shafts of the most slanderous tongue; and his lady, in her own sphere, is equally as clever as himself. Mr. O'Donnell illumines the land of his nativity from one extremity to the other, by means of an unsullied reputation, unbending integrity, good disposition, and agreeable habits that unquestionably correspond with his manly and noble appearance. Mr. O'Donnell keeps a first class hotel in Baltimore, where the higher class rendezvous to refresh and recreate themselves. I met with a gentleman named Mr. Andrew Carroll, from Ballynacorra, county Tipperary, but cannot posititively determine where, still, I must candidly acknowledge him to be a genuine Irishman. Mr. James O'Reilly, Woodsfield, county Cavin, another undegenerated son of the Emerald Isle. Mr. John Chapman, from the immortal county of Longford, a constituted gentleman in all his habits.

Mrs. S. Lucas' brewery, corner of Hanover and Conway streets. In this brewery I met with a number of my countrymen, from different parts of that down-trodden Isle; and as their customary habits are immovable, I found them exceedingly generous, patriotic and clever. Their names, if I mistake not, are as follows: Mr. Edward Lanahin, born inthe parish of Morea, county of Roscommon, came to America when eight years of age, and ever since resided in Baltimore; and the rest of the gentlemen in that establishment are equally entitled to my praise and approbation; but owing to the destruction of the notes I had taken of them, their names are entirely omitted or misplaced, that are not inserted in the proper place. The Irish Social Benevolent Society, established in Baltimore: President, Mr. James Lawn; Vice President, Mr. Christopher Mullen; L. E. Gill, third Vice President, Felix Trainer; Recording Secretary, William Higginbothom; Corresponding Secretary, Charles McColgan; Treasurer, ———. Finance Committee: William Ward, P. Holden, John O'Conner, P. McHolbrook, Investigating Committee: Jeremiah Kenedy, John Mullen, Hugh O'Brien, John McShein, John Kerrand, Alexander Cummings. All concerned in this association, individually and collectively, are men of incorruptible habits, religious propensities, unblemished reputation, learning, and strict varacity; all are men of high standing in society, universally known and universally respected; and any laudable constitution framed or governed by such men must remain permanent and beneficial in all its operations and tendencies. Charles McColgan, Esq., is an Irish gentleman; and comparatively speaking, is one of the wealthiest men in the city of Baltimore. Mr. McColgan & Brothers, bear in front testimonials and mouuments of hereditary distinction and unmistakable integrity, and have been of incalculable benefit and encouragement to Catholic clergymen, to religion, and to their countrymen in the city of Baltimore. One of the brothers is one of God's anointed, and has been a priest in that city for a long time, to whom I thought it prudent to call during my rambles in Baltimore; and I candidly aver, and honestly declare, that there is no reasonable man who would sit in his company an hour and take cognizance of his sentiments, pious conversation, guileless appearance, and agreeable manner, but would emphatically pronounce him an angel in human form; and my description of this benevolent gentleman is as far from illuminating his attributes or himself, as the most remote star in the firmament of heaven is inaccessible to the brilliancy of the sun that illuminates the globe which we inhabit. May God grant him long life and a happy death. In my rambles through the city of Baltimore, I called in to see a young widow of surpassing beauty, whose proportions are handsomely arranged; her skin is fairer than the driven snow; her raven tresses are thick, silky, heavy, and clustering, and inimitably adjusted; her own teeth are beautifully arranged, which she shows to great advantage when she gracefully smiles. Her ways are artless, her conversation modest and unassuming, and her countenance serene, and seems entirely divested of those tempestuous surges and earthquake explosions which some women can command in the hour of extremity or irritation. In a word, the beauty of her features would command the respect and affection of any man conscious of the superiority of her attributes and appearance. The lady I mean keeps the first rate hotel in Crab street; her bar is well supplied, and her viands are full, to their utmost capacity, of everything that is rich, rare, and reviving. No doubt some smitten distinguished gentleman will soon place his affections upon her, and make her his wife, to crown his future happiness with matrimonial ecstacies. Mrs. Kennedy is of Irish birth; a consummate lady and a Catholic in practice. Beauty is a dangerous neighbor; dangerous to others, and dangerous to its possessors, unless fortified by immovable virtue, the unerring daughter of devotion. In my travels in another part of the States I met with an unmarried lady of consummate beauty and perfection. I viewed her in silence and with astonishment, as she brought my youthful freaks and folly fresh to my recollection, which has been the cause of the following burst of poetic inspiration. In consequence of a treacherous memory, I hurriedly wrote the lines on a slip of paper; and in doing so, she carefully watched my assiduity, and when I had done, she expressed a desire to know what I had written. I answered the lady, and said: "It has been written with a soft lead pencil; the reading of it would be attended with much difficulty." And, said I, again. "Madam, if you have no objection, I will read it for your consideration; for I can do so with more poetic ease than you can, as it is no more than the sudden explosion of momentary fancy." She answered and said: "Sir, I have no objection." The lines ran as thus:

Ah! fate, what mischief you can play,
And which no mortal hand can stay,
As, you directed me this day
To view Diana's fences.

When youth has left me in decay,
You sent an angel in way,
More bright than Sol's meridian ray,
To captivate my senses.

O'DONOVAN.

When she heard the lines read she gracefully smiled and accused me of flattery, which I strenuously denied and said, that, flattery was incompatible with both my nature and years, and added, that the comeliness of her symmetry and personal charms attracted my attention, and merited my approbation. It must be understood that this young lady purchased before this time a copy of every publication I had, and read a considerable portion of my lamentation in search of my angelic Jane, and it appeared evident that she sympathized in my misery and misfortune. After some further conversation I bowed submissively and with some reluctance departed. Mr. Daniel Connelly, parish of Ross Enerver, county Leitrim, landed in America in 1847, an unblemished Irish gentleman, and has continued so until this day. Mr. John Kelly, grocer, corner of Pratt and Bothel streets; I emphatically challenge history to record a more genuine Irish gentleman than Mr. Kelly is. His appearance recommends him and also attracts the attention of a philosophic eye, as well as the most incurious. His generosity is well known and established, and his disposition unruffled, and even his structure harmoniously corresponds with his disposition, and both accord admirably together. Mr. Kelly is married to a lady of unparalleled beauty and virtue, and I may add, of fine intelligence, and to sustain the fidelity of my testimony that such is the case, she is from universal Cork the nursery of theology and mathematics. As I am determined to take especial notice of Mr. Kelly and of his lady in the forthcoming metrical history of my travels, I will say no more at present concerning themselves or their happy union. Mr. Kelly recommended me to call on his father who resides in 288 Monument street, who was a long time in government employment in his native country, and also in the country of his adoption, as being a mechanic of high professional abilities, incorruptible habits, strict integrity and unsullied reputation; I did so, and found him to be a genuine Irishman, and that definition is sufficient to divest a man of all human imperfections, and render him, if possible, a perfect mortal. Mr. Anderson, who keeps the Black horse tavern, hails from the county Antrim and has been only three years in the country, and I must candidly acknowledge that Mr. Anderson is an honour to Antrim, and also to the whole of the Green Isle. There are two brothers of the name of Flinn below the city of Baltimore convenient to the railroad that leads from the city to Philadelphia, who are unquestionably of a superior grade, they are generous, warm-hearted, patriotic and intelligent, they possess a genuine and incorruptible principle, which in a manner, is the exclusive inheritance of the Irish; they came from either the King or Queen's county, and have been fifteen years in America. These brothers are deserving of the most unbounded applause, more about them by and by. Below the residence of these gentleman at the edge of the water, there is a cluster of houses which show something of a princely appearance at a distance, and which approximation diminishes. After making some inquiries about the inhabitants in some distant locality from the place, those of whom I made the inquiry thought to dissuade me from going there, as they considered the attempt to terminate in a perfect abortion, but being informed that a Mrs. Morgan was a Tipperary lady, although married to a Welsh gentleman, and that she kept the principal and most distinguished house in the place, I thought I would visit it rather from curiosity than any expectation of gain, although when the word Tipperary sounded in my ear it gave unspeakable encouragement to know the result of my adventure.

Mrs. Morgan had been regulating her domestic affairs when I arrived, and after an Irish salutation, and some abridged conversation, I found her to coincide with my opinion. She is a lusty, beautiful lady, friendly, affectionate, and national, and seems to have everything at her command that would make her comfortable; she is also blessed with a fine family of daughters. Mr. Crimmin, or Professor Crimmin, who teaches at the corner of Orchard street, is a mathematician of brilliant abilities, and deservedly bears the name of a professor, to distinguish him from other professional men of ordinary abilities. Mr. Crimmin is as useful as he is popular in Baltimore, and his name is mentioned, wherever he is known, in venerated terms; he is a native of the county of Kerry, a place where education is cultivated, admired, and cherished. Mr. Hughes, editor of the *True American*, close by the city post office.—This gentleman is one of the Green Isle's unflinching sons; he is as sincere an Irishman, as uncorrupted a patriot, and as sound a democrat, as can be found in the land of our "adoption"; he is a brilliant writer, a finished gentleman, and a man of fine attaiments; he is also obliging, affectionate, and friendly; more about him hereafter. Mrs. Cawley, First street.—This lady is an ornament to society, and any attempt, in a literary form, to immortalize the land of her nativity, is cherished and encouraged with indescribable tenacity and enthusiasm by her, and in my forthcoming poetic history of my travels I intend to say a great deal concerning her. Mrs. Russell, corner of Chew street, near the market.—I had been warmly recommended to this lady, and was very anxious to see her, for her noble sentiments and fine feelings had been reduced to a proverb in Baltimore; after an interview with her, I soon discovered her patriotism and sincerity; she is one of my reserved friends, and I think I can do her more justice poetically than otherwise. Mrs. McQuirk, corner of Orchard and Ross streets. —This is another of the favorite daughters of Erin, and her virtue, friendship, cleverness, and patriotism are of such magnitude and sterling worth, as to obliterate the maculations of thousands of her sex; more about her hereafter. Mr. Michael Duffy, from the townland of Mulloghave, county Monaghan, No. 108 Bank street, Baltimore, and only four years from his native land.—Mr. Duffy is one of those men that can accumulate money and friends wherever his lot may be cast, or energy appreciated; he is exceedingly popular in Baltimore, by means of his persevering industry, sober habits, and noble principle. There is an Irish gentleman at the extremity of Pratt street, which is leading out to the country, I think of the name of Cotter or Manning, and a more popular man there is not living in the city; speak of his name wherever you will, or wherever he is known, and you will know by the applause and approbation of the people, how he is venerated, admired, and respected; he keeps the first rate inn, which is considered a house of refuge and security for the traveller and citizen. The notes I had taken of this gentleman and others in Baltimore disappeared, and that accident has given me much uneasiness, yet I hope to make amends for the catastrophe. In Baltimore lives another gentleman who sustains an honorable fame, and has been an established citizen of that city for many a year; he keeps the first class hotel which is the rendezvous of the rich and respectable portion of the citizens, whenever recreation is necessary; he is far advanced in years, though his character is still immaculate. I was directed by my invaluable friend, Mrs. McDevitt, to a young gentleman of the name of O'Reily, in Baltimore, whom I consider to be a constituted gentleman.

Mr. O'Reily is a tailor of a high order, professionally speaking, and has been always employed as a cutter; he is a very handsome young man, pregnant with patriotism and friendship. There are many names omitted here, of which I had taken notes in Baltimore, but the omission must be considered unavoidable, and as I am determined, God willing, to see Baltimore again, if I shall discover the names of those I have omitted, I faithfully promise them a double burnish from my poetic battery. The cause of the omission will be made evident before the conclusion of my travels. There is another gentleman, Mr. Furlong, at the foot of Hill street, whose name disappeared in the catastrophe that happened, an accident I sincerely regret. This gentleman keeps two large groceries on the opposite corners of Hill street, and seems to be doing exceedingly well. I think he is a native of the noble and patriotic county of Longford, and a better or a more genuine Irishman is unnecessary. This gentleman did as much for me as my brother could, were he placed in the same situation, and I have no hesitation in saying that he is one of the most popular men in Baltimore and deservedly so. Opposite to this gentleman's grocery, lives an Irish gentleman, a fine mechanic and patriot, of the name of Mr. Low. O! how he sympathized in the bondage of his native country; I am sure he would sacrifice his life to restore the Emerald Isle to her original position and brilliancy —I shall think of my friend and countryman in my next effusion. There is a lady located in the same vicinity, somewhat like Kennedy or Keenan, whose patriotism and ineffable desire for the emancipation of her native country from British oppression, should be admired and applauded. Her husband was from home, when I called at his place, but that only facilitated the sale of my poetic history. She is a magnanimous, patriotic, and an affectionate lady—more hereafter about her. I called to see the Rev. Mr. Earl, Superior of the Jesuit College in Baltimore, and in my humble opinion, his distinguished cast and beautiful appearance are an appendage to humanity, and such personal beauty of course, is heightened by education, sanctity and devotion; to speak of his abilities is to understand all about them, when it is known that he is a Superior in a Jesuit College, as that Order, or body of Ecclesiastics, are the most literary men in the world, and the greatest acquisition for the promotion of religion and learning, now in existence, or that existed in by-gone days.

I took my departure in the cars from Baltimore and pushed for Washington, the capital of the District of Columbia, and put up, according to direction, at Mr. Michael Brady's Hotel, not far from the Capitol. Mr. Brady is a native of the county Caven, that noble and patriotic division of the Emerald Isle, and an ardent encourager of any literary attempt which would have a tendency to give brilliancy to the oppressed land of his nativity. Mr. Brady is married to a lady of inexpressible worth, whose maiden name was Collins, a country born, of course of Irish parents. After presenting my credentials to Mr. Brady, both he and his lady received me with great attention and respect, though his house, at the time, was inundated by an overflow of boarders, principally natives of the Emerald Isle. After making some inquiries the following morning, of Mr. Brady, to whom I could make the first application which would prove encouraging in the commencement, Mr. Brady directed me to a gentleman who kept a formidable hotel in the city, of the name of Mr. Francis Ward, an Ulster gentleman, whose patriotism and cleverness were proverbial in the city and elsewhere. Mr.

Ward was at this time an old bachelor, advanced in years and long since ejected from Cupid's bowers, by the advice and approbation of the fair sex, although the day passed by when he was a great favorite with the ladies, and Cupid's Elysian bowers were deficient in point of attraction, without the appearance of the same Mr. Ward, for at this age he displays Herculean dimensions. I was so sooner seated, than invited by my countryman to .take a glass of something that would dislodge any interruption in the passage, moisten the clay and invigorate the constitution. I strenuously refused, and declared my inability to do so, and as a fortification to render my testimony impregnable, I presented Father Matthew's invulnerable medal, which at sight, silenced any further exposulation on the subject. Mr. Ward took my metrical history and commenced looking over its pages, with much pleasure and avidity, which after a little, was reduced to a kind of settled melancholy; no doubt he met with some passages which reminded him of his own suffering in that unfortunate and misgoverned land, and also, of the woes and ineffable suffering of others. Mr. Ward after a short examination of the merits of the publication, discovered an original grammatical blunder, as he considered, in my publication; although there was enough of original blunders and typographical errors in the production, Mr. Ward, unfortunately, did not light on either, and when I confronted him, and sustained the propriety of the sentence and parsed it with some facility, Mr. Ward compromised, and tacitly acknowledged its propriety. Mr. Ward extended his cleverness to me, in common with all other adventurers, and I departed with a promise of calling at some future period.

Agreeably to directions, I called on others, yet found no encouragement to recompense poetic inspiration, and I was on the verge of returning to Baltimore, when a happy consideration suggested procrastination. There is an Irish gentleman living in Washington, whose literary attainments are of a very high order, and his classical education is refined, brilliant, varied and correct, and his inherent qualities, also, stand in an exact ratio with his educational abilities, and no man can be better known or more respected, than Doctor Philip Smith is, in Washington, D. C. No preliminary is necessary, to get acquainted with a noble Irishman, and I had no introduction that would attract or conciliate the notice or favor of Dr. Smith; yet I considered, and justly so, that so distinguished a scholar, as he is, would encourage any laudable production, be it ever so humble; particularly, any essay touching the woes and afflictions of the land of his nativity. I repaired to Dr. Smith's residence, and fortunately found him at home at the time of visitation, and as soon as he knew my errand to that great metropolis, he displayed much anxiety for my welfare, which coincided exactly with my expectations. When the Dr. knew that I was a Pittsburgher by location, his kindness seemed on the increase, and he affectionately inquired concerning his mother, brothers and friends living in Pittsburgh, and in its vicinity. Mr. Henry Smith, the Doctor's brother, is living in Pittsburgh, and I emphatically say, that a better neighbor, a better citizen, or a more sincere friend is not west of the mountains, taking both native and adopted citizens into consideration. Dr. Smith cheerfully sat down and gave me a list of the better class of the population of the great Washington, and also, permitted me to use his name where and when I thought essential or convenient. This list and permission animated my declining spirits and intrinsically gave assurance of success, and the exhalation that had been hovering over the horizon, immediately evaporated by the consideration of having an interview with so many distinguished gentleman, all, with few exceptions, natives of the Emerald Isle, and each of them holding an office of trust and emolument under the administration of President Pierce.

As soon as discretion suggested my departure, I withdrew from my friend's residence, but before I did, he cordially invited me to come on the following day to dine with him, which was an appendage to the compliments hitherto conferred upon me by the Dr., and with which I could not acquiesce, in consequence of some unavoidable impediments I had to encounter. I pushed towards my lodgings as the rays of the sun were longitudinally projected, which was a sure indication of approaching night. Lawrence, Mass. and Washington, D. C., are the arctic and antarctic boundaries of my travels, rambles and perambulation, and the cleverness of my countrymen at both extremities is entirely beyond the reach of my groveling description, though if I can do them any thing like justice, it will be poetically.

On the following morning, and in the month of March, I adjusted matters to pay a visit to my friends. The snow fell, but to no considerable depth, as the latitude of Washington is of southern nature, and the weather shows less inclemency there, than in latitudes of more northern aspects. I pursued my way without experiencing the least impediment or interruption from the snow-covered streets, and after few visitations, ascertained the imperishable patriotism of my countrymen in Washington, who received me with indescribable kindness, veneration and respect. I pursued my way on the following morning, to the great capitol, ascended the steps with interior pride and satisfaction, entered the majestic building, viewed with intense anxiety, its magnificence, hieroglyphics and signs of incorruptible liberty. I prayed fervently for its perpetuation and invincibility, as I considered it the shield of the oppressed, the dread of tyrants and the nucleus of our glorious constitution.

After viewing with avidity and unspeakable pleasure what I mention, I ascended in search of two gentlemen who were holding offices in the legislative hall of this great metropolis, whose names had been inserted in my catalogue, and of whom I received an extraordinary irreproachable character. I was soon directed to their offices, and found each of them with great assiduity performing the duties pertaining to his office. I paid the first visit to Mr. Fitzpatrick, as the nearest at hand, and at first sight I became convinced of his inexpressible worth. His appearance and distinguished attitude attracted my attention, and respect, as he sat there, divested of supercilious airs, and the offensive symptoms of aristocracy ; there he sat a plain unassuming gentleman, edifying in his conversation, and pleasing in his manners. I need not mention how he encouraged my publication or the cordial reception I received at his hands, as such can be deduced from my former demonstration, although in my opinion he is a native, he entertains for Ireland an imperishable love, and deeply sympathizes in her woes and afflictions. After leaving Mr. Fitzpatrick, I entered Colonel Hickey's office, which was quite convenient, and found him also busily adjusting matters pertaining to his office. When the Colonel saw me, he relaxed his assiduity and in a friendly and affectionate manner he bid me be seated ; I took my seat according to his request, and after interchanging some courteous terms or expressions, I made my intention manifest to the Colonel, and at his request handed him Ireland's woes and sufferings poetically written, and after looking carelessly over a few pages of it, the Colonel unquestionably became a purchaser. The Colonel's personal appearance affords much gratification to the beholder, and is much to his advantage, for a neater or a more perfect gentleman never came within the limits of my inspection. I think Colonel Hickey is a native American, still he entertains an immortal love for the Island of Saints and the sky over it. The Colonel has a brother in Baltimore, one of God's anointed, who is admired, revered, and by some almost idolized for his age, sanctity, and spiritual admonitions to those who are under the control of his spiritual jurisdiction. I had the pleasure of seeing the Reverend gentleman in Baltimore, and although he being very far advanced in years, no visible debility could be constitutionally observed, and in his motion he displayed an agility which was admirable in a man of his years. I have discovered that the offspring of the better class of my countrymen born in America entertain an extraordinary respect for the inhabitants of the Emerald Isle, and this is owing to intellectual culture, mental accomplishments, and religious training. I knew a venerated gentleman, Captain James May, a Missourian born, who would sacrifice his existence to establish the independence and freedom of that unfortunate and oppressed country. Captain May lived for many years in Pittsburgh, Pennsylvania, and a better neighbor or a better citizen never lived in it, and his absence from the city is much lamented by the rich and poor. Captain May did extensive business in Pittsburgh as a commission merchant, and owned many a fine steamboat, employed thousands of hands, and paid them with a punctuality that gained credit for himself. Captain James May is an incorruptible democrat, a devoted friend and a supporter of the established laws of our glorious constitution. He has located himself in Deavenport.

While perambulating the great city of Washington, I met with four brothers* of the name of O'Donoughue, who are citizens of that city, and who are also county and countrymen of my own, and I honestly and emphatically aver, that the cleverness of those gentlemen is sufficient to gain

---

* The four brothers, to omit the O, when writing their names, is a culpable omission, as O'Donoughue has a high elevation in the scale of Milesian dignity.

applause and shed lustre on the entire land of their nativity. They are wealthy, religious, charitable, hospitable and generous; they are known, admired, and respected; they are immovable democrats and patriots, and much devoted to the welfare of the glorious land of their adoption; the education of their family is of a very high order; they are blessed with abundance to render existence easy and comfortable, and they live contented and happy. When I called at Mr. Patrick O'Donoughue's residence, one of the brothers, who has gained a world-wide renown for his incomparable cleverness and liberality, very much astonished me, for when he knew my errand, he without hesitation took an armfull of my books and handed them around with surprising generosity, and gave some to those not included in his own family. A daughter of his, a young lady of great promise, who sat conveniently, received one of the books, and at her father's request, read a few pages of it with admirable ability. Oh, with what surpassing propriety she observed prosody, punctuation, and pronunciation! and I think eternity would steal away from me if she continued reading. I am determined, God willing, to write my travels in epic verse, and then, I think, I can do more justice to Miss O'Donoughue and to the rest of the family in Washington than I have done in this dull description; I shall try it, however. The O'Donoughues in Washington are wealthy and remarkable for their cleverness; but, if the cleverness of the whole were centered in one, the combination when compared to their father's cleverness, would stand in magnitude to his as that of a wren to an eagle, or that of a mole-hill to a mountain. I knew the gentleman in my early days, and have been well aware of his cleverness and worth. Mr. Samuel Reiney, First street.—This gentleman is an invaluable friend, a philanthropist, and an ornament to society. Mr. Richard Redit, or Pedit, Second street.—Here is another distinguished gentleman, distinguished for his goodness, accomplishments, and social intercourse. Mr. Matthew McLeoud, Fayette street, another distinguished and imperishable star, who is respected at home and admired abroad. Mr. P. O'Byrne, a native of the city of Dublin, and an indisputable gentleman in word and in deed. Mr. W. O'Byrne landed in America in 1814, and was on board the Shannon, commanded by Captain Brooks when she encountered the Chesapeake, commanded by the ill-fated Captain Lawrence, and in that memorable contest he received three desperate wounds; he is now living in Georgetown, the home of religion, theology, and science.

In sailing on one of our rivers not long since, and as being determined to notice everything I could hear and see—two men were on the boat, and if judged by their conversation, they were undying enemies to the Catholic Church; one of the men was called Lion, and the other answered to the name of Assmith; their conversation was the cause of the following fugitive poem:

What mighty things of late have come to pass,
The roaring Lion and the braying Ass—
Have both combined to desolate the fold
Of saints and angels since the days of old;
Their mighty efforts will of course decay,
The Holy Church will keep them both at bay.
Tho' oft attacked by strong repulsive arms,
She steers her course and weathers out the storms.
The promise made is a substantial bail,
That hell cannot against His Church prevail.
We know the Lord abominates a lie,
His Church, therefore, is fated not to die.

Mr. Sweeney, Jefferson street; one of Erin's sons, distinguished, admired and venerated by one and all who have the pleasure of his acquaintance. Mr. Dennis O'Neill, Fayette street; descendant of the illustrious house of O'Neill, and well he sustains the dignity of his ancestors. Mr. John Boyce, convenient to the market place; it is not an easy matter to find a more generous or more sincere patriot than Mr. Boyce. He has gained an imperishable renown for himself, for the land of his nativity, and is an acquisition to the land of his adoption. Mr. James Mager, Dumbarton street. Any eulogy concerning this gentleman would not be considered extravagant or out of order by those who are acquainted with him. Mr. William Barton is another gentleman, and one of the Green Isle's patriots, whose fame is widely circulated, whose character is irreproachable, and whose habits are temperate and unsullied. Mr. John Laffin, Alexandria; I met with this gentleman in Washington, and I never can forget his courtesy and patriotism. His bearing commands respect, and the dignity of his symmetry, together with a fine open countenance, will secure the approbation of any assembly. Mr. Garrett Sweeney, from the Parish of Ballycullen, County Kilkenny, landed in this country twenty-six years since. The expression or sentence comprising individual panegyric will answer the collective mass of my countrymen in Washington, D. C., and no encomium, be it ever so extravagant or lofty respecting them can be considered in the least exaggerated. Mr. Peter Grady, Twelfth street and New York avenue, is another noble Milesian who is deservedly honored for the noble principle and unbounded patriotism he displays on every commendable occasion. Mr. James Riordain, in Fifteenth street, convenient to St. Matthew's Church, another Milesian, and a full-fledged, finished and confirmed gentleman. Mr. Matthew Hegarty, another scion of the regal stock, and a genuine patriot who loves Ireland in her sorrows, and vehemently denounces English laws and British tyranny. Mr. Martin Renihan; this genuine Hibernian is indisputably a gentleman of a very large calibre, a credit to the Emerald Isle, an ornament to society, a patriot, a prince and a peasant, as he lives in a rural district. Mr. William Heany, Twentieth street, another of my countrymen whose faults are few, and whose redeeming qualities are many. Mr. Heany loves the land of his nativity, and clings with much tenacity to the land of his adoption. Mr. John Ously, Thirteenth street, is another gentleman, and an incorruptible democrat and patriot who would at all hazards attempt the emancipation of the Green Isle if well seconded. O, wicked England! beware of the irresistible union of such men. Mr. Gregory Ennis is a gentleman of distinguished parts, sublime ideas and lofty attainments; he is also a democrat and a patriot, and, in one word, a constituted gentleman. Mr. John J. Joice, Thirteenth street; this is an exceedingly clever man, who is exceedingly popular for his many amiable qualities; his friendship is unbounded, his patriotism imperishable, and his democracy unpolluted, and no man can be more respected than Mr. Joice. Mr. Andrew J. Joice, Thirteenth street and if I am not mistaken, this gentleman is a brother to Mr. John J. Joice, and the eulogy that answers the one will indisputably answer the other. These brothers are much esteemed, and in high standing in society. Doctor Michael Shine, Land Office, D. C.; this gentleman, to the best of my opinion, is from the City of Limerick, a city rendered memorable by the defeat of William, Prince of Orange. If anything could add to the fame and glory of this city, it is giving birth to so distinguished a gentleman as Mr. Shine.

> This worthy mau is noble, free and kind,
> And very hard another Shine to find;
> He left the spot where women stood the fire,
> And made the Dutchman from the place retire.

Mr. Reaney, Navy Department; it is unnecessary for me to pronounce a eulogy on this gentleman, as the situation he holds vindicates his respectability. Mr. Reaney is an honor to the land of his birth, and an acquisition to the land of his adoption, and an ornament to society. Mr. J. O'Sullivan, Seventh street.

A glance at this gentleman is sufficient to identify his Milesian origin and conclusively prove him to be lineally descended from the illustrious family of the O'Sullivan. Mr. O'Sullivan is as much the gentleman in appearance and unquestionably in principle as any I met with in my travels. Mr. M'Guire is a descendant of the illustrious lords of Fermanagh whom military skill and ineffable bravery placed in the meridian of fame, and in the ramifications of that noble family all over the world, patriotism and bravery are discovered, without the admixture of anything resembling alloy: location between Third and Fourth streets, First avenue. Mr. Francis O'Reilly, Capitol Hill, this is another branch of an ancient illustrious Milesian stock, who is well known and respected for his incomparable social habits, manly principle and patriotic feelings. On this hill reside Mr. Fitzpatrick and Colonel Hickey of whom I have spoken already. Mr. M'Ginty or Ginity corner of Thirteenth and D, this gentleman is as true to the land of his nativity as the needle is to the north pole, and clings with as much tenacity to it as the bark clings to the tree; he is a worthy Irishman, and no other name would answer his uncontaminated principle but that only. Mr. Thomas Ginity, near Georgetown bridge; here is another gentleman, who is known and distinguished for his unparalleled friendship and patriotism, and the most exalted fame is due to his meritorious actions, habits and appreciated worth. Mr. John McGinity, near the aforesaid bridge; probably these two gentlemen are brothers; if not they are congenial spirits, and entitled to the same laudations. In the poetic history of my travels I mean to describe these gentlemen more properly, and with poetic candor. Mr. Philip O'Reilley, living conveniently to the aforesaid bridge. O'Reilley is a constituted gentleman, and a descendant of an illustrious family, that gave as many priests and prelates to the Church of God as any other name on the page of history. Mr. Forsyth, engineer, First street and Ward avenue; this is a gentleman of high attainments, universally revered for his expansive mind, experience in his undertaking, and social habits. His worth is known and admired, and he is precise, prudent and patriotic. Mr. Henry Cassady, from the Parish of Drumconrie, County Meath; I will forbear saying much of this gentleman until such time as I will galvanize him with my poetic battery. I would be ungrateful if his kindness slumbered in the shade of oblivion or security. Nothing could dim his lustre or obscure his intellect; he is as brilliant as the star Deneb, and neither adversity nor prosperity could make him any other thing but a consummate gentleman. Mr. Thomas Denemy, from the sweet County Cavan, the home of patriots and soldiers, and also the home of fine men and fair women. I need say no more of Mr. Denemy, as he is from the invincible County Cavan; more about him hereafter. Mr. Moriarty, from the Parish of Asketow, County Limerick. Any man who has read the History of Ireland must be conversant with this ancient and illustrious Milesian family, and with the vast possessions that family held, and should hold, in the County Kerry, if Irishmen were not robbed of their estates by the oppressive might of unrelenting strangers. Lawrence Mahon, from the County Limerick, and now residing in C street, Washington, D. C. This gentleman's name should be written McMahon, as the destruction of the "Mc," the same as the "O'," has been caused by neglect, ignorance, or a perversion of religious sentiments, but I think they should be restored to their original dignity and position by the Milesian Irish. But this gentleman of whom I speak is neither perverted nor ignorant, and is indisputably a descendant of that illustrious family. Mr. Denis O'Leary, Millstreet, County Cork. The

O'Leary family held vast possessions in West Carbury, County Cork, and conscientiously maintained the faith of their ancestors in spite of racks and tortures, for which alike the rest of the noble Irish were deprived of their estates, and in a thousand instances, of their lives for their fidelity.

Mr. Michael Joice, is another distinguished Hibernian, that no panegyric could overreach his worth. May such men live long and die happy. Mr. P. Fordan, War Department, D. C.; the distinguished office that this gentleman occupies at present, and which he fills with unerring capacity, is sufficient to signify his standing in society. Mr. Fordan is much esteemed and deservedly so, as he possesses in himself all the qualities and attributes that constitute the gentleman. Mr. Thomas O'Gready, Winder's Buildings. O'Gready is an ancient illustrious name of a Milesian stock, which is allowed a high position in the scale of Milesian dignity, and this descendant, Mr. Thomas O'Gready of that illustrious line, has not in any manner tarnished the dignity of his ancestors. Mr. John O'Sullivan, Navy Department. Here is another invulnerable lion who is unquestionably descended from illustrious ancestors, and whose qualifications entitle him to the distinguished office he holds at present under President Pierce. I will try hereafter how I can poetically describe those gentlemen of whom I speak. Mr. Martin Foley, Eighteenth Street between H. and F. This is another bright star of Erin, who left his country in consequence of the oppressive demands of unrelenting oppressors. Still he lost nothing of his patriotism nor of his other sterling qualities since he left the land of his nativity. Mr. John J. Joice, born in the town of Fermoy, county Cork, Ireland, and has been thirty-five years from the land of his birth; yet at present, you would know him to be an original Irishman in appearance, in language, in principle, and in faith. Mr. Michael McDermott, coachmaker, between Third and Four and a half Streets, D. C. This worthy gentleman through his ineffable kindness and assiduity to the community at large, is revered and appreciated; he is an honest man, a good neighbor, a worthy citizen, and much admired for his professional abilities; he has a son now married, who inherits all his father's qualities and qualifications. Mr. Mortimer Keating,* from the city or county of Limerick. This gentleman is distinguished in Washington for high and varied attainments, for his strict integrity, social habits, immovable patriotism; he governs in a manner all the operations carried on in Willard's inimitable mansion house in that city, and oversees every thing with a correctness inaccessible to description; he is a poet of a high order, a fine writer, and an incorruptible Irishman. I met with a certain gentleman in the Willard House, in Washington, who strenuously assisted Mr. Keating in the management of affairs in that great establishment, and it seldom came to my lot to meet with a more generous, a more sincere, or a more affectionate countryman. I had been very particular in taking notes of this gentleman, and of others with whom I met in this House, which is the rendezvous of the higher class of our American people, and also of foreigners, but to my mortification and chagrin the notes were accidently lost, and the cause of their disappearance, ere I take leave of Washington, I'll make manifest, and this accident left me to the mercy of a treacherous memory to give a description of those I met with in that far famed House of which I have spoken. The gentleman of whom I speak

---

* Every man is familiar with this name, as a Keating fell, and met with an untimely death by the hands of the unrelenting California murderer, in Willard's Mansion House, Washington, D. C.; whether this be the man or not, is not in my power to ascertain. Yet this much I know, if Mr. Mortimer Keating be not the man, his brother fell a victim in that unprovoked and cruel murder.

is a Mr. Smith, from the noble and patriotic county of Cavan, the home, the cradle, and the nursery of brave men and fine women. Mr. Smith is a patriot, although invariably adheres with ineffable fidelity to the laws of our glorious constitution. Mr. Smith has two sons, perhaps of Irish birth, in this establishment. I candidly aver I never saw in the whole course of my life and travels, more promising lads than they. As my intention is to write poetically my travels, I will say no more until then, concerning Mr. Smith or his two promising sons. In the great Hotel that I have spoken of, and, as I also expressed, the rendezvous of the better class of our American ladies and gentlemen, and also of foreigners, whom I viewed, I think, with a philosophic eye, such as came within my inspection, and I must candidly acknowledge that both ladies and gentlemen are entitled to my warmest approbation. The ladies generally speaking looked exceedingly fair and modest, without the least appearance of affectation or pride, and the gentlemen displayed every thing that is noble, dignified, national, and agreeable.

At that time, an Irish lady of the name of Mrs. Maden, or Headen, in company with her husband, stopped in this hotel; this lady had been introduced to me, probably by Mr. Smith, and when she read a little of the poetic history of Ireland, she soon became with much alacrity a purchaser; as soon as she made her appearance I knew her to be an Irish lady, and although her size was large, her proportions were so admirably and equally adjusted; her size contributed much to the completion of her beauty, and whether she had been long or short from the land of her nativity, her native charms suffered no injury from the changes and severity of her adopted climate. Mr. Bernard Fitzpatrick, parish of Dumblane, county Cavan.—Mr. Fitzpatrick is lineally descended from the kings of Ossary; he is á finished, indisputed gentleman, and a brave patriot. Mr. John O'Neil, a native of Gallard, parish of Kilkerry, county Tyrone.—Where I met this gentleman I am unable to tell; but, wherever I met with him, I recollect him to be a noble specimen of humanity, a warm-hearted friend, and a descendant of the noble and illustrious family of O'Neil. In Washington I met with another gentleman, an extensive grocer, of the name, I think, of Mr. Hays, and also with a Mr. O'Conner, from the county of Kerry, whose patriotism is invulnerable; and I met hundreds of my countrymen in Washington, of whom I can give no account at present, in consequence of the accident that happened my trunks, and the annihilation of the notes I had taken, in forwarding them from Rochester to Buffalo. In Washington I met with an extraordinarily clever Irishman, of the name of Mr. Coleman a native, I believe, of the county Meath, who gave me a letter of introduction to a consummate gentleman in Easton, Pa, of the name of O'Connell; I think I never met with a greater patriot than Mr. Coleman, in the whole course of my travels. Now, I am going to speak of a gentleman with whom I met in Washington, perhaps of the name of Barry; he is a young man of intellectual culture, and a mechanic, (carpenter,) of the highest order; his appearance is splendid, and his popularity unbounded. As I intend to visit Washington shortly, I may learn all the particulars about him, and if so, in the poetic history of my travels I will pay him a tribute, to which he is justly entitled.

To take my departure from Washington city without paying a visit to the far-famed College of Georgetown, would be a culpable mistake that no sacrifice would be an equivalent atonement to banish my intrinsic contrition for such a mistake, as I was exceedingly anxious to see the Rev. Mr. McGuire, president of said College, who is known throughout the western world as an orator, a scholar, and a theologian of the highest grade;

when I arrived there, I was introduced into an apartment to await the arrival of the president of the College, who ere long made his appearance, and received me with that courtesy which is peculiar to Ecclesiastics of the Roman Catholic religion. I was astonished to see so young an ecclesiastic president of one of the greatest colleges on the continent of America, but brilliant attainments and religious devotion are the cause of his elevation. Oh Ireland, my native country, Oh land of hospitality, Oh gem of the ocean, what a host of literary men you have produced, in spite of the cruel enactments manufactured in the pandemonium councils of British cabinets!

After bidding adieu to my friends in Washington, I immediately took my seat in the cars, and owing to their incredible speed we soon arrived at Philadelphia, and there I repaired with indescribable anxiety to my old quarters, where I met with a warm reception from my unflinching friend, Mrs. Griffin—himself being from home on some unavoidable business—when I spent a few days in the city of Brotherly Love, among my friends. I got into the cars again, and according to Mr. Coleman's directions, I soon arrived in Easton, a considerable town on the banks of the Delaware, Pa. When I entered the town I cautiously inquired of the first of my countrymen with whom I met, was there a house of entertainment in the town of Easton kept by any of my countrymen? he replied affirmatively, and emphatically promised me comfort and security, where he would recommend me to stop, during my stay in Easton. I promised invariable tenacity to his recommendation.

My countryman then gave me the name of the gentleman who kept the house, and of the street in which it was located, to which place I directed my steps; and without navigable efforts or traverse sailing, soon found myself at the port of destination. After a little sedentary posture, my uneasiness cooled and my doubts evaporated, as the appearance of the landlord gave indisputable evidence that the recommendation of my director had been saturated with sincerity; and I therefore made myself contented under the friendly dome of my countryman. Retired early to rest, a clear conscience and a soft pillow attracted Morpheus to my sleeping apartment, where he threw me into one of those imaginary slumbers; during which time I ranged, if imagination could be infallibly sanctioned, all night with some fascinating companion through the Elysian fields of indescribable happiness; but when Sol's brilliancy in the morning chased away the exhalations beneath the horizon, I awoke and found it all a dream. I think, therefore, that this dreamy, illusory happiness that suddenly evaporates is not to be accredited. After breakfast, as directed by Mr. Coleman, I went in quest of Mr. O'Connell's residence, and as a clever Irishman's house is easily found, I soon found the object of my search; when I entered, he received me as Irishmen are accustomed to receive strangers; he received me with that courtesy and friendship he himself received as an inheritance from his ancestors. After some terms of courtesy reciprocally passed, I presented him with Mr. Coleman's introductory note, and after a momentary pause he got pen, ink and paper, and wrote the following note to an Irish gentleman in Easton, with incredible dispatch and avidity:

"Patrick McGloin, Esquire.

"Sir:—A splendid Irishman, a poet, author of the History of Ireland in verse, has come amongst us, and we feel it our duty to patronize him, not by words or pretensions, but by forking out the cash, and taking as many numbers as possible. Now you, Mr. McGloin, you as being one of the most influential men in this locality, and one, too, of whom we are proud, in consequence of your manly and spirited opposition to Ned Buntline, in Easton, on a former occasion, you, I say, we deem alone competent to extend the circulation of this history, and thereby render a service to our worthy visitor.

"THOMAS O'CONNELL.

February 19*th*, 1855."

My feelings, after leaving the residence of my friend, may be more easily imagined than described, as I consider it a revolution in times and circumstances to find such a brilliant countryman as Mr. O'Connell, bleaching himself on the declivity of a Pennsylvanian hill, whereas he should be in his native Emerald Isle, feasting with his friends and kindred in the royal halls of his progenitors. I proceeded without delay to see Mr. McGloin, my distinguished countryman, and without much exploration I inadvertently met him, and he acted conformably to the account I received of his cleverness. After leaving him, I returned to the house of my friend, as it was then verging on dinner time, for Sol was meridian high, and his incomparable steeds were anxious to descend and take a view of the globe we inhabit. As I entered, everything was in readiness; an abundant dinner, seasoned and embellished with Irish hospitality, that would do justice to an oriental prince or a Grecian epicurian; and as time insensibly stole away, I think eternity would too, could I live during that time in the enjoyment of such company. I went to Easton when all the public works were suspended, and everything in that line in a state of stagnation; notwithstanding, my visit to that region was not unprofitable. As I lost the most of the notes I had taken of my friends in Easton, and as they disappeared as if in the Carthagenian conflagration, I think it more prudent to withhold the few that remained, than to give them publication, as my intention is, God willing, to write my travels in epic verse, and to visit Easton, before then, which will give me an opportunity of seeing them, or those who were acquainted with them, and then their names will appear unquestionably in that poetic composition. The notes I had taken of my host and hostess did not disappear, and are still in my possession, and in some place among my papers; but they will show themselves ere long, or I am much mistaken in my calculations; but this much I know and recollect, that he is a native of the county Meath, and I think from the vicinity of Tara, Royal "Tara," which inspired him with invincible patriotism, and an anxious desire for the restoration of his native country to her freedom and independence; he is a true-hearted Irishman and Providence has provided him with a helpmate of the same disposition.

There is a splendid Catholic Church in Easton, large enough to accommodate a considerable congregation, and the Rev. Mr. O'Riordin officiates in it, who was then from home for the benefit of his health, which, I was informed by some of his parishioners, was much damaged and impaired. The Reverend gentleman, if I could consistently with my faith make use of the expression, was idolized by his congregation, not exclusively by his congregation, but by all who had the pleasure of his acquaintance. During his absence a worthy young priest officiated there, of the name of Mr. O'Hern, who was also beloved by the congregation for his attention and spiritual assiduity. I called at the priest's residence one blustering morning when the Reverend young gentleman was called upon to visit a sick man who was about thirty miles away from Easton, and if the information could be accredited, the sick man was in a dying condition. The young priest immediately saddled his horse and complied with the urgent call with that willingness that no other could, but the minister of God. Agreeableness, urbanity and humility are the inheritance of a priest, and that combination can be found wherever he is located. I often considered the lot and slavery of a priest the most difficult to be endured; he eats little, fasts a great deal, and has to arise from his bed at every hour he is called upon, even in the most inclement season of the year, and brace himself against the raging storm, ride and sometimes travel long journeys; he approaches the bed of sickness where perhaps the contagion is alarmingly spreading, to prepare the sick person to appear before the tribunal of divine justice, and all this toil and danger without the smallest hope of a pecuniary remuneration; nevertheless, he does his duty with unspeakable resignation, blesses his Divine Master who suffered more than he, and prepares also himself for eternity. He continues in this manner until perhaps old age and infirmity restrain his exertions, still he keeps on doing all the good he can until he is called upon to receive a glorious reward, a reward that no tongue can utter or no heart comprehend. After selling a few of my books to a promising young Irish lad who keeps a Catholic bookstore for Catholic accommodation adjoining the church, I got every thing in readiness, took my seat in the cars, and in a few hours found myself in the city of Brotherly Love, well satisfied with my visit to Easton, which is situated on the declivity of Mount Olympus, in the State of Pennsylvania. As usual I recreated myself in Mr. Griffin's hospitable residence, and in a few days I departed again in the cars, for the summit of Allegheny mountains, where I met with pure Irish patriots.

This land is bless'd with blessed liberty,
And yet, 'tis full of sin and heresy.
Here are assembl'd, to the Christian's woe,
A spawn ascended from the pit below,
Still here and there, are sparks of heavenly fire,
In course of time will leaven the entire.

O'Donovan.

Among my countrymen on the mountains, I met with a gentleman of the name of Mr. M'Loughlin, a native of Donegal who keeps a large establishment of dry goods, &c., on the Summit for the accommodation of the inhabitants of that region, whose position in society is high and unsullied, and I met with others of no mean or narrow calibre.

It is gratifying to think that a wise Providence has given everywhere an opportunity to Catholics, to prepare themselves for eternity; even the summit of the Allegheny Mountains affords them that spiritual consolation. On the summit I got into the whale's belly, which while puffing steam in the elements, descended the declivity of the Allegheny Mountain with a velocity that is incredible to those unacquainted with that bounding Pegasus, until we came to a station house, situated on the side of the hill opposite Johnstown. I got out to breathe the fresh air, and after a momentary pause, gave orders to have my trunks taken to Mr. Carnahan's, who kept an orderly and respectable temperance house, and there I remained during my stay in the town. Mr. Carnahan is a native and a worthy Catholic, as far as I could learn, and keeps many respectable boarders, principally all Protestants, who deported themselves with propriety and discretion, during my stay in the place. The following morning, I paid a visit to the Rev. Mr. Kearney who is very popular in Johnstown for his urbanity and social habits, and I need not say that he received me kindly, as kindness and humility are the unquestionable inheritance of a priest. The Rev. gentleman of whom I speak, did much to faciliate the sale of my books; he bought himself, and directed me to others whom he considered likely to purchase, and in this town; I found my countrymen full of kind feelings and patriotism. But the accident that dispersed the notes I had taken of my friends in Johnstown will become evident before the conclusion of my travels, and a prudential consideration prevents me from giving publication to such as adhered to memory, as I could not give the entire. There is a county and a countryman of mine living in Johnstown for many a year, on whom I called,—having some previous knowledge of him. I knew his parents in my youthful days, and I fear no contradiction, neither do I exaggerate when I emphatically aver that they were rich and respectable and stood high in public estimation. Mr. Kingston is the gentleman I mean, he is a convert to the Catholic church, and I sincerely think, a good member of it too, and if I mistake not before or after his departure from the Emerald Isle, his parents and the rest of the family became also converts to the same faith. I made one great mistake on leaving Johnstown, that I sincerely regret, and though it happened in 1855, I feel uneasy through the means of it to this day, and that feeling will continue until I make an adequate atonement for the same mistake, when I got my baggage removed back again to the station house situated on the declivity of the hill, and as the cars were momentarily expected, and seldom make any delay there, I solicited the aid of two boys that were standing by, to put a large chest that I had on the cars, which they did with surpassing fidelity. The alarm was given to get into the cars, and I like others immediately mounted, completely forgetting my obligation to the boys, who faithfully assisted me in the hour of extremity. One of those lads was a son to the gentleman with whom I boarded in Johnstown, and the other I think, was of the name of Glorie. I will never rest satisfied until I pay them for their trouble, with compound interest. The cars were under way when I thought of this egregious mistake, which was then irremediable, and which mortified me beyond description. A few hours race in Pegasus brought us to Pittsburgh. This is not the end of my travels, and I am going to rectify the omission I mentioned before, that I came to the summit after leaving Philadelphia, but it was not so, I only came to Harrisburg, and there took my quarters with my brave and generous countryman Mr. McCabe, who keeps an orderly house of entertainment, convenient to the R. R. Mr. McCabe is a native of the noble county of Longford, and a clever man is not easily found, as he is generous, hospitable, and temperate, well-known, and indisputably popular.

The following morning I went to the residence of the Rev. Mr. Meagher, the distinguished orator, theologian and ecclesiastic, who is the officiating Catholic clergyman of the place, and fortunately found him at home ; he knew me, as I had called on the Rev. gentleman in 1848, and as a priest, full of kindness and humility, he received me with marked veneration, which I thought myself unqualified to receive at the hands of so distinguished a divine. The Rev. gentleman did every thing in his power to dispose of my books in Harrisburg ; he bought of me himself, he traveled with me, he animated the inanimate to do the same, and when I was in the cars ready to start for Altoona, the Rev. gentleman followed me to the place, to inform me of a new discovery he made, where I could dispose of some of my books. I was much surprised at the Rev. gentleman's poverty, or at the limitation of his means, which proved at once, that pecuniary accumulation was not his object. His poverty manifestly appeared when he purchased of me. Like his Divine Master, who made application to the fish of the sea, to pay a wonted tribute, or to give Cæsar his due, the Rev. Mr. Meagher was compelled to make application for the purchase money, to a boy whom he had, I think for the purpose of going errands. I would then, far sooner, the sum should remain unpaid, but I well knew that terms of negations would not suit the Rev. gentleman's disposition—

O ! inimitable Tipperary—

As friendship reigns in every bosom there,
To ease the mind that's burdened with despair ;
There all in need, would get their wants supplied,
The truth of this was never yet denied.

My countrymen and women (making use of a general expression,) in Harrisburg, are spirited, generous, respectable and patriotic, and also religious, as they faithfully adhere to the faith of their ancestors.

To great mistakes the human mind is prone,
The cause of it to some must be unknown;
With fewer thoughts, we could advantage gain,
For oft, too many paralyze the brain—
The quick succession that they come and go,
Must be the cause of all our blunders so—

After starting from Philadelphia in the cars, I halted in Lancaster, where I met with some of my countrymen of the right kind; among whom, was a Mr. Timothy Farrell, a professional boot and shoe maker, born in the county Longford, got married in said county, and took his departure from it for America, eighteen years since. I honestly aver, if a greater patriot than he, be in existence, he should be embalmed, and in that state of preservation, presented to future generations, to inspire them with love for the country which gave birth to their progenitors, and as I intend to write my travels poetically, I will reserve Mr. Farrell for a poetic shock, which will shake Lancaster city to the very centre.

During my stay in Lancaster, I took up my residence with my inestimable friend, Mr. Richard Mc.Grann, whom I mentioned in my first travels, and by referring back, the reader will find a pretty exact illustration of the same gentleman in the indigested history of my travels in 1848. Mrs. Hannah born in the town of Donegal, has been during six years a widow and has a large and respectable family. Excepting the county Caven, I got more encouragement in my travels from the natives of Donegal, than the natives of any other county in Ireland. It is a certain fact that I met with more of my countryman from there, than from any other county in the nation; all clever fellows at that.

Mr. Roger Sheeley, from Tralee, county Kerry, married in Lancaster, and has been eighteen years from his native land. Unquestionably he left a county which is renowned for generosity, song and science. Mr. Philip Fitzpatrick, from the parish of Columkill, County Longford; Mr. Fitzpatrick is a worthy citizen of Lancaster, and keeps in it a respectable inn, signalized by the sign of the lamb, which is notorious as being a safe harbor for citizens and travelers, and a more obliging, generous and manly landlord, could not be found, than my friend and countryman Mr. Fitzpatrick.

Mr. James Fitzpatrick, parish of Nocknotney, Farmanagh, left his native country ten years since, and as yet, has preferred a life of celibacy. Mr. Edward McCann, Carberry, County Kildare, seven years from his native place, and has preferred a single life, and of course, follows the same direction as his predecessor. Mr. Thomas Rooney, from the parish of Kinawley, has been twenty-five years in the land of his adoption, and acted quite contrary to his two predecessors, as he has taken to himself a wife, and a Lancasterian at that; this gentleman is an indisputable Milesian. Messrs. Patrick, Michael and Richard O'Kelly; no man of the lowest capacity will dispute the Milesian origin of those gentlemen; they are Irishman of a high grade, and exceedingly popular. Mr. James Caffery* is universally known to the community at large, and admired and respected by others, as well as his own countrymen. Mr. James Peoples, a democrat of high standing in society, invulnerable in his political principles, and unerring in his social habits. Mr. Hugh Corkeran, a Leitrim gentleman, an honor to his country, a friend to his race, and an acquisition to Lancaster. Mrs. Taylor, an amiable lady

---

* Mr. Caffery—this gentleman is a boot and shoemaker, of a high grade.

The man who climbed the great poetic mountain,
And largely drank of that inspiring fountain.

saturated with patriotism, and fervently prays for the freedom of the Emerald Isle. Mr. McGunnigal, an Irishman, whose fond desire of seeing his native country exonerated from the cruel and unrelenting grasp of the ruthless stranger. Mrs. Flinn and Mrs. McGunnigal, two widows residing in Lancaster, I think, who signified more veneration for the Emerald Isle than I could demonstrate within a limited space; may God help those holy widows. Messrs Healy and Flinn, two gentlemen of an ancient Milesian stock, who love their country and the sky over it. Mr. Gallaspie, a fearless democrat, an honest, generous man, and an Irishman in the bargain. Mr. Hugh Kennedy, a county Galway gentleman, and a full fashioned, finished Hibernian. Mr. John Rose, born in Spratton, Northamptonshire, England; Mr. Rose is a converted gentleman to the unerring faith of the Catholic Church, and in him, and in other English converts to Rome, I discovered more sorrow for the condition of the Irish nation, and for its downfall, by means of English tyranny, than I discovered in thousands of my own countrymen. O! may they all soon be converted from the errors of their faith, which is, and will be, the fervent prayer of the author.

I left Lancaster in the cars for Harrisburg, and continued my travels in them until they came as far as Altoona. I have already mentioned my stay in Altoona, where I remained over night with a countryman of mine, an Ulster gentleman, who kept an inn in the town for the special accommodation of the traveling community, and for the accommodation of his neighbors, who often rendezvous at his house to recreate themselves. Although this gentleman, with whom I stopped, and I, differed in faith, it made not the slightest difference on either side, for I found him to be a finished gentleman, and were it not for losing the notes I had taken of him I would say more; but as I am determined, God willing, to write my travels poetically over again; and to see Altoona ere long, and get some information, so as to identify the gentleman's name, as well as the names of others who are neglected here; then, and not till then, can I do him or them anything like justice. On the following morning I proceeded to the Rev. Mr. Twigg's residence, who officiates there as a Catholic clergyman, and fortunately met him on the way to the Church to celebrate mass. This happened in the middle of March, when a partial dissolution of the snow had taken place, which made the vicinity of the Church, as well as other parts of the town, display a disagreeable and dreary appearance, for the town is new and received but very little improvement from the improving hand of man; still, in despite of all impediments, there was a comfortable gathering in the Church that morning to hear mass. From Altoona I went to Hollidaysburg, and thence to Newry, of which places I will give a graphic description ere long, and which will be the end of my second travels. I went from Altoona to Hollidaysburg, Blair county, a considerable town situated somewhat on the declivity of a hill, and possessing the advantage of an immutable stream of pure atmospheric ramification, which expels and prevents the proximity of malignant and contagious distempers, so often fatal to man, and which sometimes confound the skill of doctors of distinguished abilities, and lie inaccessible to the prescriptions of superficial empiric.

In this town, I met with many of my countrymen and women of no ordinary grade, who individually and collectively entertained immovable love and respect for the land of their nativity, though not lessening nor interfering with their allegiance and fidelity to the land of their adoption. After taking a hasty view of Hollidaysburg, I paid the first visit to the Rev. Mr. Walsh, who officiates there as a Catholic clergyman, and this I did unaccompanied by my usual timidity when approaching a

Priest, or the messenger of God; this reservation I entertain for a Priest, which I know is indisputably due to his sacred dignity and situation; and as a collateral annuller of timidity, another circumstance faciliated its extermination, it is this: I knew I was within the circumference of Bishop O'Conner's jurisdiction, and as his Lordship, at sundry times, had given proof of his kindness to me and that the friendship of a Bishop of such distinguished eminence and ecclesiastical power would support me in Hollidaysburg, as it did throughout my travels; when I arrived at the Rev. gentleman's residence, I fortunately found him there, and I exaggerate not, when I say that that Rev. gentleman and amiable young Priest, received me with marks of veneration and respect to which I considered myself not entitled, and he with alacrity became a purchaser; nay, did more to facilitate the sale of my productions, as he gave me the names of such as were likely to purchase. But, my dear reader, I have to state that the notes I had taken of my friends in Hollidaysburg, disappeared by means of a great accident I met with in my travels, an illustration of which will appear before the conclusion of my travels, but, I will give the names of the few that had not escaped a treacherous memory. Mr. John McCullough, born in the parish of upper Bodona, County Tyrone. Mr. McShea, Rilegh, County Cork, Barony of Imokillea, nineteen years in this country, and is blessed with a virtuous wife and three fine children; Mr. Charles Canney, from the parish of Carn, Donough, County Donegal, eighteen years in America; Edward McHaugh, born in Mifflin County, Pennsylvania; Mr. Peter O'Heagan, formerly of Dungiven, County Londonderry, a citizen of the United States for the last twenty-three years. I visited Newry, a small town only a few miles distant from Hollidaysburg, March 7th, 1855, and in said town, or rather a village, I met with some sterling countrymen of mine. Mr. Slaterly, from the Kings County; I can't exactly inform my readers, where I met this gentleman, whether it was in Newry town or elsewhere; Mr. George Kearney, parish of Glendeherky, County Donegal; Mr. John Doughan, parish of Killan, County Meath, six years in America. Mr. Patrick McKin, county Louth, also six years in the land of liberty; Mr. John Talbot, parish of Dunkerrin, County Tipperary. My dear readers, an individual praise or applause is unnecessary, as the eulogy that would answer individually, would answer collectively, as they are all men of unexceptionable character and high standing in society. From Newry, as I stated before, I came to the Summit, from the Summit to Johnstown, hence to Pittsburgh. End of my second travels. No obscure writer could have greater success than I had, and this was partially or entirely owing to the distinguished friends, with whom I met in my travels, or as I should say in the commencement of my second travels. The first of these had been Roger Brown, Esq., of Market street, Philadelphia, who has since departed this life, and whose demise is much lamented, by an extensive circle of relatives, friends, and acquaintances, and I fervently pray and beseech God, if not there already, to restore him to the communion of the seraphim, in heaven.

As I stated already, when on the verge of taking my departure from Philadelphia, I asked Mr. Brown, would he recommend me to any of his friends, in that city, as I knew that an introduction from a man of his high standing in society, would have a powerful effect. Mr. Brown cheerfully answered that he would give me one, to one of the most popular Irishman in the State of New York, Archbishop Hughes, excepted, and who can, and will do more for your promotion and proficiency, than any other gentleman in the city or State; the above exception to be considered. Mr. Brown, sat down and gave me a letter of recommendation, though sententious, it was to the point, to Cornelius Dever, Esq., who is associated with an extensive and impregnable firm, in No. 10, Pearl street, New York. Though his private residence is located in Brooklyn. This remark was more of a prophecy, than a conjecture, or an accidental saying, on the unparalleled merits of Mr. Dever, and this opinion had been corroborated by the unspeakable kindness he displayed to promote the sale of my productions. Cornelius Dever, Esq., whom I consider the Irish Achilles, might have an existing parallel, but, can have no superior.

Men may pretend to be as good as he,
For pity sake, do let the maniacs be.
Fair fame that travels on the wings of air,
Would soon confront them, if they would compare.
Yes, fame indeed, that could the like control,
Would make my friend, the monarch of the whole.

I had been absent from home better than twelve months before I returned to the city of Pittsburgh, and although being absent during the specified time, my stay in the city was limited, as I came to the conclusion of returning to the city of Philadelphia, to dispose of the remainder of my works. Conformably to this resolution I entered the cars or flying Pegasus in Pittsburg, and took my departure for Philadelphia. Our journey was rapid, agreeable and safe, and no obstruction marred our rapidity until we arrived at the city of Brotherly Love, and on our arrival in that city, I repaired immediately to the great printing establishment of Messrs. King & Baird, in Sansom street in that great metropolis, where many of my books was unbound and insured. I remained in Philadelphia enjoying the friendship and hospitality of my friends until I got some of my works bound, and then I started for Phœnixville, a small town not far distant from Philadelphia, and there I met with some genuine ladies and gentlemen from my native country, the far-famed Emerald Isle. During my stay there I put up at the house of Mr. Hughes who keeps a respectable tavern in that small town, for the accommodation and security of the community at large, and also, for all travellers whom chance or design would direct to his elysium. The notes I had taken of my friends in Phœnixville, as I stated before, disappeared in the wreck, and left me nothing to draw upon, but such as clung with indelible tenacity to a treacherous memory, and here I set down their names in order: Mr. James Fitzgibbons, born in Wales, married in Wales and has one beautiful little girl; although this gentleman is a Welshman born, he is an Irishman in appearance and principle; he has been eight years in America. Mr. Edward Wallace, wine and liquor merchant, north Thirteenth street; I have already spoken of this gentleman who is now located in Philadelphia. Mrs. M'Alier; this old lady displayed as much patriotism as any lady or gentleman with whom I met in my travels; she ought to be embalmed for the immortal love she entertained for the land of her nativity. Mr. Mananey is from the parish of Donoughmore and has been six years in the land of liberty. Mr. Owen Devlin, a fledged, finished and constituted Tyrone gentleman also six years from home. Mr. John M'Kee, another Tyrone gentleman. Mr. M'Cullough, tailor. Mr. Bernard O'Neil. Mr. Samuel O'Neil, this gentleman came from the Emerald Isle when six years of age, got married in Manayunk to a lady whose mother was Irish, and father English. Mr. O'Neil is a boss or superintendent in a factory in Phœnixville, and a better man in his sphere is not in existence; he is exceedingly well known and his social habits and intercourse are much appreciated and admired; more about him hereafter. Rev. P. O'Farrell is located there as Catholic clergyman, and much respected by those who differ with him in religion, and dearly beloved by his own congregation; the reverend gentleman is a native of the noble county of Longford. Mr. James from the county Derry, has been seven years from his native country. Mr. M'Quade from the parish of Aragal, county Monaghan, and married in his own Emerald Isle. There is a very respectable family* still living in Phœnixville of whom I have already spoken, and my approbation of that family can be seen during my travels in 1848. In my forthcoming poetic history, I intend to do some justice to my friends in Phœnixville. From Phœnixville I returned to Philadelphia and instantly concluded to embrace the first opportunity that would take me to Albany, the capital of the State of New York.

Although my decisions are momentarily, I generally carry them into execution. This was a long and terrific journey, and to commence it, I crossed from Philadelphia into Jersey, where I entered the cars, which moved with incredible velocity until they left us in Jersey city, opposite New York, and after crossing, we got into a steamboat which ploughed with might and majesty up the North river, until she cast anchor near the city of Albany. The transmission of myself and baggage was rapidly effected, and I took shelter under the friendly roof of my friend and countryman, Mr. Patrick Murphy, who is located, according to my understanding, in Church street, and who keeps there, as good, as comfortable and as respectable a hotel, as any in the city. After recreating myself and hearing the musical strains of my countrymen; Mr. Murphy illustrating his youthful perambulations and rambles through the verdant and Elysian fields of the Evergreen Isle, the unfortunate land of my nativity; I went earnestly on my mission, and that with an interminable alacrity, as all my countrymen in the city with whom I had the plea-

* O'Kelly.

sure of an interview, possess the most charming reminiscence of the once blessed land from whence dire oppression, the legitimate daughter of British tyranny, banished them, and to write an individual panegyric on the Irish Albanians would be superfluous, as the eulogy which answers individually, answers collectively, as they are all men of irreproachable character and equally and perpendicularly stand on the same horizontal level, though there being a disparity in their worldly circumstances and position in society, nothwithstanding, there is no supremacy adopted. I paid my first visit to Mr. Patrick O'Donovan, a native of Saint Mary's parish, county Limerick. In that county, the royal palace of O'Donovan was located when Irish kings and princes reigned supreme. Mr. John Franklin Dune, born in the county Limerick also, in the year 1801, and has been twenty-one years in the United States. Mr. Michael Clarke, born in the town of Ballybarren, county Cavan, emigrated to the United States on the first day of June, 1833, married in Ireland. Mr. John Walsh emigrated from the parish of Dungarven, county Kilkenny, and landed in America, in 1830, married in Albany, resides at No. 57 Pearl street. Mr. John Murphy, born in the parish of Dromen, county Limerick, emigrated in the year 1835, married in this country and now resides in Albany, where he keeps an extensive hat establishment. Mr. Henry Mulholland from the county Derry, left there when two years old and now resides in Albany, keeps a hotel of considerable magnitude and respectability, in Beaver street, has a brilliant wife and a young family, consisting of two girls and one boy. Mr. Hugh J. Hastings, born near McGuire's bridge, county Farmanagh, and emigrated to this country, where he has resided since his emigration, I think in Albany or contiguous to it, and his emigration took place in 1829. James Cotter, another clever Hibernian, and resident of Albany. Mr. James O'Loughlin, another Irish chieftain of an indisputed Milesian origin, also a resident of Albany. Mr. Joseph Clinton; it admits of no controversy, when I affirm that Mr. Clinton is a distinguished son of the Evergreen Isle, renowned for its sanctity and hospitality to strangers. Mr. Reed another distinguished citizen of Albany, a wealthy spirit and wine merchant, and a patriotic Irish gentleman. Mr. Henry O'Kelly, a noble descendant of Milesian progenitors. Mr. Bartley, an honor to the land that gave him birth and an ornament to society. Mr. Michael Rogan, another Irish comet of brilliancy and fame. Messrs. John and Owen Lynch, two gentlemen of irreproachable fame and unsullied character. Mr. Patrick Bready; I have spoken of this gentleman already in the best and highest terms I could command, though in terms inadequate to his worth and unspeakable cleverness.

Mr. Bready had been inspired by two impulses in my favor; the first of these was because I am an Irishman, and the second as being a Cork man; because Mr. Bready is married to a lady from the same county,—a county which has produced theologians, statesmen, poets, mathematicians, and linguists in countless numbers, and in the forthcoming poetic history of my travels, I mean to galvanize, not meritriciously but solidly, my distinguished friend, Mr. Patrick Bready and his lady, my amiable county and countrywoman. Captain Michael Conway was born in the parish of Little Longford, Kings county, emigrated in the year 1817, and has been ever since a resident of the city of Albany. The Captain married the daughter of Mr. Delany in said city in 1840, and has been many years connected with a military department; the last fourteen years he has been captain of the fourth police district in Albany. I intend to describe him poetically with more force and ability. Mr. Michael Larkin, from the parish of Ballynakill, county Galway; Mr. Larkin is a finished gentleman, and this positive declaration admits of no controversy. Mr. Kearney, attorney-at-law, is on of the distinguished sons of the Emerald Isle; h is thirty-seven years of age, and in the vigor o manhood. Messrs. H. and T. Kearney; these brothers keep an extensive clothing and provision store at the Little Basin, near Albany. They are lineally descended from Milesicus, and this distinction they display in an admirable manner. Their patriotism is unquestionable and like all other genuine Irishmen, they are generally known and respected. Mr. John Meehen, from Edgeworthstown, county Longford, a town rendered illustrious and universally known by the inimitable effusions of the celebrated novelist, Miss Edgeworth. Mr. Meehan is a married man, and lacks nothing of being a gentleman. He is engaged in the great Stanwix Hall or Hotel, in Albany. Mr. Patrick Fitzsimmons, an illustrious Irishman, has been engaged in the same establishment. Mr. James Nugent, a Cavan gentleman, who left his native country six years since for America. Mr. Nugent is an addition to the galaxy of the Irish population in Albany. Mr. Nugent is a full finished Irishman, and that sentence constitutes a gentleman of the highest grade. Mr. Saift, merchant tailor, emigrated with his parents when he was only three years of age. He came from the county Tyrone, a county rendered illustrious by the host of eminent men it has produced. Mr. Saift, though but a child when he left his native country, is still an incorruptible patriot, and a friend to his country and countrymen. Mr. Edward Rodgers, from the county Longford, is a gentleman who is every day shedding lustre on the land of his nativity. He and his brother Patrick, another irreproachable character, are extensive business men. They are justly considered men of strict integrity, and every confidence is placed in them. Oh Longford, what a multitude of such men you have produced! Mr. Patrick Daly, from the county West Meath; this is another gentleman who is worthy of applause for his social habits and affections. Mr. James Brady, from the parish of Killroan, county Ross-common; married in that county in 1827, and has been these last twenty-six years in West Troy, in the State of New York. I have already spoken of Mr. Brady in the highest terms that my cloudy and defective abilities would permit, yet they are inadequate to his worth, as no panegyric, be it of the most exalted character, could be too extravagant respecting his applause. Mr. Brady's fame should be sounded weekly, monthly, and yearly in consequence of his virtue, generosity, and admirable cleverness, and he stands next in patriotism and goodness to the inimitable Mr. Cornelius Dever, whom I have styled the Achilles of my countrymen in America, and who is now a citizen of Brooklyn city, in the State of New York. I hope I will do more justice to Mr. James Brady in my forthcoming poetic history.

This worthy man, from Erin's ancient shore
Has been as kind as he had been before,—
When now,* I meet him in his favorite Troy,
He has received me with amazing joy;
Although he's wealthy, and has much in store,
May God consent to make his riches more.
O'DONOVAN.

I have no doubt but the Messrs. Rodgers, of whom I have spoken, are also residents of West Troy. Captain B. Griffin, from the wealthy and far-famed county Limerick; this gallant son of the immortal Emerald Isle is captain of the Montgomery Guards, in Albany, and is considered a finished gentleman by all who have the pleasure of his acquaintance. Mr. Richard Bulger, from the county of Kilkenny, was a merchant tailor in Albany; the eulogy that befits any good and great man befits Mr. Bulger, and his external appearance, in the eyes of any keen physiognomist, will

---

* 1854.

prove him to be a man of no ordinary firmness or magnitude; his words are few and well-directed, and he is none of those hypocritical creatures whose friendship is located on the extremity of their tongues, without any possibility of a nearer proximity to the heart; whatever he promises he is prompt in the fulfilment of it; and the solid thoughtfulness, and serenity of his countenance, evidently show his fidelity; he loves the land of his nativity, and every genuine son of the Emerald Isle. Mr. John Higgins, a lawyer of distinguished abilities, from the philanthropic county of Cavan; perhaps a more genuine son of the Isle of Saints never crossed the Atlantic, than Mr. Higgins; this gentleman has been of infinite service to his countrymen in his professional career; he is a consummate lawyer, an unchangeable democrat, an invulnerable patriot, and an indisputable Irishman. Mr. Higgins gave me a note of introduction to Mr. James Brady, of West Troy, of whom I have already spoken. Messrs. Patrick and Anthony McQuade, I think, are brothers, and natives of the parish of Tempo, county Farmanagh. These gentleman have been for a long time citizens of Albany, and during their stay in that city nothing can be said, even by the foul breath of calumny, to stain their characters. They became wealthy by persevering industry; they deservedly bear the name of honest, pious, and charitable men, and are much valued by their respective friends and the community at large. I got an introductory letter from one of these brothers to another brother living in Utica city, State of New York, who had been, previously to my arrival in that city, mayor of it; and I honestly aver that he received me with approbation and applause. Mr. Francis McQuade, corner of Swan and Lumber streets, is a native of the immortal county Tyrone. Mr. McQuade is a gentleman of no vulgar magnitude or calibre; a more gentlemanly man cannot easily be found in Albany city than he is; he is saturated with unsullied friendship, which is hereditary in every genuine Irishman, and all his social affections, habits, and intercourse, are much admired, esteemed, and appreciated; his wife is a lady of immovable virtue, and is handsome, amiable, and courteous.

Mr. Molowny, professor in St. Mary's literary department. Teachers, generally speaking, are possessed of some noble aspirations inaccessible to vulgar minds, and this inheritance they display on every occasion. Education would refine and elevate the most uncultivated boor, and dispel the sediments of ignorance located on his brain. Mr. Maloney, with his assiduity, perseverance, and ability, often performed this miracle. All men would be boors in the absence of education. Mr. Walsh, an extensive grocer; Mr. Walsh is indisputably an Irishman in shape, size, and principle; he is well known, esteemed, and venerated, and his absence from Albany would be felt and very much regretted. Mr. O'Connell, another of the imperishable Milesian race, is a democrat, an Irishman, and a gentleman. Mr. Doyle; this gentleman is another of the Milesian chieftains, and a native of Archstoven, county Meath, and keeps an intelligence office in the city; his very appearance commands respect, as in his countenance are legibly written—fortitude, faith, and fidelity. Mr. Wallace; this gentleman keeps a very extraordinary and extensive grocery in Albany, and it is no digression from either truth or justice, to style him a perfect gentleman; he is an honor to his native country, and a credit and acquisition to the land of his adoption. Mr. Thomas Murry, Green Bush; this gentleman, to whom I had been introduced by my friend Mr. Murry, lives opposite Albany city, at the other side of the river, and as a true and noble countrymen of mine, he strenuously exerted himself to facilitate the object in view, though but partially succeeded. Mr. Murray is a star of considerable magnitude among his countrymen. Mr. Thomas McCarthy, professor in St. Joseph's Church; this gentleman is a branch of the illustrious McCarthy family, and like the general run of professors in that city; he is an honor to his native country, profession, and creed. Mr. John Ewers, Athlone, West Meath, emigrated thirteen years since, and has demeaned himself with distinguished correctness, continued success, and persevering industry, since he landed in America. Mr. Read, State street; this is an Irish gentleman, of a high order and unsullied reputation; also, if I am not mistaken, a wine and liquor merchant; his circumstances are easy and flattering, and his noble principle and social habits are admired and appreciated. Mr. Matthew McMahon, attorney and counsellor-at-law; Mr. McMahon is a native of the city or county of Limerick, and no man who had or has the pleasure of his acquaintance will say that I prevaricate when I pronounce him a perfect gentleman. Mr. McMahon stands high in his professional sphere; he is also a fine neighbor, a good citizen, an unflinching patriot, an incorruptible democrat, and is prompt in favor of his client, and in sustaining his case in the hour of extremity or litigation. In my forthcoming metrical history I mean to do him and others some justice. Mr. John McCormick, a native of the parish of Mullengar, county Meath, landed in this country eighteen years since, and married in Albany, and by the exact correctness of his social affections and habits, he has made himself known, honored, and respected. Mr. McAnally; I met this gentleman in my travels, perhaps in Albany, but wherever I met with him, I met with an Irishman, a profound patriot, and a gentleman.

Mr. Patrick Coyle, No. 86 Church street; Mr. Coyle is from the county Tyrone, and alike the rest of his countrymen sheds lustre on his native land, perhaps as much as any other in his sphere, his honesty and persevering industry, have detained him during 22 years in the far-famed Delevan House, Albany. Mr. O'Connell, wine and spirit merchant, William street, Albany; this is a magnificent branch of the Milesian family, and the very name he bears, entitles him to respect and veneration, and to the approbation of his countrymen, he is a distinguished gentlemen and could be nothing else. Mr. O'Connell has been eight years in this country, and the sweet county Cavan gave him birth, a county which gave birth to numberless philanthropists besides him. Mr. Thomas Keefney from the county Sligo; for the county Sligo gave birth to one of the greatest orators that ever gazed with an eagle's eye on the brilliancy of Sol—Counsellor Phillips,—Greece or Rome never produced his equal; he is a poet of a very high order, and his "Emerald Isle" is inimitably considered by competent judges, although he wrote it when young. Counsellor Phillips wrote for a long time for the Catholic cause in Ireland, sustaining it with the brilliancy of his talents against the cruel usurpation, infringements and inexpressible tyranny of the British Parliament, which induced the English by that incomparable craft and treachery for which they are notorious, to buy him over in order to silence his irresistible pen, and that they managed by giving him in marriage to a lady of an extraordinary and illimitable means, a fortune which had the desired effect,—that moment Phillips fell from the zenith of his glory, and sank in obscurity beneath a horizon so cloudy and so invisible, that it is impossible for him to emerge from his gloomy obscurity. The counsellor as well as Mr. Keefney, are natives of the county Sligo,—still they singularly differ in patriotism. Mr. P. Barrett corner of Canal and Cross streets; Mr. Barrett is another Irish gentleman, who bears an irreproachable name and an extensive fame; he maintains a clear conscience, peace of mind, and a sound judgment, a better man is unnecessary, and a better neighbor, or a better citizen is not in Albany. Mr. Coyl, 146 Arch street; Mr. Coyl is another Irish comet displaying Irish brilliancy, and no panegric can be too extravagant for his merits and worth. Mr. Bryce, counsellor at law; I shall not during my existence forget the interest this gentleman had taken to facilitate the object I had in view; in all my travels, I received very liberal encouragement from all members of the legal profession with whom I had the good fortune to meet. Mr. Bryce did every thing in his power to promote my interest, and my ingratitude is not of that magnitude that can make me ever forget it; there is another gentleman and a counsellor at law, in the office with him and perhaps in partnership, who aided faithfully in favor of my interest; he is considered a gentleman of admirable professionable abilities. Mr. Richard Brown, No. 5 Windle street; this gentleman is another Irish primary planet worthy of the most flattering encomiums, for he is a patriot, a democrat, and a prince, and no man is more deserving of applause than he. Mr. Cahill, 245 Green street, is another worthy countryman of mine, and a brilliant star of Irish confederation; he puts me in mind of one of the stars of the first magnitude, even in the milky way, displaying an admirable and unextinguished brilliancy. Mr. J. Carmady, north of Lumber street, west side; this gentleman paternally and maternally, is a Milesian; O happy combination,—is a scion of the persecuted sons of the Emerald Isle, yet incorruptible in his faith, unshaken in his resolution prompt in his promises, and immutable in the shrine of democracy.

Mr. H. O'Carroll, ah! my friend; this gentleman is so high in the scale of Milesian dignity that something alike Jacob's Ladder must be ascended to touch him. His principle is sterling and noble, his character is irreproachable, and his Milesian pedigree can be clearly demonstrated; he dwells in No. 700 Albany or New York. Mr. William D. O'Carroll, another distinguished branch of Milesian dynasty, that has secured a high position in society. Mr. O'Carroll lives in No. 113 Lumber street in the enjoyment of universal fame and approbation. Mr. Cashman, 157 Elm street; this gentleman has added a brilliant jewel to the uncancelled dignity and reputation of his countrymen; few men are more esteemed and perhaps none more worthy of estimation than he. Mr. Peter Cassady; this is another noble and invincible gentleman, that has shed lustre on the Evergreen Isle, the land of his birth. O! my country, in spite of oppression, injustice and heresy, what luminaries you have produced who were and are in the ranks of unblemished society! Mr. John Gannon, Canal and Chapel streets; this gentleman is indisputably inaccessible to the calumny of the most slanderous tongue; he is upright, prompt, persevering, industrious and patriotic; he loves his friends, forgives his foes, and is at peace with the world. Captain Cassidy; it is unnecessary for me to make any comment on the unsullied merits of Captain Cassidy, as it would require an abler pen than mine to speak correctly, or in adequate terms of this distinguished gentleman. Ireland, may be proud of such men, and Albany too, as he is an honor to its population. Mr. John Castigan, attorney and counsellor at law, residence 68 State street: Blackstone was not more successful in analyzing the intricate points of litigation than Mr. Castigan; his knowledge placed him on the very summit of his profession, and his suggestions and irresistible eloquence throws opposition in the shade, and gains victory for his client. Mr. Castigan should be consulted in all civil, criminal and critical cases. Mr. Thomas Kelly, Orange, Montgomery; this remark defies contradiction, and admits of no controversy, when I suggest that Mr. Kelley descended from noble ancestors, and a Milesian stock, his own cleverness proves the lustre and dignity of his originality; he loves the Emerald Isle that gave him birth, and the land of his adoption for its freedom. Mr. James Condon, 36 Orange; this gentleman anxiously awaits the restoration of peace to his native country. Mr. Condon has both the heart and feelings of a genuine Irishman, he loves liberty, admires honesty, and is a friend to every one in adversity. Mr. John Harrigan, Orange; this gentlemen is a noble specimen of an Irishman, he drifted like the rest of his countrymen from the unspeakable tyranny of English avarice, and awaits with patience the hour of revenge. May Providence give him strength and fortitude in the hour of extremity. Mr. James Allen, undertaker, No. 615 Broadway, Albany; Mr. Allen is the only benefactor or purchaser I met with in all my travels of his professional class; they seem to me to differ singularly and astonishingly in feeling and generosity from all other mechanics in this country. Their propensities are as dead, avarice excepted, as the dead by whom they live, and it appears to me that poetic harmony sounds harshly in their ears, and nothing can please them but orisons for the dead, but Mr. Allen is an honorable exception. Mr. John Lamb, Church and Cherry streets; this Lamb escaped the jaws of British vultures, and the claws of an insatiable Lion; he is an honor to the green Isle, the land of his nativity, and an acqusition to the land of his adoption.

Mr. Wasser, between Arch and Rensalaer street. Although Albany is blessed with men of good will and with noble societies, Mr. Wasser is indisputably a brilliant appendage to the whole. Mr. James Lamb. This is another Lamb, that suffered the same punishment as his namesake and predecessor; he emigrated to shun the insufferable tyranny of despotic strangers. Such men should be encouraged as they fearlessly and courageously fight for our constitutional rights, and maintain the elevation and necessity of the stars and stripes of the American Union. Mr. F. F. Kearney, 173 Montgomery street; Mr. Kearney, is another offspring of the Milesian race, and he shows, on all occasions, the nobleness of his origin. He is extensively known and highly appreciated for his indefatigable and honest perseverance, and rigid integrity. Such brave men as he should be encouraged, and such, with few exceptions, compose the population of Albany. Mr. Jeremiah O'Kelly, Broad and Arch streets. My opinion of that illustrious name has been signalized before, and this gentleman's universal fame added lustre to the dignity ond elevation of his ancestors. Mr. John F. Mahar, grocer, 196 Pearl street. O! my country, here is another of your comets, to whom you gave birth and to whom all praise is due, for his urbanity patriotism and social habits. Mr. James McNally, Arch street, Albany,—

The Irish were composed of Macks and O's,
Until polluted by egregious foes,
Who landed there, to set the Isle in flames,
And introduce a thousand other names.
Still, some unfaithful had been to the creed,
That was imported by this foreign breed.

Mr. Patrick Quinlan, St. James' Cemetery, Albany,—

Patrick!—
The very name, a christian should desire,
The very name that Irishmen admire.
He gave us faith, aloof from pride or leaven,
The only faith that leads a man to Heaven.

Mr. James McGovern; another of our noble Irishman, who is much beloved, respected, and admired. Mr. McGovern loves the world, and indisputably at that rate he loves his friends, he has no foes. Mr. Michael Doyle, Archerston, County Meath, keeps his office in No. 9 Howard street, opposite the Centre Market House, Albany. I have already spoken of this gentleman. Mr. James Weldon. It is admitted on all hands, that Mr.

Weldon, is a gentleman of an irreproachable character, and that based on immovable pillars. He is an honest man, a worthy citizen, and a kind neighbor. Here comes the last, though not the least, Mr. Joseph Clinton. This gentleman holds a high position in society, and who is much beloved, and deservedly so by all who had the honor of his acquaintance, his appearance entitles him to notice and consideration, and his principle to favor and affection. He is an honor to his native, an acquisition to his adopted country, a friend to the distressed, and a good provider for his family, more about him poetically.

Albany!
The Irish there, are worthy of applause,
They help to make and regulate the laws;
To what I say, exceptions may be few,
That all are moral, honest, faithful, true.
They love the Isle had given them their birth,
The greenest Isle that can be found on earth;
Though hard it be to split true love in two,
They love the land of their adoption too.
And that they'd prove, if foreign foes would dare,
With their adopted soil to interfere,—
No wound behind could be distinct or scar,
But all before, from the effects of war.
Albanians then, would prove the sons of Mars,
In the support of our adopted stars,—
They deadly spurn the oppressor's yoke,
A well adopted instrument to choke,—
A yoke intended to destroy their race,
And make a desert of their native place.

In consequence of the disappearance of the notes I had taken of my friends and countrymen in Albany, which accident will be made manifest in the sequel of my travels, I have omitted the names of many of them; but my intention is, God willing, to write my travels poetically, in which I can give a more glowing description of my countrymen, than I have given in my loose, irregularly indigested prose. In my poetic history all omissions will be accurately taken into consideration, and finally adjusted. Among the omissions in Albany is to be found the name of Mr. Hussey, a merchant tailor of fame and renown, and a worthy, meritorious gentleman. Farewell Albany!

I took my departure from Albany for East Troy, accompanied with all the introductory preliminaries I could accumulate among my friends in Albany, and although being in this city in 1848, the gentleman under whose friendly roof I had then taken shelter, had been in the interim called to happy eternity, viz.: Mr. Russell a Tipperary gentleman, of whom I have spoken in my first rambles with applause and approbation. This information had been made manifest to me before I left Albany, and according to instructions I took lodging in Mr. Cassady's house, East Troy, and found him to be an accommodating, friendly and worthy gentleman, and his lady in her own sphere was obliging, attentive and conveniently agreeable. One evening after returning from my perambulation, while conversing in the bar room with my host, a gentleman entered and called for a small glass of brandy and water to animate and refresh the system, and banish the drowsiness that sometimes hangs heavily on our humanity. After doing so Mr. Cassady showed him one of my books, and after passing some flattering encomiums on the poetical powers of the author, he turned himself around and asked me pensively did I ever get acquainted with a man of his name in my travels, and said he, "I have been these sixteen years in quest of some intelligence concerning his whereabouts, and never came to any positive information respecting him," and added to his inquiry in rather a melancholy manner, "I suppose he is dead." As soon as he made the inquiry, some internal manifestation caused an irresistible emotion in my bosom, which silently made me, as a physiognomist would, examine his countenance, to see could I discover therein originality or cousinship; after a pause I asked him the particular spot of the Emerald Isle whence he came, he said he came from the southwest extremity of the county Cork, and also mentioned the township in which he was born. My second inquiry was respecting his name, which he told me was Robert Gould; this information was sufficient, my cousin stood before me, a great distance from the scenes of my childhood, the thoughts brought confusion and sorrow to my mind, and it was with unspeakable struggles that I suppressed the elementary bubbles located in my eye. Oh! many a strange and hazardous revolution I encountered since I left him a child or a small boy in the land of his nativity. There I stood somewhat debilitated by declining age and deprived in a manner of my strength and agility, before my cousin, unknown and unseen by him for many a year. "Robert" said I, "I am that Jeremiah O'Donovan whom you have been inquiring after since you landed in America." As soon as he heard my declaration he rushed into my arms, and our emotions may be more easily conceived or imagined, than described. The landlord and others in the bar-room seemed to be much affected at our meeting after the expiration of many a year. When our emotions had subsided and nature resumed her original dignity and composure, home with him I should go, and there I remained during my stay in famous Troy, in the enjoyment of friendship and the best of accommodations and comfort, free of all expenses. Mr. Gould is married to the second wife, a lady of amiable qualities and great worth, who received me with unbounded joy and marked veneration.

Mr. Thomas M'Kenny from the county Tyrone, left it thirty-six years since, married in East Troy, and is a brother-in-law to Mr. Bulger of Albany. Mr. M'Kenny corroborated the testimonies previously circulated in his favor, as I found him a friend, an Irishman and a consummate gentleman. I paid Mr. M'Kenny the first visit conformably to the directions of Mr. Bulger. Mr. Thomas Davis, from the county Carlow; residence, No. 31 Museum Buildings. This young gentleman, I think, is unmarried and I make no hesitation in saying, nor fear no contradiction when I pronounce him a very brilliant and accomplished young gentleman. Mr. Davis treated me with peculiar respect and unspeakable friendship, for which, in my forthcoming poetic history of my travels, I intend on a larger scale, and in the most glowing terms to do him honour and justice. Mr. Davis keeps an extensive boot and shoe establishment in No. 397 River street, East Troy. Mr. Patrick O'Kelly, a native of the county West Meath, has been thirty years in this country. Mr. O'Kelly is an illustrious branch of the Milesian race, and well he identifies his claim to royalty, in principle, in practice, and in communion with his fellow-man. Mr. Daniel Lousey, otherwise Squire Lousey, I am happy to state that he is a countyman of mine, Cork, and was born not far from the scenes of my childhood. The inhabitants of Troy applaud him to a man, and universally appreciate his merits, and unquestionably deservedly so. Mr. James O'Reilly, grocer, Troy. This is another gentleman whose blood for its purification passed through a Milesian worm until its corruption, or the corruption peculiar to human nature became as pure as amber and free from all dregs and sediments. Mr. O'Reilly is worthy of unbounded applause. Mr. Magovern, grocer; this gentleman is a genuine Irishman in the strictest sense of the word, and an honor to the population of Troy. Mr. Magovern's appearance is a recommendatory letter to him wherever he goes, no honorable society would object to a man of his confirmation or symmetry, and his internal qualities exactly stand in the same ratio with his exterior dignity, more about him by and by. Mr. Murphy and son, brewers, East Troy, the terms I make use of respecting Mr. Murphy and son are irrefragible, and they are thus; I candidly say without committing any debauch on the responsibility of truth, that he is, as far as I can judge, an irreproachable character, a finished gentleman, an unchangeable patriot, a sound democrat, a constituted gentleman, and a genuine Irishman; his son though young, bids fair to rival the father in all laudable actions. He is a young man of fine appearance and great promise.

Mr. James McCaffery, from the county Monaghan, left home in 1842, and emigrated to America. Mr. McCaffery is a boot and shoemaker, mechanically considered, and no man could be more anxious for the restoration of freedom to his native country than he. Mr. McCaffery is a gentleman, possessing a sterling principle, and no condition in life, high or low, could contaminate his patriotism. Mr. Moley, a contractor; I never met a contractor in my travels but had been impregnated with a large share of liberality, and also of patriotism; contractors are generally men of large minds, fine feelings, and sound understanding, though very often those men are disturbed and made angry by a set of unmanageable customers who labor under their superintendence; contractors are generally great patriots and unflinching democrats. Mr. Dexter, born in Windham county, Vermont, married in Boston, October 7th, 1837, to a Miss Dix, a native of Vermont. I met with this gentleman in East Troy, and had been much pleased with his conversation and principle. Mr. Dexter seems to possess a great regard for my countrymen, and such of them as I heard speak of him did so in a very flattering manner. Mr. Dexter and my countrymen, in regard of friendship, stand in the same reciprocity of terms. Mr. Edward Murphy; I had an introductory note to this distinguished young gentleman from a friend in Albany, who described him in a glowing and satisfactory manner, and I must candidly aver, though lucid and brilliant the description, it did not overreach the mark. Mr. Murphy is a credit to all young men of the same maturity, an ornament to society, and an honor to the population of Troy. Mr. James Cavanan, from the parish of Killidan, county Mayo, emigrated nineteen years since from his native country, and now resides in No. 320 River Street, Troy. This gentleman is another star of the first magnitude that can never sink beneath the western horizon. Mr. Cavanan, every way you take him, is a genuine Irishman, and no man loves his native country better, still it does not lesson his love and devotion for the land of his adoption. Mr. Patrick Wilkinson, from the parish of Glenworth, county Cork; Mr. Wilkinson landed in this country twenty-one years ago, and brought one son, Patrick, who was then but two years old. Mr. Wilkinson has two daughters married in the same locality he resides. I am happy to be able to state that Mr. Wilkinson is a countyman of mine, and a more devoted man to his native country never left it, or never existed, for an egg was never more impregnated with matter than he with the pure and genuine friendship which is peculiar to his countymen. I got acquainted with some of his family, particularly with his son Patrick, and they all inherit the same propensities with the father. There is a terrific manufacturing establishment convenient to Mr. Wilkinson's house, wherein he works twenty-three days in two weeks which denotes his persevering industry. Mr. William Hall, from the noble and incomparable county Tyrone. Mr. Hall left his native soil when very young, nevertheless, Mr. Hall, like the rest of his countrymen is a true and incorruptible patriot, who laments the woes and afflictions of his countrymen with sorrow and dotestation. Mr. Curley; this gentleman is in the employment as book-keeper or cutter of Mr. Bulger, Albany. Mr. Curley honestly speaking is a genuine Irishman. Mr. Charles Grayham, of Castle Palace; This gentleman is another Hibernian comet, that sheds lustre on his native land, and also illuminates the Trojan multitudes, and the entire land of his adoption. Messrs Leonard and Dornett, extensive manufacturers of coaches and other vehicles, located at the corner of Seventh and Congress streets. Mr. Leonard has been sixteen years from his native country, got married in the land of freedom to a lady from the Emerald Isle, a native of the county Sligo. Throughout my travels it seldom fell to my lot to meet a more genuine or a more spirited Irishman than Mr. Leonard; he indefatigably exerted himself to facilitate the object I had in view. Mr. Leonard is affectionate, friendly, facetious, and conversable, and is also saturated with patriotism. Messrs. Leonard and Dornett are universally known and respected, and by their assiduity, thorough and comprehensive knowledge of mechanism, they have secured for themselves a tremendous patronage. Mr. William McCleland, from the county Kerry. This young gentleman now working in the establishment of Messrs. Leonard and Dornett, is from that part of the Emerald Isle which has been distinguished since time immemorial for producing some men of the brightest talents that had, and have been, not only of benefit to other parts of Ireland, for the disseminating of arts and sciences among them, but to all the world, as their prominent education invites them to every department of learning, both classical and mathematical, and which departments they ably fulfill. They are also famed for generosity, hospitality and poetry. Mr. John Galagher, from Fermoy, county Cork.

This county claims the brightest men on earth,
Cork they claim, and Cork that gave them birth;
Such we can claim till every thing is blue,
And we can claim good many blockheads too;
Still every whale as well as every shark,
Must grant applause to universal Cork.

Mr. McKernon, from the parish of Aughabaugh, left his native country twenty-four years ago, and has been ever since inhaling the balmy air of liberty.

Mr. McKernon is unquestionably a gentleman of a high order, who loves every thing that conduces to the welfare of his native country, as a true patriot should. May Mr. McKernon live to see the day that his native country will be exonerated from the grasp of unrelenting tyranny. Mr. Owen Clark, from the parish of Baliabero, county Caven; I met with many a gentleman of this name in my travels, and I never met with any that did not display an extraordinary share of patriotism, and I must say also, that I never met with a native of the county Cavan that had not been fully saturated with it. I am more indebted for their inexpressible kindness to those who emigrated from that county, than to the inhabitants of any other in the Emerald Isle. Mr. Clarke left his native country sixteen years ago, is a married man, and where I met him is a matter of conjecture. Mr. Philip McGovern, Correlehanbeg, county Cavan; here is another unsetting star, philanthropist, patriot, and democrat, and it is unnecessary to give an illustration of his ancestral royalty, as I gave it a thousand times before, and where we met is also matter of conjecture. Mr. Thomas O'Donovan, from the parish of Killinan, county Galway, two years from his Island of Saints. This gentleman is lineally and illustriously descended from the Milesians dynasty, he has been two years from the Saintly Isle, and during that time, he has resided in America, the land of his adoption. West Troy, in the western division of this city reside some very distinguished Irishmen. In this part is the residence of Mr. James Brady, of whom I have already spoken, and many more of worth and consequences.

The destruction of the notes I had taken of my friends in this section of the city mostly disappeared, whether through design or accident I am not able to establish positively. When leaving every city I tied in separate parcels the notes I had taken of all the Irish inhabitants with whom I had the opportunity of an interview, before I took my departure from said city, and for fear they should interfere with each other, this separation of the parcels I considered prudentially, and wanted only an opportunity to transfer them in a rough historical form, where they would remain indelibly for future improvement, or rather amendment, in their style of writing and diction. The notes I had taken, I generally carried in my travelling trunk until I arrived at Rochester, and there I transferred them to a huge case, together with my books, to be forwarded to Buffalo. Whatever hands attended the loading of the boats, they had broken the case that contained them, and when I arrived at Buffalo the notes that did not disappear altogether, were in one promiscuous heap at the bottom of the case, which gave me indescribable chagrin. It is by this catastrophe, and the commingling of the notes, that the notes that are the property of one city, are inserted in that of another. However, in the forthcoming poetical history of my travels, all omissions will be adjusted with considerable deliberation and accuracy. My first visit I paid to Mr. Keane an extensive manufacturer and cooper in West Troy, and found him to be an honorable Trojan and a gentleman in all his transactions. Mr. Keane is considered an honorable and genuine Hibernian, and worthy of the most exalted praise. Mr. Murry, grocer, West Troy; this gentleman is a grocer of considerable means, and his strict integrity together with his assiduity to business secured to himself an astounding patronage. What a great loss such a man as Mr. Murry is to his native land, and what an acquisition to the land of his adoption! Messrs. M'Clarren and Donnelly, two honest relatives of an honest and learned profession, who are noble and generous, incomparable in rebutting testimonies, acute in the examination of witnesses, lucid, clear and convincing in debate, true and honest to their clients. Ah! to such men, or to such lawyers, an application should be made, by those who fall into difficulties and dangers, as they can exonerate them from the meshes of rascality and the intriguing sophistry of the law. Messrs. Edward and Patrick Rodgers, West Troy; whether these are the gentlemen I have already spoken of, or not, I am not candidly able to decide; this is owing to the confusion of the notes I have already established; but I am of opinion they are different parties; these two brothers are rich and respectable and hold a high position in society. Although they are among the most industrious and persevering of the inhabitants of West Troy, I went into the residence of one of these brothers which was richly furnished, and indisputably adjusted in the neatest possible manner, and in addition to the unspeakable arrangement of the furniture, the graceful and beautiful appearance of Mrs. Rodgers completed the exhibition. Mr. Patrick Rodgers; here is another gentleman of the name, and it is probable I met with him in West Troy; wherever I met with him I found him to be a consummate gentleman, and indeed I must say that every man of the name with whom I met throughout my travels was of a superior grade, and possessed an uncommon degree of generosity. I have mostly omitted saying anything respecting the ladies; but in the poetical history of my travels I will speak of them in the most brilliant and glowing terms I can command.

Mr. Clarke, druggist. — Druggists, generally speaking, are a class of men of fine taste, solid education, refined manners, and invariably democratic, who would relieve, if possible, the woes and afflictions of an oppressed nation. Mr. Clarke is one of this class, that would lend his aid and deliberation in its accomplishment. Mr. Golden.— This is another of my countrymen who is a double distilled genuine olive branch, fully saturated with patriotism and democracy. Oh, you unhappy Lord John Russell! Oh, you improvident vulture! Oh, you accursed, unmerciful, and unrelenting tyrant, who strenuously helped to enact laws to banish such men from the land of their nativity, and who suffered such of those who remained behind to perish from hunger, starvation, and pestilence! No wonder the Queen's rank should be attenuated and incapable of resistance. Mr. Patrick Day.—To describe this gentleman according to his merits and worth would require a lucid, clear, and forcible pen, or a brain free from sediment or ignorance, as I consider him an honor to the land of his nativity, an acquisition to society, and an unflinching adherent to our glorious institutions. I think I have the honor of this gentleman being a countyman of mine, and if so, I swell in my own estimation, and also in the estimation of others who are acquainted with the fact.

Mr. P. O'Kelly, a Milesian chieftain.—

The Macks have suffered, and the mighty oo's
From the spleen of their offending foes.
A stranger's brand, a blemish and disgrace,
To every man of all the human race.
Yet made the Irish more than all to bleed,
For nothing else than for their holy creed.
Ah! Satan's throne must surely get a fall,
'Tis built on sand and has no solid wall,
Alas! alas! this counterfeiting stall.

O'DONOVAN.

Mr. Henry Bingham, a Milesian chieftain.—No eulogy pronounced favorably to this gentleman could diverge from truth or fidelity, or overreach his worth. Such is due to thousands of the Irish inhabitants of West Troy. Mr. Martin O'Gorman MacSavin.—This gentleman adds another refulgent star to the brilliancy of West Troy:

This man, renowned for honor and for fame,
Left his own Isle and to this country came;
Though hard to rive each strong endearing tie
That held him fast, he was compelled to fly—
And safe across the vast Atlantic sea,
To seek a balm for all his misery.
His vast estates the vultures now possess,
Ah! time, I hope, will make him a redress!

O'DONOVAN.

Mr. John Sedly, from the famous county Longford.—It is unnecessary to multiply words to sketch this gentleman's character and merits, as they are well known and appreciated, and well supported by the approbation and applause of all his friends and acquaintances. Mr. Sedly has been fifteen years from home, and married in South Troy. Mr. Patrick O'Reagan, supervisor.—Mr. O'Reagan is another illustrious branch of the Milesian race, and has ascended in the scale of Milesian dignity by the indisputed distinction of his progenitors. Many bright stars of the first magnitude illuminate West Troy, which have arisen in the Emerald Isle.

The Isle that nature with much beauty paints,
The gem that was and is the Isle of Saints.

Mr. Gleeson, South Troy. Many perhaps would doubt that Mr. Gleeson is not lineally descended in a direct line from Milesius the fifth adventurer that inhabited Ireland, and that he is not entitled to an O' the emblem of eternity and distinction, but, I fearlessly say that he is, and for that reason, I annex it by way of distinction, as a memorial appendage to his name. Mr. William Gleeson, left home on the 22nd of May, 1837; married in Troy, February 2nd 1842, and is now a resident of West Troy. Mr. Curry; this young gentleman is book-keeper to Mr. James Brady, in West Troy, of whom I have already spoken; he is a young man of promise, and deservedly loved and respected.

Mr. Hugh McCully, County Louth,—

This comet gives a bright and brilliant blaze,
Makes Erin's sons with much attention gaze
Upon the man who often leads the van,—
And shapes his course to organize a plan,
To free his country from ignoble toil,
And drive the tyrants from his native soil,
He is loved by all, who love a patriot's will,
Though long from home he is a patriot still.

Mr. Crowley, sadler. This gentleman should have

the annexation too, but as he forgets his privilege, and dignityby omitting the O', I am not to blame for omitting it also, although Mr. Crowley, is justly and honorably entitled to its annexation.

Mr. George O'Sullivan, from Limerick City,—

This is a place of an unbounded sway,
That kept the Dutchman and his troops at bay,
A-near this place, brave Sarsfield scourd the plain,
And gazed with pity on the heaps of slain,—
Though being his foes, and weltering in their gore,
He prayed for them he never saw before
While William pour'd against the wall his lead
Till he considered every man was dead;
Still being determined to prolong the siege,
But no admittance for a German Liege,
They cried within, "Approach us if you dare;
Our wives are ready now to interfere,—
And with assurance, we as thus can tell,
If we will fall, our wives can fight as well."
This made the Dutchman to withdraw his force,
Retire at once, and take another course.

Mr. Crumm, from the parish of Dromgoon, County Cavan, nineteen years from his native country. In this gentleman, I discovered more earnest assiduity towards the promotion of my cause, than in many with whom I met in my travels. The preliminaries which I had carefully taken of Mr. Crumm, disappeared, and I have nothing to help or animate a hebetated memory, but the recollection of his friendship. Mr. Crumm kept a grocery in East Troy, and also a victualing shop, and to both public professions, he attended indefatigably, and in consequence of being a warm hearted Irishman and generous to a fault, he secured to himself unlimited custom. A man more liberal is not in existence, and as respecting patriotism and democracy, he stands unsurpassed, and in the poetic history of my travels, I will endeavor to do Mr. Crumm, something like justice.

Before I bid adieu to the noble and illustrious Trojans, I have a few words to say concerning a distinguished theologian and writer, with whom I had the honor of an acquaintance in my cousin's house in East Troy—I mean the Rev. Mr. Quigley. He is known to the literary world as a writer of a very high order, and many that would wish to compete with him as such are in dread of the force of his irresistible pen, and from a prudential consideration shrink from competition. A Protestant divine had the temerity to attack Catholicity, or, as he had the audacity to say, its enormities; but the Rev. Mr. Quigley opened his demolishing battery on this Protestant divine, and his irrefragible and convincing arguments made him pull in his horns the same as a creeping snail in one of the dew-bespangled meads of the Emerald Isle would from an electric touch. The Rev. Mr. Quigley officiated as a Catholic clergyman in Lansingburg, in the year 1855. After leaving Troy I directed my course to Waterford, a small town in Saratoga county, State of New York, not many miles distant from Troy. On entering this town I felt an original settled melancholy agitating me, which clung tenaciously to my mind and r ollection since I left my native country. The cause is as follows: Waterford quay was the last spot of the Emerald Isle, on which I stood when departing from the Elysian scenes of my dear Erin, and looking back since that date when youth and agility kept my feet in their proper directions, and taking a retrospective view of my meanderings and rambles since, through the wilds of America, my sensation may be easily conceived. However, after some ineffectual struggle to stifle those fond recollections, I proceeded to business, and having an introductory note to Mr. Thomas Preston, a long and respected resident of Waterford, who emigrated from the parish of Rathkall, county Limerick, in 1836. On presenting my introductory document to Mr. Preston, and after looking over its contents with avidity he received me with marked attention and respect, and immediately prepared himself to promote strenuously, and to my advantage, the object I had under consideration, by disseminating my works among the inhabitants of Waterford; and for his exertions I acknowledge I owe a debt of gratitude, for which I will make him honorable amends when the first opportunity favorably presents itself. Mr. Matthew Sheridan, a Cavan gentleman. Mr. Sheridan has been, I believe, a resident of Waterford for some time, and is universally liked there and elsewhere. Mr. Sheridan, although national, is a friend to every person in the hour of extremity; no matter what country or clime he came from, his reception will be agreeable to his condition if he happen to become acquainted with him; he is unmarried. Mr. Thomas Howley, from the parish of Kildee, county Limerick, has been living in Waterford fourteen years. Mr. Howley is much distinguished in Waterford and in all parts for his worth, that is wherever he is known, and his intercourse and social habits are deservedly appreciated; he is a patriot, a democrat, a philanthropist, an Irishman, and a gentleman. Mr. Howley loves well the land of his nativity, and unmistakably regards the laws and institutions of the land of his adoption. Mr. Daniel Murry, from the parish of Cilashee, county Longford, emigrated in the year 1829, then in the sixteenth year of his age. Mr. Murry is one of those unsullied characters whose merits are known and estimated in the scale of nicety and distinction, and found to be of favorable worth; his high position in society entitles him to the remuneration of the community at large; he lives happy and comfortably and his means are no way straitened.

Mr. Daniel O'Driscoll, from Capaquin, county Waterford, arrived in this country in 1829, married at home, and has been a resident of the town of Waterford mostly since his emigration had taken place. Alas! how the abominable enactments and the corruptible legislation of a corrupted parliament scattered the chiefs and chieftains of the Milesian race, without thinking of making the slightest atonement, or manifesting the least symtoms of compunction for the enormity of the woes and afflictions they enjoined on them. However, the natives of the Emerald Isle thrive and prosper under any government, civilized or savage, that is established on this habitable globe, but to thrive or prosper under the iniquitous and heretical government of England is incontestably impossible. Mr. O'Driscoll is in easy circumstances, and no way circumscribed by pecuniary embarrassments. Mr. John Duffee is a resident of Waterford, and of much advantage to the place, as his industry and perseverance demand the highest applause, and neither adversity nor prosperity could make him alter his course or change his habits. Mr. Duffee's principle is noble and straightforward, and where ever he is known he is respected. Mr. John O'Driscoll is another Milesian chieftain, and worthy of the same applause and veneration that a man of worth deserves. I believe all the principal men in Waterford are coopers, who carry on the business extensively. Mr. McKean another Irish gentleman, who shines constantly in the asterisk of Irish brilliancy in Waterford. Mr. McKean is an honest neighbor, a sound democrat, a steadfast patriot and indisputably an Irishman. May God bless him and the like. Mr. Patrick O'Kelly, another branch of the Milesian and illustrious Irish, and also a resident of the quiet town of Waterford. I spoke already in the history of my travels in 1848, of Mrs. O'Kelly, and of her amiable daughters in the most glowing terms I could command, as I much prized the amiable qualities and friendship of Mrs. O'Kelly, and also the appearance, manners and politeness of her daughters. I called the second time in 1855, and found them as usual. I have made a slight mistake in my route, which I mean to rectify on leaving Troy. I stopped in a small town situated mid way between Troy and Waterford, which turned out to be an abortion. Still I was perfectly satisfied in doing so, as the Rev. Mr. Quigly, of whom I have already spoken, was located there as a Catholic clergymen, and stopping there gave me both the pleasure and honor of an interview with this distinguished theologian and writer within the limits of his own residence. As was natural, I asked his approbation of my metrical history of Ireland, and the Reverend gentleman answered as thus. "My friend and countryman," said the Reverend gentleman, "I am much pleased with your productions, the preface to your Irish history, excepted, and if you took a little more care of what you were doing, your works would indisputably immortalize you, and your name and fame would be handed down to posterity, as a poet of a very high order." This encomium was highly satisfactory, as it fell from the lips of a most celebrated and distinguished writer, who is the same as all other priests, the deadly foe of pernicious flattery, and I would sooner have the approbation of one distinguished writer, than if a thousand asses were braying its praise and commending it to posterity. I effected no sale in Lansingburg but one, and I soon ceased my assiduity as I saw at once the improbability of effecting another. This sale I effected in the wine and liquor store of Mr. Patrick Fitzgerald, from Ballymahan, county Longford, a gentleman of mind, means, and principle, all of a high order. I like the name, as no other imported name suffered more for the cause of Ireland than the name of Fitzgerald, and the only hereditary duke we can mention regarding the nation is Fitzgerald, the Duke of Leinster; all the rest are created titles conferred on some shoe blacks that followed the fortunes of Elizabeth of blessed memory, or others who signalized themselves for having committed atrocious crimes, or by murdering some helpless women and children, or emboweling some religious priest, while in the service of honest Bess, or while following the adventures of Cromwell. In a solemn breath I poured out my benediction on the inhabitants of New Waterford, on the Jew and on the Gentile, and then departed for the Cohoes, which brought me again in proximity with Troy.

Mid way between Waterford and the Cohoes are the great Falls bearing the appellation of the Cohoe Falls, one of the grandest exhibitions the human eye can contemplate. It cannot be called a cataract as the fall is not perpendicular enough to be so considered, but its longitudinal declination and the rapidity of the water flowing with such ecstacy, makes the scene admirably grand, and its beauties inaccessible to vulgar description. This sublime scene should be reserved for poetic fancy and poetic sublimity. The Cohoes is a small town; still there are some choice spirits from my country living there; when I arrived I paid the first visit to Mr. Henry Lyons, a county Leithrim gentleman, a noble and generous minded man, and a philanthropist, a patriot, and democrat. Mr. Lyons became a benefactor at once, and readily offered his assistance to facilitate the sale of my works in the town. This kindness I am not ungrateful enough to forget, and shall think of Mr. Lyons in the poetical history of my travels. Miss Fitzgerald; the conversation and expressions of this young lady certify the brilliancy of her talents, and her high accomplishments. Miss Fitzgerald lives unknown to pride, pomposity, and supercilious airs, which disgusting fog is the atmosphere of many of her sex; her disposition is exceedingly calm, even mellow, and well tempered; more about her by and by. Mr. McAfee, here is an unflinching patriot, and after patriotism comes democracy, unadulterated and undefiled. Mr. McAfee is indisputably a gentleman in appearance, conversation, habits, and manners, and the most obtuse physiognomist, after an hours interview with the gentleman, would second my approbation. Such a man is an honor to the community at large, and particularly to the inhabitants of the Cohoes. Mr. Atchison, another distinguished inhabitant of the town of Cohoes. Mr. Atchison is deservedly honored for his strict integrity, social habits, and calm moderation, such men living in a small town will soon establish and also circulate its fame and raise its population to distinction. Mr. Scally is another unblemished Hibernian, and no man could be in his sphere more respected and valued than he, or more admired for his unsullied principle, practice and persevering industry. Mr. Hugh McAfee, from Rathoath, county Meath,. emigrated to America twenty years since, married in Cohoesville, and is a resident of the place ever since. I have perhaps spoken already of this gentleman, and if not, he is indisputably entitled to the same respect, applause, and approbation of his namesake and predecessor. I got in the cars in the Cohoes, and after a short space of time found myself again in East Troy, and after emerging from the subterraneous abode, if I may be allowed the expression, I occupied in the belly of my Pegasus, I proceeded immediately to my cousin's residence, where I rested for a few days, conversing with my cousin on the beauties and miseries of the Emerald Isle, the land of our nativity, and still consoling ourselves while illustrating on the grandeur and royalty of our ancestors.

After a few days, rest at Mr. Gould's residence, I took my seat in the cars for Saratoga Springs, the celebrated rendezvous of all persons, rich and poor, for the preservation as well as the restoration of impaired health and debilitated constitutions, as the water of these springs is considered an infallible cure for a thousand diseases which are entirely beyond the reach and skill of the most eminent physicians, and found myself after the expiration of a few hours at the Springs, and although I arrived there rather early in the season, a great many had been already collected to try the medicinal virtues and efficacy of these celebrated Springs, and also for securing for themselves proper and convenient accommodations for the season. When I started for the Springs, I had two introductory letters for presentation to two distinguished Irishmen, residents of this celebrated spot, which I got from my cousin, which indisputably proved to facilitate the sale of my productions, and establish myself or reputation as an honest man among the inhabitants of the place. The letters conclusively showed that I was the author, which many doubted in my travels to whom I presented them. This removed the ambiguity from the minds of illiterate men who generally judge abilities by bombastic terms and butterfly dress, and very frequently know or think they know the obscurity or brilliancy of your brain by the hat you wear. My cousin being extensively known and deservedly valued in that section of the State, cancelled all diffidence respecting the like, although all my countrymen residing in Saratoga with whom I met or had an interview, are men of a high grade and brilliant capacity. One of these two distinguished gentlemen to whom my document directed me, was Mr. Simon Flanigan, born at Daily Hill, Conamara, county Galway, emigrated to this country May 10th, 1840, and resides at the renowned Springs at present at the age of forty-three. He is also emigrant and ship agent to the famous ship establishment of Williams and Guion, No. 40 Fulton Street, New York. Mr. Flanigan sells drafts at sight on England, Ireland, and Scotland, without discount, which are readily accepted in all the solvent and impregnable banks in the three kingdoms. Now let me express my own opinion and approbation of Mr. Flanigan, as an opportunity has offered that I can do so without committing a debauch on my conscience or consideration. I stopped at the house of my friend and countryman during my stay at the celebrated Springs, and I honestly aver that a cleverer man is hard to be found, or if such a man exists that his cleverness is unnecessary and uncalled for to be of service to humanity. Mr. Flanigan is married to the second wife, an amiable lady, who sits now in the midst of all the necessaries of life that could render her comfortable or useful, not surrounded with unnecessary extravagance or luxury, which only tend to destroy the appetite and debilitate the constitution. The other gentlemen to whom I had been favorably represented in the introductory letter of which I have already spoken, is another Mr. Flanigan, and a countyman of my own, and an excellent yoke-fellow for his namesake and predecessor, and no panegyric could be uttered in his favor, would overreach the honor and established reputation of Mr. Flanigan. Mr. Hugh McComes, born in the parish of Lavy, in the sweet county Cavan, and has resided in Saratoga these five years past; he is yet enjoying the mist and mysteries of a single life. This gentleman and patriot is from the county Cavan, a county that has produced legions of brave men and fine women. My dear reader, let it be remembered that I hardly ever met with a Cavan gentleman, but possessed the genuine principle of an Irishman at home and abroad, he has shed lustre on the land of his nativity. Mr. William Hector, from Purtumnah, county Galway, emigrated with his parents when six months old. Left home May 16th, 1833, which leaves him twenty-one years old, and with a privilege of self-government. Mr. Hector is a good scholar and a fine pensman.

The brave bold Hector who defended Troy,
Which warlike Grecians labor'd to destroy ;
In the attempt, he had resign'd his life,
And Hector fell in an unequal strife :
Another lives to vindicate his fame,
And keep unsulli'd fated Hector's name;
What clime produc'd him? Erin's sacred soil.
Though forc'd to fly from tyranny and toil,
He now resides at Saratoga Springs,
Beyond the reach of tyranny and Kings.

Mr. Patrick Cogan, born in the town of Aughlin, Castle Roghan; and has been residing in those parts seven years, at the Springs.

This man indeed, has never sold his creed,
Nor is accountable for such a deed;
His holy creed, and such a creed as this,
Must be the source of everlasting bliss.
His Church is built upon a solid base,
With truth and virtue chis'ld on her face,
As the Church is built impregnably so,
She is at variance with the wicked foe,
By whose allurements ceaseless sinners stray,
Who after death, will go the broader way.

Mr. McDonough, in Mr. Mitchel's grocery; here is a young man who promises fairly to hold a high position in society. He is a young gentleman of very happy and steady habits, strict honesty, and unceasing industry, and is deservedly respected for all his qualities and qualifications. Mr. James O'Daily, from Drounsnee, county Leitrim, now at the Springs.

O'Daily is a great Milesian name,
In ancient days, he held a vast estate,
Till Godless tyrants came, and to their shame,
Had left them nothing, such had been his fate;
But, now I prophesy the day will come,
When they'll repay the interest and sum.

Mr. Lawrence Dolan, from the Parish of Aughade, county Down. If misfortune, bad management or revolutionary circumstances would strip him of all other effects; still nothing could rob him of his natural inheritance, the genuine principle of an Irishman. Mr. Dolan is altogether a finished gentleman. Messrs. John and Charles McColgan, Gay street, Saratoga Springs; my dear reader, this is a name with which I met in various parts of my travels; and justice compels me to acknowledge that there is something inseparably connected with it. I met a family of this name in Baltimore, who is among the wealthiest in the city, and this family is also remarkable for patriotism, liberality, charity and religious proclivities.

One of the family is the Lord's anointed, and is distinguished for his piety and all other stainless virtues, pertaining to an ecclesiastical life. I met with some of the name in the city of Brooklyn, in New York and elsewhere, as well as at the Springs, and I discovered in one and in all some elementary principle of a very high order, and of a superior quality; and I mean in my forthcoming poetic history, to do the name as much justice as the obscurity of my abilities will allow,

When at Saratoga Springs my countrymen and friends pressingly advised me to pay a visit to Chancellor Walworth, who has a summer residence there of his own, where he remains during the summer months for the benefit and preservation of his health. I made strong objections against paying a visit to so distinguished and exalted a gentleman in society, as Chancellor Walworth, as I considered the cultivation of his mind, the brilliancy of his talents, and the superiority of his judgment would cancel his liberality from becoming a benefactor to my grovelling and sterile production; and whereas, Homer, the king of poets, has been deservedly censured for the imperfections of his composition, by the eagle eye of criticism, why not the poetic works of a man of my obscurity receive condemnation, who never wrote in his life time in neither prose nor rhyme in the English language but a few fugitive sentences until my abilities were on the decline, except all the love-letters I had written, and those generally dictated by the lunacy of the strongest affection which would only charm the ear of those who were equally affected. From my youth up to the time I took my departure for America, I composed in my own native tongue with some ease and facility, for the Irish language is more expressive, charming, and soothing, than any other language spoken at the present day. Nevertheless, I yielded to the entreaties of my friends, and paid a visit to the Chancellor;

and another consideration that induced me to do so is made manifest in the following explanatory sentence. I was under the impression that Chancellor Walworth was a Catholic, as knowing his son, who is known throughout Christendom, for his piety, orations, theology, and immaculate virtues, to be a convert to the Catholic Church. Although having the most flattering prospects before him that could attach him to the world, he forsook them all to magnify and participate in the sufferings of his crucified Lord, and is now not only a member, but also a distinguished priest officiating in that Church that has for nineteen centuries successfully withstood, with unspeakable magnanimity, the furious hostility of Satan and his followers. Sure enough I went accompanied with some timidity to the residence of the Chancellor, whom I met outside; and being something of a physiognomist, his humility at once struck me with surprise and veneration; and the habits of this great man would be a useful lesson for arrogant fops to study, who arrogate to themselves haughty supercilious airs and lofty pretensions, without having the cultivation or necessary achievements to support such terrific demonstrations as they display.

After making use of some courteous terms to the Chancellor, I presented him with the poetic history of Ireland, which he hurriedly opened, and the first couplet that came under his inspection made him shake his head and bitterly exclaim as thus: "Ah! my friend, your countrymen have suffered." This exclamation evidently shows how much this great man sympathized with my countrymen for their servitude and subjection. But, my dear reader, I was entirely mistaken respecting the religious belief of Chancellor Walworth, as he is not a Catholic, for he sticks as fast and as tight to Protestanism as Prometheus did to the mountain, yet his lady and children are good Catholics, and it is to be hoped that the Chancellor will be one too, and may God through his infinite goodness and mercy convert him from the errors of his ways, and make him a member of the one Holy Catholic and Apostolic Church, out of which there is no salvation. I departed from Saratoga Springs in the cars for Utica, and on my route I formed an acquaintance with a gentleman who told me there was a Catholic settlement within one or two miles of the next station that would encourage my literary production, so said he. He also strenuously maintained they were all original Irishmen or their offsprings; to fail in the enterprise would be impossible. This address had been so oleaginous and kind, caused me to comply with his disinterested advice, as such, I considered it to be.

At the station I got out of the cars, and proceeded according to his directions to explore this Catholic settlement, and in my route I made considerable inquiry respecting the locality, but could get no information that could make me believe that my informant had been saturated with integrity or candid in his admonition. Prudence cautioned me to retrace my steps, and while doing so, I observed a number of ladies conveniently seated close to a beautiful country residence, without one of the opposite sex to beautify and bespangle the combination of the young and old ladies that had been collected together. I approached the rendezvous with timid steps and manifest humility, touched a consumptive hat I wore, and lowly and submissively in a reverential position bade the ladies good morning. The ladies offered in the most graceful and respectful terms the same salutation. At this moment I felt exceedingly dry, which compelled me to ask a respectable matron for a glass of water to slake my thirst, to which she acquiesced without the slightest appearance of reluctance, and I must acknowledge I drank the necessary beverage with avidity. The lady asked me would I take another, and then like the conquered Yankee, I cried enough. After a momentary pause, the clouds lowered frowningly, which we considered an indication of an approaching shower, and as soon as such a revolution in the atmosphere was observed, we shifted our quarters to avoid a disagreeable drenching. When seated inside, then a lady, perhaps the Mrs. of the tenement, asked me if I had any connection with those two young men who preached the Gospel lately in our vicinity. I answered her inquiries negatively, and then asked her which of the innumerable sects now extant they supported in their doctrine. She answered none of them; they preach a new doctrine altogether. She then asked me, did I decidedly fix my mind on any religious belief to obtain salvation? I told the lady that I was something of a latitudinarian respecting religion, and for that reason made no particular decision, neither could I, with safety to my own salvation, make choice of any among the modern sects which are as thick in number at present throughout the land as stars in the firmament. "Well," said the lady, "it is true you should look out for your future happiness, and these gentlemen who preach at present in this neighborhood would be very glad to meet a man of your undecided notions respecting your religious belief, and added, if you stay here this night, you will have an opportunity of hearing them, and we will use you as well as we know how. "Madam," said I, "your kind invitatation I appreciate, and confident I am that the entertainment would be brilliant and sumptuous, and your attention unsurpassed, still it would be useless for me to delay, as their preaching could make no alteration on my mind, or alter my determination; for Madam," said I, "it does not require any great stretch of imagination or metaphysical disquisition to show forth the absurdity of their undertaking, for common reason would dictate that the unerring ways of Providence after the lapse of nineteen centuries, have only been revealed to those young men who very probably left some country school house vacant, or who are for selling their carpet bags which had been in use by them, for the purpose of peddling essence. It would therefore be of no use for me to stay for the special purpose of hearing them preach, as their preaching would not avail as touching myself; they are nineteen conturies too late, and therefore can be nothing else but counterfeiters." At this moment, an outlandish looking gentleman issued from an adjoining apartment in his stocking-feet, and with a bare head, uttered the following inquiries, which I knew had been hypostatically intended. "My friend," said the intruder, looking sternly at myself, "what brought you here, and who are you?" I answered him, without embarrassment or hesitation, as follows:

An honest man, and something of a sage,
Annoy'd by women and declining age.
O'DONOVAN.

I made use of the noun in the plural number for fear I should implicate the lady who had been speaking to me, as I suspected she was his wife, and if so, may God help her, as she paid too much for her whistle. The gentleman who made his appearance asked the lady gruffly, some questions, which she answered with unspeakable meekness. However, I arose from my seat, submissively bowed, and bade farewell to the ladies, forgetting the compliments due to the intruding hippopotamus, and soon arrived at the station, and patiently awaited the approximity of the cars, into which I got and soon arrived at Utica. Before arriving at any city I made it an indispensable duty to inquire of travelers who left the city to which I was going to direct me to some house or tavern where my safety or security could be established during my stay in that city, and I took especial care not to rely infallibly on individual testimony, without other corroborating information; however, from concurring recommendations I concluded to stop at Mrs. McAvoy's house, which is conveniently located to the city, and only detatached from it by a bridge which is erected across the Mohawk river. When I got out of the cars in Utica I immediately crossed the bridge and inquired of the landlady could I board with her during my stay in Utica; she facetiously answered that I could with pleasure. I secondly asked her concerning the capacity of the house, or had she room for my baggage, &c., which was of considerable magnitude, and she answered "yes." When these arrangements were made, and every impediment removed, I recrossed the bridge and got the necessary conveyance to take my trunks to my lodgings, and placed them in a position inaccessible to approaching calamity. As it was late in the evening, I put off the inspection of the city until morning, and after viewing it, as I considered it with unerring exactness, I was pleased with the manifest improvement of the city, since the first time I had an opportunity of seeing it. Some thirty years since, I failed in the mercantile line, in Upper Canada, and then crossed the St. Lawrence to retrieve my fallen state in the land of freedom, and in passing through Utica I called on John C. Devereux, Esq., an illustrious countryman of mine, who was one of the wealthiest men in the State, and the founder and owner of most part of the city. The worthy gentleman received me with such attention and veneration, such as I thought myself unworthy of receiving at the hands of my illustrious countryman. Mr. Devereux despite of his vast wealth and distinction was one of the plainest men I met with in all my travels, and as soon as I made him acquainted with my downfall in business he immediately sympathized with the calamity that befel me, and although a stranger to him, he seemed also to place implicit confidence in the history I gave him of my total defeat in business; but this last time I called my friend and countryman was no more. He is, it is to be hoped in one of the mansions in his Father's house, in communion with angels and saints, as he fed the hungry and clothed the naked. This is a happy consideration that his good works followed him, and also, the prayers of the poor that he relieved, ascended to the throne of mercy in his behalf.

Having an introductory note to Mr. John Cantwell, a resident of Utica, it was to him I made the first application. This note I received of Mr. Robert Gould of East Troy, whom I have already exhibited as my cousin, and as Mr. Gould spoke of him so exaltedly, so extensively, and so eulogistically that I must acknowledge I considered his approbation sprang from too warm an imagination, although Mr. Gould said his remarks of him were only preliminaries of his worth. I called on Mr. Cantwell and found him busily engaged in his establishment. How Mr. Cantwell appeared at first sight to me, was thus, a large man with a well constructed frame beautifully knitted together, and preserving an admirable ratio, his countenance serene, although displaying inexpressible resolution in the hour of extremity, and his eye beaming with love and affection. The first glance taken of him was sufficient for a physiognomist of accuracy and experience to draw his conclusions from, and I immediately rested satisfied that my cousin's approbation of Mr. Cantwell was not imaginary, nor a fiction, but reality. After some conversation I mentioned to Mr. Cantwell the cause of my coming to Utica, and presented him with a metrical history of the Emerald Isle, my own production, and no sooner had he read a little than his countenance flushed with patriotism, which at once indicated his intrinsic feeling. It is needless to mention that Mr. Cantwell became a purchaser, and that with much alacrity; nay, did more, as he animated others to follow his example, and by his admonition some of his journeymen were also purchasers. Mr. John Cantwell is a native of Carrick, a section in the inimitable County Tipperary, and now a citizen of Utica, in the State of New York, where he carries on the largest, most complete and most fashionable boot establishment in that section of the State; and he not long since, and in the time of competition secured a patent right for the superiority of his workmanship. I paid the second visit to Mr. Michael McQuade, to whom I had a letter of introduction from his brother, a respectable citizen of Albany. I found no difficulty in finding his residence, as it was known, the same as the residences of all distinguished men, by the citizens in general. After arriving at his dwelling, Mr. McQuade was not there, as he was from home on some unavoidable business, but I had the pleasure of seeing him the same day in Mr. Cantwell's shop, where he expressed his good wishes towards me, and promised to use indefatigably his efforts to facilitate the sale of my books. Mr. McQuade, to make use of a Yankee phraseology, is a nice man; but I go farther, and pronounce him a constituted gentleman. Some time previously to my arrival in the city, Mr. McQuade had been mayor of Utica, and by his just, cautious, fearless and impartial administration of the laws pertaining to his office he acquired the applause and good will of those who came within the limits of his jurisdiction. In my first interview with Mr. Cantwell, I gleaned from his conversation that he doubted my success in Utica, and said they would rather listen to the discordant sounds of any other music than to the pensive, soothing, pathetic and inspiring strains of the worshippers at Mount Helicon, the rendezvous of Apollo and the Muses, whenever they wanted to slake their thirst for the inspiration of poesy. Nevertheless, there is no town or city in America but some spirited Irishman can be found, and the following is a list of all the men who encouraged my productions. Mr. Patrick Cogan, Mr. Owen Brady, Mr. John Looby; Mr. James Daily, Oneida County, N. Y., has been 18 years in America, born in Adair, County Kilkenny; Mrs. McAvoy, a native of the County Cork; this is the lady with whom I boarded during my stay in Utica, and her fame and reputation are so well established that encomiums pertaining to her are altogether unnecessary. Mr. Michael McQuade, from the parish of Clougher, County Tyrone, has resided in America for the long term of 32 years, and during that time has been a resident of Utica. Mr. John Rowe, from the County Cornwall, England, emigrated to this country 10 years ago. Mr. John Cantwell, born in Carrick-on-Suir, County Tipperary, married in the Emerald Isle and emigrated to this country 20 years since. Mr. Patrick Day, Lismullen, County Meath, 6 years in America, still unmarried. Mr. Patrick McCabe, from the Parish of Aughnamullen, County Monaghan, has been 12 years in this country, yet unmarried. Mr. O'Connor, from the patriotic County of Wexford, at present in Mr. Cantwell's employment, emigrated to this country 4 years since. Mr. Thomas Cody, Mr. Patrick Mathers, Mr. Michael O'Cavanagh, are also employed in Mr. Cantwell's establishment. My dear reader, I have remarked in my travels that whenever and wherever I met with any gentleman bearing the sacred name of Patrick, he displayed unusual patriotism, as if it had been hereditary. Mr. John O'Donoughue, grocer, Fayette street, Utica; this gentleman is indisputably clever.

Messrs. Devereux and Kernan, counsellors-at-law; these two gentlemen have formed a law association in the city of Utica, and it is the consideration of competent judges that they thoroughly and profoundly understand all the avenues and ramifications pertaining to jurisprudence, and that they now bask at the summit of the legal profession. Those gentlemen never interfere with petty cases; they grasp only at knotty mysteries, law questions which are inaccessible to vulgar conceptions, and they are as renowned for their strict integrity as they are for their knowledge of the law. Another thing which should be considered and which will go far to corroborate my assertion, is this; these gentlemen are neither greedy nor needy, as Mr. Devereux is, I believe, a brother's son to the late lamented John C. Devereux, of illustrious memory, and of whom I have already spoken, and he dying without any issue, bequeathed the most of his vast estates to his brother's children, and Mr. Kernan being married in the family, which of course entitled him to his share of Mr. Devereux's stupendous estates. Messrs. Devereux and Kernan are unlike some of the hungry vultures, who rescue a man's property from the obtrusive and avaricious grasp of his neighbor and keep it themselves. They always give Cæsar his due, and are always true to their clients. I had not the pleasure of an interview with Mr. Devereux, as he was not in the office when I called, but I was exceedingly pleased with Mr. Kernan, who happened to be there at the time, as a more finished gentleman, I seldom, or perhaps never had an opportunity of meeting in the whole course of my life, than he; and another remark I am going to make, which is this, and which excited my curiosity very much; I mean the rapidity of his pen when putting it to paper, it outstrips electricity, and yet the writing appeared quite legibly written. In the office at the time, there was a law student, a Mr. Browne, who wore the finest specimen of a mathematical head on his shoulders, I ever saw, and the serenity of his countenance would gain him admittance in the higher circles of society. Mr. Browne is unquestionably a promising young gentleman. Before taking my departure from Utica, I'll pass some remarks on a certain gentleman with whom I got acquainted in that city. Although I had taken accurate notes of him, they disappeared in the catastrophe, and his name vanished from my memory; therefore, nothing can be expected but omissions. The gentleman of whom

I speak, is a lawyer of considerable talents, and conducted affairs of the most intricate complexion, for many years in the city of Utica, still by some misfortune, which is sometimes the revolving satellite of brilliant talents, he fell from the zenith of glory, and when his declination became manifest his friends forsook him, and their ingratitude made a deeper impression on his mind than all the injuries he received otherwise, yet no adversity could obscure the honorable principle implanted in his bosom, or his friendly disposition, which was always uppermost. I have the honor of claiming him as my countryman, and I hope his ascension will be as rapid as his lamentable declination. I hope to know his name before my forthcoming epic history of my travels will make its appearance, and then we will faithfully give it publicity.

After I bade farewell to the inhabitants of Utica, I got in the cars and after a short time found myself in modern Rome, and before arriving there, I hoped in its construction, it would bear some resemblance to ancient Rome, yet after a hasty inspection of the place, I came to the conclusion it would never have the same extension, or vast proportions, or display the unparalleled grandeur and glory of its original or ancient Rome. American Rome, is a small town, and the location is not a desirable one; however, a stranger by a cursory inspection can hardly foretell its future greatness or prosperity. I halted at the western extremity of the town at a very respectable inn, and the host and hostess, as far as I can judge, could live in no other dwelling than one that would display respectability. The landlord, and I regret I cannot give his name, visited in company with me, all the places where he thought there would be a probability of disposing of my work, but all a miscarriage, the Romans displayed no taste for epic composition, nor could Homerian invention or his poetic strains, make any impression on their minds, remove their obduracy, or induce them to purchase. Nothwithstanding, among them I met with one star of the first magnitude, lineally descended from the illustrious family of the O'Neills. Mr. John O'Neill, of Ardinagh, parish of Tagriven, Barony of Shelmalier, county Wexford, has been fourteen years in this country, thirteen of which he has resided in Rome.

Feint and declining probabilities induced me to quit Rome that evening for Syracuse. After emerging from the bowels of Pegasus, I inquired of some of the citizens who there gregariously met, where I could find a respectable resting place, during my stay in Syracuse, and being strenuously advised to stop at Mr. McGuirk's house, I at once directed my steps to the place, to ascertain if a vacancy offered to receive me. No sooner did I enter the house, than I met the landlady, of whom I made particular inquiries respecting my entertainment during my abode in Syracuse, and she answered familiarly, and said that I could be accommodated. I was glad to hear her affirmation, as she was inexpressibly handsome, and her manner indisputably agreeable. In my travels through life, I cared not how sour and repulsive the landlord appeared, if the landlady were otherwise, although in my travels through life, I avoided too much familiarity with strangers, as my habits are shy, distant and reserved. While traveling, bright and early on the following morning, I sauntered through the city to inspect its construction, dimensions, and its private and public buildings, which unquestionably excited my surprise and gratification, as the city is constructed on a superior scale, its dimensions extensively projected and its public buildings beautiful and imposing. The most part of this city is inhabited by the sons and daughters of the Evergreen Isle, and it gives me unspeakable pleasure to proclaim to the world that they are healthy, wealthy and sober; I use the expression in a general form. In this city are at present, three diffirent and distinct families, who are among the wealthiest of my countrymen in Syracuse. These families are of Milesian origin and if we believe history, their progenitors ranked high in the most distinguished circles, and their genealogical descent can be traced to the illustrious Milesians. The ancestors of these families, the McCarthy family, the Lynch family and the Murphy family held vast and indisputable possessions in the Emerald Isle, and it is a fact that the illustrious McCarthy's in South Munster, for forty generations elected their own kings, framed their own laws, and were the undisputed lords of the soil, and all the O's in South Munster, though powerfully posted, were under the necessity of acknowledging their vassalage to the illustrious house of McCarthy, and the O'Briens, who were kings of North Munster, and oft contested supremacy with McCarthy, were always obliged to surrender to the irresistible prowess and conquering arms of McCarthy.

Before leaving East Troy, I got a note from my inimitable friend and countryman, James Brady, Esquire, introducing me to the notice of Doctor O'Brien, or O'Byrne, an eminent and distingushed Doctor of Syracuse. The Doctor might be called Burns, but Burns is a Scotch name, and all the Irish bearing that name are O'Byrnes, and are indisputably lineally descended from the illustrious chieftains of Wicklow, and I consider it an insult to the descendants of the illustrious chieftains to be deprived, through ignorance, of the O' as being a distinctive sign of their illustrious Milesian origin. When I entered on my mission I paid the Doctor the first visit, and fortunately found him in his office ; and I consider him a very close student, for Esculapius was never more attentive in his application to books than he. Notwithstanding he received me kindly and courteously, dropped every thing pertaining to his own affairs, and gave me a list of the principal men in the city, where a sale, or the probability of a sale, could be effected. The following list contains the names of my benefactors in Syracuse; I suppose many omissions have been made of names that are entitled to publication, which is an inevitable consequence arising from the dispersion of the notes I had taken of my friends in Syracuse, but the cause of their dispersion will manifestly appear as soon as I will arrive at Rochester, as it is in that city the dispersion happened. Mr. Thomas Coleman, a gentleman and pensman of superior talent. Mr. James Martin, from near Navin, county Meath, emigrated to this country fifteen years since, and got married here. Mr. Bernard O'Reily, from the Parish of Donuskeegh, has been seven years in this country, and married here also. Mr. Patrick Boland, from the Parish and townland of Ballymuck, county Sligo, married in Ireland, has been seven years in this country, and now resides in No. 101 Mulberry street, Syracuse, State of New York. Mr. Boland is a constituted gentleman. Mr. P. Lynch, born in Selina, and is at present twenty-one years of age. Mr. Lynch is a young man of extraordinary promise, with fine prospects before him. Mr. Thomas McCarthy, from the Parish of Carrick-on-Shannon, county Roscommon, has been ten years in this country, and married also, in Syracuse. Mr. McCarthy is also an eminent penman. Mr. John Gorman, from the Parish of Cashel, county Tipperary, has been eight years in this country, and married in Syracuse in 1849, where he now resides. Mr. William Drum, from the county Kilkenny, has been thirteen years in this country, and married also, in Syracuse. Mr. Peter Maguire, of Selina, Syracuse, left the Parish of Knockbride in 1827, and married in Canada in 1833. Mr. Martin Hogan, junior, born in the townland of Killadangan, county Tipperary, in 1843, and now living in Selina. This young gentleman, by his social habits, is deservedly appreciated, and by means of his many virtues, and strict integrity, though young, has reflected honor on the land of his birth. This young gentleman is a great patriot, and a genuine Irishman, he is still unmarried. Mr. Moloy, Ranger Block, No. 16 Montgomery street. Miss Savage, Selina; Miss Savage is a finished lady, and a dress-maker of a very high order; she emigrated from the county of Kerry, the soil of song and science. Ah! she is beautifully fair,—

Ah! were I young, I'd give her both my hands,
To have us joined in matrimonial bands,
If she'd comply, how happy would we be,
Upon this earth, and in eternity.
No jarring discord should commence or strife,
No end to happiness with such a wife.

Mr. Simon O'Donovan, from the Parish of Dreenagh, county Cork. In my youth, and in my native country, I had been well acquainted with Mr. O'Donovan's father and grandfather, who were both Doctors, and I must honestly say, were gentlemen who bore, in spite of unceasing malice and calumny, untarnished reputation for truth and strict integrity. Mr. O'Donovan is respectably connected by marriage in the city of Syracuse, and I can indisputably myself bear testimony to his worth. Mr. O'Donovan is without one stain on his character, and is deservedly respected and applauded by all the citizens in Syracuse. Mr. John Boyle, Professor in a Catholic College, Selina. Mr. Boyle is a gentleman of rare abilities, and adds as a collateral aid to his brilliant talents patriotism, liberality, social affection, and sobriety. Mr. Boyle deviates not an inch from the established maxims adopted by professors and teachers, generally speaking, which are social affections, good conduct, humility, and brilliant acquirements; and no man in his sphere could be more respected than he is by the clergy and laity. Mr. Michael Dolphin, now a resident of Selina.

Irish stars, the biggest, brightest, best,
Rise in the east, illuminate the west,
The darkest clouds they banish in despair,
And where they shine no mist can settle there.

Mr. Peter Colvel, Selina; another Irish comet. Mr. William Drum, a star of much magnitude and lustre. Mr. Corbitt, from the city or county of Limerick; this young gentleman had been my bed-fellow during my stay in Syracuse, and is considered, though young, to be one of the best bootmakers in Syracuse. Mr. Corbitt is a young man of great promise, and his appearance, humility, and sober habits go far to sustain the expectation. Mr. James Burke, civil engineer in the collector's office in Syracuse, and I aver most candidly, that in my travels I met but with few of his equals. Mr. Burke sheds lustre on the land of his nativity by his conduct, deportment, and qualifications; he was born in Hospital, county Limerick. In St. Charles Hotel, in Syracuse, I met with some of my countrymen that the highest applause or encomium respecting them could have no tendency to exaggeration. In these I discovered patriotism in full blast, and they also possess liberal principles, warm and friendly dispositions, and bear an untarnished reputation. Their names are as follows: Mr. John Gorman, Mr. John Harrington, the prime bootmaker of Syracuse, and another gentleman whose name I forget, who has preferred a life of celibacy to the unspeakable elysian happiness of matrimony. Mr. Thomas Hall, Montgomery street; Mr. Patrick Boylan, Mulberry street; Mr. John Covely, Mulberry street; Mr. Thomas Maloney, Mr. Phelan, Mr. Coffee, Mr. Terrence Kearnan, Mr. Patrick Malone, Mr. Patrick Burke, a descendant of the illustrious House of Burke, Mr. Robert McCarthy, Mr. James McGuirk, Mr. Rodgers, from Sligo, came to this country in 1831, married in Ireland, and keeps an extensive grocery at present in Syracuse. Mr. Thomas Drum, from near Navin, county Meath. Mr. Browne, a constituted gentleman. Mr. William Magher, from the famous and inimitable county Tipperary, emigrated thirteen years since, and is now a resident of the City of Syracuse.

Adieu to all in Syracuse that dwell,
With all my heart I wish them all farewell;
The scattered race, by vile oppressive laws,
Who settled there, are worthy of applause;
Success and sunshine on their efforts smile,
Who with reluctance left their native isle,
But, Godless tyrants made them cross the sea,
And hail!!! with joy, the land of Liberty.

I know I have omitted many valued names that contributed to my benefit and to the purchase of my books in Syracuse; but, a satisfactory apology will soon appear illustrating the cause of such omissions; and, I also hope, in the forthcoming epic history of my travels, to make an ample atonement for all the omissions that happened in my travels through various States of the Union. After taking leave of my friends in Syracuse, I took my seat in the cars and soon found myself in Auburn, and as the evening clouds foretold the proximity of night I took my lodging there that night, and after some inspection I discovered it to be a small place, without any phenomenon to draw attention, or excite curiosity, with one exception, —the Penitentiary, or place of incarceration for offenders for a time, or for life, if the magnitude of their crimes be of such a nature as to merit such punishment. The one exception I have already mentioned is the Penitentiary, and the most incurious eye would indisputably be satisfied after the inspection of the Auburn Penitentiary. On the following morning I called on the gentleman who is there appointed to convey travellers who have the curiosity of seeing the interior of this formidable edifice, and found him at his post, and he readily, for the small sum of twenty-five cents, showed me all the different rooms occupied by different mechanics in that stupendous building. My guide was an American gentleman, who displayed a good deal of urbanity on our first interchange of civilities, and when he took his cane in his hand and stood erect, I have no hesitation in saying that he made an exact angle of ninety degrees on the horizontal plane on which he stood, and confident I am that he stood six feet five inches in his stocking vamps. My explorer proceeded with cautious steps, and made all the necessary observations clearly demonstrating every thing that appeared mysterious to my inspection. He showed me the different rooms of the different mechanics which in number was astonishing, and all other marvellous things pertaining to this formidable structure that could excite either curiosity or surprise. However, my examination of this tremendous dungeon or place of incarceration was more mournful and sad, than satisfactory, while contemplating the unhappy state of the confined, without the liberty of exchanging one word, as I considered with each other, and busily employed in their different capacities, dragging out a miserable existence, inaccessible to pity, piety or friends, all wearing fawn-colored clothes, as a mark of degredation and felony, sleeping in iron bedsteads without the ramification of air, deprived of the privilege of casting one glance at the by-standers, who visit the place for the melancholy novelty of the scene. Alas! what a consideration! what a lesson of instruction this awful scene should be to those who are not as yet in jeopardy, and to those who are not yet adulterated with the commission of crimes, that would provide for them a loathsome dungeon, a disgraceful confinement which would render them unfit for any other society but that of felons, crimes that would bring their parents to a premature death, and leave their broken-hearted wives and children to desolation and at the mercy of this merciless and unfeeling world! What a lesson of morality can be drawn from this awful and disgraceful scene!

I withdrew from the dismal place with nearly a

broken heart, from the shameful and melancholy condition of my fellow creatures, and made an inflexible resolution never to visit the like again. While examining the dormitories of the incarcerated victims in Auburn State Prison, my conductor advised me to go into one of the cells, so I would be able to inform my friends that I had been confined in the Auburn Penitentiary. To acquiesce with his request I entered the cell, and no sooner had I been seated, than my conductor locked the cell, and I sat down in an iron chair for the accommodation of the occupier, which was fixed convenient to a small iron bedstead with scanty covering, and this was all the furniture to beautify a narrow contracted cell, with a small orifice to give ventilation to this inhospitable contraction. While in this predicament I felt some unaccountable shuddering, and I thought my blood stopped from circulating in my veins. This strange and uncomfortable feeling was engendered from contemplating on the melancholy and insufferable situation of the occupier of the cell, in which I was confined. The conductor immediately opened the cell, and when I got out I felt an unutterable change in my system, and all for the better. As I considered Auburn to be unfavourable to the sale of my prose and poetical works, I formed a resolution to leave it on the arrival of the cars, as

> There, Homer's works could not effect a sale,
> And how could my own barren rhymes prevail.
>
> O'DONOVAN.

Accordingly I went to work instantly, and got my trunks and baggage brought to the depot. On approaching the baggage master I soon discovered by his countenance that he was a Celt, or of Celtic origin; I asked the gentleman to put away in some place of safety my trunk, and by so doing that he would confer a compliment on his countryman, &c. My friend answered in friendly terms that he would unerringly attend to my instructions, we both being

Irishman, and I suppose both national, brought our friendship to a close proximity, and his interrogatories gave me an opportunity of expounding my mission to my countryman. The gentleman at once requested to see one of my books, and knowing by his manner of speaking that his intelligence was of a high order, and such I knew would facilitate the sale of some of my books. This internal conviction was not engendered by prophetical vanity or conjectures, as sales were effected. However, the whistle of the cars informed me they were approaching with incredible rapidity, and as soon as they arrived my countryman put my trunks in safety in the cars and also accompanied myself into them, and after taking my seat he with great urbanity and deference shook hands with me, and wished me an affectionate farewell.

In an instant, the cars were in motion for Canandaigua which was my next place of destination, and where I was to stop, and examine the magnitude and situation of the town, but, as it always had been customary with me, I paid the first visit to the Rev. Mr. O'Conner, who is located there as a Catholic clergyman, and much distinguished for his learning and theological proficiency, I need not inform my readers that he received me with more kindness and respect than I considered a wandering, romantic, muse had been entitled to receive at the hands of so eminent a theologian and philosopher. After a short interview with his reverence, he informed me that the Rev. Mr. Dean was the officiating Priest at Penn Yan, a small town at the distance of some thirty miles from Canandaigua, the Rev. Mr. Dean being ordained in Pittsburgh, Pa., and so universally beloved by the entire population of that city, and so much my friend, induced me to pay him a visit in that region of the State of New York, and when I arrived there, and made some inquiries respecting his residence, I understood that the distinguished and amiable young Priest, was boarding at the principal Hotel in the town, to which place I hurriedly directed my steps, and as soon as I entered the hotel, my first application was to the barkeeper, as he is always in possession of every intelligence respecting those who board or frequent the house, and inquired of him was the Rev. Mr. Dean in the hotel at the time. He answered that he was, but, at the same time, that he was inaccessible to proximity, as being confined to a sick bed. "Sir," said I, "I am his friend and came some distance to see his reverence, and my proximity could be no way objectionable to him, therefore, permission to see him would tranquillize my feelings." "Well then," said the young man, "that shall be granted." Then he gave me directions, respecting the course I should go, to find out the number of his bedroom. I knocked gently at the door, and he being incapable by his sickness to leave his bed, he cried languidly, "Push," and when I entered, he cried in spite of his debility and prostration, "Ah! there comes a Pittsburgher." At seeing him, my intrinsic agitation and feelings were beyond the reach of my illustration, for seeing him prostrated on a sick bed without the necessary attendance to render his situation more easy and comfortable. I remained with his reverence for some time, and never tried to effect a sale in the place, as I learned from the reverend gentleman, the hopelessness of the attempt, and the only sale I made in Penn Yan, was to himself, for which I was well paid, although, I stoutly objected to any compensation or compromise, but all to no purpose. As my feelings were considerably hurt by the indisposition of his reverence, I made no long delay, and I bade farewell to my reverend friend, and after receiving his benediction, I took my seat in the cars and returned to Canandaigua, where I stopped over night, and on the following morning after effecting few sales, I entered the cars and departed for Rochester, or the land of promise. After emerging from the cavity of my Pegasus, my first object was to look for a place of safety and accommodation where I could cast anchor during my stay in Rochester, which after a diligent search I found, and when I removed my baggage to it, I inspected the magnitude of the city, and the private and public edifices which embellish and magnify Rochester. I had lived in this city about 26 years since, and I thought I had still, its configuration and dimensions imprinted on my memory, but, after a hasty inspection of its present splendour, I mentally exclaimed, all my original ideas of this city have evaporated, as the city since I lived in it has been inconceivably enlarged and beautified.

The heavy clouds of night appeared and the last ray of Sol's brilliancy sunk below the horizon; and such symptoms induced me, like all birds of passage, to return to my roosting place, and at the proper and appointed time, for boarders to rendezvous and prepare themselves for bed, I was not found absent, for I always made it a point of duty in all my travels, not to infringe on the established laws of my host or hostess. I retired to bed early and slept soundly, and on the following morning, after partaking of a hearty breakfast, I started on my mission to try the poetic taste of my countrymen in Rochester, and as usual I paid the first visits to all the Catholic clergymen, and found them as I expected, amiable in their manner, edifying in their conversation, patriotic in feeling, and each with an extraordinary share of piety and humility depicted in his countenance. From the Rochester asterisk of learned ecclesiastics I received such encouragement and applause as flattered my ambition, and had, as I considered, prognosticated my progress and proficiency. The next visit I made was to Mr. Gafney, who is not only known in Rochester, but also throughout the State of New York, as being one of the most extensive merchants or dealers in dry goods in the western region of the State; and I can say for myself, that I seldom, if ever, saw so varied, so splendid, and so fashionable an assortment as I had seen in Mr. Gafney's store; and what I say is this, and it is a manifest illustration of its capacity and of the amazing amount of business daily transacted in his store, as it requires thirty handsome young gentlemen to attend to his customers and to others who come there for the purpose of supplying themselves with all valuable necessaries. As I cannot ascertain the number of young ladies employed in this establishment, I have omitted conjectures. Mr. Gafney is a fully finished gentleman, friendly, facetious, national and patriotic; these are the true characteristics of a genuine Irishman, and is free from all lofty and imaginary ideas, pomposity, affectation, and disgusting airs, and also of those heavy, haughty, and impenetrable mists which surround potentates;—I mean those who are extravagantly wealthy. All such things are repugnant to his feelings and disposition. Mr. Gafney did everything in his power to accommodate my design, and facilitate my efforts, and some of the young men in his employment bought of me with seeming alacrity. As I have noticed heretofore, the disappearance, whether accidentally or otherwise, of the notes I had taken of my countrymen in Rochester; and as this city is the place where the catastrophy occurred, and which occurrence will now be illustrated in its truest colors, and which I hope will be an ample apology for all omissions respecting Rochester and elsewhere. I sent by canal a case of huge dimensions, full of my books, from Utica to Rochester, which I received in safety and unhurt, and nearly all the notes I had taken in my travels were in it, and divided in several packages; that is, every town and city through which I travelled had been in a separate parcel and negligently wrapt in a newspaper; as fearing no imminent danger or unavoidable accident, I gave directions in Rochester to continue the transportation of my huge case, or hippopotamus, to Buffalo, which the same company did, but on my arrival in that city I found the case in the forwarder's office, and by its external appearance no man could believe that a separation of its parts had ever taken place, it had been so well adjusted, or put together; and whoever the Surgeon may be, he must be a pupil of Sir Astley Cooper, as he surgically knew every joint in the composition of my modern ark. When I considered it to be in a perfect state of preservation, I reached the manifest or receiving ticket I got from the forwarder in Rochester, to the clerk who was in the office at the time, and being unconscious of the disaster which befel it; but no sooner did he receive it, than with unspeakable avidity he tore it to pieces, or rather to mathematical points, accord-to Euclid's definition. When I approached the case and touched it, it magically fell apart, and in a fractional manner, to my great astonishment; and in the case my books and notes were in one promiscuous confusion; many of the books I am certain lost, and thousands of the notes I had taken throughout my travels had also disappeared. My consternation and fury became unlimited and unrestrained, and particularly when I inquired of the clerk how such a disaster had happened he answered with an air of affectation and seeming consequence, "accidentally." I was at the time lamentably fixed, as I took no inventory of the number of books I had in the case, and also had not the forwarding declaration; situated thus, I had no compensation to get, and therefore made an immediate application to patience, which after a short consideration turned out a complete balm to calm my misfortune. Mr. Foot was the name of the forwarder in Buffalo.

Here follows a list of all my contributors in Rochester, and before commencing my catalogue I will state by way of abbreviation that a panegyric in a collective capacity must suffice instead of individual encomiums, until I write my travels poetically. Mr. Daniel Crowley, from the county Cork, and has been five years in America, yet unmarried. Mr. Cunningham, a salesman in Mr. Gafney's establishment. Mr. James McMahan, who keeps an extensive book establishment near the depot. Mr. Thomas Commiforel, born in Kingston, Upper Canada, in 1839. Mr. Patrick O'-Meara, No. 11 Centre market, from Banagher, Kings county, barony of Parry Castle, left his native country on the 7th of June, 1847. Doctor McCay, from Ballenderry, county Londonderry, left his native country five years since, and is now a respectable and useful citizen of Rochester city. Mr. Peter Quonen, born October 6th, 1834, in the parish of Augnamullen, county Monaghan, came to this country September 2d, 1844; he is a mechanic, bearing the appellation of a machinist. Mr. John Rigney, a contractor, born in the parish of Lemenaghan, Kings county, emigrated to America in 1836, and married a lady of Irish extraction; I mean to say, God willing, something poetically respecting this gentleman, as I saw him shaking with unparalleled violence in the ague. Mr. Hugh Mulholland, from Londonderry, emigrated in 1847, and lived in Rochester since June 5th, 1855. Mr. Bernard O'Reilly, from the parish of Rossminigree, county Wexford. Mr. John McKanna, from the county Longford. Mr. James Leahey, born in the townland of Grovine, parish of St. Patrick; married in the same parish in 1850, and left on the 4th of July the same year. Mr. Timothy O'Donoughue, born in Canada West, in the town of Kingston, came to the United States and married June 8th, 1855. I met with this young gentleman in Messrs. Cunningham & Co.'s great coach factory in Rochester, where he had been engaged as a clerk, and as soon as he made known his name to me, and who his father and grandfather were, I felt an indescribable sensation of a melancholy nature, as his grandfather and I lived on the most amicable terms for a series of years in Upper Canada, with one another, and a more friendly man never existed; he died lamented by all who had the pleasure of his acquaintance; and his father I knew when he came from his native country, quite a promising boy, but I came to the United States before his maturity or manhood became manifest.

Miss Jane Rooney, born in the Parish of Kin awley, Farmanagh. Mr. Michael McRoden, born in the Parish of Arigal, County Monaghan, married in Rochester, May 4th, 1846. Mr. Patrick Hogan, born in the Parish of Cloney, County Clare, has been 9 years in America, and married in freedom's home, and keeps at present a large dry goods store in Rochester. Mr. Michael Fitzsimmons, from the Parish of Crosserlaugh, County Cavan, married in Rochester, and is one of the firm of Hogan & Co., 55 Main street, Rochester. Mr. Joseph Kavanagh, clothier, from the Parish of Craighnemernano, County Kilkenny, has been 24 years from his native country; married here. Mr. O'Beirne, Ohio street, Mr. James O'Sullivan, corner of Elk street. Mr. P. O'Byrne, Gothic Hall; perhaps I met with this gentleman in Gothic Hall, Buffalo, of which I shall speak hereafter. Mr. Patrick Gannon, Sixth street; Mr. Gannon, is a distinguished gentleman and citizen of Rochester, who has a son a student in the Eternal City. Mr. Edward Berery, of the firm of Hogan & Co., No. 55 Gaffney's Block, Main street; he was born at Nenagh, County Tipperary, married in Canada, and and has been five years cogitating in freedom's own empire. Bartholomew Crowley, born in the Parish of Castle Lyons, County Cork. I have faithfully given a list of all the gentlemen's names who contributed to the sale of my works in Rochester, or at least of all that remained after the destruction of my modern ark, and of the dispersion partly of the notes it contained. I have already made an ample apology for all my omissions, and have also suggested that in the forthcoming poetic history of my travels, all the omitted names shall receive due attention; not meretriciously, but sincerely and solidly. I would have also illustrated this beautiful city with all the scenery and embellishments that surround it, but, being determined to reserve this part for poetic illustration and fancy. Before I left Rochester I received a letter from my son, that since my departure from home he had taken to himself a wife and also the responsibility of housekeeping, and expected my immediate return to assume the dignity of a patriarch over the rest. This news, coming so unexpectedly from an only son, frustrated my future design, and prevented me for some time from carrying out my intended enterprise. Accordingly, I hastened home, and acted conformably to my incumbent duty. On the morning of June 12th, 1855, I took my departure in the cars from Rochester and proceeded to Lockport with a speed that slightly fell behind the velocity of the sun when drawn by his incomparable chargers, and when I emerged from the hollow space which I occupied, I inquired, as usual, of a native bystander, if he knew of any of my countrymen keeping a house of entertainment in Lockport. Any house of the kind was without the limits of his knowledge, but he knew of an American house, and other houses of rare attractions for the accommodation of travelers. Notwithstanding, all these attractions did not suit my propensities, for I would rather lie under the shade of a weeping willow with my countryman than enjoy all other rich and sumptuous attractions and luxuries, even at the same cost elsewhere. At last, after making some further inquiries I discovered that a countryman of mine, a Mr. Mangin, kept a boarding house in the place, and directed the driver to take me there, which he obeyed agreeably to orders. Luckily enough, Mr. Mangin was in his house at the time, and assured me of an Irish reception during my stay in Lockport; all rightly and satisfactorily understood. I paid the driver, and instantly removed my traveling budget and baggage into the house, and placed them under the protection of Mr. Mangin, and made but a transitory stay, as I labored under ineffable uneasiness from a desire of seeing the Rev. Mr. Credon, of whom I knew so much and heard so much in my travels, and all to the advantage of his reverence. I proceeded immediately to his residence, which, I may say, is adjoining the church, and, as good fortune would have it, his reverence was at home at the time of my arrival.

> Bright science shown upon his noble birth,
> Which made the priest an ornament on earth;
> Such being the fate of the illustrious star,
> Immortal fame his name has borne afar.
>
> O'DONOVAN.

The reverend gentleman at the time had some hands papering his room, and making some other necessary arrangements, which gave me unspeakable pleasure, as I thought his reverence lived contented and happy among his parishioners. His reverence received me with that pleasing courtesy and unspeakable kindness which are the inseparable companions of this distinguished theologian. I instantly communicated my mission to his reverence, and also that I was a Pittsburgher. This I did to bring things to his recollection, as I considered that his knowledge of me had been drowned in the stream of oblivion, but quite to the contrary, and no further recommendation was necessary than being a Pittsburgher, whose keen maternal inspection is necessary to recognize her offspring among a crowd of the same age and maturity. I heard of the reverend gentleman's generosity and cleverness throughout all my travels, which I discovered to be the case, and which will appear before the conclusion of my narrative concerning Lockport. The reverend gentleman cordially invited me to dine with him, which I refused, as being after dinner at the time. I had some of my books along, which he bought at first sight, without the least examination of their merits. His reverence bought also some of my books for others, and gave me a sum of money far exceeding my demand and the original price. His reverence said he would give every encouragement and help to effect sales for my works in Lockport. This encouragement coming from so distinguished a theologian and gentleman as the Rev. Mr. Credon was noble, and with that he sat down and wrote the following with incredible rapidity: "I have the honor of knowing Mr. Jeremiah O'Donovan, author of a Metrical History of Ireland, these many years, and feel great pleasure in testifying to his worth as a man, as well as to his abilities as poet and author." To this he added other encomiums which were exceedingly flattering. This recommendation to his parishoners conveyed an assurance, had a tendency leading to conviction, which effected considerable sales among his parishioners in Lockport. His reverence also gave me the names of a few respectable men, and said they would undoubtedly introduce me to others, and added the reverend gentleman by way of admonition, "If you should find the times hang heavily on your shoulders, go to the Falls of Niagara, and call on the Rev. Mr. Stephens, and he will contribute by his influence to the sale of your books;" and again added his reverence, "Be sure to be here next Sunday at church, and let no unavoidable business detain you." The mariner's needle never pointed to the true north more unerringly than I did to his admonition.

All my countrymen to whom I called in Lockport, with few exceptions, purchased a copy of me with astonishing alacrity; perhaps in my travels in America, I seldom met their equals. They all seem friendly, affectionate, and truly patriotic, and down the line I found them generous and anxiously inclined to purchase. On the line I met with a young gentleman by the name of Mr. Thomas Rooney, who requested me to write something panegyrically respecting Lockport, and I promised him to comply with his request, and after arriving at Buffalo, I composed extemporally and epically on the noble and unparalleled inhabitants of Lockport, which I sent him according to promise. In this I mentioned their names, individually and metrically, which will appear in the forthcoming poetic history of my travels. It should be amended, but in dread that the original has been already in circulation, it shall appear without pruning in its original state. My success in Lockport may be attributed to the goodness of the Rev. Mr. Credon. May God in his mercy watch over him, and grant him long life and a happy death. A second thought induces me to give the bungling explosion or poetic burst I sent to Mr. Thomas Rooney insertion at present, without alteration or amendment. It is as follows:

O! Lockport, Lockport, is at present blest,
With pious people and a heavenly priest,
Here mass is said, and with devoted care,—
And prayer and incense, sanctify the air;
The priest and people, altogether kneel,
And show externally their inward zeal,
And as the church is built upon a rock,
The church and priest, both sanctify the flock;
The worthy pastor without stain or guile,
Is a pure gem, from Erin's verdant Isle;
May he long prosper and continue there,
To fill the office of his sacred sphere,—
As the good priest is candid, kind and true,
And so I found his congregation too.
O'Connell's there, of pure Milesian race,
Who had been honored in his native place,
And a brave chieftain of the name of Burke,
And Mr. Tobin from the City of Cork;
In rank comes Bulger, and his Vulcan brow,
And gives his anvil a tremendous blow,—

And worthy Dapson, from my native Isle,
And Glinn divested of intrinsic guile,
Next comes McGrath, of universal fame,—
And Mr. Boland, who enjoys the same:
These are patriots of the deepest dye,
Who loved their country, still were forced to fly,
And next the last, which rather seems unkind,
Is generous Duffy, with a generous mind;
Far down the line, through motive or desire,
I met the son,* of a respected sire,†—
The various virtues, mankind could adorn,
He does possess, though being Canadian born.
Onward still, determined not to tarry,
Until I met with a tremendous quarry.
There awful thunder shook the mighty earth,
And each explosion gave a stony birth.
There Brazel stood, and with assiduous care,
To measure stones with his unerring square;
There rocks are drilled, by a superior race,
Whom tyrants banished from their native place.
All their names, hereafter, will appear,—
That Erins sons may hold their memory dear;
Since tyrants drove them from their native soil,
They are doomed to labor and excessive toil,
But time and patience will again restore,
To them possessions they possessed before,—
Descended then unto the planes below,—
Where wheat and barley, in abundance grow,—
There met O'Ready with amazing care,
Showing each plowman, how to plow his share.
He left that city, all with diamonds set,
As being unconquered by no tyrant yet,—
'Twas there, proud Billy, raised the siege and left, (Limerick.)
Next in order comes their noble boss,
Whose loss would be a very serious loss.‡
Who shook with patience, which I did admire,
And that convenient to a blazing fire.
'Tis there, indeed, great Vulcan's bellows blow,
Or else the son of great Tipperary,§ O!
Undoubtedly he's clever, free and frank,
And modest Melegan,|| have closed the rank.

To comply with the advice of the Rev. Mr.

---

* *Sire*—Mr. Patrick Rooney, a respectoble Irishman and contractor. † Mr. Thomas Rōoney.

‡ This section is under the superintendence of Mr. Mathew Rigney, who had the ague.

§ Mr. Lonegan, blacksmith.

† Mr. Melegan, is another boss.

Gredon,* I took my seat in the cars in Lockport, and departed for the Niagara Falls, and after arriving there, I inquired for the residence of the Rev. Mr. Stephens, expecting as usual a warm reception; and this I expected from a priest, and particularly on the strength of the Rev. Mr. Credon's recommendatian, but, unfortunately his reverence had been in bad humor, or governed by some malign star, at the time which led him out of the usual course of his humility and courtsey, as the reverend gentleman is universally admired for his urbanity, kindness, and polished manners, still, I must acknowledge, he concealed them from me individually and collectively. This I considered very strange as being backed, and as I thought, rendered inaccessible, to this reception, as having a letter† of approbation, from one of the most distinguished priests and theologians in my travels. I withdrew from his reverence, somewhat dissatisfied, and went to the Rochester House, kept by a Mr. O'Holoran, who gave me a very poor description of the place, and indeed, I attributed infallible belief to his testimony. My host directed me to Mrs. Calidan, whose maiden name was Harding, native of the County Kilkenny, who lived conveniently; and I instantly repaired to her house or place of abode, and unquestionably she was Irish of the genuine kind, and also a devoted Catholic, though married to a Protestant, or some other extravagant thinker of the Reformation. Of course she purchased with incredible cheerfulness, and exclaimed "that no price, be it ever so exorbitant, could keep from me a book of such Catholic tendencies." She had in her bookcase, exclusively of Catholic books, the accumulated works of the most eminent poets of ancient or modern times, and I thought my own poetic pro-

* Rev. Mr. Credon, is a native of Charleville, County Cork

† Either a letter, or a verbal introduction.

duction would get no admittance among the powerful productions of those luminaries who decorated poesy, with their incomparable effusions ; but, I was mistaken, as she was kind enough to saturate mine with the most flattering applause.

A German music professor attended her little daughter, so as to impress on her mind the musical art, and she attentively devoted herself to her religious instructions. I crossed the suspension bridge that day about noon, and visited the Canadian soil, and strange it is to say that, in spite of all my prejudices, I felt some warm feelings in my bosom towards the flag I utterly abominated thirty years since. O ! what a sensation came over me, and what strange imaginations crowded into my head, when thinking at that time I had youth and agility to give proper directions to my velocity when I first saw the falls, while encumbered during my last visit, with declining age and other impediments! alas ! what an extraordinary change in the constitution of man takes place during thirty years! When first I visited the tremendous Falls, I took an accurate observation of their terrific grandeur, sublimity, and construction, and I had at my last inspection concluded that the powerful element had since my first visit fearfully worn away my landmarks. When I crossed the bridge and paid twenty-five cents for the privilege, at the Canadian side I met with an Irish gentleman from the county Roscommon, who purchased one of my books with surprising readiness, and read distinctly a page of it in the presence of some Englishmen, which undoubtedly must have been disagreeable and repugnant to their feelings, and I must acknowledge I would far rather he had been silent on the occasion, as the subject under consideration was a manifest chastisement to the English government, and fearfully condemning their invidious enactments and unrelenting barbarity, which would in days gone by implicate me in their inexorable power.

His name was Devinny, and one of the finest looking men I saw in my travels. I went that evening in the cars to St. Catharine's, but not until I paid a visit to a gentleman of the name of Mr. Geary, from the county Meath, who is extravagantly wealthy and good with all, and living in the vicinity of the Falls, and is also blessed with a wife of noble feelings and fine qualities here unspecified, though an American born, and seems to fondly cherish any essay that would embellish the Emerald Isle. I visited another man in the same vicinity of the name of Mr. Quinn, a full finished gentleman, and afterwards took comfortable shelter under the friendly roof of Mr. Nugent's house in St. Catharine's who came to this country at an early age, and married in the prime of manhood a Canadian lady, one of the best women in her station of life that can be found. In such hotels travellers find safety and protection, and in such places their property and themselves are safe under the unerring protection of Providence. On the following morning I paid a visit to the Rev. Mr. Grattan, who officiates there as a Catholic clergyman, and whom I found friendly and affectionate, and an original Irish gentleman. His reverence purchased of me without hesitation, and also gave me all the information he could to facilitate the sale of my poetic history of Ireland in St. Catharine. His reverence sent one to a young and interesting gentleman of the name of Mr. Manahan, who dwells in the quality of a teacher in St. Catharine, who also purchased with avidity, and gave me the names of the most prominent men in the place. Mr. Manahan is a Canadian by birth, and I found in him as I did in teachers in general, which is a hereditary principle and privilege pertaining to this class, and this principle and privilege comprise dignity, science, and edification. The names of my contributors in St. Catharine will not appear in this abridged history of my travels, notwithstanding, I will make particular mention of one gentleman's name I met with in St. Catharine, and who left that part of the Emerald Isle, not yet obliterated from my recollection, as it had been the enchanting scenes of my childhood and youth, when the flight or gyrations of a butterfly conveyed more pleasure and astonishment to my mind, than the terrific and stupendous Falls of Niagara do at the present time. His name is Mr. Daniel Maguire, a gentleman of literary taste, edifying conversation, and polished manners, he is also a merchant in St. Catharine. Mr. Maguire did every thing within his province to dispose of my metrical history in the town of St. Catharine, Upper Canada, and the inhabitants of this town, as far as I could judge, are honest, sober, industrious, and persevering, and uncommon friendly in their manner and expressions, and I am confident that any person acquainted with said population will, by his affirmation, corroborate my testimony.

As my intention is, if Providence spares me, to write the history of my travels in epic verse, where I mean to do justice to St. Catherine, I will desist from lavishing further encomiums on its inhabitants till then. In the afternoon I took my seat in the cars to return to the land of promise, and to pass in them the terrific suspension bridge, fearless of danger, and acted accordingly, though we passed over in sloth-like manner, and then found myself sheltered and shrouded by the brilliant, invincible, impregnable and immortal flag of our Union, the terror of tyrants, and the protector of freemen. I stopped again at the Rochester House, where comfort, abundance and attention, were duly administered to me; and early in the following morning, I arrived at Lockport. On leaving Lockport for Buffalo, disagreeably disappointed in the pleasure of a second interview with the Rev. Mr. Credon, whose residence is convenient to the depot; but this disagreeableness entirely evaporated, as I had the honor of seeing him at Buffalo, immediately after my arrival in that city. In Syracuse, Rochester, and Lockport, I made a diligent enquiry of my friends, respecting their knowledge of any distinguished and prominent countryman of mine in Buffalo city, to whom I would apply for instructions that would enable me to dispose of my poetical works, and my friends in the aforesaid places unanimously and emphatically directed me to Maurice Vaughan, Esquire, and spoke of him in terms of the highest adulation. I was much astonished at the universal approbation and applause he sustained everywhere, which made me think that he was a man of uncommon goodness and conservative power. When I arrived at Buffalo, I went immediately to his office, which is in Quay street, and fortunately found him sitting leisurely, and as I considered in his happy element, and to give utterance candidly touching the matter, I think his sociability and familiarly happy manner of expressing himself, would render him a welcome guest to the most exalted society. After the courteous terms of reciprocity had subsided, I simply and unequivocally declared my intention to Mr. Vaughan, and he was not the man to discourage or undervalue my patriotic efforts, as he cheerfully and without hesitation, became a purchaser; and also offered his assistance to establish its indisputable success. After some conversation I discovered him to be a native of the universal county Cork, and when I took a survey of all the luminaries that county produced, in ancient and modern times, I was not astonished at the term universal; and still thinking it gave birth to men of every grade, from a needle to a thunderbolt, I felt happy in being a Corkman myself. Mr. Vaughan is still a bachelor, and his appearance displays dignity, and commands respect; his eye is large and expressive; his features comely, though slightly marked with the small-pox; his frame is gigantic and geometrically constructed, and his accent is mellow, musical, and to the point. Mr. Vaughan has a brother living in Buffalo, who is his equal in all the points heretofore specified with one exception, being a married man. Mr. Vaughan gave me a list of gentlemen residing in different streets in the city, among whom I found very clever men, exceedingly so, and patriots bold, courageous and incorruptible, whose names will appear in succession; still if all the gas that has been evaporated in that city, were of an inflammable nature, the human family would suffer in one general conflagration, and time indisputably would have its limits. Purchasers' names: Mr. M. Vaughan; Mr. Vaughan is a brother to the aforesaid. Mr. Sweeny, pawnbroker, a native of the town of Murckroom, county Cork; Mr. Sweeny is a distinguished citizen of Buffalo, distinguished as a linguist and mathematician; particularly as he is a self-taught man, more about him poetically. Mr. Hughes, a counsellor and attorney at law; Mr. Hughes is a genuine Irishman remarkable for his nationality and patriotism, and also for his professional talent. Mr. William Carland, a native of the city of Cork; he came to this country twenty-one years since, and married in Buffalo. Mr. Carland keeps one of the most extensive clothing establishments I met with in all my travels; he is unquestionably much respected, and deservedly so.

Mr. James Boland, No. 104 Main street, born in St. John's, Lower Canada, aged 22 years; a more promising young gentleman is hard to find. Mr. Ronald McDonald, born in the Parish of Raphael, County of Glengary, Upper Canada; I met with this gentleman in some place, and whether in Buffalo or elsewhere it must be left to conjecture. Mr. Peter Mullins, Kanturk, 18 years in the land of freedom, and married in Buffalo. Mr. George O'Deal, born in Limerick and emigrated 23 years since, married in Buffalo. Mr. Augustine Keogh, a native of the city of Dublin, has been 25 years in America, and married in Buffalo; Mr. Keogh keeps the best and most extensive establishment of musical instruments, particularly his piano department, such are appreciated for the harmony they yield and their enchanting melody and sound. Mr. F. O'Byrne from Athlone, County Roscommon, 13 years in freedom's home, and married in Buffalo. Mrs. Roach, corner of Main and Genessee streets, is an indisputable lady, and a patriot of a high degree; she is also beautifully fair. Mr. Finagin, No. 62 Ellicot street. Mr. Patrick Cannon from the Parish of Temple Michael, left his native country 27 years since, married in Quebec and is now a citizen of Buffalo City. Mr. Michael Morresy, Clashmore, County Waterford, has been 12 years in this country, and married in Mill Street, County Cork; Mr. Morresy is an indisputable gentleman. Mr. John Canty, a native of the County Limerick, and born in the Parish of Bruff, has been 7 years from home, and married in New York. Mr. James McCook, from the County Derry, married in Buffalo, 11 years since. Mr. John Galvin, a native of the County Galway, married in Rochester, State of New York. I met with another gentleman of distinction in Buffalo, and the mention of his name will be an additional lustre to the rest of my contributors in Buffalo, and although he is a native of Pennsylvania, he is an Irishman in principle and practice; his name is Mr. McBride, and is both Captain and Commander of the Queen of the West, one of the most splendid steamboats sailing from Buffalo. Mr. McBride is beautifully formed by nature, or by nature's God, his size is of considerable magnitude, and his parts and proportions stand in exact ratio to each other, his countenance shows much fortitude in the time of danger, and also shows generosity, frankness, and decision. Although Mr. McBride, as I mentioned heretofore, is a Pennsylvanian by birth, he is an inflexible democrat, and an Irish patriot. Mr. McBride offered me, with unspeakable kindness and urbanity, a free passage from Buffalo to Erie, and also all other necessary accommodations, which I refused, as, being determined to come around the lake by land, an expensive and profitless journey; he also recommended me to Mr. Murphy in Erie, an indisputable gentleman, and to another gentleman in Cleveland, who will be hereafter mentioned.

I took my seat in the cars in Buffalo and with a rapidity surpassing my sanguine expectations we came to Dunkirk, a small and new town on the verge of the lake, without any considerable improvement and its appearance divested me of all hopes of success: I took up quarters at an inn in this place, kept by a gentleman of the name of O'Donoughue, I think a native of Kerry, and felt myself comfortable and happy under the friendly roof of my countryman, but I could with as much facility stop the revolutions of the planet Jupiter with its revolving satellites, as dispose of any of my books to any of the inhabitants of Dunkirk. Notwithstanding this disappointment, I was otherwise requited. As the last blush of the sun's refulgence had been sinking from my view beneath the horizon, the moon, which arose diametrically opposite, with the pleasing and beautiful lustre pertaining to her magnitude, and meeting the sun's reflection which formed a straight line across the lake, and caused the most beautiful illumination, which phenomenon would inspire a poetic fancy in the most sterile bosom, though it were as repugnant to versification as a saw-mill. On the following morning I started in the cars for Cleveland, Ohio, and on my arrival there, I called on Mr. Dougan, to whom I had been strenuously recommended by Captain McBride, commander of one of the most magnificent steamboats on the lakes, and he received me with ineffable kindness, and also, did as much to advance my purpose as could be expected. I did some business in Cleveland, but not so extensively as I expected. In this place I met with a young amiable priest, the Rev. Mr. O'Neill, and his conversation and generosity convinced me that he was lineally descended from the illustrious house of O'Neill. After spending a few days perambulating and inspecting the beauties of Cleveland, and travelling on the lake shore, which, with reference to the lake, is a brilliant scene, I then returned to Pittsburgh, and found my son married, and my wife and the rest of my family in good health and anxiously awaiting my arrival. After a short time with my family, as I had still some of my books unsold, on the 7th of August, 1855, I took my departure from Pittsburgh on the steamboat Brazil for Cincinnati, and considering myself robbed by riding in the cars for nearly two years in succession, in an unavoidable business, and that, through the various States of the Union, I thought, as a counterpoise to the enormous expenses I incurred during my travels, to take a deck passage, which would lessen the bill descending the Ohio River, and being also induced accordingly to realize another expectation which I am going to demonstrate. I always entertained and will entertain, some lofty conceptions of my own dignity, from the uncontested royalty of my ancestors, although my inheritance is totally obliterated by the cruel and relentless tyranny of strangers, which must be considered the intrusion of irresistible might, still, I see as through an impenetrable mist, the vast possessions and dignity to which I am entitled, though being inaccessible at present to my grasp. On the steamboat descending the Ohio at this time, was an Indian king, of the Caw tribe, whose appearance and construction bespoke incredible strength and agility; he was accompanied by his queen, and some of the royal family, and his majesty had been returning from Washington City, which place he visited, to see our good President, to obtain some privileges respecting his tribe; this is the demonstration, for, as the noble Roman said, "I would prefer to be king of the most deserted village in Europe, than to be viceroy of London." For the extremities of travelling in the steamboat, I made no preparations, as in such cases, I always depended on my purse, though often its specific gravity was of that quality, that, if thrown high in the air, it would display many gyrations before returning again to our earth. I omitted mentioning that the royal family had taken a deck passage. When night approached and threw her dark canopy over our part of the terrestrial globe, and human nature wanted its natural repose, by order of the captain an elevated bed was made down stairs for his savage majesty and family, on which I threw a covetous glance, as no accommodation had been provided for me, but the permission of reposing on two flour barrels which were up-ended, as if kind Providence placed them there for my comfort and convenience. I felt more happiness in my situation, as being in company with royalty, than I could enjoy in the cabin in company with the captain and his mistaken nobility.

In the course of some time the luxury of reposing on the extremities of the two barrels had been disturbed by a growl from his savage majesty, by means of my approximation to the couch of royalty, which I consider arose from a knowledge of his dignity, or from an indication of his morose disposition, rather than from my intrusion, as my situation rendered it impossible to be coveted. My anxiety to be in company with the royal family, undoubtedly, may be considered aristocratical, and such ambition in some is to say the least of it to be dreaded, and should also be despised, but when it is commingled with honor, devotion, and liberality, it becomes harmless and inoffensive. All the rest of deck passengers formed themselves in communities in other parts of the boat, and amused themselves with some old-fashioned stories, and also with occasional drops of old rye whisky, until twelve o'clock, when they individually and collectively fell into the arms of Morpheus, in which position they remained in the enjoyment of imaginary happiness until Sol's brilliancy and intense heat aroused them from their slumbers in the morning. When I arose from my hard bed early in the morning, whether it had been occasioned by the disqualification of years, or the hard and limited position of my bed, I felt myself very uncomfortable and unhappy in mind for the humble situation I enjoyed, and knowing that I descended from an illustrious line of ancestors, by both sides, paternally and maternally, that adored, long since, the Emerald Isle with virtue, power and science, and also being an unflinching citizen of the United States of America, still I found myself placed below the level and meridian of a savage son of the forest, as he was well provided with accommodations, whilst I remained unseen, unknown, and neglected. In every extremity there is an invisible help, as will appear from the following manifestation. From my youth up to the present time, I have been a very early riser, which I found conducive to health and meditation; and on rising from my hard bed this morning, though of my own choosing, I made my appearance on deck, and no sooner there than the engineer of the boat espied me, and identified his old teacher, and then with anxiety and unutterable kindness, approached and asked me how I did. His size and maturity prevented me from recognizing my former pupil, Mr. D. W. Carroll, a Pittsburgher born. My friend related my situation, and gave an abridged history of my life to my countryman, Mr. John McGrath, who was watchman on the boat at the time, and a more faithful selection could not have made. Some little investigation made me sensible of my kind, noble, industrious, and obedient pupil, Mr. D. W. Carroll. Messrs. Carroll and McGrath altered my condition at once, and at that moment my manacles and all other impediments disappeared, and my comfort descending the Ohio river became very evident. This change fortunately happened, as will appear from the following testimony which is entitled to credit.

The cooks on all the steamboats on the river then were restrained by the captain, and prohibited from giving anything to eat to deck passengers for love, commisseration, or money, and had been compelled by an established and inflexible injunction to throw everything overboard pertaining to victuals; yet, through the assiduity and kindness of my friends, my living and accommodations were in close communion with extravagance, until I reached Cincinnati. Although my bed and boarding were free of all expenses, with the exception of some delicacy for putting my friends to such unnecessary trouble. We had a considerably tedious passage descending, and we felt it, as the weather was oppressively warm, and the ramification of air afforded us no comfortable fanning. At last the steamboat sounded a loud blast, informing us of our proximity to Cincinnati, for which we returned thanks to the invisible hand of Providence for our preservation during the passage. As soon as the plank was adjusted for all the passengers to debark, I went ashore and instantly proceeded to the O'Connell House, which is situated on River street, and kept by Mr. Richard Walsh, my former friend and acquaintance who immediately recognized me. After the lapse of some years, it is needless to say that Mr. Walsh received me with that warm affection and hospitality which Irishmen entertain in all climes and countries they inhabit. After terms of friendship and courtesy had subsided, I asked Mr. Walsh some questions concerning Mr. Patrick Collins; and as soon as I learned from him that his immortal spirit was carried on angelic wings to the regions of bliss, and that some more of my original friends died and disappeared since my last interview with them, I felt intrinsically uncomfortable when meditating on the joys and meretricious trappings of a transitory and uncertain existence. Ah! unhappily I felt then, bereft by death ando ther causalities, of my best friends, and placed under the necessity of creating new ones. I was strongly advised by my remaining friends to call on Mr. Nugent, who stopped at the far-famed Burnet House in that city, and all spoke of him panegyrically, and I acted accordingly, and found him to corroborate the extravagant encomiums heaped upon him by the sincere sentiments of my worthy friends. Mr. Nugent is a gentleman of rare and distinguished abilities, professionally speaking, and makes the Burnett House his home, as being a conservative bachelor, and unquestionably a close inspector and admirer of beauty, as is naturally the case with bachelors of art; and I am happy in announcing him a native of the universal county of Cork. Mr. Nugent with much alacrity recommended me to the following gentlemen, and assured me that they were cast in the right mould, and composed of the right kind of clay. Captain McGroarty, between Race and Elm streets, on Fifth street; Lieutenant Thomas Lavender, Webb street, Western row, between Third and Fourth streets; Mr. P. Molowney, on Fifth between Plum and Western row; Captain Conohan, of the Sarsfield Guards, corner of Laurel and Western row; Mr. Tobin, Broadway. These are few in number; still they reflect honor on the land of their nativity; and they were selected with admirable judgment by Mr. Nugent, for the individual cleverness of this brilliant constellation would cancel the infirmities of ten thousand men, or, in other words, that human depravity would be overlooked by taking into consideration the individual merit of the aforesaid constellation. Mr. Groarty is a native of Donegal, and left it exceedingly young, and keeps at present an extensive dry goods store at the above mentioned place.

This asterisk is composed of noble Irishmen, universally known, universally admired, and universally respected. Captain Thomas Lavender is a native of the parish of Ballybracken, county Roscommon, emigrated in 1827 to this country, and is now living in the Western row, Cincinnati, Ohio, married in the Emerald Isle to a very amiable lady, by the Rev. Mr. Hanly, and has a large and flourishing family. Captain Conahan, of the Sarsfield Guards is truly a specimen of an Irish gentleman; his parts and proportions are geometrically adjusted; his complexion is fresh, and his constitution robust and vigorous; he does not afford himself any disgusting airs, the inseparable companions of aristocracy, and the extensive range of his military skill is indisputably acknowledged.

Mr. Charles Conahan, banker, and keeps his office in Third street: this gentleman is brother to the aforesaid captain, with whom I had the honour of an interview in his office, and I must say, that he reflects honour on his dear Erin, and also on the land of his adoption; he is calm, courteous, unpretending, liberal and cautious in sentiments; in a word, he is a genuine son of the Emerald Isle. Mr. P. Moloney and lady; I think they both are natives of Waterford, but spent some time in France, whence they emigrated to America. They are as affectionate, happy and comfortable as any other lady and gentleman with whom I met, united in the bonds of matrimony, and are blest with a young and beautiful family. Mr. Tobin, Broadway; I have the pleasure of announcing that Mr. Tobin and his lady are both natives of the county Cork, and bred convenient to the haunts of my childhood, and if there be either leprosy or stain on the individual character of any who came from there, the well merited reputation of Mr. and Mrs. Tobin will cause it to evaporate from the minds of the most contaminated, malicious and perverted of our race. Mr. and Mrs. Tobin live in easy circumstances, and

I think have a flourishing young family. Mr. Charles O'Conner is a native of Yogal, county Cork, and came to this country thirty-one years since, and married here. He possesses a surprising faculty as being an antiquarian and a man of an expansive mind. Mr. O'Conner possesses another priceless jewel of incomparable value, which surpasses all his other qualifications in worth, which is his immovable attachment to his religion and religious duties, which will keep unsullied his reputation, and prepare him for everlasting happiness. Mrs. O'Conner died not long since, a noble Christian, and it is to be hoped that she is now enjoying the reward derived from a well spent life; she left behind her a large family to mourn her irreparable loss. I met in that city with a gentleman from the noble county Tyrone, of the name of Mr. Peter O'Neill, who proved himself to be a descendant of that illustrious family, whose magnanimity, eminence and hospitality, will remain on the page of history in spite of the devastation of time, tyranny or prevarication, until printing be abandoned. The recollection of the glory of that race will survive until then. Mr. O'Neill keeps a large grocery in Cincinnati, and is doing considerable business therein. Mr. Peter Griffin, a native of the county Longford, left home in 1832 and now keeps a large establishment in Vine street, of manufactured boots and shoes of the latest fashion and of the best quality. Mr. Griffin's name is incorporated with every laudable and noble institution in Cincinnati, and a more generous or a warmer-hearted Irishman never crossed the Atlantic. When I left that city for Louisville, I left Mr. Griffin hearty, healthy and vigorous, with a robust frame and a strong constitution, but after the expiration of a few days, I returned and found him no more, the relentless arm of death terminated his mortal career, and left a void in society which will not be easily supplied. The vain man who highly values this transitory life, and takes not into consideration its real worth, and never thinks of the outstanding debts against him on the unerring book in the hands of a Divine Calculator, must be in a state of lunacy. Mr. Griffin left a large circle of friends behind him, lamentingly mourning his demise, and particularly his wife and children, who are rendered inconsolable by the loss of an affectionate father, and a faithful and devoted husband.

Oh! cruel Death, how false, without alarm,
You came unseen, with an uplifted arm,
Which nothing mortal on this earth can stay,
E'en the power of kings the blow cannot delay:
While we're in health, this thought should interfere,
As we act here, we'll be rewarded there.

O'DONOVAN.

I was introduced by Captain Daniel Kelly, of whom I intend to speak hereafter to the Rev. Mr. Ford, the officiating priest of Chillicothe who happened to be in Cincinnati then, in whom is combined the priest, the patriot, the gentleman the scholar and theologian; but agreeableness, urbanity and humility, are, it seems, the inheritance of the priesthood, and the aforesaid combination can be found wherever a priest is located. The Rev. Mr. Ford, M. A., is both president and professor in St. Peter's College, Glen Mary, Chillicothe, Ohio, which is enough to show the brilliancy of his intellectual acquirements, and the fame of Ireland can never receive cancellation by the wasting hand of time, or from any other revolutionary disadvantage, while she gives birth to men of such distinguished fame and abilities as the Rev. Mr. Ford. Mr. Richard Walsh, in whose hotel I took up my residence during my stay in Cincinnati, and of whom I spoke in my former travels with respect and approbation, is a native of the county Kilkenny, and a gentleman well known to the traveling community, and also, to a large number of his countrymen and to others, whom he fed and sheltered in the hour of extremity. No recommendation of mine is necessary to add to his fame, as he is well known to be an honest man, and an excellent landlord, whose desire is to administer to the comfort of all who call upon him, and his charges are comparatively moderate, if we take into consideration the profusion of delicacies we receive in exchange. Although Mr. Walsh is young, he is married to the second wife, and I verily believe and conjecture by her declining health, that she is approaching the verge of eternity, and I think she is aware of her condition herself, as I observed her always on her bended knees and in the attitude of praying, and acquiescing with perfect resignation to the will of Providence. One day while traveling in the streets of Cincinnati, I was asked by some of my friends and countrymen had I paid a visit to my namesake Mr. Daniel O'Donovan, residing in No. 312 Main street. I answered negatively, but as they spoke of him eulogistically, I lost no time, but steered loungingly my course to his residence, to see my namesake, and to learn how a man of that illustrious race felt among the heterogeneous population of that city.

After interchanging some amiable terms, he asked me my name, and when I told him my name was O'Donovan, he looked at me with some peculiar admiration, and grasped my hand with a degree of affection and tenacity only known to Irishmen. I knew by his accent he spoke the Irish language as it had been taught classically in that part of the country that gave him birth, notwithstanding the accursed legislation, of an unhallowed government, which made him a part of the wreck that drifted to America to find shelter and security within the folds of the flag of freedom. When Mr. O'Donovan mentioned where he was from, I could hardly restrain my tears, as being born within two miles myself of his father's residence, and well I knew his father and grandfather, who lived in easy circumstances when I took my departure from the Emerald Isle, and also sustained a high and unsullied reputation, and I have no hesitation in saying as they religiously lived that they happily died. Mr. Daniel O'Donovan omits putting an "O" to his name, which is a culpable omission. Mr. O'Donovan is wholly entitled to it, and in the forthcoming history of my travels, I will demonstrate his unquestionable authority for the annexation. My friend and namesake is happily married and doing well, and is much respected by all his acquaintances. Mr. Walsh often summoned his recollection to discover opportunities and places where I could dispose of my poetic works, and I depended much on his sententious definitions, and considered an abortion incompatible with his analysis, as he had been well acquainted with men and manners. I had been directed by him and others to Messrs. O'Daley & King, who keep a very large assortment of liquors, groceries, and other saleable commodities in the city, and as being acquainted with the irreproachable reputation of these gentlemen, I was very anxious to see them, particularly as being my countrymen. I entered the office and fortunately both were there at the time, busily engaged with affairs pertaining to the establishment; and after the simple terms that give brilliancy to a warm reception had subsided, I opened rather timidly and languidly my commission, and after listening patiently to me for some time with concealed admiration, as they were undoubtedly astonished that I would attempt a production which no man attempted before; this was no surprise, as their intellectual attainments showed them all the difficulties I had to surmount. Notwithstanding all the original and typographical blunders contained in the work, they seemed highly satisfied with its contents and became liberal contributors at once. The gentlemen, by way of encouragement, gave me a list of meritorious gentlemen entitled to applause and popularity. Mr. O'Daley is from the Metropolis of Ireland, the nursery of literary men, and Mr. King is from Limerick, or from some part of the Province of Munster, a province where many of its inhabitants are as well acquainted with the course of higher fluxions as they are with the soul-inspiring strains of Ossian their countryman, the bard of bards. Mr. Michael Walsh, born in the county Cork, September, 1818, emigrated to America, 1842, married in New York in 1845, and now a resident of Cincinnati, Ohio. As I intend, God willing, to write in epic verse the history of my travels, and particularly that of some distinguished men whom I met with in my travels, I will give no more illustrations of my friend than to say, he is one of Ireland's noblemen, and as an addition to the embellishment of the foregoing expression, and to demonstrate his real worth he came from Cork, or the county Cork, the birth place of prelates, priests, theologians, poets, orators, philosophers, barristers, and of some of the most incorruptible patriots that ever suffered in struggling for the emancipation of their country from the grasp of the most daring, doubtful, damnable, desolating despots that ever held the reins of government or shaped the destinies of nations.

Messrs. Henry & Poland; the firm of Poland & Henry, is favorably known to the whole population of Cincinnati, as they keep the most varied and extensive assortment of groceries, liquors, and various other kinds of mercantile commodities, and I say, without infringing on veracity, or without any intention to indulge in extravagant encomiums or unnecessary exaggerations, that these gentlemen cannot be excelled in honor, honesty and industry, and indisputably in fair dealing. Mr. Henry is from the inimitable and unterrified county Tipperary, and coming from that part of the Emerald Isle, will place his character beyond the reach of the most unscrupulous calumny. Mr. Henry is candid, friendly, generous, and national, as far as discretion will permit, and much revered by men of high standing in society, and who entertain the most lofty conception of themselves. Mr. Poland is a Leinster gentleman, and it is not in my province to tell which of the twelve counties gave him birth, but it matters not what part of the Island of Saints gave him birth, as he is an Irishman of a high order, admired, beloved, and respected, and reflects credit on the land of his nativity.

Now, my dear reader, I am determined to give an illustration of a certain gentleman in Cincinnati, but it would require the incomparable pen of a Fenelon to do him justice or to define his cleverness, as the most unbounded applause, or meritorious panegyric could not overreach the mark. His name is Captain Daniel Kelly, and a native of the county Kilkenny, a county where hospitality is established without ostentation, industry without admiration, wealth without pride, and religion without alloy. I was asked by many in Cincinnati had I been with Captain Kelly, and when I answered negatively, they seemed astonished in consequence of his popularity, that I had not visited him before; but I will illustrate the reason of not making an earlier application to my friend and countryman. It is thus: good men who acquire great popularity are continually annoyed from all wandering applications, and unless supported by fortunate circumstances and inexhaustible funds, their pecuniary means will inevitably suffer, and no class of men having a downward tendency should be more regretted than liberal good men, because when they fall they draw others who prey on their liberality into the same vortex with themselves, and instead of helping them in the time of peril they are forsaken by their friends and left to be crushed under the weight of their misfortunes; such considerations chilled me, and kept me frequently from visiting them. At length I paid a visit to Captain Kelly, and as I suspected, he more than sustained the dignity of his reputation, and the extravagant testimonials I received in his favor. Mr. Kelly became a liberal contributor to my works, and also introduced me to gentlemen of high positions in society, from whom I received great encouragement; Mr. Kelly also gave me a preliminary note to James Looby, Esquire, a conservative bachelor in Louisville, backed by a very respectable Irish gentleman, Mr. McCormick, which operated significantly in my favor, and he also directed me to Mr. J. McCabe, No. 312 Main street, a gentleman of honor, responsibility and renown. Mr. McCabe is wealthy, and keeps an extensive tannery in the city; more about Captain Kelly by and by. By the advice of my friends and countrymen I called on a young gentleman of the illustrious house of Burke, son to Dr. Burke, residing in that city, where his professional abilities are the theme and admiration of such as call upon him in the time of sickness and danger; that young gentleman displays admirable and noble qualities, which predict his future greatness, and it requires but little knowledge of human nature to sustain my opinion, for one glance at this young gentleman would vindicate my opinion to be more of a prophecy than a conjecture, and if Providence spare him until his faculties be developed, he will irrefragably shed light, honor, brilliancy and lustre, on the land of his nativity. There is another gentleman in No. 3 Broadway in whom I found an inexhaustible source of Irish elements, namely, candor, honor, liberality and patriotism, and to attempt a definition vigorously of his professional abilities would demonstrate my absurdity in the extreme, for they are inaccessible to vulgar conceptions, and only within the knowledge of men of profound abilities who are moving in his own sphere, still I am of opinion if he be not Esculapius himself, there must be some proximity in the line of consanguinity as he can inevitably cure cough, colic, costiveness, consumption, cholera, &c., &c., &c., and has the most extraordinary success in all his professional undertakings. The Doctor is incontestably a Milesian, and a bachelor as yet, and to add another jewel to his coronet, he is from the black North.

Mr. Walsh directed me to call on another gentleman, Mr. Nories, or Norris, who keeps an extensive establishment in the dry good line, I think on Fifth-street, and to his advice I readily acquiesced; and his lady bought a history at once, and read a few verses of it with propriety, elegance, and astonishing sweetness, and I had enough to do to conceal the intensity of my feelings, or restrain my tears; thinking then that millions of her sex that emigrated from that unfortunate country that gave her birth, would display the same towering abilities that she did, had they the same opportunity, and such they would show had they the same opportunity; but such had been stunted in the bud by fell tyranny, the offspring of an accursed government. This lady and her husband are young, national, affectionate, courteous, and patriotic, and consequently natives of the Island of Saints. My host and countryman also directed me to a constituted gentleman named Mr. Sheehan, a native of Kilkenny, (which county is made beautiful by nature, and alas! cursed by the unhallowed hands of strangers,) who keeps a very extensive grocery not far from the observatory. Mr. Walsh spoke of him in adulatory terms, not hypothetically, but from conviction. Mr. Sheehan is an Irish gentleman whose position in society is high and towering, and he will bear blossom in spite of adverse gales, or the whirlwind put in motion by the foul breath of prejudice. Mr. Michael O'Daily who superintends Mr. Walsh's establishment, is from Carignavar, a short distance from the City of Cork, and formerly the ancient residence of one of the great McCarthy family, and if I am not mistaken, the present proprietor of the place is of that illustrious race; and if so, he must have bartered his birthright or eternal happiness, for a faint flash of transitory glory, Oh! eternity of immeasurable length, Oh! eternal duration.

Alas! alas! what a sad consideration to barter the inexpressible happiness and enjoyment of perpetual bliss for a gleam of momentary splendor; but my brave O'Daily, whose ancestors held large and ample possessions, relinquished them to the robber, and in spite of fraud, force, fines, forfeitures, and punishments held to his faith. Mr. O'Daily is an honest, industrious, clever man, and a true patriot, who has been a long time in this country, and tried every state but that of matrimony, and is still patiently awaiting the opportunity of getting united to some peerless lady of pure Milesian extraction; if she come in his way happiness awaits her. There is another gentleman named Mr. Denworth, a boot and shoemaker, in Broadway near Sixth street, who is a staunch patriot and an Irishman in full; he loves his country, sighs over her present bondage, and hopes anxiously for the restoration to her of her original dignity. Mr. Denworth is a native of Kilkenny, and an honor to the land of his birth. I met a gentleman in Cincinnati of fine intellectual culture and indisputable talents, whose natural and acquired abilities display much brilliancy and edification. He is unquestionably a genuine Irish gentleman, and a native of the City of Dublin, and reflects inexpressible credit, not only on that City, but on all parts and portions of the Emerald Isle. Mr. McCormick is the gentleman's name, who is at present the proprietor and editor of a daily newspaper in that city called the "Sun," in which he gave a very favorable notice of my Poetic History of Ireland; and, although sententiously conveyed, it proved the fertility of his imagination, and the powerful and inexhaustible source he commands, and whence it emanated. Mr. McCormick's editorials, and the profound scientific brevity of his composition, are much admired by the literary men of our country, including both foreigners and natives. Mr. McCormick, if I mistake not, is one of the cautious, conservative bachelors of the present century. Mr. McCormick is one of my reserved stars for poetic views and illustrations. There are more of my friends and countrymen in Cincinnati, on whom I called, that no eulogy, be it ever so flattering, respecting them, could be immoderately considered, as the mere mention of their names demonstrates their respectability and high position in life, viz.: Mr. P. Cody, grocer; Mr. William O'Sullivan, 253 Main street; Mr. Thomas O'Sullivan, 124 Walnut street; Mr. Thomas O'Sullivan, Chase Buildings; Mr. Barry, and if I mistake not, another gentleman named Mr. White, of each of these gentlemen I mean to speak in the forthcoming epic history of my travels.

Under the oppressive heat of a July sun, I crossed the Ohio river to Covington, Kentucky, to know if my countrymen in that city, possessed the same invincible spirit and patriotism I witnessed in the meritorious population of Cincinnati, and a little time, patience and opportunity conclusively proved that they were of the same stamp, and possessed the same abilities and propensities. There I met with an American gentleman of lofty and noble conceptions, fine feelings and of the most refined education, in Covington; he is also a worthy member of the Church of Rome, and a lawyer of high professional abilities, and the most fertile imagination would be necessary to do him justice in description and to show the dignity of his mind. After entering his office and after a partial examination of my poetic works, he calmly remarked and said as follows: "My dear friend, I hope you will excuse me for making any remark on your public and professional career at present, I only mean to fortify you against the wanton intrusion of unscrupulous men, who, for the sake of a pecuniary consideration, would inform against you, for a violation of our laws, for such is the case with you at this present moment, for you cannot offer one of your books for sale in the state of Kentucky, with the approbation of our established laws, and your mode of disposing of your books is at variance with them. On yesterday," said this good and great man, "quite a young fellow called into this office, and offered me a newly printed book for sale, which, after examining its contents, I found to be very much against my faith and religious conviction, and although both have been assailed by the author, with reproach and in a polluted manner, he conjectured his book would be of infinite service to the present and future generations, as the enormities of the Church of Rome were demonstrated in it, and the perusal of it would be the cause of many substantial conversions to the Protestant faith. In consequence of his youth, I was conscientiously induced to put him in mind of the violation of our State law, and the danger of his being mulcted in the sum of fifty dollars, for said violation. I insinuated caution to him or a total departure from his way of doing business. Regardless of advice, he continually kept selling in an unguarded and public manner to the best advantage; but to be candid on the subject," said this gentleman, "he soon got entangled in the meshes of one of those gentleman of his own calibre, and of his own way of thinking in a religious light, to whom he offered his book for sale, and who adjudged him to pay the above sum according to law, and would have compelled him to pay the amount, were it not for my interposition, and after demonstrating to him his youth and inexperience, the gentleman suffered him to depart with impunity." Now, my dear reader, take into consideration the feelings of these two gentlemen; the one a rigid Catholic and the other a consistent Protestant, and judge which of them showed mercy to the offender. This gentleman's name will hereafter be made manifest. Thence I steered my course to Mr. John White's extensive grocery, and I fortunately met him there attending to his customers with incredible politeness and dispatch. No applause is necessary to certify his cleverness, and as a proof of it, it is only necessary to say that he is a native of Tipperary; a better or more generous Irishman is incontestably unnecessary. In Mr. White's grocery store I got acquainted with a gentleman of the name of Mr. James Murray, who gave me special invitation to call at his house in Covington, and expressed an anxious desire of seeing me there, he also passed a flattering opinion, through a partial examination of my poetic works. Conformably to his advice I did so, and no sooner had I entered his house than he and his lady received me with unspeakable veneration and respect. This is the warm and invaluable inheritance of the genuine Irish, which inheritance in spite of prejudice, is sustained by the sons and daughters of that Isle which is renowned for religion, hospitality and literature.

A momentary pause and a fugitive glance made me sensible of their intrinsic worth and of their unassuming sancity, and also a revolutionary motion of the eye made manifest that Mr. Murray kept a Catholic book store for the use of the Catholic population of Covington, and others who would be glad to be supplied with the like. A view of the various kinds of religious books gave me an internal animation. Although an unworthy member of the Catholic church, still the works of devotion and departed worth, was the cause of an agreeable and increased sensation, I felt stronger and more forcibly than I can describe. Mr. Murray and his lady made no boast of what they could do to facilitate my intention, but took an armful of my books and placed them on a shelf, and bade me call some day in the commencement of the following week to know the result of the sale of my poetical works placed in their hands.

During my short stay in the house several Catholics came in to purchase some religious books, and I thought the obliging, unassuming humility of the honest couple rendered them unfit for the office they held, but when I saw the buyers taking everything they said for granted, the idea of incompetency evaporated from my mind, and while indulging in this meditation an opportunity afforded which gave an ample testimony of Mrs Murray's mode of selling, before I departed, which immediately changed my opinion, and conclusively proved my cogitation to be unfounded and imaginary. At the verge of my departure a gentleman whom she knew came in, and being well aware of his patriotism, as I thought, she instantly introduced to him in a lucid, pleasing and happy manner, one of my books, and logically illustrated its merits, as she kindly so expressed, and this evidence of her abilities satisfied me, and supplanted my original opinion, and I departed agreeably surprised and fully convinced of the folly of passing an immediate opinion on things and circumstances unfathomable to our shallow conceptions. However, this prompt and momentary decision sometimes arises from the want of consideration, and sometimes from the depravity of our nature. I recrossed the river and continued my perambulation among my friends in Cincinnati until the Sunday following, and on that morning I came to the conclusion to hear mass in the Cathedral in Covington, and as Mr. Murray's house is opposite the Cathedral, unquestionably, as in duty bound, I called in to see how Mr. and Mrs. Murray were before entering the house of the Lord. At that moment Mr. Murray was preparing himself to go to church, and then cordially invited me to a seat in his pew, which was convenient to the altar, to which, after some objections, I acquiesced. I felt exceedingly happy for having it in my power to contemplate the magnificence of that splendid and sacred edifice, and also of having the unspeakable pleasure of seeing the venerable Bishop Carrell. His Lordship looked exceedingly well, and stood as straight as an arrow, with a constitution which appeared to me to be invulnerable, and his countenance beamed with dignity, though blended with humility and devotion. After mass he addressed his congregation from the altar steps, in language sublime, religious and instructive, which brought conviction to the minds of his hearers. When mass was over I returned to Mrs. Murray's house, and I must candidly acknowledge that I received the amount of my books at the hands of Mrs. Murray without the deduction of a single cent for her trouble from the amount, and as an additional testimonial of her kindness, she advised me to leave her some more of my books until my return from Louisville, and she thought probably they would also disappear. I complied with her request, and after mutual benedictions had been pronounced I departed and recrossed the Ohio river, when, in spite of solar attraction my perspiration was heavy, which made me seek some gloomy, sequestered shade to gain advantage of the oppressive heat of the day, but such delightful refreshment remained unknown to my strenuous explorations. On the following evening I took my departure for Louisville, entertaining strong hopes of a successful trip to that city, being strongly backed by recommendations to the Rev. Mr. Boyce, to J. Dooly, Esq., and to others living in that city. My backers were Captain O'Kelly and Mr. Walsh, of whom I have spoken already. I know I have mistaken the names of some of my contributors in Covington, as all the notes respecting them were taken with a soft lead pencil, which after some friction entirely disappeared. It was late in the night when we approached the Louisville wharf, which compelled me to remain in the boat until morning.

Quite early next morning, ere the luminary of heaven sent forth his soft blushes and radiant beams to chase away the heavy exhalation from the mountain's brow, and clear the vale of the impenetrable mist that seemed to settle on its bosom all night, the industrious portion of the City of Louisville began to show themselves indiscriminately on every street and corner, while some others were detained in bed either by intoxication, extravagance, or some other irreclaimable habits, such as squandering wealth, destroying health, and sacrificing character at the expense of wives and children, who sorrowfully and shamefully suffer, and are objects of pity and commiseration.

Louisville is not an exception, as such nobility as the above mentioned can be found in all cities in the world. In Louisville the carters are up very early, for they delight in the accumulation of dimes and dollars, and when one of the gentlemen of this class came to the wharf, I asked him to take my trunk to Mr. John Gaul's boarding house, but he at once confessed his ignorance of the location, "But," said my friend, "I will take you to a gentleman's house where you can leave your trunk, which will be perfectly safe until you can find out the residence of your friend." I immediately agreed to his proposal, which I considered both reasonable and honorable. While on our journey, I understood from him that he was a Pittsburger, and then we soon identified each other. The gentleman was a Mr. Jackman, and indisputably an original Pittsburger, and Irishman of course, and by all means a gentleman. After leaving my trunk in another Pittsburger's house, I think named Mr. Murray, I went in quest of Mr. Gaul's boarding house, and found it to be located on the corner of Market and Sixth streets. The first sight I got of my friend, I felt some strange and affectionate feeling towards the man in whose hands I experienced so much kindness in the time of sickness and danger. After having a short interview with my friend, and when our feelings subsided, I asked Mr. Gaul if I could remain under his friendly roof during the time I would remain in the city, and although his house had been filled to its utmost capacity with boarders, he answered affirmatively, and immediately bought a patent spring bed, not more singular in its construction than in its capacity, for my comfort and accommodation, and to give a proper definition of its usefulness and importance to the occupier, is not within the limits of my talent, notwithstanding I will make a feeble effort to do so, and if I fall short or get confounded analytically, the reader must debit my ignorance, and not my propensity. On lying on that bed, much like the flow and ebb of the tide, and contrary to all other beds that I, through accident or design, met with in my travels, it gradually acquired a great elevation in spite of the weight and gravity of the slumberer, and on its descending tendency to regain its original level, it displayed the same slow motion that it did when ascending, and before the two motions expired or evaporated, the slumberer or occupier had been in the arms of Morpheus, enjoying the imaginary happiness of another sphere, where sin, shame, sorrow, or sickness can never contaminate or disturb our peaceful career, or perhaps ranging until morning through the enamelled meads of perpetual spring. On the following morning, refreshed and invigorated after a sound sleep in Elysian shades, I prepared myself as was my customary habit, to pay a visit to the Rev. Mr. Joice, and fortunately met him in the church, to whom I presented my credentials, and a slight acquaintance satisfied me that I was introduced by my friends to a distinguished priest, and to an Irish gentleman. I positively aver that a priest is the greatest ornament on this globe of ours to society, though well knowing his dignity, his religious and theological virtues, and his other attainments all are well balanced and kept under control by his piety and humiliation, and his mind is calm and without the reach of tempestuous irritation, and his conversation is plain, edifying, and always based on charity, and indisputably his benediction is invaluable to the living and to the dead. After leaving the reverend gentleman, I steered my course immediately to James Dooly, Esquire, whom I found in his grocery and much engaged with his customers, giving out groceries and other merchantable commodities in abundance, and at first sight I knew he corresponded with the favorable illustration I heard respecting him. Mr. Dooly, I believe, is a bachelor of the high school, and immutably devoted to the life of celibacy, but the lady who would be fortunate enough to frustrate his design, and invite him to the Elysian fields and walks of matrimonial alliance, would confer an ineffable happiness on Mr. Dooly, and secure her own happiness during her own existence. No doubt Mr. Dooly did everything in his power to advance my promotion, and promote my interest, and an Ulster gentleman who is in his store, strenuously exerted himself in my behalf. This gentleman's name is Mr. McMahon.

I should not wonder if a consanguinity is not subsisting between himself and the great general of his name, whose military renown will descend to the latest posterity, as also his magnanimity and achievements in the French service, under the gallant leadership of Napoleon III., when resisting the determined legions of Austria. Mr. McMahon is a native of the county Cavan, and I emphatically aver, that I received more encouragement from the illustrious natives of that county, than from any other county in Ireland. They are all patriots to a man in that county. When the evening came, and the brilliant luminary of the firmament was descending and gathering his scattered and declining rays below the verge of the western horizon, I returned to my boarding house, to relate the adventures of the day to my friend, Mr. John Gaul, and after a little while, the boarders commenced to collect, and were as strong and as thick in numbers as swallows in a sand bank at the time of incubation. I seemed much astonished where my friend could find accommodations for the whole, but my astonishment soon abated, when I saw the apartments and conveniences ready for their reception. A young lady named Miss Campbell was his housekeeper, and her superior method of cooking, and of making tea and coffee, attracted boarders to participate in the incomparable and sumptuous entertainment afforded in Mr. Gaul's boarding house. There is a young gentleman, Mr. William White, and a native of Pittsburgh, residing in Louisville City, whom I found necessary to my welfare. He is in Louisville the same as he was in his native city, much respected for his social habits, urbanity, and cleverness. Another Pittsburgher, Mr. O'Sullivan, with whom I met in that city distinguished himself in my behalf, and in his establishment can be found the most fashionable boots and shoes, made to order and composed of the best materials. In Louisville I called at a gentleman's house, and I emphatically aver that I feel much abashed for the omission of his name, as it disappeared unaccountably from my possession, although I consider I had been very careful of its preservation, both in memory and on paper. When I called at the gentleman's house, I had not the pleasure of seeing him, as he was unavoidably from home; but his lady was there, an excellent substitute for her absent husband. When I first saw his lady and children, although some of them were grown to maturity, and the magnificent dwelling in which they lived, I was impressed with the opinion that their circumstances were large, easy, and unlimited, as everything familiar to the eye indicated the like; the gentleman himself is a native of the State of Maryland, and the issue of Catholic parents, but his lady, I think, is a native of Kentucky, who had been educated in the principles of Protestantism, yet her conversion took place shortly after her matrimonial alliance with her husband; the change which had taken place in her creed and sentiments was of her own selection, without the interference of her husband, who solemnly adhered to his own, in principle and practice, and never had taken the least trouble to impress on her mind the deficiencies and corruptions of Protestantism. The first glance at this lady made me sensible of her repugnance to aristocracy and its annexations, and though after raising a promising and flourishing family, she stands exceedingly straight, and is pretty tall, and her symmetry is beautifully constructed, her features pleasing and agreeably delineated, and chiselled by nature. After some conversation, I made my vocation known to her, which she with unspeakable alacrity immediately encouraged, and I soon discovered that she was a worthy member of the Catholic Church. In the forthcoming history of my poetic travels, my illustration of this noble family will be more concise, elaborate, brilliant, and entertaining. My stay in Louisville was not as long as I expected, for all hopes of future proficiency evaporated from my mind, and this prognostication afterwards appeared to be very fortunate. On the following day there was an election of major importance to take place in Louisville city, and the distinguished Breckenridge, a Kentuckian, who is now our vice-president,* was to address that evening a large audience in favor of democracy, to whom, by invitation, I listened with inexpressible zeal and attention; but. the evening before the election day forbode something very calamitous, as Native Americans gregariously came into the city, and if we are allowed to judge from outward ap-

* 1856.

pearances, the most incurious observer would conjecture that they were a part of the inhabitants of Acheron, who crossed the lake Avernes to display the hellish inhabitants of Pluto's accursed dominions in the city of Louisville.

Each of these gentlemen had his own peculiar faculty of ornamenting his chin and other parts of his face with beard; some of them only embellished the chin, some were favorably inclined to do justice to the upper lip, while others encouraged the growth of the entire fleece, which proved them in part or in whole, to be fools or philosophers. This assembly, though differently marked, could not be considered heterogeneously, as they had the same errand and application under consideration, or in other words they were unanimously bent on destruction. They were from different States, determined to massacre inoffensive men, women, and children of foreign birth, although the men were naturalized and should be protected by the laws of our country. Still, no force was formidable enough to shield them from the undeserved wrath of the natives. Their emblematical banners and hieroglyphics displayed very unpromising aspects, and foretold imminent and approaching danger; but I beg leave to mention, that Native Americans, taken as a mass, should not be considered to entertain any feelings of friendship towards those of whom I have already spoken; this consideration is to be omitted, as the real Native Americans cannot be surpassed in dignity, tender feelings, and humanity, by any portion of inhabitants existing on our globe; but every wood, be it ever so green, has its own complement of rotten, sapless limbs and branches, and also every nation, be it ever so civilized, has its share of the dregs of society. I frequently mentioned, that in matters of consequence and consideration, my decisions were invariably momentarily, which proved to be the case in Louisville, as I returned immediately to my boarding-house and referred the matter to Mr. John Gaul, who approved of my resolution, and strenuously assisted me to take my trunks to the river. That evening I took my departure for Cincinnati, where on the following morning we were informed of the unscrupulous murder of foreigners, and the destruction of property by the inhuman acts and barbarity of Native Americans, which is a stain on themselveson and their posterity, that neither time nor distance can obliterate. After spending some time with my friends in Cincinnati, I returned to Pittsburg, and my arrival at that city put an end to my travels.

O'DONOVAN.

THE END.

APPENDIX.

To Louis Napoleon, Prince President of the French Republic.

Prince,—As the contemplation of human events has occupied the serious attention and consideration of theologians, historians, philosophers, statesmen, and all other sound thinking men, since time immemorial, and that that combination of learned men, with the exception of those whose conceptions and understanding are clogged, or defiled by religious animosity, or altogether deprived of any belief of Christian principles, came to the conclusion that there is an invisible hand, agent, or power, that governs the action of men, and all acknowledge that government as the special and unerring arrangement of Divine Providence. Prince, that providence raises some of his creatures to dignity and circumstance, and secures to them the full estimation and universal approbation of their cotemporaries for some special purpose beyond the reach of human comprehension, and if those men will not claim that elevation to be peculiarly due to their own actions and qualifications, but will consider it an undeserved blessing bestowed upon them by the hand of Providence, the Author of all goodness, the Giver of all gifts, and the Architect of the universe, such men will continue in the administration of justice, and their names will be transmitted to posterity; the prayers of millions yet unborn will follow them to their graves; their memories will be religiously observed and commemorated by the good, the wise, and the virtuous of all Christian denominations throughout the Christian world. Prince, there can be no reasonable man but will acknowledge, and believe in the goodness of Divine Providence, if we only look to the liberation of St. Peter the apostle, from confinement, we must believe it had been effected by Divine Providence; and if we look back to your own former predicament, when implicated in the meshes of a ferocious and unapproachable tyranny, confined within the limits of an impregnable fortress, we must acknowledge emphatically, that some invisible Divine interposition effected your escape, and placed you on a throne more grand and glorious than those of kings and emperors, a throne created in the hearts of seven millions of Frenchmen; a throne more substantial and exalted than any acquired by hereditary humbug or any other stratagem. Prince, as Divine Providence has placed you on the pinnacle of fame, power, and dignity, basking in the brilliancy of a meridian blaze, your position will only be rendered permanent by the wisdom of your government.

A president of a great republic should know his dignity, and should also divest himself of ambition, intolerance, and all unjust severity incompatible with justice. By ambition, I mean a desire for a higher and more flourishing appellation, or title, than that of president. By intolerance, I mean restrictions placed on the religious observance of those who religiously differ with us in religious opinion; for men, or any body of Christians, that sincerely and solemnly love the Lord, can hate no individual, or will do no harm, and are incapable with divine assistance, of injuring a fellow-creature, with outrageous severity. By severity, I mean, those who have offended the State, by the dissemination of vice, and the corruption of virtue, as well as all other political transgressions, should not be tortured with excessive punishment, or excessive incarceration. Prince, I do not accuse you of either ambition, intolerance or severity, and the way to fortify yourself against such misfortune, is to adhere to the admonition of that church, in which you were baptized, in which you believe, in which you live, and in which you hope to die, as she will point out to you, the vanity of earthly and temporary distinctions and declarations, the shortness of time, and the length of eternity. Prince, I am happy to think, that the discretion of your government, so far, is marked with prudential consideration, and merits great applause, and that your actions indicate fortitude, faith and fidelity, and that the political stretch of your imagination, is considered unequalled and impregnable, as you dispelled, and I may say annihilated forever, the framework of a fearful combination, that enveloped, not only France, but all Christendom, in the clouds of death and eternity, an illegitimate and unhallowed scheme, hatched by the vilest combination of organized corruption, the most dreadful, and the most wicked, that ever polluted or infringed on the laws of humanity. A dangerous faction leagued together to destroy peace, security, and morality, and to sap the foundation of religion, under the hypocritical and assumed title of socialism, that body has been disorganised with one blow by your assiduity, and the altars of the Most High protected from sacrilegious hands, Europe saved from convulsions and unheard of atrocities. Prince, as you are chosen the successful candidate, or rather an instrument in the hands of Heaven I hope, there is another intervention I would suggest to your consideration, and that is, the emancipation of my unfortunate country. I am an Irishman, thank God, and proud of my native land, though being in chains, and enslaved by the unjust tyranny of unhallowed rulers, yet a devoted citizen of the United States of America, my adopted country, and I know, Prince, you know the history of my native country to perfection, and any further demonstration is unnecessary, and that by her emancipation, she would be restored to the elevated position to which she is entitled, and her position then would be, as it had been before her cancellation by British misrule, great, glorious and free. Prince, Ireland has for a long time groaned under the oppression and intolerance of strangers. The most cruel, the most sanguinary, and the most desperate government that ever existed in any part of the civilized, or uncivilized world, has crushed and impoverished my native country for centuries, and Prince, if you adhere to my admonition, the freedom of that country will be obtained without the effusion of much blood, losing much time, or expending much treasure. Harvest would be the best time for the invasion of Ireland, when provision would be most abundant and within the reach of the inhabitants, and by landing fifty thousand men, and five hundred thousand stand of arms in any two places in Munster, that is, twenty-five thousand at the mouth of the Shannon, and the same force in any point in the county Cork, the forces that would land at the mouth of the Shannon, to push with impetuosity through the province of Connaught, and reach Ulster as soon as possible, to save the inhabitants of that province from the fury of their remorseless enemies, and the army that would land in the county of Cork to make a vigorous push for the capital, and confident I am, that that division of the force would be reinforced by five hundred thousand fighting men, before it would reach Dublin. After the subjugation of Ulster, it would be necessary to leave fifteen thousand effective men there to maintain the independence of the place, and render it impossible for the Scotch, England's vassals, to interfere, and the other ten thousand to march to the capital to join the rest of the army. Prince, there is another scheme I would suggest to your consideration, in connection with the invasion of Ireland, and that is, the invasion of England: make a simultaneous attack on the kingdom, send across to England three hundred thousand men, well disciplined, and under skilful commanders, and let them land in three different points; one-third the number would do, yet to do the business with dispatch, as you have men in abundance, and then each division to push with intrepidity to the capital of the kingdom, and in one week after the landing of the troops, the independence of England will be within the limits of your grasp. One hundred pieces of heavy cannon will be necessary for the invasion of England, and fifty of the same calibre for the invasion of Ireland. By making an attack on both England and Ireland simultaneously, England could receive no assistance from Ireland, neither could Ireland receive any from England.

Prince, after the restoration of the two kingdoms to their freedom, or independence, let the government of the two kingdoms be liberal, solid and protective, somewhat similar to the established laws of this great and glorious republic. Let there be no restriction of religion, except in those imitations that would be dangerous to social order, and christianity. Let every sect support the ministers pertaining to that sect, such liberality will secure individual happiness and universal esteem ; peace, order and harmony will triumphantly reign in both kingdoms, and nothing will mar the perpetuity of that happiness—particularly when sanctioned by man, and blest by Divine Providence. Prince, if you consider that I, as an individual, would be of any assistance in that enterprise, I am at your service, although advanced in years I think I would. My ambition and fortitude are as yet undiminished. I know my native language and can speak it with force and rapidity, and tactics are not beyond my comprehension, and to crown all, I am an honest, faithful, incorruptible patriot, who would not violate your confidence. I am willing, determined and venturesome though sometimes cautious, and prudentially restrained, and my age could be the only impediment; but mind you, Prince, that an old fox commits more depredation than all the cubs in his den. Prince, I am not actuated by pomposity or any lucrative desire, or motive, when I offer myself, or my feeble assistance, for the achievement of the emancipation of my country. No, prince, I wish for no consideration, no office, no honors, all I will request is to put me in the front of the battle along with my countrymen, and if I fall the sacrifice is nothing. I am willing at any moment to shed my heart's blood to gain the independence of my native land, which has been polluted, oppressed, impoverished, and persecuted for centuries, by an ambitious, tyrannical, unscrupulous, sanguinary and inexorable government whose atrocities for centuries are beyond the power of my feeble and grovelling illustration. Prince, although there can be no man more devoted to the welfare of his family than I, or more attached to my adopted country, yet I would commend all to the protection of Providence, this instant, to join the invasion for the redemption of the Emerald Isle. Prince, were I to fall in the attempt, in that unfortunate country, I would be sure of one thing which would give me unspeakable consolation, expecting when the last trumpet would sound, I would arise in the association of a million of saints, who suffered martyrdom for the faith originally believed by Saint Patrick, and has been ever since unerringly preserved, and taught in all parts of the Christian world. Prince, I am paternally descended from the ancient family of O'Donovan, and maternally descended from the illustrious house of McCarthy, though living conveniently in my native country, to the vast estates and inheritance of both families, the day I left my native land, which has been twenty-eight years ago, I could not openly declare, without implicating myself in the meshes of official spies, who had inundated that unfortunate country at the time, and each more venomous and subtle than the seven-headed monster destroyed by the matchless strength of Hercules, that one rood of those extensive possessions had been originally in the hands of my ancestors, or should be mine by inheritance. Prince, if you act in conformity with my suggestions your memory will be embalmed in the affections of posterity, and when the memory of Alexander, of Cæsar, and even the memory of the late and great Napoleon, your uncle, who suffered persecution and premature death in an impregnable prison at St. Helena by the treachery of the English government, will be buried in oblivion, or withering in obscurity, yours will be green, unblemished, and undiminished, in the hearts of all good men, and commemorated by the lovers of peace, order, freedom and religion, throughout the Christian world. Prince, with profound respect and veneration for your wisdom, justice, judgment, unerring sagacity and incomparable abilities, I subscribe myself, your humble, submissive and obedient servant,

JEREMIAH O'DONOVAN.

MY SECOND LETTER TO LOUIS NAPOLEON, EMPEROR OF FRANCE.

The love of liberty, the undying hatred I entertain for oppression, and other considerations induce me to adress your Imperial Majesty on a very important subject. Illustrious sire, your invincible courage in the field as a soldier, your skill and discipline as a tactician, your inspiring oration to your army in the hour of extremity, and the intrinsic desire you cherish for the welfare of wretched humanity all over the world, are universally admitted and established in the bosom of the fool and the philosopher. Illustrious sire, the combination of so many qualities, qualifications, and attributes uniting in one illustrious sovereign, at the head of irresistible legions, can by gradual steps, like the mighty Hercules, clear the world of monsters, tyranny, and infidelity, and leave no signs of either on the face of the globe we inhabit. Illustrious sire, you have already shown admirable skill and ability and religious feelings in abolishing the baneful influence and ungodly tendency of sanguinary socialistic conspiracies and red republican systems, who formed a confederacy to confound religion, annihilate virtue, and contaminate, if possible, the immaculate practice of the Catholic Church, for which you have the respect and prayers of millions, the communion of angels and saints, and the benediction of Heaven. Illustrious sire, as you have sympathized with the Italians, and by your invincible arms, restored to them their original equality, though but a short time under the government and dominion of Imperial Austria, a Catholic sovereign who is notorious for his Christian fortitude, Catholic principles, and noble disposition, by which he gained the universal appellation and venerated title of Saint Francis Joseph. Now, illustrious sire, I hope you will take into consideration the indescribable tyranny, oppression, and abominable servitude of my countrymen for several centuries past, groaning under an invidious, accursed, and relentless government, that excels in atrocity, savage barbarity, and cruelty all other governments, whether christian or infidel, civilized or savage, under the canopy of Heaven. Illustrious sire, I am an Irishman, and proud of the appellation, and some of the wood that drifted from the shores of the Green Isle, an island remarkable for its sanctity, eminent for its learning, distinguished for bravery, illustrious by the purity of its daughters, and notorious for its hospitality to strangers, though in chains and in bondage at present by the unhallowed enactments of tyrants. Illustrious sire, it is unnecessary for me to picture to your mind the woes, afflictions, and sufferings of my countrymen for centuries past, caused by the unjust legislation of the British Parliament, and by the unscrupulous enactments manufactured in the pandemonium councils of British peers; I say, imperial sire, unnecessary, as you are the better historian of the two, and no man can be more conversant with British perfidy than your Imperial Majesty; Illustrious sire, turn the victorious arms of your conquering legions against the ancient and formidable enemy of your empire, the robber of every hamlet, town, and city in the world, the scavenger of the high seas, the dreadful scourge of humanity, and the murderers of your illustrious uncle. Illustrious sire, fear not defeat, for the prayers of the virtuous of all nations will follow your arms, the angels and saints will intercede for your success, and an unerring Providence will grant you victory. Illustrious sire, if you act in conformity with my directions, you will gain immortal renown for yourself in this world, and eternal happiness in the next.

With profound respect for your Imperial Majesty, I subscribe myself your very obedient servant,

JEREMIAH O'DONOVAN.

MY THIRD LETTER TO LOUIS NAPOLEON RESPECTING ROME.

SIRE,—The intensity of my feelings commingled with astonishment would not permit me to let so favorable an opportunity pass, without addressing your Imperial Majesty on the importance of the subject under consideration throughout all christendom respecting Central Italy. Sire, my prayers often ascended to the tribunal of the Most High in your behalf, in behalf of your Empress, and for the preservation of your royal heir. I also prayed fervently and frequently for the perpetuity of the Napoleon dynasty, and for the safety of your government and throne, and add to mine the fervent and frequent prayers of Catholic christendom, and consider seriously did they move or had they any effect on a crucified God, to interpose his unerring Providence to shield you from the terrific danger that threatened you in the hour of extremity. Meditate, great sire, only for a moment, that nothing human could save you in the time of inexpressible danger, and that there must be some supernatural though invisible agent that saved you from falling a victim to your implacable enemies. Alas! sire, how little we value the invisible interposition of Him who suffered and died ignominously on the cross, and between two notorious malefactors, and left us an immaculate guide, his Church, to secure for our immortal souls everlasting rest in the kingdom of his father, if we adhere to her holy laws, and harken to her unerring admonition. Great sire, from the present appearance of things, how are you determined to act your part towards the infallible Church which I have mentioned, and towards her spiritual head, the vicar of Jesus Christ upon earth? In the commencement of your career, you seemed favorably disposed to sustain the Church, and to maintain the supremacy of the Pope, both spiritually and temporally, but when you find yourself basking in the meridian blaze of an almost unbounded applause, and anticipating an augmentation of power and an extension of your realm, you turned around without having the fear of God before your eyes, or the thoughts of Him in your heart, and thought to rob the Church of God of what was left for her support, and the support of her mission, many centuries since, an act surpassing even the rapacity of your illustrious uncle. Oh, great sire, pause for a moment and try to divest yourself of that inheritance which your uncle left you, and seriously think of his downfall, and of his ignominious captivity in the sterile and inhospitable island of Saint Helena, by the inhuman acts of an infidel government, your present immortal foe, and the ancient foe of your empire, a foe that is at this present moment meditating your captivity or personal destruction, as well as meditating the subjugation of your empire. Sire, deprive yourself of this inheritance if you can, and think of the plunder and ungodly efforts of your uncle, and also think how a just and merciful God rewarded him for his vandalism and sacrilege, and from such meditation and from his humiliation, you can draw a moral which may be profitable to yourself, to your Empress, and to your royal heir. Sire, what do you expect to benefit by your usurpation and treachery if you persevere in your unhallowed design? The Pope will be under the disagreeable necessity of excommunicating you from the Church, and you will come under the same ecclesiastical curse and censure with all visionary wanderers from the truth, and indisputably under the ire and curse of Heaven; then the annihilation of your power is inevitable. Sire, how do you think the Catholic world will be affected by your treachery and prevarication, and how Catholic France will feel at your invidious ambition? Seven million votes given in your favor by gallant Frenchmen raised you first to the presidency of France, and half that number will chase you away from that throne you unjustly occupy by your usurpation, treachery, and by revolutionary circumstances. Sire, the irresistible arms of France tumbled your predecessor from his high position, and the same arms, after a hard struggle, can accommodate you with a passport to cross the channel to Queen Victoria, who will be very happy to witness your humiliation; therefore pause, sire, in your mad career, or dread the consequences.

Respectfully yours, &c.,

JEREMIAH O'DONOVAN.

PITTSBURGH, PENNSYLVANIA.

WRITTEN ON THE DEPARTURE OF BISHOP O'CONNER, FROM THIS CITY, FOR HIS OWN EMERALD ISLE.

Our Bishop's gone and left us all in gloom,
Through his devotion to the Church of Rome;
His Lordship's gone to edify some flock,
Adhering still, to the unerring rock;
The imps below, combin'd with those on earth,
Well know her age and know who gave her birth.
The church will stand until the end of time,
She has no faults, and she commits no crime—:
Ah! stand she will, impregnable and fast,
Unchanged, untarnished, while the world will last.
May stronger hands, than Neptune's rule the main
And aid his efforts till he come again,—
Oh! may they calm the ocean's angry roar,
Until he'll land upon his native shore,
That gem-like Isle, from tyranny undone,
Will welcome home her own immortal son,
Whose wide renown and unaffected grace,
Shed lasting lustre on his native place.

O'DONOVAN.

PITTSBURGH, PENNSYLVANIA.

Two holy men,* from Erin's verdant shore,
Are here to-day, were never here before;
Inspired by faith, and not the love of gain
Impelled the priests to cross the raging main;
Each being determined to extinguish sin,
And build a church to worship God therein.
My friends disburse, and give the Saints a share,
For few there are but can a little spare;
Refuse them not, as you'll receive in lieu,
The sum you'll give with heavy interest too
From Erin's Isle there went in days of yore
To foreign climes, a thousand saints or more,
There preached the word, and there salvation wrought,
And holy converts that salvation taught,
'Till heathen hearts had softened to the lyre
Attuned and managed by the sacred choir.
Such was the case, and such the case will be
With those two Saints who crossed the boisterous sea.
Their usual practice is to fast and pray,
And pen the sheep without the fold that stray.

O' DONOVAN.

---

* Rev. Mr. Croghan, and Rev. Mr. Quigley; both North Carolinians.